UNDERSTANDING
GROUP BEHAVIOR

Consensual Action by Small Groups

Volume I

UNDERSTANDING GROUP BEHAVIOR

Consensual Action by Small Groups

Volume I

Erich H. Witte
University of Hamburg, Germany

James H. Davis
University of Illinois, Urbana–Champaign

LAWRENCE ERLBAUM ASSOCIATES, PUBLISHERS
1996   Mahwah, New Jersey

Lawrence Erlbaum Associates, Inc., Publishers
10 Industrial Avenue
Mahwah, New Jersey 07430

Library of Congress Cataloging-in-Publication Data

Understanding group behavior / [edited by] Erich H. Witte, James H.
   Davis.
      p.   cm.
   Based on papers presented at a conference held at the University
of Hamburg, Nov. 1992.
   Includes bibliographical references and index.
   Contents: v. 1. Consensual action by small groups — v. 2. Small
group processes and interpersonal relations.
   ISBN 0-8058-1639-9 (v. 1 : cloth : alk. paper). — ISBN
0-8058-1640-2 (v. 1 : pbk. : alk. paper). — ISBN 0-8058-1641-0 (v.
2 : cloth : alk. paper). — ISBN 0-8058-1642-9 (v. 2 : pbk. : alk. paper).
   1. Small groups—Congresses. 2. Decision-making, Group—
Congresses. 3. Interpersonal relations—Congresses. I. Witte,
Erich H., 1946–   . II. Davis, James H., 1932–   .
HM.133.U526 1996
302.3′4—dc20   96-12707
                                                                  CIP

Books published by Lawrence Erlbaum Associates are printed on acid-free paper,
and their bindings are chosen for strength and durability.

Printed in the United States of America
10 9 8 7 6 5 4 3 2 1

CONTENTS

PART III: SOCIAL INFORMATION-PROCESSING MODELS

PREFACE

The project that was to become the two volumes, *Understanding Group Behavior*, began as a conference, emphasizing theory and conceptual issues in empirical research on small group behavior. Held at the University of Hamburg, November 1992 (and sponsored by the Deutsche Forschungsgemeinschaft), conference presentations were later amplified and considerably expanded as a consequence of discussion among participants and subsequent exchanges. The two volumes present original theoretical works that address a variety of important current problems, both applied and basic. Contributions to both volumes are up-to-date accounts of original theory: Those comprising Volume 1 tend to be rather specific in character; those of Volume 2 are similar, but the work described is of a more general conceptual nature.

The special emphasis of Volume 1 is on "consensual action by small groups." Juries, panels, and committees of many kinds are ubiquitous in the affairs of societies, and have been the target of considerable research by social psychologists, as well as researchers from a variety of other disciplines. The chapters collected in Part I present theories and models stressing the process of *aggregating* preferences and *combining* member contributions in achieving consensus. Part II contributions emphasize the social processing of information and interpersonal exchanges, as well as member reactions, during the consensus process. Together, these chapters offer a wide range of theoretical perspectives on the process of "individual-into-group" behavior characteristic of consensus.

Small groups (two to a dozen or so) are not only primary agents for performing many of the tasks of organizations and institutions, within which they are embedded, but they can play a major role in promoting subsequent acceptance of their actions. In any event, whatever the interpersonal phenomenon of interest, the small group is surely one of its primary habitats. Although many research problems of social behavior have been abstracted from that "natural setting," and reformulated as intraindividual problems for close experimental study, research on the intact group continues to be of fundamental importance. The aim of the two volumes comprising *Understanding Group Behavior* is to provide a picture of relevant current theory.

Erich H. Witte
James H. Davis

INTRODUCTION

1

SMALL-GROUP RESEARCH AND THE STEINER QUESTIONS: THE ONCE AND FUTURE THING

James H. Davis
University of Illinois, Urbana-Champaign

The very notion of social behavior implies more than one person. Both the individual and interacting individuals have been a focus of research in social psychology, although the study of very large assemblies and social movements were generally the province of sociology and anthropology. For some years, the concentration on mental phenomena has increased throughout psychology, including within social psychology. The result of this shift in emphasis has been an ever increasing focus of research effort not on interpersonal behavior per se, but on cognitive representations and stored information *about* interpersonal behavior and associated cognitive mechanisms within the individual.

BRIEF AND RECENT HISTORY

Against such a background, a closer look at research developments in social psychology suggests the unfolding of two major trends in the study of social behavior, and both beginning, roughly, just after midcentury. The first trend, as implied earlier, has been a great conceptual turning inward such that questions about *intra*individual life became paramount. Part of this inward shift was surely due to the change in psychology at large where behaviorism was being rejected and a reawakening of interest in mental life was gaining in popularity. Indeed, cognitive conceptual notions had never altogether vanished from social psychology, and it can be fairly said that cognitivism lived on in social psychology after its defeat elsewhere by the behaviorist revolution early in the twentieth century. Norms, values, attitudes, intentions, and so on endured and prospered at the hands of social researchers even during the period in which such ideas were anathema to experimental psychology at large.

Ironically, it may have been the preeminent group dynamicist himself, Kurt Lewin, who actually laid the foundation for the great turning inward of social psychology. For example, much of the import of Lewinian (e.g., 1958) experiments on groups can be traced to the subsequent consequences for individuals (e.g., attitude change) attributable to exmembers' participation in group decision making. (Actually, Lewin's groups rarely made explicit, collective decisions in these experiments—e.g., Lewin, 1943; rather, discussion revealed the prevailing consensus, providing, in a sense, "group" decision by implication; Bennett, 1955.)

Considered loosely, *commitment* (cf. Kiesler, 1971) was the label for these postgroup phenomena, and the "group-induced-change" research tradition itself soon led to an entire social movement (some might say industry) emphasizing personal change through (guided) group interaction (see the review of "T-groups" and derivatives by Back, 1972). However, commitment was soon followed by the theory of *cognitive dissonance* (e.g., Festinger, 1957) that focused even more closely on the individual, and researchers in the associated research tradition quickly dispensed with an actual group setting altogether in the experimental operations that generated the relevant data (e.g., see Aronson & Carlsmith, 1968). Cognitive dissonance was in turn succeeded by *attribution theory* (e.g., Jones & K. E. Davis, 1965; Kelley, 1967), a conceptual approach that, although initially emphasizing *perception*, subtly introduced additional cognitive operations, especially inferential processes, thereby enlarging the span of cognitive mechanisms to be considered. Finally, the emergence of *social cognition* (e.g., see Wyer & Srull, 1984), the most recent development in this conceptual line, signaled the emergence of a very general concern with social phenomena as intraindividual events, and indeed, has at the same time come increasingly to encompass many of the traditional topics of personality—such as emotion and motivation. In fact, under the social cognition umbrella, various theories large and small now address virtually all intraindividual phenomena that have much of a social referent, and exclude only actual social/interpersonal behavior.

The second trend was the rise of a general behavioral science on a broad front. The kind of empirical (often experimental) methodology and theoretical style typical of science in general were increasingly employed in a variety of disciplines that were necessarily concerned with social and interpersonal behavior: organizational behavior, speech communication, administrative science, and systems analysis, to name only a few. Even some areas of economics have come to use experimental methods for gathering data (e.g., D. D. Davis & Holt, 1993). Although it seems fair to say that psychologists pioneered many behavioral science research methods (especially experimental techniques) and approaches to the study of human cognition and behavior, many disciplines now pursue similar research agendas in similar ways, albeit often in pursuit of highly pragmatic goals.

The preceding scenario is worth noting, because the disciplines at issue generally consider task-oriented groups of various sizes and types as among their fundamental objects of study, although surveys and other individually oriented research methods are not unknown. After all, committees, panels, and many other kinds of small groups are fixtures of organizational and institutional life. It should have come as no surprise when Levine and Moreland (1990) concluded their incisive literature review by asserting that small-group research was "alive and well" after all, but much of the work was now located in organizational studies of one sort or another, rather than in its ancestral home, psychology. A number of disciplines now share an interest in group research, and are actively investigating small-group behavior in many contexts.

Finally, it is worth asking after the engines that might be driving these two trends. First, the immediately preceding discussion makes fairly obvious that the *conceptual* and *practical needs* of the areas in question made inevitable their eventual focus on small, task-oriented groups, and in time the effort came to rely heavily on empirical research.

Second, it is important to note that the progression of rich *theoretical* developments, outlined earlier, fueled much of the evolution toward the intraindividual, in contrast to empirical discoveries or practical problems. Of course, it is difficult to imagine that extraordinary empirical events did not sometimes figure in the evolution of intraindividual conceptual approaches. Consider the theory of cognitive dissonance and its early relation to the famous study by Festinger, Riecken, and Schachter (1958) of an end-of-the-world cult whose members displayed a paradoxical increase in a belief, following its apparent disconfirmation. Moreover, these theories, of which cognitive dissonance is highly typical, are clear, uncomplicated, and parsimonious constructions that are immediately available to the researcher, even those without a substantial background. That is, such theories are highly compelling prima facie, and fit well with conventional conversational explanations of human behavior, among other appealing features. We return later to theoretical considerations, because theory is the main thrust of this volume.

A third intraindividual trend engine is the less intellectually lofty, but very serious, problem of subject costs in group research. Sample sizes adequate for research on individuals are increased by a factor of group size. A simple, commonplace experiment of 2×2 cells containing 20 subjects each means a total of 80 required for research on individuals, but 400 subjects are needed if five-person groups are the research target. Actually, the problem is more serious than the foregoing implies. Imagine a reasonably high individual show-up rate at the laboratory—for example, suppose that .80 is the probability of assignees actually showing up. Under typical random assignment of subjects to experiments, conditions, locations, and times, subject arrivals at the laboratory are independent events; the probability of staffing a five-person group is thus only $(.80)^5 = .33$. (The tempting strategy of overscheduling subjects is not only potentially wasteful, assuming no backup projects can use overflow, but likely to irritate research colleagues.)

Such mundane facts are as unpalatable as they are intellectually dreary. Yet, it seems highly plausible that the subject-shortage problem, worsened by ever more competition from other topic areas of the discipline that have been increasing their use of human subjects, is at least as serious a damper on group research within the typical psychology research department or institute as any (more intellectually interesting) conceptual features associated with the two trends themselves. Because subject availability appears to be a problem unlikely to resolve itself, and creative solutions are not now evident, research using actual groups of actual subjects will face major challenges for some time to come. In the meantime, the appeal of research strategies that concentrate on simulating others or addressing those group-related concepts and phenomena that do not immediately require multiple sets of subjects, is likely to endure. (See J. H. Davis & Kerr, 1986, for a discussion of simulation within the subject-shortage context.)

Summary. The proposal here is that the *relative* incidence of group-level research in social psychology has declined over the past 40 years or so, because (a) Straightforward theories addressing individuals proliferated inside social psychology and successfully competed for researcher attention, and (b) the lack of sufficient numbers of subjects makes group studies highly unattractive to potential investigators. During the same period, other disciplines increased their empirical research on small groups; this development accompanied the decline in social psychology, but did not contribute much to it.

THE STEINER QUESTIONS AND ANSWERS

Steiner's (1974) famous question, "Whatever happened to the group in social psychology?" has provoked much discussion. His own answer was predicated upon socio-historical forces; he posited that a group focus, after some temporal lag, was likely after periods of social conflict in the surrounding culture, and thus forecast a resurgence of research on groups during the late 1970s. Later Steiner (1983) qualified this hypothesis, using attributional notions, in order to explain why the predicted upsurge had not occurred. Still later (Steiner, 1986), he seemed pessimistic about any upturn in the near future, citing probable paradigm shifts in social psychology that favored a continued intraindividual emphasis. Likely to be permanent, he further implied that these changes fostered a concentration on individuals and immediate internal causes of behavior at the expense of external causes, multiple-person units, and sequences of behavior over time.

Obviously, our earlier analysis does not agree with Steiner's (1974, 1983, 1986) original and later proposals that the rise and fall of group research is closely tuned to larger societal concerns and phenomena that in turn stimulate social researchers. As a supporting counterexample of sorts, consider the deep distress among social observers of many kinds about possible changes in the United States judicial system during the late 1960s and 1970s—especially those focusing on the role and structure of the criminal jury. (During the same period, similar social and scientific issues stimulated considerable concern in Canada and the United Kingdom; see Muller, Blackman, & Chapman, 1984.) In particular, much research was stimulated by U.S. Supreme Court decisions about jury size and assigned decision rule (see discussions by J. H. Davis, 1980, 1989; J. H. Davis, Bray, & Holt, 1977; Vollrath & J. H. Davis, 1980), a very great deal of it focusing on studies of mock juries. However, the furor was about the jury as special social agency, not as small group, and once the excitement surrounding the political and ideological concerns of the period abated, the interest in group research declined as well. Most telling of all, research interest did not generalize beyond the jury to other collective behavior topics and environments.

The Steiner questions were recently very thoroughly addressed by Moreland, Hogg, and Hains (1994), who surveyed publication trends in several primary journals in social psychology. In light of our earlier discussion, as well as Levine and Moreland's (1990) earlier conclusions, it is regrettable that Moreland et al. did not also include communication and organizational research journals, among others. However, Moreland et al. did incorporate certain *social cognition* topics and the general area of *intergroup relations* ("European approaches") in the "group research" category, areas not ordinarily thought to be involved with the Steiner questions. Their results showed a recent upsurge in group research, but only if the two new areas were included; otherwise, the relative incidence of group studies remains fairly constant—and small. Finally, although the long-time group research topics indeed may not be studied at earlier rates, one can only applaud the Moreland et al. expansion of conceptual horizons—especially because there has been a related merging of research interests quietly taking place in at least one corner of the general area of group behavior and interpersonal interaction. An expansion of sorts, this new development is marked by the tendency of investigators to refer to "social decision making"—a broad category of interpersonal research that includes social dilemmas, bargaining and negotiation interactions, and experimental games, as well as consensual decision making. One could further make the case that a mature science of group and interpersonal behavior would eventually include as well such methodological topics as block models (Wasserman & Galaskiewicz, 1994) and cluster analysis (e.g., Arabie, Boorman, & Levitt, 1978), largely conceptual topics such as voting models (e.g., Grofman, 1981, 1987), social/public choice theory and research (e.g., Brams & Fishburn, 1983; Fishburn, 1973), and so on. However, only time will tell whether or not these and related areas, now often located in various disciplines outside of psychology, will emerge as part of a new synthesis.

In any event, it now seems that the time has come to put the Steiner questions to rest, especially the lamentations that have often surrounded their discussion. Just as the intellectual anguish associated with the "crisis in social psychology" (e.g., Baumgardner, 1976; Elms, 1975; Silverman, 1971) eventually became tiresome and finally dwindled (without any noticeable "resolution" of anything, including whatever it may have been that produced the sense of "crisis"), the time has come to talk less *about* the rise and fall of group-oriented research, and to act instead on the significant theoretical and methodological problems in the area.

THE QUESTION OF THEORY

Although there is not now an obvious solution to the subject-supply problem on the horizon, one can be much less pessimistic about the prospect of new theories and conceptual developments—a point to which we return later. There has always been a strong theoretical tradition in small-group research, but it has differed in significant ways from theory that has generally guided research in intraindividual social psychology.

First, group theory has tended to be relatively *formal*, often expressed as a mathematical or computer model. Second, group research in general has tended to be *problem oriented*, and of course, theoretical explanations have been similarly oriented. In contrast, as detailed earlier, intraindividual theory is quite *informal* in format (although there exist some striking exceptions—e.g., in attitude theory, Anderson, 1959, 1971; Hunter, Danes, & Cohen, 1984), and the related empirical intraindividual research is perhaps more likely to be *theory oriented* in the sense that studies are so often expressly motivated by the goal to demonstrate how the hypothesized theoretical process works in various contexts. Just after midcentury, cognitive dissonance theory (Festinger, 1957) appealed widely not only because it was (perhaps deceptively) simple and clear, but also because in principle it was virtually unbounded—thereby giving rise to the possibility of applications in a very wide variety of situations. Considerable effort was devoted to devising new situations to which the theory might potentially apply.

During the same period, group-level research, in contrast, tended to be organized around various (often unrelated) problems, and to be composed in mathematical or computer language. For example, consider the following problem-oriented, formal theories addressing questions associated with: (a) *group performance*, by Lorge and Solomon (1955, 1962), Thomas and Fink (1961), Smoke and Zajonc (1962), and Restle and J. H. Davis (1962) on group problem solving, and more recently, Gelfand and Solomon (1974, 1975, 1977), and Hastie, Penrod, and Pennington (1983) on jury decision making; and (b) *interpersonal processes/group structure* by Simon (1952), Harary, Norman, and Cartwright (1965), and Horvath (1965), and more recently, Stasser (1988) and Galam and Moscovici

(1991 in press-a, in press-b). Moreover, note that the foregoing discussion does not even include the equally problem-oriented and highly formal theoretical developments associated with research on social dilemmas, negotiation/bargaining, and voting models, to name only a few appealing possibilities.

Finally, the inclination to formal theory and the disposition to problem-oriented research will probably continue, and indeed is likely to be promoted further by the increasing involvement of such disciplines as organizational behavior, social choice, and economics. The applied nature of such disciplines is likely to foster a continued propensity for investigating particular problems, and given the academic training of researchers from those disciplines, the inclination to mathematical and computer models seems likely to continue.

CONCLUDING REMARKS

The preceding discussion aimed to identify general trends in recent past and present group research and theory, and to reflect upon possible influences that have helped shape those trends. Like all such summaries, it must be imperfect. Intraindividual research can of course be problem oriented (e.g., Hamilton, Sherman, & Ruvolo, 1990) and intraindividual theory can be formal in character (e.g., Anderson, 1971). Additionally, much of what has been said is more characteristic of North American social psychology, than elsewhere. For example, group-research problems of many kinds have been and continue to be the source of strong research themes in European and Japanese social psychology. General cultural differences may account for some of the relative differences in intra- and interindividual research focus, but other, less obvious, causes may also be involved. Such additional issues deserve further exploration.

A central aim here has been to argue against the imputation often associated with the Steiner (1974, 1983, 1986) questions that group-level research has declined because something went wrong, and by implication needs to be put aright. The thesis here is that the "original" group-level research topics have evolved into multidisciplinary problems of different kinds, have attracted investigators from a wide variety of areas outside social psychology, continue to stimulate theory phrased in languages not popular in most circles in social psychology, and, perhaps most of all, continue to require subjects in numbers that cannot easily be satisfied by the usual sources that feed most psychological research projects. The current relative incidence of group and intraindividual research is an evolutionary consequence of these factors. Nothing is wrong; change is inevitable. However, changes in relative emphases that would favor research on intact groups is currently unlikely due to the persistence of the influences discussed previously, especially subject shortages.

This volume offers a sample of current theory addressing group and interpersonal behavior, especially within that subtopic we might call "consensual action." These chapters also illustrate both the problem-oriented feature discussed earlier, and the inclination to mathematical and computer models. Although there are some interesting similarities in conceptual approaches among these chapters, there is also a challenging diversity in the theorizing herein, suggesting that the trends and influences discussed in this chapter indeed do not capture all that is going on in the field.

ACKNOWLEDGMENT

Portions of this paper were prepared with the support of National Science Foundation Grant NSF SBR 93-09405.

REFERENCES

Anderson, N. H. (1959). Test of a model for opinion change. *Journal of Abnormal and Social Psychology, 59*, 371–381.
Anderson, N. H. (1971). Integration theory and attitude change. *Psychological Review, 78*, 171–206.
Arabie, P., Boorman, S. A., & Levitt, P. R. (1978). Constructing block models: How and why. *Journal of Mathematical Psychology, 17*, 21–63.
Aronson, E., & Carlsmith, J. M. (1968). Experimentation in social psychology. In G. Lindzey & E. Aronson (Eds.), *The handbook of social psychology* (Vol. 2, pp. 1–79). Reading, MA: Addison-Wesley.
Back, K. W. (1972). *Beyond words: The story of sensitivity training and the encounter movement.* New York: Russell Sage Foundation.
Baumgardner, S. R. (1976). Critical history of social psychology's "crisis." *Personality and Social Psychology Bulletin, 2*, 460–465.
Bennett, E. B. (1955). Discussion, decision, commitment and consensus in "group decision." *Human Relations, 8*, 251–274.
Brams, S. J., & Fishburn, P. C. (1983). *Approval voting.* Boston: Birkhauser.
Davis, D. D., & Holt, C. A. (1993). *Experimental economics.* Princeton, NJ: Princeton University Press.
Davis, J. H. (1980). Group decision and procedural justice. In M. Fishbein (Ed.), *Progress in social psychology* (Vol. 1, pp. 157–229). Hillsdale, NJ: Lawrence Erlbaum Associates.
Davis, J. H. (1989). Psychology and law: The last fifteen years. *Journal of Applied Social Psychology, 19*, 199–230.
Davis, J. H., Bray, R. M., & Holt, R. W. (1977). The empirical study of decision processes in juries: A critical review. In J. L. Tapp & F. J. Levine (Eds.), *Law, justice, and the individual in society: Psychological and legal issues* (pp. 326–360). New York: Holt, Rinehart & Winston.
Davis, J. H., & Kerr, N. L. (1986). Thought experiments and the problem of sparse data in small group research. In P. Goodman (Ed.), *Designing effective work groups* (pp. 305–349). San Francisco: Jossey-Bass.
Elms, A. C. (1975). The crisis of confidence in social psychology. *American Psychologist, 30*, 967–976.
Festinger, L. (1957). *A theory of cognitive dissonance.* Stanford, CA: Stanford University Press.
Festinger, L., Riecken, H. W., & Schachter, S. (1958). When prophecy fails. In E. E. Maccoby, T. M. Newcomb, & E. L. Hartley (Eds.), *Readings in social psychology* (pp. 157–163). New York: Holt.

Fishburn, P. C. (1973). *The theory of social choice*. Princeton, NJ: Princeton University Press.

Galam, S., & Moscovici, S. (1991). Towards a theory of collective phenomena: Consensus and attitude changes in groups. *European Journal of Social Psychology, 21*, 49–74.

Galam, S., & Moscovici, S. (in press-a). Towards a theory of collective phenomena: II. Conformity and power. *European Journal of Social Psychology*.

Galam, S., & Moscovici, S. (in press-b). Towards a theory of collective phenomena: III. Conflicts and forms of power. *European Journal of Social Psychology*.

Gelfand, A. E., & Solomon, H. (1974). Modeling jury verdicts in the American legal system. *Journal of the American Statistical Association, 69*, 32–37.

Gelfand, A. E., & Solomon, H. (1975). Analyzing the decision-making process of the American jury. *Journal of the American Statistical Association, 70*, 305–310.

Gelfand, A. E., & Solomon, H. (1977). An argument in favor of 12-member juries. In S. S. Nagel (Ed.), *Modeling the Criminal Justice System* (pp. 205–224). Beverly Hills, CA: Sage.

Grofman, B. (1981). The theory of committees and elections: The legacy of Duncan Black. In Gordon Tullock (Ed.), *Towards a science of politics: Essays in honor of Duncan Black* (pp. 111–133). Blacksburg: Virginia Polytechnic Institute & State University, Public Choice Center.

Grofman, B. (1987). Group decision making: The theory of committees and elections [Mimeographs]. Irvine: University of California, School of Social Sciences.

Hamilton, D. L., Sherman, S. J., & Ruvolo, C. M. (1990). Stereotype-based expectancies: Effects on information processing and social behavior. *Journal of Social Issues, 46*, 35–68.

Harary, F., Norman, R. Z., & Cartwright, D. (1965). *Structural models: An introduction to the theory of directed graphs*. New York: Wiley.

Hastie, R., Penrod, S., & Pennington, N. (1983). *Inside the jury*. Cambridge, MA: Harvard University Press.

Horvath, W. J. (1965). A mathematical model of participation in small group discussion. *Behavioral Science, 10*, 164–166.

Hunter, J. E., Danes, J. E., & Cohen, S. H. (1984). *Mathematical models of attitude change: Change in single attitudes and cognitive structure* (Vol. 1). New York: Academic Press.

Jones, E. E., & Davis, K. E. (1965). From acts to dispositions: The attribution process in person perception. In L. Berkowitz (Ed.), *Advances in experimental social psychology* (Vol. 2, pp. 220–266). New York: Academic Press.

Kelley, H. H. (1967). Attribution theory in social psychology. In D. Levine (Ed.), *Nebraska symposium on motivation* (pp. 192–240). Lincoln: University of Nebraska Press.

Kiesler, C. A. (1971). *The psychology of commitment*. New York: Academic Press.

Levine, J. M., & Moreland, R. L. (1990). Progress in small group research. *Annual Review of Psychology, 41*, 585–634.

Lewin, K. (1943). Forces behind food habits and methods of change. *Bulletin of the National Research Council, 108*, 35–65.

Lewin, K. (1958). Group decision and social change. In E. E. Maccoby, T. M. Newcomb, & E. L. Hartley (Eds.), *Readings in social psychology* (3rd ed., pp. 197–211). New York: Holt.

Lorge, I., & Solomon, H. (1955). Two models of group behavior in the solution of Eureka-type problems. *Psychometrika, 20*, 139–148.

Lorge, I., & Solomon, H. (1962). Group and individual behavior in free recall verbal learning. In J. H. Crisswell, H. Solomon, & P. Suppes (Eds.), *Mathematical methods in small group processes* (pp. 221–231). Stanford: Stanford University Press.

Moreland, R. L., Hogg, M. A., & Hains, S. C. (1994). Back to the future: Social psychological research on groups. *Journal of Experimental Social Psychology, 30*, 527–555.

Muller, D. J., Blackman, D. E., & Chapman, A. J. (1984). *Psychology and law*. Chichester, England: Wiley.

Restle, F., & Davis, J. H. (1962). Success and speed of problem solving by individuals and groups. *Psychological Review, 69*, 520–536.

Silverman, I. (1971). Crisis in social psychology: The relevance of relevance. *American Psychologist, 26*, 583–584.

Simon, H. A. (1952). A formal theory of interaction in social groups. *American Sociological Review, 17*, 202–211.

Smoke, W. H., & Zajonc, R. B. (1962). On the reliability of group judgments and decision. In J. H. Crisswell, H. Solomon, & P. Suppes (Eds.), *Mathematical methods in small group processes* (pp. 322–333). Stanford, CA: Stanford University Press.

Stasser, G. (1988). Computer simulation as a research tool: The DISCUSS model of group decision making. *Journal of Experimental Social Psychology, 24*, 393–422.

Steiner, I. D. (1974). Whatever happened to the group in social psychology? *Journal of Experimental Social Psychology, 10*, 93–108.

Steiner, I. D. (1983). Whatever happened to the touted revival of the group? In H. H. Bluberg, A. P. Hare, V. Kent, & M. F. Davies (Eds.), *Small groups and social interaction* (Vol. 2, pp. 539–548). Chichester, England: Wiley.

Steiner, I. D. (1986). Paradigms and groups. In L. Berkowitz (Ed.), *Advances in experimental social psychology* (Vol. 19, pp. 251–292). New York: Academic Press.

Thomas, E. J., & Fink, C. F. (1961). Models of group problem solving. *Journal of Abnormal and Social Psychology, 68*, 53–63.

Vollrath, D. A., & Davis, J. H. (1980). Jury size and decision rule. In R. J. Simon (Ed.), *The jury: Its role in American society* (pp. 73–106). Lexington, MA: Lexington.

Wasserman, S., & Galaskiewicz, J. (1994). *Advances in social network analysis: Research in the social and behavioral sciences*. Thousand Oaks, CA: Sage.

Wyer, R. S., & Srull, T. K. (Eds.). (1984). *Handbook of social cognition* (Vols. 1, 2, & 3). Hillsdale, NJ: Lawrence Erlbaum Associates.

II

SOCIAL AGGREGATION AND COMBINATION MODELS

2

A Probabilistic Model of Opinion Change Considering Distance Between Alternatives: An Application to Mock Jury Data

Helmut W. Crott
Joachim Werner
Christine Hoffmann
Albert-Ludwigs-Universität Freiburg

Social decision-making research studies the mutual influences exerted by group members upon each other. To investigate this social decision schemes were postulated, which implicitly or explicitly transform the differing opinions of individuals into group decisions (Davis, 1973, 1982; Isenberg, 1986; Kaplan & Miller, 1983). For a brief review of the history of that research see also the contribution of Davis in this volume. The research on social decision schemes, if it considers the process of social judgment, includes process characteristics as a part of the scheme. The schemes, however, usually are not conceptualized to describe or to predict the process itself.

Of course, the question might arise whether the study of the process is useful per se. But, in our opinion, the study of the process of opinion change can contribute to the understanding of the principles underlying interpersonal communication, collective decision making, and problem solving. Hence, the theory of group behavior might benefit from the analysis of the process of change.

Several studies have been conducted to get insight into the nature of opinion change. To mention only a few studies, the works of Hastie, Penrod, and Pennington (1983), Kerr (1982), Stasser (1988), Stasser and Davis (1981), and Stasser, Kerr, and Davis (1980), for example, focused on the process of forming judgments and decisions in mock juries. Kaplan and Miller (1983) in their review suggested that models dealing with the process of collective judgment should be extended to situations involving more than two alternatives, including those in which the alternatives are ordered along a continuum (Kaplan & Miller, 1983;

see also Kerr, 1992). That implies that proximity or distance should be introduced into a model of social change.

INDIVIDUAL TRANSITION PROBABILITIES

The central objective of this chapter is to develop a generalized probabilistic
model of the social group interaction process including a distance function. This
model is derived in two steps. In the first step, individual transition probabilities
are determined on the basis of theoretical assumptions. The set of individual
transition probabilities consists of the probabilities for each individual to change
from alternative i to any alternative j from time t to time t + 1. These transition
probabilities need not be constant over time, because the probabilities might
depend on the composition of the group to which the individual belongs.

In the second step, the transition probabilities for group constellations (distinguishable distributions of group members over alternatives) are derived. To
calculate the probabilities of change from a group constellation k at time t to
any other group constellation at time t + 1 requires the derivation of a combinatorial algorithm. As long as the individual conditional probabilities of change
for any individual preferring a certain alternative in a given constellation are
independent of time, these theoretical transition probabilities between group
constellations are necessarily constant over time.

We first say something about the general concept of individual probabilities.
To prevent misunderstanding, it should be stated that by individual probabilities
we do not mean personal probabilities that are dependent on a person's characteristics, attitudes, and so forth. It is rather supposed that all persons have
the same individual probabilities of change if they are exposed to the same
influences relevant for the tendency to change. The framework of individual
probabilities of change can be depicted by a general additive composition of
sources of influence and their concatenation with a proximity or distance function. It should be noted that the notion of distance would have no meaning if
the alternatives are not fixed by context or definition and any permutation of
them is as reasonable as any other.

This general formula for the individual probabilities of change from alternative i to j, (i ≠ j) for m alternatives denotes as follows:

$$p_{ij} = (w_1 I_{1ij} + w_2 I_{2ij} \dots w_e I_{eij}) * f(d_{ij}), \qquad (1)$$

with each w-weight ranging between 0 and 1 and the sum of w-weights being
≤1.00.

The probability to stay in the original position (p_{ii}) is then defined as

$$p_{ii} = 1 - \sum_{\substack{j=1 \\ i \neq j}}^{m} p_{ij}. \qquad (2)$$

The terms of the expression in parentheses, I_{1ij}, I_{2ij}, and so on are different sources of influence exerted by alternative j on holders of alternative i. Such sources might be the instrumentality of an alternative, its social desirability, its truth value, its overt attractiveness, or the number of group members who plead for it.

The w values are weights that are attached to the influence sources, but are not dependent on i. The sizes of the w weights also account for the fact that the readiness to change will depend on several task characteristics. For example, w weights will depend on the time interval between polls, because it seems plausible that changes of opinion are less likely to occur within shorter time intervals. Additionally, one might suppose that persons are less ready to change when the subject of discussion is an important issue.

The weighted sources of influence then have to be combined by a function of distances in one- or multidimensional cases. For example, if the alternatives can be arranged in a one-dimensional continuum, then persons with different points of view can approach each other step by step (Crott, Szilvas, & Zuber, 1991; Crott, Zuber, & Schermer, 1986; Zuber, Crott, & Werner, 1992). In this way, alternatives in between also may be chosen even if they have no attractiveness (informational or subgroup) in themselves. The sign * indicates that the combination of distance with the weighted influence sources is not just a multiplication but a special concatenation. We comment on this concatenation in more detail in the following section.

THE DISTANCE FUNCTION

The definition of the distance function can be illustrated by an object that is drawn along the continuum of alternatives by several forces, arranged one behind the other. The force of all sources pulls the object to the location of the first source. From that point, the force exerted by the first source lapses. The remaining sources draw the object to the location of the second source, then the third, and so on. Because the force of the sources decreases gradually with increasing distance from the object, the force has to be adjusted in each case by a distance factor. Such a kind of distance function is best illustrated by an example (see Fig. 2.1).

In the example in Fig. 2.1, assume that there are five alternatives, i is fixed as $i = 2$, and consider the group constellation is 21011. A group constellation 21011 indicates that two people at the moment prefer alternative 1, one person alternative 2, no persons alternative 3, one person alternative 4, and one person alternative 5. For reasons of simplicity, further assume for the moment that the influence potentials depend on one kind of force only, for example, the relative faction size r_j/r. Then the relative faction size of alternative 1 is 2/5, that of alternative 3 is 0/5, and that of alternatives 4 and 5 is 1/5 for each. The actual influence of the relative faction size on the subject at alternative 2 depends,

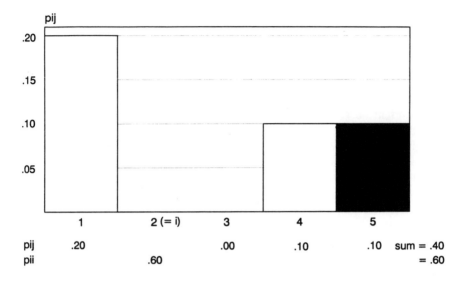

	1	2 (= i)	3	4	5	
pij	.20		.00	.10	.10	sum = .40
pii		.60				= .60

a) probabilities of change <u>without</u> distance

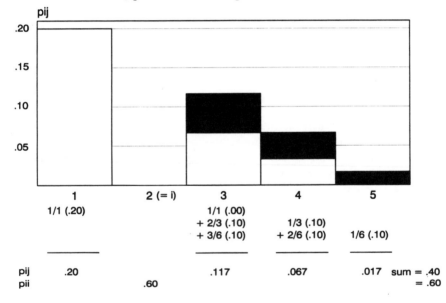

	1	2 (= i)	3	4	5	
	1/1 (.20)		1/1 (.00) + 2/3 (.10) + 3/6 (.10)	1/3 (.10) + 2/6 (.10)	1/6 (.10)	
pij	.20		.117	.067	.017	sum = .40
pii		.60				= .60

b) probabilities of change <u>with</u> distance

FIG. 2.1. Example for the modification of probabilities of change (pij) by the introduction of distance for an individual presently on alternative 2 (i) in constellation 21011.

among others, on the task characteristics and the time interval considered. Therefore, the relative faction sizes (r_j/r) have to be adjusted by a parameter w, which ranges from 0 to 1. Assume for example a w value of .50, for the purpose of calculating the probability p_{2j} of changing to any of the remaining alternatives 1, 3, 4 or 5. According to such a pure subgroup model without distance (see number under the continuum in Fig. 2.1), the person at alternative 2 cannot change to alternative 3. This possibility, however, will be created, as can be seen from the example in Fig. 2.1, by the concatenation of the influence potentials with the distance function. Observe how the influence potentials of the alternatives given by the numbers under the continuum in Fig. 2.1 are redistributed over the alternatives according to their distance to i. As seen from the example in Fig. 2.1, 100% of the influence potential of alternative 1 is effective for the change to alternative 1 $(p_{21} = 1.0 \times .50 \times 2/5)$. The same is true for alternative 3. The influence potential of alternative 4 is distributed in inverse proportion to the absolute distance between alternatives 2 and 3 $(= \mid 1 \mid)$ and the absolute distance between alternatives 2 and 4 $(= \mid 2 \mid)$. That results in 2/3 of the influence potential of alternative 4 being effective on alternative 3 and 1/3 on alternative 4. Analogously, the influence potential of alternative 5 is distributed in inverse proportion to the absolute distances between alternatives 2 and 3 $(= \mid 1 \mid)$ and alternatives 2 and 4 $(= \mid 2 \mid)$ and alternatives 2 and 5 $(= \mid 3 \mid)$ into 3/6, 2/6, and 1/6 of the influence potential of alternative 5 for alternatives 3, 4, and 5 respectively. The corresponding influence components in each line of the example in the bottom of Fig. 2.1 are summed to obtain the p_{2j} values. This procedure results in the probabilities of change p_{2j} given in the last row of Fig. 2.1. The total influence potential of any alternative remains preserved; it simply becomes redistributed over all alternatives. Thus the probability of maintaining a stable opinion (inertia) $p_{ii} = 1 - \Sigma \ p_{ij}$ will remain constant after application of the distance function. Note that by including the distance function, the *probabilistic model of opinion change including distances* (PCD) model allows a person at alternative i to change to any alternative j, even if the faction size of j is zero (alternative 3). This is a desirable property of the model, because such changes obviously occur in group discussions. It is further evident that taking distance into consideration drastically reduces the probabilities of changing to more remote alternatives in favor of the alternatives nearer to the current opinion. For example the probability of changing from alternative 2 to 5 reduces from .10 to .017, whereas the probability of changing from 2 to 3, which was zero, becomes .117 after the distance function is added.

APPROACHING GROUP PROCESSES

It should be noted that the individual probability of changing from alternative i to alternative j cannot remain constant over time in a model that incorporates the relative size of a subgroup. Because the size of a subgroup at alternative j can change from one point in time to another, the probability of switching from alternative i to alternative j also varies from one point in time to another. Actually, small-group research does not focus on the individual's probability of changing from alternative i to alternative j, but on the changes in group constellations. Previous research has used computer simulations to describe this process of change. Such simulations fix a unit of observation (e.g., a time interval); the factors of influence (e.g., informational value or faction size) are estimated from the nature of the experimental system, and the whole process is then simulated on the basis of path independence and stationarity of transition probabilities with random generators (Stasser & Davis, 1981). It appears worthwhile, however, to solve the matrix of group constellations in terms of probability theory. In order to determine the probability that a group will move from one constellation to another, the individual probability vectors have to be combined. This allows one to ascertain the probability with which any constellation (e.g., 20210) will change into any other constellation (e.g., 30200). By this procedure the process is expressed theoretically as a stationary Markov chain. The result is a cross table that contains for each state k the probability to remain stable or to change to any other state l from time t to time t + 1. Details of this method of combining the individual probability vectors are given in the Appendix.

DERIVATION OF A SPECIFIC MODEL (NORM-INFORMATION-DISTANCE MODEL)

The Norm-Information-Distance (NID) model yields a simple model for judgmental tasks that focuses on three components: the influence of the faction size on alternative j, the influence of the overt attractiveness of the alternative j, and the distance between alternatives i and j.

The social influence that is exerted by an alternative j on proponents of alternative i is supposed to be a function of the informational value that alternative j has for proponents of alternative i, the relative faction size within the group on alternative j, and the distance between i and j. More precisely, in Formula 3 that follows the τ_{ij} values (or respectively in the concatenation with the distance the τ_{ik} values) describe the informational attractiveness that any alternative j has on a representative of alternative i. The value $(r_j/r)^c$ describes the normative effect of a subgroup holding alternative j. With regard to the results of Godwin and Restle (1974) and Stasser and Davis (1981), the normative component is shown by a power function $(r_j/r)^c$. The parameter c takes the possibility into account that the influence of subgroups is an exponential function of their size. The term $(r_j/r)^c$ should be standardized to guarantee that the sum of all subgroup influences equals 1.00, so that the sum is not dependent on c. The w_1 and w_2 weights express the relative contribution of the informational and the normative components. Finally, the expression to the right of the parentheses of the formula summarizes the distance function as it was described in the section on the distance function.

$$p_{ij} = \sum_{k=j,1}^{m,j} \left[w_1 \tau_{ik} + w_2 \frac{\left(\dfrac{r_k}{r}\right)^c}{\sum\limits_{l=1}^{m}\left(\dfrac{r_l}{r}\right)^c} \right] \frac{2(|k-j|+1)}{(|k-i|)(|k-i|+1)} \tag{3}$$

$i < j \leq k \leq m$, or $i > j \geq k \geq 1$ respectively
$0 \leq w_1$, w_2 and $w_1 + w_2 \leq 1$, $\Sigma \tau_{ij} = 1.00$

In the application given that follows, the individual transition probabilities are specified to depend on three components: faction size, informational value, and distance. It is apparent, however, that depending on the type of problem any additive combinations of an arbitrary number of components could be chosen to define the individual transition probabilities. Thus the general framework allows expression of various theories in terms of individual transition probabilities.

Several possibilities for applying the NID model to the data were developed: pure information models (including τ_{ij} or τ_j), pure subgroup models [including the (r_j/r) component only], and mixed models incorporating both informational and subgroup components (including both components). Regarding the informational component, it appears reasonable to test whether informational attractiveness of an alternative j depends on i, or not (τ_{ij} vs. τ_j). Following the idea of the bias sampling model of Stasser and Titus (1985, 1987), it makes sense to analyze whether the informational attractiveness of all m alternatives influences the process or only the informational attractiveness of those alternatives exerts influence on the process that are held by at least one group member at a certain point in time. Such models are called conditional models, because the effectiveness of the informational component depends on the existence of at least one proponent for that alternative within the group. Conditional models exist for pure information models and for mixed models; pure subgroup models are conditional per se.

Again depending on the choice of the c parameter—as, for example, 1, 2, or 3—different manifestations of the subgroup component can be tested, each of them with or without consideration of the distance function. Mixed models result from the combination of the informational and subgroup components.

We introduced a pure random model as a baseline model assuming that the individual probabilities of change from any alternative i to any alternative j are equal for any i and any j. The combination of the random model with the distance function would yield a pure distance model. It describes a situation in which the effects of equally attractive alternatives depend only on the distance of alternatives from each other.

The model fit analysis will determine those w weights that fit the empirical data best for any of the models. The estimation of the w values was done by an iterative maximum-likelihood function in steps of .01 from 0 up to a maximum of 1 with the restriction $w_1 + w_2 \leq 1$.

METHOD

This chapter does not focus on the presentation of experimental results. We do, however, use some results from two mock jury experiments, one of which has already been published (Crott & Werner, 1994), to demonstrate the possibilities of using Markov chain analyses to describe the process of group interaction. For the present purpose it appears sufficient to mention that subjects in the two mock jury experiments had to discuss in five-person groups for about 20 minutes in the role of mock juries. The task was to deliberate about the appropriate sentence. The sentences for each of the two cases are determined by German law to range between 1 and 5 years in prison. At the outset, subjects were asked to give their opinion about the appropriate sentence: 1, 2, 3, 4, or 5 years (it is a characteristic of the German judicial system that jury members determine the sentence). Additionally, subjects had to evaluate each sentence (alternatives 1 to 5) by distributing 100 points over the alternatives according to their attitude toward the respective sentences. Every 90 seconds an acoustic signal indicated that subjects had to mark their present opinion, that is, to indicate which sentence they preferred at that moment. Of the 47 five-person groups, 23 discussed a taxicab robbery case (an attempted robbery with physical injury resulting from negligence) and 24 discussed a traffic offense (a dispute about the right of way, followed by intentional physical injury).

RESULTS

Originally, the experiments were run under four conditions. However, experimental variables had no significant effects, either on the judgmental process or on the final discussion.[1] Therefore, in the following analyses we report the results for the joint data (see Crott & Werner, 1994).

We do not consider any of the results from this study except the process data in order to assess the NID model as a predictor of the observed changes

---

[1]In these two conditions, 47 groups of five persons each were involved. The complete experiment included two further control conditions—"no intermediate measurement and group decision" and "no intermediate measurement and no group decision"—to check whether the intermediate measurement influenced the group process. We do not discuss these conditions in the present text, because no effect could be found according to several criteria (Werner, 1992).

of verdicts. Thus, the sample of observed mock jury processes is compared with the theoretical predictions of the best fitting versions of the NID model and with the predictions of a random model as a baseline.

It is our intention to derive predictions on the distribution of group constellations over the 10 points in time. In addition, we strive to attain information about special features of the process itself by applying Markov chain statistics to a limited number of assessments. For example: How often do the groups change from one state into another before the end of the experiment? How many different states do groups enter before the end of the experiment? How long do groups stay on the average in a certain transient state before the end of the experiment?

As described earlier, many different versions of the NID model can be derived from the basic model. Whereas the measurement of the parameters (r_j/r), c, and the distance is obvious, there exists no obvious measure for the informational values τ_{ij} or τ_j. To estimate τ_{ij}, we took the mean number of points attributed by holders of alternative i to alternative j, and divided it by the total number of points, that is, 100. If informational attraction of the alternative j is considered independent of the first preference i of the judge, then τ_j can be defined by averaging the τ_{ij} values for the holders of the different alternatives i.

Altogether, we tested 40 different versions for both items. Considering the c parameter deviations were smallest for c = 1 for all 10 models containing the c parameters (with values 1.0, 2.0, and 3.0). It should also be stressed that all versions taking distance into account provided a better approximation to the data than models without distance (see Crott & Werner, 1994). To decide between the several models at disposure we used a multistage statistical evaluation process. In a first analysis, we determined the w weights that best fit the empirical data for any of the 40 models. The second analysis calculated the goodness of fit for each model. The third analysis consisted of a pairwise comparison among all those models that did not deviate significantly from the data (for details, see Crott & Werner, 1994). According to that multistage statistical evaluation process, a mixed conditional model with distance resulted for the taxi item (for the definition of this model, see Crott & Werner, 1994). The w-value for the faction size (r_j/r) was .07 and that for the informational effect (τ_j) was .01. For the traffic item, a pure subgroup model provided the best fit. The w value for the faction size effect (r_j/r) was .07 and the w value for the informational effect was accordingly .00.

The theory of Markov processes allows one, however, to derive several statistics that describe processes in more detail (see Kemeny & Snell, 1965). There are Markov processes that contain both transient states and absorbing states. The transient states have the property that one can switch with a certain probability to another state, whereas the absorbing states, once reached, can never be left. The two best fitting versions of the NID model, the mixed conditional model with distance for the taxi item and the pure subgroup model with distance for the traffic item, both imply the existence of an absorbing state. This is evident for the pure subgroup model with distance. For the mixed conditional model with distance, the absorbing character results from the conditional effect of the τ_j parameter. Alternatives that are not occupied have no informational attractiveness according to the conditional definition of the τ_j. The absorbing states then are the states of consensus. That is the case, because according to these two models, there exist no more forces that could cause a change to another alternative.

For groups of five persons and five alternatives there exist 126 distinguishable distributions. Therefore the matrix of transition probabilities consists of 126×126 cells. The size of that matrix makes it almost impossible to gain an overview. For that reason, we searched for meaningful criteria to aggregate the large number of states. Among all criteria considered (see Crott & Werner, 1994), the most informative one was the number of occupied alternatives. That is, all states with one alternative occupied fall into the first category, all states with two alternatives occupied fall into the second category, and so on up to the fifth category.

By doing this, we could reduce the 126×126 matrix of transition probabilities to a 5×5 matrix. In the following, we calculate all the Markov statistics on the basis of the original 126×126 matrix, and afterward combine them into the 5×5 matrix.

We conducted the following investigations separately for the taxi case and the traffic case and then combined them for both items. Because the direction and the strength of the effects are comparable for the two items, taxi and traffic, we report only the combined results. First, we investigated whether the process is a stationary (independent of time) Markov process, which is a prerequisite for the application of the PCD/NID model. This was achieved by comparing the matrix of transition probabilities for each single point in time with the matrix of transition probabilities averaged over all 10 points in time. The condition of stationarity was fulfilled with $\chi^2 = 28.2$, $df = 31$, $p > .60$. Next we checked how the transition probabilities predicted theoretically by the best fitting versions of the NID model compared with the observed transition probabilities (see Table 2.1). We found a sufficient correspondence for both items with $\chi^2 = 5.76$, $df = 4$, $p > .20$.

That is, the results in general met reasonable statistical criteria, so that we could analyze the dynamic processes using Markov chain analysis. First, we predict the development of group constellations over the 10 points in time by the transition probabilities provided by the best fitting versions of the NID model. Then we compare these predictions with the observed data. Finally, the random model serves as a baseline to compare the empirical data with data generated by a pure chance process. The random model implies that subjects jump with the same probability to any of the alternatives j ($i \neq j$). To illustrate the development of the process, we selected 4 points of measurement, namely, the starting point, and the 4th, 7th, and 10th points in time. Figure 2.2 combines the frequencies of both items. It becomes evident from Fig. 2.2 how the frequen-

TABLE 2.1
Observed and Expected Transition Probabilities (Expected in Parentheses) Averaged Over the
10 Points in Time

	1	2	3	4	5
1	1.000 (1.000)	0.000 (0.000)	0.000 (0.000)	0.000 (0.000)	0.000 (0.000)
2	0.040 (0.018)	0.896 (0.924)	0.064 (0.059)	0.000 (0.001)	0.000 (0.000)
3	0.008 (0.000)	0.083 (0.064)	0.892 (0.894)	0.016 (0.042)	0.000 (0.000)
4	0.000 (0.000)	0.000 (0.004)	0.151 (0.150)	0.849 (0.833)	0.000 (0.012)
5	no entries (0.000)	no entries (0.000)	no entires (0.019)	no entries (0.268)	no entries (0.712)

cies (bars) with one to five occupied alternatives changed over the four chosen points in time. Obviously, the predictions of the best fitting versions of the NID model (solid line) corresponded to the observed changes quite well: $\chi^2 = 2.14$, $df = 6$, $p > .90$. In the course of time, the frequencies of group constellations with less occupied alternatives increased. These changes over time could not, however, be predicted by the random model (dashed line): $\chi^2 = 83.32$, $df = 6$, $p \leq .001$. The shape of the development that is visible in Fig. 2.2 was similar for both items, and the corresponding statistics provided equivalent results. The analyses so far, which were conducted with commonly used Markov statistics, indicated that the best fitting NID models were able to predict the deliberation process and its results well.

It is desirable to extract more detailed information about the process in order to generate new ideas for developing group process models further. With this objective in mind, we consider some more specific aspects of the process. From all possible Markov statistics, four appear to be especially instructive: (a) the number of groups that reach a majority (three or four persons on the same alternative) or a consensus (all five persons on the same alternative) at the end of the experiment, (b) the number of new transient states (i.e., states not entered by the groups before; including the states at the starting point) entered by the groups at the end of the experiment or before the absorbing state is reached, depending on the number of occupied alternatives at the beginning, (c) the number of times the groups change to transient states (from this number it is possible to derive further measures), and (d) the number of trials the groups remain in certain transient states until the end of the experiment or before the absorbing state is reached.

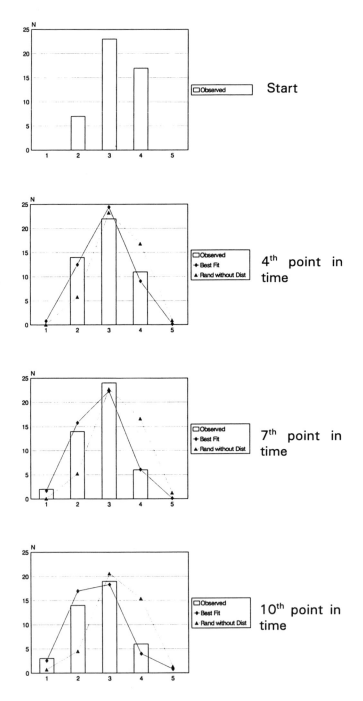

FIG. 2.2. Frequencies with which 1, 2, 3, 4, or 5 alternatives are occupied at the start and in the 4th, 7th, and 10th points in time ($n = 47$, at the start).

TABLE 2.2
Number of Groups That Reach a Consensus or a Majority

| | Points in Time | | | | | |
| | 4 | | 7 | | 10 | |
	Obs.	Exp.	Obs.	Exp.	Obs.	Exp.
Consensus	0	0.772	2	1.668	3	2.613
Majority	22	21.970	26	25.118	23	24.773
No Majority	25	24.259	18	19.214	16	14.615

With regard to (a), the predicted and the observed number of groups that have reached the stage of consensus, majority, or no majority at the 4th, 7th, or 10th point in time corresponded well. For both items combined, $\chi^2 = .38$, $df = 3$, $p \geq .90$ (see Table 2.2).

As for (b), it can be seen from Table 2.3 that the observed number of transient states entered by the groups was too large in comparison to what is expected according to the Markov NID model. When the results for both items were put together (Table 2.3) the p value fell below the level for conventional testing ($\chi^2 = 17.80$, $df = 3$, $p \leq .00$). Obviously, groups had a tendency to change their composition during the course of the experiment more often than it was predicted by the NID model.

Regarding (c), Table 2.4 shows a corresponding result by indicating that groups switched too often from the present transient state to another transient state (for both items combined: $\chi^2 = 8.62$, $df = 3$, $p \leq .05$). Note that the results from Tables 2.3 and 2.4 are not just complementary. Potentially, groups could also switch too often but numerously return to transient states in which they had been before.

To answer (d), we now calculated the number of trials the groups remained in transient states before an absorbing state was reached or until the end of the

TABLE 2.3
Number of Different Transient States

| Number of Occupied Alternatives at the Start | New Transient States Not Entered Before | | Transient States Entered Before or Absorbing States | | |
	Obs.	Exp.	Obs.	Exp.	n
2	8	4.27	53	56.73	61
3	42	28.08	176	189.92	218
4	37	25.30	130	141.70	167

TABLE 2.4
Number of Times the Groups Change to Other Transient States

Number of Occupied Alternatives at the Start	Other Transient State		Same Transient or Absorbing State		
	Obs.	Exp.	Obs.	Exp.	n
2	14	8.09	47	52.91	61
3	51	44.95	167	173.05	218
4	47	38.22	120	128.78	167

TABLE 2.5
Number of Trials the Groups Remain in CertainTransient States

Number of Occupied Alternatives at the Start	Number of Occupied Alternatives					
	. 2		3		4	
	Obs.	Exp.	Obs.	Exp.	Obs.	Exp.	n
2	58	56.834	3	1.582	0	0.104	61
3	57	59.666	155	153.960	6	8.145	218
4	11	20.849	69	70.101	87	74.797	167

experiment. Table 2.5 shows these results depending on the number of occupied alternatives with which the groups started (for both items taken together, $\chi^2 = 7.389$, $df = 3$, $p \le .10$). From these results we can conclude that the number of trials that the groups stay in certain transient states do not fit with the number expected theoretically. This difference was mainly due to the effect that groups starting in group constellations with four occupied alternatives did not stay long enough in states with two occupied alternatives.

DISCUSSION

The Markov process analyses showed that NID versions of the PCD model are able to predict the process of opinion changes. The best fitting predictions were from a mixed conditional model with distance for the taxi item and a pure subgroup model with distance for the traffic item. Predictions from a random model with distance, in contrast, showed a poor fit.

The process analysis demonstrated the importance of the inclusion of a distance function, because models considering distance generally fitted better than models without distance. The existence of a distance function implies that group members have the possibility to enter alternatives that exert neither a normative nor an informative attraction.

In order to get deeper insight into the nature of the process, we investigated several internal features of the process itself. First, we checked whether the condition of stationarity of transition probabilities that is a prerequisite to apply Markov chain statistics was fulfilled and whether the empirical and theoretical transition probabilities corresponded. Comparing the observed and the expected frequencies of consensus and majority states over time yielded a convincing correspondence. According to the criteria traditionally used in Markov process analyses (stationarity of the transition probability matrices, correspondence between predicted and observed frequencies of groups in the different states over time), the NID models predicted the features of the deliberation process well. The more detailed criteria that we introduced additionally into the analysis, however, showed some deviations from the expected values. This was especially true when both items were combined for the purpose of testing. Apparently, groups enter too many transient states and switch too often from one state to another during the course of action. The duration that the groups stay in a certain transient state differs from what was expected. This difference was mainly due to the traffic item. It was caused by the fact that groups starting in a group constellation with four occupied alternatives stayed there too long. Consequently, they stayed for a too short period in states with two occupied alternatives.

The reported discrepancies seem to indicate that the NID model does not account for all relevant aspects of the group process. On closer examination, the fact that the group members switched too often appears to be caused by moving back and forth into previous states. This phenomenon resulted very often from the behavior of the same person. One possible explanation might be that persons who changed their opinions are still in the state of uncertainty and hence return to the previous alternative. That suggests that a further development of the stochastic model for group opinion change might profit from taking into account the certainty about the opinion presently held.

The observation that groups starting with four different alternatives tended to stay there too long shows that the correspondence depends on the category of states in which the groups start. The idea to improve the fit of these internal statistics by further trying to optimize the parameters of the present versions of the NID model (e.g., w weights, c value) might appear suggestive. However, the observations made so far suggest that the approximation of theoretical and empirical values cannot be improved significantly by adjusting the free parameters w and c. Presumably, such a procedure would result in a displacement of the directions of the deviations.

The stochastic PCD model is conceptualized to allow the definition of sources of influence different from those already included in the NID model. One might think of sources like social desirability of an alternative, its instrumentality, its truth value, and so on. It will be one of the tasks of future research on group processes to discover the sources of influence relevant to the dynamics of opinion changes in groups. These investigations should extend over those potential influence forces stemming from the group itself as well as those forces exerted by external sources. The development of adequate methods for the assessment of such forces will constitute a major challenge.

One further possibility for modifying the present NID model would be to change the model into a shift model instead of a rate model. Rate models like the present version of the NID predict not only the direction but the rate (in time units) of opinion change. Shift models, in contrast, predict only the direction of opinion changes when they occur while ignoring the elapsed time between change of opinion (see Kerr, 1981; Stasser & Davis, 1981). This would provide an elegant way to bypass some of the violations of the internal statistics. On the other hand, by favoring shift models one will lose valuable information and at the same time give up the option to learn about temporal aspects of the process.

Although the NID model showed a sufficient goodness of fit for the data analyzed in the present application, it appears desirable to test further models derived from the PCD. For example it might be of interest to analyze decision-making tasks and intellective tasks of varying importance and familiarity. In addition, one might think of generalizing the present stochastic model for quantitative decision making to tasks consisting of more than one dimension (e.g., for location problems, attitudinal dynamics).

It should be noted that the stochastic model described here was tested by groups of subjects with comparable status, education, and motivation. Those groups had no prior history and the group members had no commitments except to their own attitudes. There are, however, situations where members of teams or committees have to take preexisting task-relevant obligations into consideration. Such social contexts can lead to complicated phenomena, like coalition formation, decision making under the whip, pivotal power, and loyalty, that have yet to be conceptualized in interpersonal behavior theories such as we consider here. Given the encouraging results from the Markov analyses with the NID versions of the PCD model, it appears worthwhile to attempt further development of dynamic models that will address a variety of tasks in more complex social contexts.

APPENDIX

The question is, how probable it is that a certain group constellation at time t will result in any other group constellations at time t + 1. This is first illustrated by an example with the simple case of two alternatives and three group members, for the calculation of the probability to change from constellation (2,1) at time t to (1,2) at time t + 1.

According to formula A1a, we first compute all probabilities for the two people at alternative 1 to stay at alternative 1 or to change to alternative 2, that is,

$$\left(\frac{2!}{2!\ 0!}\right) p_{11}^2 p_{12}^0 \quad \text{both persons stay at alternative 1}$$

$$\left(\frac{2!}{1!\ 1!}\right) p_{11}^1 p_{12}^1 \quad \text{one person stays at 1, one person changes to 2} \qquad \text{(A1a)}$$

$$\left(\frac{2!}{0!\ 2!}\right) p_{11}^0 p_{12}^2 \quad \text{both persons change to 2}$$

Then for the one person at alternative 2 we compute the probability to stay at or to change, that is

$$\left(\frac{1!}{0!\ 1!}\right) p_{21}^0 p_{22}^1 \quad \text{the person stays at 2}$$

$$\left(\frac{1!}{1!\ 0!}\right) p_{21}^1 p_{22}^0 \quad \text{the person changes to 1} \qquad \text{(A1b)}$$

The constellation (2,1) can change in to (1,2) in two different ways. First, one of the persons at alternative 1 stays, the other changes to 2, and the person at alternative 2 stays. Second, both persons at alternative 1 change to 2, and the person at alternative 2 changes to 1. The probabilities for these two events add up to the probability to change from (2,1) to (1,2). That means, to find the probability to change from constellation k at time t to constellation l at time t + 1, add all products consisting of one component of A1a and one of A1b for which $(r_{11}, r_{12}) + (r_{21}, r_{22}) = (r_{11}, r_{12})$. For example, the probability that (2,1) will result in (1,2) is

$$2\,p_{11}{}^1\,p_{12}{}^1\,p_{21}{}^1\,p_{22}{}^1 + p_{11}{}^0\,p_{12}{}^2\,p_{21}{}^1\,p_{22}{}^0 \qquad \text{(A2)}$$

Doing this for all $[(m + r - 1)! / (r! (m - 1)!)]$ possible constellations, in the example for the four constellations 3:0, 2:1, 1:2, 0:3, results in the matrix of transition probabilities between all possible constellations from time t to time t + 1.

The algorithm for computing the probabilities may be defined more generally. Let r be the size of the group. In the upper part of the multinominal the coefficients $(r_{k1}, r_{k2}, \ldots, r_{km})$ represent the distribution of the r group members over the m alternatives in state k at time t.

For example, r_{12} means the fraction of those persons at alternative 1 in constellation k at time t who will be at alternative 2 at time $t + 1$. Analogously, p_{12} means the individual probability to change from alternative 1 to alternative 2 from time t to $t + 1$. First compute for each constellation all products:

$$(1) \left(\frac{r_{k1}!}{r_{11}! \, r_{12}! \, \dots \, r_{1m}!} \right) \quad p_{11}{}^{r_{11}} \, p_{12}{}^{r_{12}} \dots \, p_{1m}{}^{r_{1m}}$$

$$(2) \left(\frac{r_{k2}!}{r_{21}! \, r_{22}! \, \dots \, r_{2m}!} \right) \quad p_{21}{}^{r_{21}} \, p_{22}{}^{r_{22}} \dots \, p_{2m}{}^{r_{1m}}$$

$$\vdots \qquad\qquad \vdots \qquad \vdots \quad \vdots \qquad \vdots$$

$$(m) \left(\frac{r_{km}!}{r_{m1}! \, r_{m2}! \, \dots \, r_{mm}!} \right) \quad p_{m1}{}^{r_{m1}} p_{m2}{}^{r_{m2}} \dots \, p_{mm}{}^{r_{mm}} \qquad\qquad \text{(A3a)}$$

Sum all products of those m components of A3a from 1, 2, . . . m for which:

$$r_{11} + r_{21} + \dots r_{m1} = r_{l1}$$

$$r_{12} + r_{22} + \dots r_{m2} = r_{l2}$$

$$\vdots \qquad \vdots \qquad \vdots \qquad \vdots$$

$$r_{1m} + r_{2m} + \dots r_{mm} = r_{lm} \qquad\qquad \text{(A3b)}$$

Carrying out this operation for each constellation k and all resulting constellations l, results in a transition matrix of the group constellations with $[(m + r - 1)!/(r!(m - 1)!)]^2$ cells.

ACKNOWLEDGMENTS

Research was carried out at the University of Freiburg/Breisgau (Federal Republic of Germany). Special gratitude is due for financial support provided by the Deutsche Forschungsgemeinschaft, Project No. CR 68/4-3.

REFERENCES

Crott, H. W., Szilvas, K., & Zuber, J. A. (1991). Group decisions, choice shift and polarization in consulting-, political- and local political scenarios: An experimental investigation and theoretical analysis. *Organizational Behavior and Human Decision Processes, 49,* 22–41.

Crott, H. W., & Werner, J. (1994). The Norm-Information-Distance model: A stochastic approach to preference change in group interaction. *Journal of Experimental Social Psychology, 30,* 68–95.

Crott, H. W., Zuber, J. A., & Schermer, T. (1986). Social decision schemes and choice shift: An analysis of group decision among bets. *Journal of Experimental Social Psychology, 22,* 1–21.

Davis, J. H. (1973). Group decision and social interaction: A theory of social decision schemes. *Psychological Review, 80*, 97–125.

Davis, J. H. (1982). Social interaction as a combinatorial process in group decision. In H. Brandstätter, J. H. Davis, & G. Stocker-Kreichgauer (Eds.), *Group decision making* (pp. 27–58). London: Academic Press.

Godwin, W. F., & Restle, F. (1974). The road to agreement: Subgroup pressures in small group consensus processes. *Journal of Personality and Social Psychology, 30*, 500–509.

Hastie, R., Penrod, S., & Pennington, N. (1983). *Inside the jury*. Cambridge, MA: Cambridge University Press.

Isenberg, D. J. (1986). Group polarization: A critical review and meta-analysis. *Journal of Personality and Social Psychology, 50*(6), 1141–1151.

Kaplan, M. F., & Miller, C. E. (1983). Group discussion and judgment. In P. B. Paulus (Ed.), *Basic group processes* (pp. 65–94). New York: Springer.

Kemeny, J. G., & Snell, J. L. (1965). *Finite Markov chains* (2nd ed.). New York: Van Nostrand.

Kerr, N. L. (1981). Social transition schemes: Charting the groups' road to agreement. *Journal of Personality and Social Psychology, 41*, 684–702.

Kerr, N. L. (1982). Social transition schemes: Model, method and application. In H. Brandstätter, J. H. Davis, & G. Stocker-Kreichgauer (Eds.), *Group decision making* (pp. 59–79). London: Academic Press.

Kerr, N. L. (1992). Group decision making at a multivariate task: Extremity, interfaction distance, pluralities, and issue importance. *Organizational Behavior and Human Decision Processes, 52*, 64–95.

Stasser, G. L. (1988). Computer simulation as a research tool: The DISCUSS model of group decision making. *Journal of Experimental Social Psychology, 24*, 393–422.

Stasser, G. L., & Davis, J. H. (1981). Group decision making and social influence: A social interaction sequence model. *Psychological Review, 88*, 523–551.

Stasser, G., Kerr, N. L., & Davis, J. H. (1980). Influence processes in decision-making groups: A modeling approach. In P. Paulus (Ed.), *Psychology of group influence* (pp. 431–477). Hillsdale, NJ: Lawrence Erlbaum Associates.

Stasser, G., & Titus, W. (1985). Pooling of unshared information in group decision making: Biased information sampling during discussion. *Journal of Personality and Social Psychology, 48*(6), 1467–1478.

Stasser, G., & Titus, W. (1987). Effects of information load and percentage of shared information during group discussion. *Journal of Personality and Social Psychology, 53*(1), 81–93.

Werner, J. (1992). *Dynamische Analyse von Gruppeninteraktionen: Simulation von Gruppendiskussionen auf der Basis des Norm-Information-Distanz Modells*. Frankfurt: Peter Lang.

Zuber, J. H., Crott, H. W., & Werner, J. (1992). Choice shift and group polarization: An analysis of the status of arguments and social decision schemes. *Journal of Personality and Social Psychology, 62*(1), 50–61.

3

GROUP DECISION MAKING AND QUANTITATIVE JUDGMENTS: A CONSENSUS MODEL

James H. Davis
University of Illinois, Urbana-Champaign

The aim of this chapter is to address the theoretical problem of representing the consensus decision of a small task-oriented group when the outcome is not a choice among discrete alternatives, but a quantitative judgment. Our specific focus is the ad hoc group of a dozen or fewer peers who are seeking to reach agreement on a single numerical value, although members' initial views may be quite disparate and provoke some degree of conflict along the way. Civil juries awarding damages, university space committees allotting work areas, and organizational budget panels recommending monetary allocations are familiar examples within existing institutions and organizations. After a brief summary of historical developments, the sections that follow discuss the general approach (focusing on the general case and some special cases of the Social Decision Scheme model as an example applied to consensual choice), and then outline a consensus model for quantitative judgments. The final sections present some preliminary evaluations of the model, discuss shortcomings, and describe likely future developments of special cases for particularly interesting group decision environments.

HISTORICAL DEVELOPMENTS

One of the oldest empirical research traditions in experimental social psychology stems from the contrast of individual and group task performance. The focus here is on the group-level product of interaction—a consensus response. (See summaries by Geen, 1989; Zajonc, 1965, 1980; concerning individual performance before an audience or coactors of noninteracting individuals working in close proximity.)

The idea that groups are stimulating and tend to catch errors such that group work is *generally* superior (more nearly correct, optimal, etc.) to individual work is an old and compelling notion that persists despite much evidence to the contrary (see Davis, 1992, for a discussion of the persistence of such intuitions in the face of contrary evidence). However, the important issue from our perspective is not to chart the relative performance levels of individuals and groups working in this or that environment (see Davis, 1969, 1992; Hastie, 1986; for relevant literature reviews), but rather to take note of the development of statistical models for pooling individual contributions that was originally motivated by the need to address the question of group efficiency implied by the classic individual–group comparison. The idea was to construct performance baselines deduced from one notion or another (about how individual members pooled or combined their contributions) against which group performance could be evaluated. These early models translated notions about how members might, could, should, and so on, aggregate personal preferences and opinions into a group decision. These formalizations provided point predictions (explicit baselines) against which actual group performance data could be compared, and in turn laid the groundwork for descriptive theories to come. For example, Lorge and Solomon (1955) reanalyzed some of the data from Shaw's (1932) classic experiment on group problem solving that had been interpreted as supporting routine group performance superiority. In the process, they derived a model[1] based on the notion that the social interaction preceding a group answer was neither facilitating nor deleterious, but essentially neutral. Grouping was conceived as sampling from a population of subjects who were either solvers or nonsolvers, and a group "solved," if it contained at least one solver. Specifically, if p is the probability of sampling a solver, and $(1 - p)$ a nonsolver, the probability, P, of a group of r persons containing at least one solver is

$$P = 1 - (1 - p)^r, \tag{1}$$

or as a sum of relevant binomial terms,

$$P = \sum_{\forall s \neq 0} \binom{r}{s, r-s} p^s (1-p)^{r-s}, \tag{1a}$$

---

[1]We only consider the Lorge and Solomon (1955) Model A here. Their Model B was designed for problems with parts to be conjoined to achieve a correct answer, thereby permitting subtasking and scheduling of partial work, and so on, and is a straightforward extension of Model A.

where s and r − s are respectively the number of solvers and nonsolvers.

Subsequent theoretical progress was rapid. Smoke and Zajonc (1962) proposed rules or decision schemes about which preferences were aggregated and in what way; Thomas and Fink (1961) generalized the pooling idea to polychotomies (and hence Equation 1a to the multinomial), and suggested additional baselines; and Steiner and Rajaratnam (1961) found that a "second best member wins" notion (in contrast to the Lorge and Solomon, 1955, idea that is often characterized as "best member wins") was a better description of their group problem-solving data. (Unfortunately, such informal descriptive labels, though popular, sometimes obscure the task and contextual features that typically qualify theoretical conclusions about group performance.) Finally, Restle and Davis (1962; Davis & Restle, 1963) proposed a model that accurately described group problem-solving performance by assuming that a norm of equalitarianism provided discussion time (and by implication, credence) to those members on the wrong as well as the correct solution track—essentially a pooling of "chaff" as well as "wheat." These theoretical efforts, as well as those that followed (e.g., Steiner, 1972), were aimed at assessing group performance quality or efficiency (usually, but not always, in ad hoc groups with little organization or task-relevant division of labor). The collective result was the counterintuitive conclusion that, at least for the performance environments studied at the time, groups (whatever their many other virtues) tend to perform well below performance levels predicted by various notions of efficiency, including the "best member" baseline. The practical implications of this body of findings remain largely unpalatable to this day, and have served to motivate those who would engineer improvement in group performance. For example, note the lingering popularity of "brainstorming" (Osborn, 1957), despite a voluminous contrary literature (see the summary by Mullen, Johnson, & Salas, 1991), and considerable experimental evidence pointing to the *sources* of brainstorming inefficacy (e.g., see Diehl & Stroebe, 1987, 1990). Happily, recent improvement-engineering efforts have proved far more promising. For example, Valaich, Dennis, and Connolly (1994) reported that group members communicating through a computer ("electronic brainstorming") outperform nominal group baselines, at least in larger groups, perhaps by avoiding production blockages that had been identified by Diehl and Stroebe. Such procedural manipulations to improve collective functioning are among the more exciting developments in current group research.

The Social Decision Scheme Model

As indicated earlier, our interest is in the conceptual approach that takes as its general aim the prediction of a consensual outcome, given some notion of how individual task preferences are distributed in the population from which the group was sampled, or when available, given the actual preference arrays observed. (For more detailed discussions, see Davis, 1969, 1982; Stasser, Kerr, & Davis, 1989.) A very general model for groups making a discrete choice[2] among a set of mutually exclusive and exhaustive alternatives is the Social Decision Scheme (SDS) model (Davis, 1973, 1982; Stasser et al., 1989), under which most of the conceptual notions discussed previously can be subsumed as special cases.

Briefly, let π_i be the probability that the ith distinguishable distribution or faction array of r members will form. If individual response alternatives, A_j, j = 1, 2, . . . , n are distinguishable, but people are not, then i = 1, 2, . . . , m = C(n + r − 1; r) = [n + r − 1]!/[r!(n − 1)!], a situation that is probably the most typical in research. If both response alternatives and people are distinguishable (rare in research applications), then m = n^r. Let the conditional probability that a group will choose the jth alternative, A_j, j = 1, 2, . . . , n', given the ith distinguishable distribution of its members, be the conditional probability, d_{ij}. (Without loss of generality, we assume for the moment that individuals and groups face the same number of choice alternatives, and thus, n = n'.) The value of d_{ij} derives in principle from a variety of situational, social, and task parameters that depend on social norms, task features, and other characteristics of the decision environment. In research applications, d_{ij} is given by theory, or estimated from empirical data; and in practice probably derives from constitution, custom, or social norms—or some function of all three.

If π_i is fixed by theory or empirical estimate, the probability distribution of group decisions, $\mathbf{P} = (P_1, P_2, . . . , P_n)$, may be predicted by noting that

$$\mathbf{P} = \pi\mathbf{D}, \tag{2}$$

where $\pi = (\pi_1, \pi_2, . . . , \pi_m)$, and $\mathbf{D}$ is an m × n stochastic matrix,

$$D = \begin{bmatrix} d_{11} & d_{12} & \cdots & d_{1n} \\ d_{21} & d_{22} & \cdots & d_{2n} \\ \cdot & & \cdots & \cdot \\ \cdot & & \cdots & \cdot \\ \cdot & & \cdots & \cdot \\ d_{m1} & d_{m2} & \cdots & d_{mn} \end{bmatrix}$$

---

[2]The earlier notion of "group problem solving" was in fact a kind of generic label that referred to performance rather than problem solving per se, although many of the tasks emphasized information processing to be sure. Subsequently, and to the present time, group research tasks have tended to emphasize selection among options (response possibilities defined by the task), and such action is typically called "decision making." In practical contexts, most consensual group responses are actually preceded by both individual and interpersonal information processing (problem solving) and response construction/selection (decision making).

The observed distribution of decisions, $\hat{\mathbf{P}}$, may then be contrasted with theoretical predictions, $\mathbf{P}$, in order to evaluate the accuracy of the special case model (defined by the entries, [d_{ij}]) derived from theoretical notions about interpersonal behavior assumed for that model.

It is worth noting that π_i is rarely known in practice, but must be estimated empirically. *Direct* estimation is possible for experimental designs that solicit member positions prior to group discussion, because the observed relative frequency, $\hat{\pi}_i$, with which each of the distinguishable distributions occurs can be tallied by observation. *Indirect* estimation is necessary when member personal preferences are unknown prior to group discussion, but independent random samples of individuals are available. The vector π can be estimated by noting that

$$\pi_i = \left(r_1, r_2, \overset{r}{\ldots}, r_n \right) p_1^{r_1} p_2^{r_2} \ldots p_n^{r_n}, \tag{3}$$

where $\mathbf{p} = (p_1, p_2, \ldots, p_n)$ is the distribution of probabilities with which an individual chooses alternatives, $A_1, A_2, \ldots, A_n$, and the p_j may in turn be estimated from the independent sample of individuals.

Theoretical analyses involving the SDS model have ranged from the representation of the strength of various faction patterns that affect the group outcome to the prediction of decisions with changing group size, given a constant social decision scheme. A major value of these analyses has been the tracing of ways in which the best fitting (most predictive) social decision scheme varied with the decision environment, especially with the particular task demands and attendant social norms. For example, at one extreme the group facing a very difficult and ambiguous problem-solving task (i.e., no immediate solution is evident) is typically represented successfully by an "equiprobability" model that assumes equally likely choice from among alternatives advocated by at least one member (e.g., Davis, Hoppe, & Hornseth, 1968), whereas consensual decisions about the group position on an attitudinal issue (about which persons have already-formed opinions) has generally been best predicted by a weak majority model (e.g., Kerr, Davis, Meek, & Rissman, 1975). Mock criminal jury decisions (e.g., Davis, 1980), in contrast, have been found to follow a strong majority principle (e.g., agreement of at least two thirds). Summary discussions of how different social decision schemes operate with different task demands may be found in Laughlin and Adamopolos (1982) and Davis (1982).

Most important, SDS models have allowed the representation of "imperfect" faction domination. That is, a majority, or any other faction size, does not necessarily operate with certainty, but only up to some probability, depending on the social and task context. In particular, the obvious role of minorities and factions of equal size (especially in cases with some potential for conflict) can be represented within the same theoretical system.

Examples of Special Cases. Finally, various special cases of the SDS model have been derived in order to accommodate several applications of particular interest. For example, the dynamic quality of social interaction is a much-noted feature of group-level decision making. The changing factions sometimes noted in periodically voting groups (e.g., mock criminal juries) were first represented as stationary Markov processes (Davis, Stasser, Spitzer, & Holt, 1976), using a m × m transition matrix, S, to keep track of interfaction traffic. The entry $[s_{ii'}]$ is the probability that a group is in faction structure i (ith distinguishable distribution) at time t, and is in faction structure i' at time t + Δt. The value of such a conception is due in part to the possibility of predicting the final group decision distribution after T discrete time intervals (or trials), from

$$P = \pi S^T D. \qquad (4)$$

Although there were additional developments for other applications of this "traffic map" notion (e.g., Social Transition Schemes; Kerr, 1982), it became evident from empirical data that the assumption of constant transition probabilities, $s_{ii'}$, was not plausible. In practice, the $s_{ii'}$ may change, albeit in an orderly way—at least in the decision environments that have been studied to date (e.g., Stasser & Davis, 1977). A theory of how these parameters change during discussion was then developed (the Social Information Scheme model; Stasser & Davis, 1981), with the goal of predicting the $s_{ii'}$ over trials or time, and which in the end, would imply as well the final decision distribution.

Other special-case models have been developed to accommodate individual differences. One approach (Kirchler & Davis, 1986) considered *both* members and response alternatives to be distinguishable, a possibility remarked earlier but that has not figured in the various developments of the SDS special-case models discussed earlier. The results showed that the individual difference variables relevant to task performance depended intimately on the task demands, and the SDS model that successfully predicted the group consensual outcome was one that used *differential* member input to match these demands. Although other useful extensions have been developed (e.g., for the case in which the focal responses are individual and group preference *orders*), these are not discussed further here.

Summary. The preceding discussion has emphasized models of collective *choice*, reflecting the fact that the decisions were selections among discrete alternatives (although response alternatives have sometimes been *ordered* categories), and not a judgment about quantity. The evolution of SDS models for the discrete case continues for various applications, but we now turn to a very important class of decision environments where quantitative judgments are at issue. The social consensus process now must operate on member preferences that are *quantities*.

CONTINUOUS JUDGMENTS

Many decisions, of course, are naturally discrete choices—for example, guilty or not guilty; accept, reject, or postpone; and so on. In other cases, it is merely a convenience to represent that which is actually a *quantity* (e.g., a continuous response variable such as size or attractiveness) as a *choice* among a set of mutually exclusive and exhaustive ordered alternatives (e.g., n-category Likert scales, ranging from "very small" to "very large" or "extremely attractive" to "extremely unattractive"). Creation of such polytomies has often been justified on the grounds of simplicity for subjects, ease of "scoring," and so on. In practice, however, many group decisions are not choices, but judgments that fall along a continuum, potentially taking any value within some interval defined by the task. Familiar examples are budget committee fund allocations, civil jury damage awards, a commission of experts' risk assessment, and many other group decisions about distance, money, time, and so on.

Unfortunately, group decisions involving continuous judgments are rarely studied empirically, even though in practice groups that make such decisions are quite common. In addition to data recording and scoring convenience associated with categorical responses, this research imbalance may be due to the ready availability of theory addressing *discrete* choices, in contrast to relatively little theory dealing with *continuous* judgments. In turn, the relative lack of group decision models for the continuous case may in part be due to some conceptual complications that arise in the continuous case: The number of possible internal preference patterns or faction structures into which group members may array themselves at the outset or during discussion is *unbounded*. Moreover, it is argued later that it is precisely the property of infinitely many positions that members may assume that holds such important implications for groups making judgments in contrast to choices—ranging from the difference in compromise possibilities to the difference in how internal factions may form around common positions.

Recall from earlier discussion that when a task defines n discrete response alternatives for the r-person group, there are $m = C(n + r - 1; r) = (n + r - 1)!/r!(n - 1)!$ distinguishable distributions of preferences possible, if alternatives but not individuals are distinguishable; if both are distinguishable, $m = n^r$, a larger number. Consider the following examples. Respectively, if $n = 2$ and $r = 6$, then $m = 7$ or 64; and, if $n = 4$ and $r = 4$, then $m = 35$ or 256. Although m can rapidly become large (in both cases) with increases in n and r, it is generally still possible in principle to enumerate the various distributions and to contemplate for *each pattern* the social psychology at work in a group with such a preference array—whether an initial array pattern or one evolving with discussion. For example, the size and composition (e.g., particular categories of members) of a majority in conjunction with different kinds of minority factions are clearly relevant to the interpersonal (and interfactional) processes that precede a consensus decision.

Now, a considerable amount is known about "majority" (e.g., Allen, 1965, 1975; Levine, 1989) and "minority" effects on interpersonal and consensual behavior (e.g., Moscovici & Mugny, 1983; Moscovici & Paicheler, 1983; Nemeth, 1986), including the role of factions of various sizes within actively interacting groups (e.g., Davis, 1982, 1992; and especially, Tindale, Davis, Vollrath, Nagao, & Hinsz, 1990). Clearly, a comprehensive theoretical approach to consensus processes in general must encompass faction patterns and their interaction.

However, when the decision falls along a *continuum*, we are unable to inspect a finite set of arrays that constitute the possible number of member preference patterns, and subsequently hypothesize about their resolution into a group decision. In other words, the conceptual strategy so useful in the SDS model is thus precluded. Every point is potentially available, although rounding and perhaps other location preferences can sometimes create peculiarly popular points or regions. For example, an a priori formula or policy that produces a recommended budget allocation of $242,562.21 would probably be rounded to $240,000 before or during most committee deliberations. Other examples of numerical values that can be intrinsically attractive are $\frac{1}{4}$, $\frac{1}{3}$, $\frac{1}{2}$, . . . of a plausible range of the judgment.

Quantitative Judgments

As discussed previously, a number of formal consensus models are available for discrete variables (e.g., Davis, 1973, 1982; Gelfand & Solomon, 1973, 1974, 1975, 1977; Kerr, 1982; Lorge & Solomon, 1955; Smoke & Zajonc, 1962; Stasser & Davis, 1981; Stasser et al., 1989; Thomas & Fink, 1961). However, the comparable literature for consensus models addressing continuous decisions is quite small. The most relevant conceptions are summary baseline models proposed by Hinsz (1989); weighted averaging, using information integration theory (N. H. Anderson, 1981), by Graesser (1982); and the extension of social judgment theory (Hammond, Stewart, Brehmer, & Steinman, 1986) to group judgment by Gigone and Hastie (Chapter 10 of this volume). Also, a model recently proposed by Galam and Moscovici (1991) may be adaptable to the continuous case, and hence is particularly promising (see also Galam, Chapter 12 of this volume). Finally, a model of attitude change as a function of interpersonal/message discrepancies proposed by Abelson (1964) is similar in general form to the collective consensus problem, but it does not address group decision making as such.

Again, the unlimited number of preference patterns in which it is possible for r group members to array themselves implies a different conceptual strategy than pursued heretofore for choice models. Recall that SDS models (cf. Davis, 1973, 1982; Stasser et al., 1989), as a class, predict the consensus choice, *given* a particular pattern or array of preferences. This conditional probability is theoretically defined or empirically estimated from data, but depends on social and psychological factors at the core. Each possible pattern of member preferences (the m possible distinguishable distributions of r members into n response categories) could be enumerated, and the appropriate special-case model for that decision environment assigned the probability with which each of the possible decision alternatives would be selected as the group consensus decision.

The approach to the continuous case to be developed here focuses on the discrepancies (distances) among the quantities preferred by r members, and how this *pattern* of preference discrepancies may itself give more weight to some members' preferences than others. This conceptualization does not at this point (a) take into account individual differences in status, personality, or other such factors that may be imported into the group or arise from protracted interaction, (b) characterize the nature of individual member preferences probabilistically (perhaps a more realistic description at this stage of knowledge), or (c) recognize sufficiently the dynamic quality of the typical consensus process. (Such notions can be accommodated in principle, but the necessary development work is only now under way.)

In general, the current group decision-making literature is not very informative on the matter of how the pattern of intermember *quantitative* preference discrepancies might resolve into consensus in the intact, interacting group[3], although some social choice theorists have taken up the group decision problem posed by preference orders falling along a continuum (e.g., Ferejohn, Grether, Matthews, & Packel, 1980; Ferejohn & Packel, 1983).

However, there is a large body of research on persuasive communications and opinion change (see summary discussions by Fishbein & Ajzen, 1975; Petty & Cacioppo, 1981; see especially Hunter, Danes, & Cohen, 1984) that implies a relationship of some sort between persuasiveness and the *discrepancy* between one member's position and that advocated by another. (Discrepancy magnitude, of course, may now be defined for continua as the *distance* between member positions.) Moreover, this literature indeed suggests a monotonic change in influence with distance, and that this relationship is probably not linear.

Nonetheless, the "communication-persuasion" literature may be of limited value in guiding conceptualization for the case at hand. For one thing, there is likely to be a notable difference in motivation between disagreeing but collaborating group members ostensibly under pressure to reach consensus, and a set of independent individuals receiving persuasive messages discrepant with their personal positions. "Discrepancy" probably functions quite differently in the two cases.

We suspect that a negatively decelerating function of discrepancy (the distance between the preferences x_j and $x_{j'}$ of the jth and j'th subjects respectively) is the most plausible candidate in the typical *group* decision environment (see

---

[3]Self-categorization theory (e.g., Abrams & Hogg, 1990; Turner, 1982, 1985, 1991) places a similar emphasis on the importance of discrepancy and distance among ingroup and outgroup members, but does not directly address *how* individuals move as a result. That is, no particular social influence function rule, in the sense used here, is implied, and the theory does not purport to predict consensual decisions.

the middle panel of Fig. 3.1), although the particular social influence function that is the best representation may conceivably change with the task and general context. (Indeed, the impact of a given interpersonal discrepancy may be found to differ depending on where it falls along a continuum.) For example, even nonmonotonic relationships may conceivably prevail in some contexts. When an atmosphere of accommodation coupled with a strong motivation to collaborate predominates, influence might actually increase with small discrepancies, but quickly reach a maximum after which it declines with increasing distance, implying a single-peaked, positively skewed social influence function—

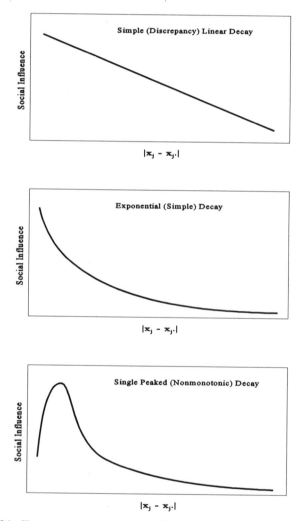

FIG. 3.1. Illustrations of how social influence might decay with distance between member positions along a continuum.

illustrated in Fig. 3.1, lower panel. For completeness, a linear decay in social influence, is represented in the top panel of Fig. 3.1. (For general discussions of social influence and relevant theory, see Tanford and Penrod, 1984; Witte, 1990.)

Under the plausible assumption that as the distance between the preference of one member and another's position increases, a constant fraction of the remaining influence is lost with each unit of distance. The well-known consequence of this assumption is that influence decays exponentially. (Recall the exponential increase that results from compounded interest, where the interest rate is constant. See any elementary discussion of the "exponential or compound interest law" or the "law of growth or decay," e.g., Smale, 1953.) Shepard (1987) argued for the universality of an "exponential law" in stimulus generalization, and its ubiquity in representing cognitive phenomena has been discussed by Restle and Greeno (1970), among others. Abelson (1964) specifically proposed attitude change as an exponential function of discrepancy in a somewhat similar approach to a rather different problem, and Witte (November, 1990; personal communication) has favored an exponential function in preference to, say, a power function (see discussion by Latané, 1981), based on conceptual notions grounded in psychophysical judgment theory (e.g., Poulton, 1989).[4]

Summary. The foregoing discussion implies two key notions: (a) Interpersonal influence declines exponentially with distance between members, and derivatively (b) influence in the final consensus depends on a member's relative centrality in the pattern of preferences. In other words, a member's weight in determining the consensus judgment is a function of the total discrepancies between that person and everyone else, relative to the total preference discrepancies everyone has with everyone else.

Social Judgment Scheme Models

More specifically, assume that the ith group's decision, G, is a weighted sum of the r member preferences, x_j, $j = 1, 2, \ldots, r$, and c_j is the weight of the jth member. That is,

---

[4]Another possibility for the social influence function is that social influence decay follows a power function, for example,

$$f(|x_j - x_{j'}|) = (|x_j - x_{j'}|)^\alpha, \quad j \neq j', \alpha < 0 .$$

The relative theoretical value of power and exponential functions for representing memory decay, and other cognitive processes is currently being debated (e.g., see J. R. Anderson & Schooler, 1991; Bogartz, 1990; Wixted & Ebbesen, 1991.) Although there is no evident rationale for a power function in the case at hand that is comparable to the appealing logic that leads to an "exponential law," it is worth noting in passing that power functions have been successfully used by Latané and his colleagues (e.g., Latané, 1981; Latané & Wolfe, 1981; Nowak, Szamrej, & Latané, 1990) in several applications to describe a variety of social influence and perceptual phenomena.

$$G = c_1x_1 + c_2x_2 + \ldots + c_rx_r. \tag{5}$$

If x_j is known (e.g., prediscussion assessment) or can be estimated (see following), only the weights, c_j, must be defined further.

The consensus weight of the jth member, as discussed earlier, depends on the centrality of the position advocated, relative to others,

$$C_j = \frac{\sum\limits_{j'=1}^{r} f(|x_j - x_{j'}|)}{\sum\limits_{j=1}^{r}\sum\limits_{j'=1}^{r} f(|x_j - x_{j'}|)}, j \neq j' \tag{6}$$

The social influence function, given the earlier discussion, is given by

$$f(|x_j - x_{j'}|) = e^{-\theta(|x_j - x_{j'}|)}, \ j \neq j' \tag{7}$$

where, θ is a positive constant. In the applications that follow, $\theta = 1.00$.

Theoretical Analyses

Among the many technical issues that can arise in theory evaluation, those associated with predictive accuracy are especially prominent. Even a theory that is only approximately accurate can be useful, either because it is the *only* description available, or because it provides the *best* predictions available. Of course, it is prudent to assume that all theories in the end are wrong, and will eventually be superseded by some construction that better accounts for data, in one way or another—or has some other compelling property, such as greater simplicity for equivalent accuracy. Ideally, then we would test a theory not only in terms of its statistical adequacy (goodness-of-fit between theoretical prediction and observation), but competitively, against other conceptual notions. To summarize: It seems desirable to evaluate *point* (quantitative) predictions, in term of both *absolute* and *relative* accuracy.

In view of the latter goal, we sought to construct baselines to aid in evaluating the SJS model, and perhaps guide subsequent development. First, however, we might observe that the SJS model (in the form discussed here) does not provide for "emergent" decisions in the sense that it does not predict a decision outside the range of member preferences. In other words, it is applicable only to decision environments where the group judgment lies within the range of the r member judgments, that is, $x_1 \leq G \leq x_r$. (We follow a subscript-labeling convention here and throughout the remainder of the chapter such that for each group, $x_1 \leq x_2 \leq \ldots \leq x_r$.) Baselines should therefore have the same property of locating the group decision, G, within the range of the r members' proposals. This constraint immediately suggests familiar central tendency measures, such as the arithmetic mean and median, that might serve as baselines or guideposts, against which the SJS model predictions may be usefully compared.

Baselines. The group performance literature does not suggest that many actual consensus decisions are reached by groups literally averaging member preferences, or that the actual consensus decision is often explicitly selected because it is the median. Some decision environments clearly foster explicit computational strategies by the group members (e.g., a budget committee anxious to avoid aversive debate may seek a general formula for routine resource assignment). Other circumstances may discourage calculations. For example, civil trial judges often explicitly warn jurors against averaging or searching for simple formulae in lieu of reaching a "carefully considered" decision when deliberating such things as damage awards. Committee chairs sometimes explicitly caution against the quick application of a formula to resolve disagreement, and encourage instead protracted discussion in order to "explore all the possibilities," and so forth. Clearly, there is no such thing as a single process for the "group"; there is always situational and personal variability to be considered, and theory applicability must be targeted, bounded, or otherwise constrained—either by the obvious context or (preferably) by explicit statement.

Nonetheless, the mean is that value about which the variance is at a minimum, and thus may serve as a guide to appreciating any interpersonal aggregation or combination process that inclines the group to minimize variability about its decision. In contrast, there may be a slightly more appealing basis for representing the group decision as the median of the r members' preferences. Crott, Szilvas, and Zuber (1991), in a study of group shifts and polarizations, derived a "Black-Median" model using results from Black (1948, 1958). Black had earlier showed that majority voting in which each alternative is pitted against every other alternative *or* each pair of neighboring alternatives are pitted against each other, produces a decision that will always be the median of member preferences. Of course, such social choice notions assume complete rationality, including consistency; useful conceptual analyses, these theories are normative, and not necessarily descriptive of group consensus behavior.

Nonetheless, in parallel to the earlier discussion of the arithmetic mean, recall that the median is that value about which the absolute deviations are at a minimum. The median thus reflects a somewhat different notion of minimization, and thus may have descriptive value for outcomes of consensus processes that tend to such a principle for resolving interpersonal discrepancies.

Finally, it is worth mentioning that there are sometimes practical reasons, unconnected with descriptive theory targeting empirical phenomena, for seeking the "best" single value to represent a set of numerical values. For example, such a case arises when a collection of experts' intuitive recommendations, expressed as a quantity, do not agree, and they are not able (or perhaps not required) to reach consensus—a common problem in group judgmental forecasting (e.g., see Armstrong, 1985; Lock, 1987). The task is to find a single value that "best" represents the r (numerical) judgments of the experts who are typically forecasting something (e.g., weather, economic activity, etc.) for which acceptable formal models do not exist. The familiar measures of central tendency (e.g., arithmetic mean, median, and geometric mean), along with other statistics, may each be favored for different circumstances (e.g., see the discussion by Ferrell, 1985). However, the goal of constructing an optimal synthetic forecast, from a set of heterogeneous individual judgmental forecasts, is quite different from our aim of describing theoretically *actual* consensus decisions.

In the examples discussed next, the arithmetic mean and median were calculated for each group, along with the SJS model predictions. As consensus-description "models" the latter are without established theoretical or empirical significance, and serve only as conceptual guidelines. (See Davis, 1982, 1992, for a discussion of baselines in small-group performance research.) In contrast, the social judgment scheme model explicitly assumes something about the cognitive consequences of interpersonal disagreement, preference discrepancy magnitude, and the particular intragroup preference pattern at the beginning of or at some critical point during discussion.

Two Examples

Data from two experiments (described next) designed for purposes different from our focus here were used to explore the predictive accuracy of the SJS model. Only the quantitative judgment results were used. In each case, predicted and observed group decisions were compared.

Example I: A Mock Civil Trial, and Jury Damage Awards. Subjects watched a video recording of a faithful reenactment of an actual civil trial, in which plaintiff was seeking damages for grievous injuries suffered in a farm accident some years earlier (Experiment 1, Davis et al., 1993). Plaintiff charged that the farm implement (a forage wagon) had been improperly designed, and his injury was thus due to the manufacturer's negligence. Six-person groups subsequently acted as juries in reaching a decision about the magnitude of the damages, if any, that were to be awarded to the plaintiff by the defendant. Task and context constraints resulted in awards falling in the closed interval ($0.00, $1,000,000).

Individual members' prediscussion preferences had been elicited (in both experiments), and prediction-observation comparisons could thus be made group by group. This *groupwise* approach contrasts with earlier work (e.g., research using the social decision scheme model), which (with few exceptions) makes *samplewise* predictions about group decisions. Thus, each of the 79 juries' verdict awards (nine hung juries were not included) could be compared with a prediction from the SJS model, and the baselines discussed earlier. By hypothesis, the expected difference between prediction and observation is zero, and of course, the mean of all such comparisons should be zero. The average discrepancy over the 79 mock juries, between the SJS model prediction and observation, was quite small, $ -26,218$; a value not significantly different from zero, by $t(78) = -.75$, even with a Type I error rate chosen appropriately large (viz., $\alpha = .20$), in order to increase power for theory testing as in the case at hand.[5] Both the "Group Median" (average discrepancy, $-\$60,031$, $t(78) = -2.36$) and "Group Mean" (average discrepancy, $-\$55,637$, $t(78) = -2.38$) baselines were significantly in error. (Variances in all tests were comparable.)

Next, following a different evaluative approach, the observed and predicted overall *distributions* were compared. The Kolmogorov–Smirnov test of goodness-of-fit showed that none of the three sets of predictions was statistically acceptable (at $\alpha = .20$), "Group Median" ($D_{max} = .152$), and the SJS model ($D_{max} = .190$), and "Group Mean" ($D_{max} = .253$). That is, the largest absolute discrepancy between predicted and observed cumulative distributions was a significant ($p < .20$) for all three comparisons.

The civil trial scenario would seem to be particularly challenging for theory, including the SJS model in its current form, because a preference for awarding no money seems to have a special meaning in contrast to preferring some amount. A "no damages" proposal implies a lack of culpability; the defendant is not responsible, rather like being innocent in a criminal trial. On the other hand, a preference for awarding some amount presumes culpability at some level, and deliberation need focus only on reconciling the conflicting magnitudes proposed. Such a consensus process might better be represented as a two-step mechanism: first, consensus on culpability/no culpability, and then consensus on an amount, if culpable. (Indeed, in some jurisdictions and circumstances the culpability and damages decisions are explicitly separated.) Further conjectures on steps or stages in the group decision process, together with some additional conjectures and limitations, are discussed later. First, however, we consider a different data set from an experimental scenario with fewer evident special circumstantial constraints on the group consensus process—and thus perhaps a better target for the SJS model as currently formulated.

Example 2: Public School Board Budget Allocations. An interesting contrast is provided by a study of four-person groups in which members assumed the role of school board members faced with a series of decisions[6] (Davis, Chen,

---

[5]Recall that in null hypothesis testing *rejection* implies acceptance of the alternative hypothesis, and that usually favors the investigator's conceptual notions. Thus, it is prudent to guard against Type 1 errors (rejecting true [null] hypotheses) by choosing α *small*, typically .05 or less. However, the investigator's hypothesis in the case of a descriptive model, such as the case at hand, is a point prediction that *is itself* the value favored by theory; it becomes prudent in this case to choose α *large*, so that even a small deviation of observation from theoretical prediction will cause rejection of the prediction/theory.

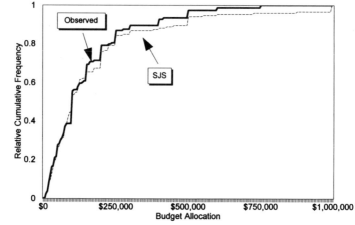

FIG. 3.2. Cumulative relative frequency distributions of award decisions observed (broken line) and predicted (solid line) by the SJS model.

Hulbert, Parks, & Nam, 1994). The mock school board was faced, among other things, with the need to reallocate money within an already tight school district budget. The critical group decision was the amount of money to be taken from the maintenance budget of the local school system, and used to support an AIDS awareness and education program. Data on AIDS and related behavioral factors were provided to board members through information sheets and video recordings of individual speakers from various interest groups opposing or favoring AIDS awareness programs that targeted teenage students. Group discussion preceding consensus on some amount of money to be devoted to AIDS awareness was frequently quite heated, and like civil juries, discussed previously, debate sometimes even continued in the hallways following debriefing.

As before, observed group decisions were compared with SJS model predictions, and baselines. The SJS model predictions did not differ significantly from observed group decisions on the average, $-\$21,848$, $t(152) = -1.23$, whereas both the "Group Mean" (average discrepancy, $\$97,331$, $t(152) = 7.48$) and the "Group Median" (average discrepancy, $\$48,768$, $t(152) = 4.04$) baseline predictions could be confidently rejected. The Kolmogorov–Smirnov goodness-of-fit test showed that the decision distribution predicted by the SJS model was acceptably close to the observed distribution, $D_{max} = .059$. (As before, $\alpha = .20$ for all statistical tests.) Figure 3.2 shows the good agreement between the cumulative distributions of SJS model predictions and observed decisions. In contrast, both base-

---

[6]Scenarios such as trial juries and school boards engage the interest of undergraduate subjects and motivate their involvement to a degree lacking in tidier task contexts that might otherwise permit better experimental control.

lines were significantly discrepant with prediction, $D_{max} = .405, .275$ for "Group Mean" and "Group Median" respectively.

In both examples, the SJS model predictions were fairly accurate, despite rather stringent evaluation conditions and standards (group-by-group predictions, large samples, and $\alpha = .20$). Although neither baseline seemed to offer much support for the notions on which they are based, it would perhaps be unwise to dismiss entirely the median of member preferences as potentially competitive, especially in view of Crott et al. (1991; see also Crott, Zuber, & Schermer, 1986) having provided a compelling conceptual rationale.

DISCUSSION

The preceding results provide some degree of support for the SJS model. The key interpersonal influence notion at the core of the model seems both intuitively plausible and consistent with the literature on basic cognitive processes: As the distance between interpersonal preferences increases, a constant fraction of remaining influence is lost with each unit of distance. Although the generality of the overall model must be established in future research, the present formulation seems to be promising enough to invite that further exploration—including development of special cases appropriate for other group decision environments. We consider next not only some problems and constraints, but especially attractive targets for further work.

Problems and Theoretical Developments

Parenthetically, it must be noted that despite the pervasiveness of groups making quantitative decisions in many institutions and organizations throughout society, there is very little empirical research on groups that must agree on a quantity. The actual experimental operations and procedures from the most closely related research tend to require *choices among ordered discrete alternatives.* That is, the group task is a choice on a Likert scale, or the construction of a preference order (frequently a focus in economics) that sometimes implies an underlying continuum; but rarely must a group decide on an unconstrained numerical value—that is, unconstrained beyond, say, a plausible interval defined by the decision problem. The lack of an empirical research literature specifically addressing group quantitative decision making is both puzzling and frustrating: puzzling because of the obvious importance of the topic, and groups making such decisions are ubiquitous; and frustrating because the absence of such a database hampers theoretical development.

Another concern is that the group-by-group focus that has been discussed here (i.e., theoretical prediction applies to each group's decision) may not be possible in many, perhaps most, research environments. For example, information about individual preferences may not be available from pregroup testing or subsequently obtained from discussion. Preferences would thus have to be indirectly estimated in some fashion. One strategy for generating a predicted group decision distribution is the use of a resampling procedure (e.g., bootstrapping; Efron & Tibrishani, 1986, 1991), using an independent sample of individual preferences from the same parent population, and applying the SJS model as described earlier to each set of r thus generated. (This application is much like the use of "staticized" or "nominal" groups familiar from studies of group performance efficiency; see Davis, 1969, 1992). Moreover, this approach leads rather naturally to a more probabilistic outlook (due to the necessary recognition of sampling error), and applies to a sample of groups, which seems intuitively more realistic than the strictly deterministic, group-by-group strategy followed in the earlier examples. In many respects, the group-by-group approach described here is "too strong" and does not sufficiently allow for error and process variability that in practice afflicts actual consensual decision making. In short, the lack of member-level information is not an insurmountable problem, if a suitable independent sample of individual preferences can be obtained.

✴ *Individual Differences.* The basic assumption that member consensus weight depends on interpersonal discrepancy, relative to the total member pattern (centrality), was noted earlier as particularly deserving of further examination in other contexts. For example, the member decision preference pattern alone may in some cases simply contain insufficient information to predict group consensus in the first place. That is, cognitive and social factors, in addition to decision preference pattern and discrepancy, may determine much of the consensus process in many decision environments. Decisions by juries or other highly task-oriented, ad hoc committees (albeit perhaps of considerable importance) are probably rather closely determined by the immediate member preference pattern. In other contexts, it is easy to imagine expertise or status from past accomplishments weighing heavily in a technical discussion aimed at achieving a consensus decision, and in the end figuring heavily in the final consensus process. Indeed, Lehrer and Wagner (1981) proposed a model of group consensus that weights each member's preference by the "respect" of other members. Their model seems particularly applicable to technical decisions by groups of experts where reputations, achievements, and accomplishments are likely to be well known to each other. Although apparently derived as a normative model for the orderly treatment of disparate opinions prevailing among members of technical advisory groups, their basic approach may have value as a descriptive model of consensus decision making for environments where members' perceptions of each other's task-relevant reputations form quickly, stand out in discussion, or are otherwise salient during consensus formation.

The SJS model may also be adaptable to the accommodation of multidimensional discrepancies, the situation implied by the inclusion of individual differences. The notion of a pattern of preference discrepancies would be retained, but interpersonal disagreement is now represented as a distance in N-dimensional space. Multiple dimensions (not necessarily restricted to person factors) would represent the relevant attributes for consensus on that decision problem. Such an approach appears quite tractable within the SJS model, and may be useful in future applications.

Factions and Stages. Up to this point, the SJS model has treated the member preference distribution within the group as a "committee of the whole." However, under many conditions, there is protracted discussion prior to group consensus—especially plausible for complex tasks involving prior attitudes, commitments, or allegiances, that might induce coalition or faction formation during debate. Specific procedures may even encourage a caucus of the like-minded before or during discussion. Faction formation and member movement in and out of factions over time were recognized as a special case of the SDS model when discrete choices were at issue (for a discussion of transition matrices for describing interfaction traffic, see Davis et al., 1976; Kerr, 1982; for an account of the Social Interaction Sequence model, see Stasser & Davis, 1977, 1981). Similarly, a dynamic version of the SJS model may be conceived for the continuous case. The process ends with a general consensus on a single value ("faction of the whole")—even though apostate exmembers may later express a personal opinion that is somewhere between their initial preference and their exgroup's consensus decision. Such "defections" among postgroup members have frequently been observed in choice tasks with ordered options (e.g., Kerr et al., 1975). Similarly, the average (quantitative) decisions of exmembers have been observed to fall between prediscussion and postgroup individual decisions as well (Davis et al., 1993).

Capturing this multistep consensus process conceptually is not as straightforward for continuous judgment tasks as for tasks requiring discrete choices, because as noted at the outset, the number of possible preference positions cannot be enumerated. However, suppose that factions of any size can form, but members cannot "leap" over each other to join different subgroups. Thus, as before, let subscripts identify members and always indicate magnitude order, that is, $x_1 \leq x_2 \leq x_3 \leq \ldots \leq x_r$. Using parentheses to indicate factions, six-person group factions may form as $\{(x_1, x_2), (x_3, x_4, x_5), (x_6)\}$, or as $\{(x_1), (x_2, x_3), (x_4, x_5, x_6)\}$, but not as $\{(x_1, x_5), (x_2, x_4, x_6), (x_3)\}$. Under this adjacency constraint,[7] there

---

[7]Although the number of faction patterns under the adjacency constraint, 2^{r-1}, can become very large as r increases, the number of structures possible without this constraint (but still ignoring distance information) becomes staggering. Moreover, for the latter case, I am not aware of a general expression for calculating the number of faction structures possible, although it is possible to construct algorithms (e.g., W. T. Au, personal communication, May 1994) for enumerating coalitions that may form, and counting them—unwieldy for large r. For example, the number of coalitions possible for r = 3, 4, and 5 is respectively 4, 8, and 16, when adjacency-*constrained*; and 5, 15, and 52, when *unconstrained*.

are K = 2^{r-1} possible faction patterns or structures for r-person groups; if r = 4 and 6, as in the earlier examples, K = 8 and 32, respectively. Note that factions are necessarily ordered, but their location or internal dispersion is not specified. Our current approach to the location/dispersion problem is to treat the faction as a subgroup that implicitly or explicitly prefers some value within the range of faction members' preferences. Each faction's position (preference) may be decided by the SJS model, yielding K (faction) positions, where K ≤ r. The K preferences are then operated upon by the SJS model to determine, as before, the group decision G. Alternatively, more than two steps may be needed to achieve consensus across factions, or factions of factions.

However, other consensus possibilities may also be operative in particular cases. For example, if a faction is some critical size (e.g., a majority of at least some order defined by constitution or contextual norms), then that faction prevails with high probability. The discrete factions, positions, in other words, may pose a problem similar to that addressed in the past by SDS theory, where there are K alternatives, each with different numbers of advocates. (Recall, too, that a SDS model includes a primary scheme and a secondary scheme to address instances where the primary scheme does not apply, e.g., nonmajorities or equal-size factions.) Obviously, some combination of faction size and interfaction distance is likely to play a role in a successful conceptual description of group decision as a consensus-of-factions process.

Finally, faction positions might sometimes be weighted by a priori considerations (e.g., organizational or agenda-related priorities), or by closeness to normatively sanctioned values. The latter is reminiscent of "taking the moral high ground." For the civil trial example, the "deep pockets bias" might suggest that those advocating higher damage awards would be more influential than those advocating lower amounts. (See MacCoun, in press, for a discussion of this response disposition characteristic of civil trials that parallels the well-known leniency bias familiar from criminal trials.) Indeed, the simple arithmetic mean of an arbitrarily chosen faction of those five of six members advocating the *highest* awards was fairly close to amounts actually awarded in the civil trial experiment discussed earlier. At the other extreme, the mean of the three of four *lowest* preferences was often very close to observation from the study of mock school boards allocating money for an AIDS awareness program. Unlike the civil trial example, there is no obvious source of normative bias for the school board decisions, and ancillary data are lacking that might assist in explaining the possible influence of lower-end factions. However, such retrospective results using arbitrarily chosen subgroups suggest potentially valuable directions for future theoretical development in normatively salient contexts, and emphasize the likely importance of research on faction dynamics.

Although we do not pursue further speculations about faction formation and re-formation, it is worth noting that faction detection or assessment is a difficult problem in cases where factions are not explicitly or formally identified (e.g., as in explicitly labeled political caucuses). Factions grouped around well-defined discrete response alternatives (e.g., guilty, not guilty; small, medium, large; etc.) are also obvious to some extent from discussion, and thus may be relatively easy for observers to tally. The continuous case would seem to be much more difficult for researchers and subjects alike; a plethora of changing numerical values (positions) are probably more difficult to perceive and process than simply noting who falls within one of two or three categories. Finally, in some cases, repeated public voting or member polling makes current member preferences public and explicit. In many other cases (e.g., those stressing diplomatic discretion, secret ballots, etc.) the researcher, like interacting group members, may be baffled about faction memberships, as well as their location and dispersion. The research literature does not lead to optimism about faction detection by independent observers alone, suggesting the value of experimental artifice— and thus perhaps limiting the generality of faction notions in practice.

Numerous other limitations and cautions could be mentioned—for example, model applicability to very large groups; extreme dispersion of member preferences or factions separated by large distances; many normatively extreme environments, such as members with deep ideological (religious, political, etc.) commitments; and so on. However, we conclude by pointing out that SJS model predictions are not invariant under linear transformations. Thus, it applies directly to numerical values to which the subjects under study themselves responded; the model makes different predictions for members arrayed in the same *pattern* of preferences, $y_1, y_2, \ldots, y_r$, but where the numerical values differ according to, say, $y_j = bx_j + a$, where a and b are real.

SUMMARY

Although much developmental work remains, the results from the examples discussed here are cause for some optimism about the possibility of deriving a general model for groups making continuous decisions. Ideally, a theoretical model, such as the SJS model, would easily admit of special case theories for particular tasks and decision environments after the fashion of the SDS model for groups making discrete choices. In particular, faction dynamics over time may mean a decision is reached in stages. Theoretical details have yet to be worked out, but the principle was anticipated by Abelson (1964) over 30 years ago.

ACKNOWLEDGMENT

Portions of this chapter were prepared with the support of National Science Foundation Grant NSF SBR 93-09405.

REFERENCES

Abelson, R. P. (1964). Mathematical models of the distribution of attitudes under controversy. In N. Frederiksen & H. Gulliksen (Eds.) *Contributions to mathematical psychology* (pp. 141–160). New York: Holt, Rinehart & Winston.

Abrams, D., & Hogg, M. A. (1990). Social identification, self-categorization and social influence. In W. Stroebe & M. Hewstone (Eds.), *European review of social psychology* (Vol. 1, pp. 195–228). Chichester, England: Wiley.

Allen, V. L. (1965). Situational factors in conformity. In L. Berkowitz (Ed.), *Advances in experimental social psychology* (Vol. 2, pp. 133–175). New York: Academic Press.

Allen, V. L. (1975). Social support for nonconformity. In L. Berkowitz (Ed.), *Advances in experimental social psychology* (Vol. 8, pp. 2–43). New York: Academic Press.

Anderson, J. R. & Schooler, L. J. (1991). Reflections of the environment in memory. *Psychological Science, 2,* 396–408.

Anderson, N. H. (1981). *Foundations of information integration theory.* New York: Academic Press.

Armstrong, J. S. (1985). *Long-range forecasting: From crystal ball to computer* (2nd ed.). New York: Wiley.

Black, D. (1948). On the rationale of group decision-making. *Journal of Political Economy, 56,* 23–34.

Black, D. (1958). *The theory of committees and elections.* New York: Cambridge University Press.

Bogartz, R. S. (1990). Learning-forgetting rate independence defined by forgetting function parameters or forgetting function form: Reply to Loftus and Bamber and to Wixted. *Journal of Experimental Psychology: Learning, Memory, & Cognition, 16,* 936–945.

Crott, H. W., Szilvas, K., & Zuber, J. A. (1991). Group decision, choice shift, and polarization in consulting, political and local political scenarios: An experimental investigation and theoretical analysis. *Organizational Behavior and Human Decision Processes, 49,* 22–41.

Crott, H. W., Zuber, J. A., & Schermer, T. (1986). Social decision schemes and choice shift: An analysis of group decisions among bets. *Journal of Experimental Social Psychology, 22,* 1–21.

Davis, J. H. (1969). *Group performance.* Reading, MA: Addison-Wesley.

Davis, J. H. (1973). Group decision and social interaction: A theory of social decision schemes. *Psychological Review, 80,* 97–125.

Davis, J. H. (1980). Group decision and procedural justice. In M. Fishbein (Ed.), *Progress in social psychology* (Vol. 1, pp. 157–229). Hillsdale, NJ: Lawrence Erlbaum Associates.

Davis, J. H. (1982). Social interaction as a combinatorial process in group decision. In H. Brandstatter, J. H. Davis, & G. Stocker-Kreichgauer (Eds.), *Group decision making* (pp. 27–58). London: Academic Press.

Davis, J. H. (1992). Some compelling intuitions about group consensus decisions and internal aggregation phenomena: Selected examples, 1950–1990. *Organizational Behavior and Human Decision Processes, Special Issue: Group Decision Making, 52,* 3–38.

Davis, J. H., Chen, X. P., Hulbert, L. G., Parks, C., & Nam, K. (1994). *Consensus in allocation decisions and judgmental forecasting by mock schoolboards.* Unpublished manuscript, University of Illinois, Urbana-Champaign.

Davis, J. H., Hoppe, R., & Hornseth, J. P. (1968). Risk-taking: Task response patterns and grouping. *Organizational Behavior and Human Performance, 3,* 124–142.

Davis, J. H., & Restle, F. (1963). The analysis of problems and prediction of group problem solving. *Journal of Abnormal and Social Psychology, 66,* 103–116.

Davis, J. H., Stasser, G., Spitzer, C. E., & Holt, R. W. (1976). Changes in group members decision preferences during discussion: An illustration with mock juries. *Journal of Personality and Social Psychology, 34,* 1177–1187.

Davis, J. H., Stasson, M. F., Parks, C. D., Hulbert, L., Kameda, T., Zimmerman, S., & Ono, K. (1993). Quantitative decisions by groups and individuals: Voting procedures and monetary awards by mock civil juries. *Journal of Experimental Social Psychology, 29,* 326–346.

Diehl, M., & Stroebe, W. (1987). Productivity loss in brainstorming groups: Toward the solution of a riddle. *Journal of Personality and Social Psychology, 53*, 497–509.

Diehl, M., & Stroebe, W. (1990). *Productivity loss in idea-generating groups: Tracking down the blocking-effect.* (Research Report). Tübingen, Germany: University of Tübingen, Psychological Institute.

Efron, B., & Tibshirani, R. (1986). Bootstrap methods for standard errors, confidence intervals, and other measures of statistical accuracy (with discussion). *Statistical Science, 1*, 54–77.

Efron, B., & Tibshirani, R. (1991). Statistical data analysis in the computer age. *Science, 253*, 390–395.

Ferejohn, J. A., Grether, D. M., Matthews, S. A., & Packel, E. W. (1980). Continuous-valued binary decision procedures. *Review of Economic Studies, XLVII*, 787–796.

Ferejohn, J. A., & Packel, E. W. (1983). Continuous social decision procedures. *Mathematical Social Sciences, 6*, 65–73.

Ferrell, W. R. (1985). Combining individual judgments. In G. Wright (Ed.), *Behavioral decision making* (pp. 111–145). New York: Plenum.

Fishbein, M., & Ajzen, I. (1975). *Belief, attitude, intention and behavior: An introduction to theory and research.* Reading, MA: Addison-Wesley.

Galam, S., & Moscovici, S. (1991). Towards a theory of collective phenomena: Consensus and attitude changes in groups. *European Journal of Social Psychology, 21*, 49–74.

Geen, R. G. (1989). Alternative conceptions of social facilitation. In P. B. Paulus (Ed.), *Psychology of group influence* (2nd ed., pp. 61–97). Hillsdale, NJ: Lawrence Erlbaum Associates.

Gelfand, A. E., & Solomon, H. (1973). A study of Poisson's models for jury verdicts in criminal and civil trials. *Journal of the American Statistical Association, 68*, 271–278.

Gelfand, A. E., & Solomon, H. (1974). Modeling jury verdicts in the American legal system. *Journal of the American Statistical Association, 69*, 32–37.

Gelfand, A. E., & Solomon, H. (1975). Analyzing the decision-making process of the American jury. *Journal of the American Statistical Association, 70*, 305–310.

Gelfand, A. E., & Solomon, H. (1977). Considerations in building jury behavior models and in comparing jury schemes: An argument in favor of the 12-member jury. *Jurimetrics, Summer*, 292–313.

Graesser, C. C. (1982). A social averaging theorem for group decision making. In N. Anderson (Ed.), *Contributions to information integration theory* (Vol. 2, pp. 1–40). New York: Academic Press.

Hammond, K. R., Stewart, T. R., Brehmer, B., & Steinman, D. (1986). Social judgment theory. In H. R. Arkes & K. R. Hammond (Eds.), *Judgment and decision making: An interdisciplinary reader* (pp. 56–76). New York: Cambridge University Press.

Hastie, R. (1986). Review essay: Experimental evidence on group accuracy. In B. Grofman & G. Guillermo (Eds.), *Information pooling and group decision making* (pp. 129–158). Greenwich, CT: JAI.

Hinsz, V. B. (1989). *Modeling group decision processes for responses having an underlying continuum: A continuous response social decision scheme model.* Paper presented at the 12th International Conference (June 1989) on Groups, Networks, and Organizations, Nags Head, NC.

Hunter, J. E., Danes, J. E., & Cohen, S. H. (1984). *Mathematical models of attitude change: Change in single attitudes and cognitive structure.* Vol. 1. New York: Academic Press.

Kerr, N. L. (1982). Social transition schemes: Model, method, and applications. In H. Brandstatter, J. H. Davis, & G. Stocker-Kreichgauer (Eds.), *Group decision making* (pp. 59–76). London: Academic Press.

Kerr, N. L., Davis, J. H., Meek, D., & Rissman, A. K. (1975). Group position as a function of member attitudes: Choice shift effects from the perspective of social decision scheme theory. *Journal of Personality and Social Psychology, 31*, 574–593.

Kirchler, E., & Davis, J. H. (1986). The influence of member status differences and task type on group consensus and member position change. *Journal of Personality and Social Psychology, 51*, 83–91.

Latané, B. (1981). The psychology of social impact. *American Psychologist, 36*, 343–356.

Latané, B., & Wolfe, S. (1981). The social impact of majorities and minorities. *Psychological Review, 88*, 438–453.

Laughlin, P. R., & Adamopoulos, J. (1982). Social decision schemes on intellective tasks. In H. Brandstatter, J. H. Davis, & G. Stocker-Kreichgauer (Eds.), *Group decision making* (pp. 81–94). London: Academic Press.

Lehrer, K., & Wagner, C. (1981). *Rational consensus in science and society.* Dordrecht, Netherlands: Reidel.

Levine, J. M. (1989). Reaction to opinion deviance in small groups. In P. Paulus (Ed.), *Psychology of group influence* (2nd ed., pp. 375–429). Hillsdale, NJ: Lawrence Erlbaum Associates.

Lock, A. (1987). Integrating group judgments in subjective forecasts. In G. Wright & P. Ayton (Eds.), *Judgmental forecasting* (pp. 102–128). Chichester, England: Wiley.

Lorge, I., & Solomon, H. (1955). Two models of group behavior in the solution of Eureka-type problems. *Psychometrika, 20*, 139–148.

MacCoun, R. (in press). Inside the black box: What empirical research tells us about civil jury behavior. Washington, DC: Brookings Institution/ABA Litigation Section Conference on the Future of the Civil Jury Trial System.

Moscovici, S., & Mugny, G. (1983). Minority influence. In P. B. Paulus (Ed.), *Basic group processes* (pp. 41–64). New York: Springer-Verlag.

Moscovici, S., & Paicheler, G. (1983). Minority or majority influences: Social change, compliance, and conversion. In H. H. Blumberg, A. P. Hare, V. Kent, & M. F. Davies (Eds.), *Small groups and social interaction* (Vol.1, pp. 215–224). Chichester, England: Wiley.

Mullen, B., Johnson, C., & Salas, E. (1991). Productivity loss in brainstorming groups: A meta-analytic integration. *Basic and Applied Social Psychology, 12*, 3–23.

Nemeth, C. J. (1986). Differential contributions of majority and minority influence. *Psychological Review, 93*, 23–32.

Nowak, A., Szamrej, J., & Latané, B. (1990). From private attitude to public opinion: A dynamic theory of social impact. *Psychological Review, 97*, 362–376.

Osborn, A. F. (1957). *Applied imagination.* New York: Scribners.

Petty, R. E., & Cacioppo, J. T. (1981). *Attitudes and persuasion: Classic and contemporary approaches.* Dubuque, IA: Brown.

Poulton, E. C. (1989). *Bias in quantifying judgments.* Hillsdale, NJ: Lawrence Erlbaum Associates.

Restle, F., & Davis, J. H. (1962). Success and speed of problem solving by individuals and groups. *Psychological Review, 69*, 520–536.

Restle, F., & Greeno, J. G. (1970). *Introduction to mathematical psychology.* Reading, MA: Addison-Wesley.

Shaw, M. E. (1932). Comparison of individuals and small groups in the rational solution of complex problems. *American Journal of Psychology, 44*, 491–504.

Shepard, R. N. (1987). Toward a universal law of generalization for psychological science. *Science, 237*, 1317–1323.

Smale, L. L. (1953). *Analytical geometry and calculus.* New York: Appelton-Century-Crofts.

Smoke, W. H., & Zajonc, R. B. (1962). On the reliability of group judgments and decision. In J. H. Crisswell, H. Solomon & P. Suppes (Eds.), *Mathematical methods in small group processes* (pp. 322–333). Stanford, CA: Stanford University Press.

Stasser, G., & Davis, J. H. (1977). Opinion change during group discussion. *Personality and Social Psychology Bulletin, 3*, 252–256.

Stasser, G., & Davis, J. H. (1981). Group decision making and social influence: A social interaction sequence model. *Psychological Review, 88*, 523–551.

Stasser, G., Kerr, N. L., & Davis, J. H. (1989). Influence processes and consensus models in decision-making groups. In P. Paulus (Ed.), *Psychology of group influence* (2nd ed., pp. 431–477). Hillsdale, NJ: Lawrence Erlbaum Associates.

Steiner, I. D. (1972). *Group process and productivity.* New York: Academic Press.

Steiner, I. D., & Rajaratnam, N. (1961). A model for the comparison of individual and group performance scores. *Behavioral Science, 6*, 142–147.

Tanford, S., & Penrod, S. (1984). Social influence model: A formal integration of research on majority and minority influence processes. *Psychological Bulletin, 2*, 189–225.

Thomas, E. J., & Fink, C. F. (1961). Models of group problem solving. *Journal of Abnormal and Social Psychology, 68*, 53–63.

Tindale, R. S., Davis, J. H., Vollrath, D. A., Nagao, D. H., & Hinsz, V. (1990). Asymmetrical social influence in freely interacting groups. *Journal of Personality and Social Psychology, 58*, 438–449.

Turner, J. C. (1982). Towards a cognitive redefinition of the social group. In H. Tajfel (Ed.), *Social identity and intergroup relations* (pp. 15–40). Cambridge, England: Cambridge University Press.

Turner, J. C. (1985). Social categorization and the self-concept: A social cognitive theory of group behavior. In E. J. Lawler (Ed.), *Advances in group processes* (Vol. 2, pp. 77–122). Greenwich, CT: JAI.

Turner, J. C. (1991). *Social influence*. New York: Open University Press.

Valaich, J. S., Dennis, A. R., & Connolly, T. (1994). Idea generation in computer-based groups: A new ending to an old story. *Organizational Behavior and Human Decision Processes, 57*, 448–467.

Witte, E. H. (1990). Social influence: A discussion and integration of recent models into a general group situation theory. *European Journal of Social Psychology, 20*, 3–28.

Wixted, J. T., & Ebbesen, E. B. (1991). On the form of forgetting. *Psychological Science, 2*, 409–415.

Zajonc, R. B. (1965). Social facilitation. *Science, 149*, 269–274.

Zajonc, R. B. (1980). Compresence. In P. B. Paulus (Ed.), *Psychology of group influence* (pp. 35–60). Hillsdale, NJ: Lawrence Erlbaum Associates.

CHAPTER

4

GROUP DECISION MAKING
AND COLLECTIVE INDUCTION

Patrick R. Laughlin
University of Illinois, Urbana-Champaign

Consider small groups of scientific researchers, weather forecasters, petroleum geologists, securities analysts, political prognosticators, market researchers, auditors, intelligence analysts, corporate board members, or air crash investigators. Although the objectives and task domains of these groups vary greatly, all of them engage in *collective induction,* the cooperative search for descriptive, predictive, and explanatory generalizations, rules, and principles. In the process of *induction,* all of these groups observe patterns, regularities, and relationships in some domain, propose hypotheses to account for them, and evaluate the hypotheses by observation or experiment. In the process of *collective* induction, all of these groups map a distribution of group member hypotheses into a single group response by some social combination process.

This chapter first presents a general social combination theory of group decision making in the form of five postulates, and then a specific theory of collective induction in the form of three postulates. Together, the eight postulates are a theory of collective induction within a general theory of group decision making. We then describe a rule induction paradigm and present support for the theory on these rule induction problems. We conclude by considering the support for the theory and the generality of the theory and rule induction paradigm.

A THEORY OF GROUP DECISION MAKING

Postulate I. Cooperative decision-making groups may resolve disagreement among their members in formulating a collective group response in five ways: (a) random selection among proposed alternatives, (b) voting among proposed alternatives, (c) turn taking among proposed alternatives, (d) demonstration of preferability of a proposed alternative, and (e) generation of a new emergent alternative.

The essential process in all group decision making, large or small, formal or informal, important or trivial, cooperative, mixed-motive, or competitive, is the resolution of disagreement among the group members. Postulate 1 proposes that there are five essential ways by which freely interacting cooperative groups whose members have equal formal status and power may resolve this disagreement. Generation of a new emergent alternative includes a wide variety of processes such as averaging, compromising, or logrolling. Postulate 1 concerns only cooperative decision making, rather than mixed-motive and competitive decision making, for which possible modes of resolution of disagreement include coercion, bribery, combat by representative champions, excommunication, and warfare. With these qualifications, Postulate 1 proposes that these five ways of resolution of disagreement are exhaustive. Following the current general term for theory and research on small-group performance and processes, Postulate 1 concerns group decision making, although the same area was previously called group problem solving, as in the comprehensive review of Kelley and Thibaut (1969).

Postulate 2. The five ways of resolving disagreement may be formalized by social combination models: (a) random selection: equiprobability model, (b) voting: majority and plurality models, (c) turn taking: proportionality model, (d) demonstration: truth wins and truth-supported wins models, and (e) generation of a new emergent alternative: specified probability of an alternative not proposed by any member.

Postulate 2 elaborates the fundamental assumption of a social combination approach to group decision making, that group processes may be considered as a social combination process that maps a distribution of group member preferences onto a single collective group response. Current social combination approaches originate in the classic article of Lorge and Solomon (1955), whose "Model A" applied the binomial theorem to predict the probability of group solution, P_G, given a population with known probability of individual solution, P_I, and the assumption of random assignment of these individuals to groups of size k: $P_G = 1 - (1 - P_I)^k$. This formalized the strong "truth wins" assumption that the group will recognize and adopt the correct answer if it is proposed by at least one individual group member.

Thomas and Fink (1961) extended this special-case binomial model for two alternatives (correct and incorrect) to the general-case multinomial model for three or more alternatives. They also tested two other assumed social combination processes in addition to truth wins (which they called a "rational" model). Smoke and Zajonc (1962) introduced the concept of group decision schemes as formalizations of the assumed social combination process, and proposed several other decision schemes besides truth wins (which they called "minimal quorum"). Steiner (1966, 1972) predicted group productivity from assumptions of the optimal process on different types of tasks and his theory of motivation and coordination process loss. Davis (1973) integrated these ideas in a matrix algebra formulation in his theory of social decision schemes (his term for the group decision schemes of Smoke and Zajonc). Shiflett (1979) further extended the social combination approach to considerations of group composition (see Moreland & Levine, 1992, for an extensive current review of the group composition literature).

In summary, the general social combination approach formalizes different assumptions of the group process and competitively tests them in a logic of strong inference (Platt, 1964). For further discussions of the general social combination approach to group decision making see Davis (1982), Hastie, Penrod, and Pennington (1983), Laughlin (1980), Penrod and Hastie (1979), and Stasser, Kerr, and Davis (1989).

Postulate 3. Cooperative group tasks may be ordered on a continuum anchored by intellective and judgmental tasks.

Postulate 3 was first proposed by Laughlin (1980). Intellective tasks are problems or decisions for which there exists a demonstrably correct solution within a verbal or quantitative conceptual system. Examples include object transfer problems (e.g., Shaw, 1932), water jar or gold dust problems (e.g., Davis & Restle, 1963), anagrams (e.g., Faust, 1959), mathematical problems (e.g., Laughlin & Ellis, 1986; Stasson, Kameda, Parks, Zimmerman, & Davis, 1991), and most of the tasks in the group problem-solving literature summarized by Hackman and Morris (1975), Hastie (1986), Hill (1982), Kelley and Thibaut (1969), Lorge, Fox, Davitz, and Brenner (1958), and McGrath (1984).

Intellective tasks emphasize the solution of a problem by a series of permissible operations within some set of constraints. Problem solution is defined by the relationships of the conceptual system within which the problem is embedded. The objective for the group is to achieve the correct solution, and the criterion of group success is whether or not the solution is achieved.

Judgmental tasks are evaluative, behavioral, or aesthetic judgments for which a demonstrably correct response does not exist. Examples include virtually all of the tasks in research on decision under uncertainty, the choice shift and group polarization, mock jury decisions, and attitudes (for reviews see Burnstein, 1982; Davis, 1980; Hastie, Penrod, & Pennington, 1983; Lamm & Myers, 1978; Miller, 1989; Myers, 1982; Myers & Lamm, 1976; Penrod & Hastie, 1979). On judgmental tasks the objective for the group is to achieve consensus, and the criterion of group success is whether or not consensus is achieved. For example, a jury that fails to reach consensus ("hangs") has failed to achieve the objective of a jury trial.

In summary, Postulate 3 proposes that intellective and judgmental tasks are the endpoints of a continuum rather than a dichotomy. For further discussion and relationships to other task taxonomies see Kaplan and Miller (1987), Laughlin (1980), and McGrath (1984).

Postulate 4. A demonstrably correct response requires four conditions: (a) group consensus on a conceptual system, (b) sufficient information, (c) that incorrect members are able to recognize the correct response if it is proposed, and (d) that correct members have sufficient ability, motivation, and time to demonstrate the correct response to the incorrect members.

Postulate 4 was first proposed by Laughlin and Ellis (1986). Demonstrability presupposes previous group consensus on a conceptual system. A verbal conceptual system such as a language or constitution assumes consensus on the vocabulary, syntax, and relationships of the system. A mathematical system such as a geometry or algebra assumes consensus on the primitive terms, axioms, and operations of the system. Tindale and his associates (chapter 5 of this volume) consider Condition 1 a *shared representation*, which they define as "any task/situation relevant concept, norm, perspective or cognitive process that is shared by most or all of the group members."

Given this consensus on the system, there must be sufficient information for solution. For example, a system of two simultaneous equations in two unknowns has a unique solution, but one equation in two unknowns does not. The group members who do not know the correct response must have sufficient understanding of the system to recognize and accept a correct answer if it is proposed by another member (this was an implicit assumption for the Lorge & Solomon, 1955, Model A). Finally, Postulate 4 specifies the characteristics of the group members that are necessary for them to demonstrate the correct response to the incorrect members.

Postulate 5. The number of group members that is necessary and sufficient for a collective decision is inversely proportional to the demonstrability of the proposed group response.

Postulate 5 was first proposed by Laughlin and Ellis (1986) as a generalization from their review of the best-fitting social combination processes on various classes of group tasks.

Two-thirds majority, in which the group decision is that favored by two thirds of the group members, is the best-fitting social combination process for jury decisions (e.g., Davis, 1980, 1992; Davis, Kerr, Atkin, Holt, & Meek, 1975; Davis, Kerr, Stasser, Meek, & Holt, 1977; Hastie et al., 1983; Kerr et al., 1976; Kerr & MacCoun, 1985). Juries without a two-thirds majority typically either are unable to come to a decision ("hang") or give the defendant the benefit of the doubt and acquit (MacCoun & Kerr, 1988). Jury decisions are judgmental tasks because conviction or acquittal is typically a matter of the more credible and persuasive rival scenario rather than a demonstrably correct response (Hastie et al., 1983).

Simple majority, in which the group decision is that favored by more than half of the group members, is the best-fitting social combination process for attitudinal judgments and preferences among bets, especially when the majority position is in the direction of prevailing values or norms (e.g., Cvetkovich & Baumgardner, 1973; Davis, Kerr, Sussmann, & Rissman, 1974; Kerr, Davis, Meek, & Rissman, 1975; Lambert, 1978; Zaleska, 1978). Attitudinal judgments and preferences among bets are judgmental tasks because they are based on values rather than demonstrably correct answers.

Most of this research with jury decisions, attitudinal judgments, and preferences among bets has involved two response alternatives, such as conviction or acquittal. An important exception is the four verdict categories (first-degree murder, second-degree murder, manslaughter, not guilty by reason of self-defense) of Hastie et al. (1983). Although a majority social combination process fit very well for decisions of guilty (collapsing over the first three verdict categories) versus not guilty, a plurality process fit quite well when there was no majority for one of the four verdicts. This suggests a simple majority, plurality otherwise, social combination process for tasks with nondemonstrable answers and more than two response categories.

Integrating a social combination approach and the social choice tradition of Black (1958), Crott and his associates have considered social combination processes for more than two alternatives with bets (Crott, Zuber, & Schermer, 1986) and choice dilemmas (Crott, Szilvas, & Zuber, 1991; Zuber, Crott, & Werner, 1992). This research has found that a reduced-paired comparison median model provides the best fit on bets and choice dilemmas. Based on Black's demonstration that the median alternative can prevail over all other alternatives for single-peaked preference distributions, this process follows a majority if a majority exists, and a paired-comparison process for adjacent alternatives in which a plurality prevails if a majority does not exist. This may be interpreted as support for a simple majority, plurality otherwise, social combination process for judgmental tasks with more than two response alternatives. Most recently, Crott and Werner (1994) found support for their norm-information-distance model on mock jury decisions. This model extends a static social combination approach to a dynamic model of changes in member preference distributions during the process of group decision.

Equiprobability, in which the group response is equiprobable among all responses advocated by at least one group member, is the best-fitting social combination process on relatively uninvolving decisions, such as predicting which of a number of lights will occur on each of a series of trials (e.g., Davis, Hornik, & Hornseth, 1970; Zajonc, Wolosin, Wolosin, & Sherman, 1968). Such tasks do not have demonstrably correct answers, and probably do not engage strong values. The best-fitting equiprobability social combination process may thus represent an attenuation of a majority process on more involving judgmental tasks that do engage strong values. More generally, we may conjecture that the size of majority required for group decisions on judgmental tasks is directly proportional to the importance of the values engaged by the decision.

For example, unanimous verdicts of guilty are typically required for jury decisions punishable by death, whereas nonunanimous majorities may suffice for less serious charges and sanctions. Under the U.S. Constitution larger congressional majorities are required for override of a presidential veto than for initial enactment of legislation. Maxim's requires a higher order of majority than does McDonalds for participants at an academic conference (say, on group decision making) who are trying to decide where the group will go for dinner.

Truth-supported wins, in which two correct numbers are necessary and sufficient for a correct group response, is the best-fitting social combination process on general world knowledge, vocabulary, and analogy items (Laughlin & Adamopoulos, 1980, 1982; Laughlin, Kerr, Davis, Halff, & Marciniak, 1975; Laughlin, Kerr, Munch, & Haggarty, 1976; see Hastie, 1986, for a review). These tasks fit the four conditions of demonstrability of Postulate 3, but the correct answers are not intuitively obvious or immediately evident once proposed, so a correct member must be supported by another member to persuade the incorrect members to adopt the correct answer as the group response.

Bottger and Yetton (1988) used the "moon survival" problem to assess their theory of expert weighting, which is related to the optimal weighting approach of Einhorn, Hogarth, and Klempner (1977). Astronauts have crash landed on the moon 200 miles from base. Fifteen items of equipment (tank of oxygen, rope, etc.) are ranked in order of contribution to survival walking to the base. The criterion of task success is correspondence to the previous rank order of the Crew Equipment Research Unit of NASA. Individuals ranked the items alone and then in groups of size four, five, or six. Group performance was successfully predicted by the ability of the two most expert group members, corresponding to a truth-supported wins social combination process.

Correct answers on complex group tasks such as the "moon survival" problem, "island" problem (Tuckman, 1967), or "mined road" problem (Tuckman & Lorge, 1962) are directly defined by correspondence to the answers of an external group of experts and only indirectly defined by demonstration within a conceptual system. Such tasks may be considered intermediate on the continuum of Postulate 3 between intellective tasks that are defined by demonstration within a conceptual system and judgmental tasks on which no correct answers exist and the criterion of success is the consensus of the group members themselves, whatever their expertise, such as juries. Alternatively, correspondence to the judgments of a group of experts may be considered to be a temporal dimension of group consensus, in which the criterion of successful performance for current groups is correspondence to the consensus of previous groups. In this sense intellective tasks presuppose the consensus of previous groups on judgmental tasks.

Truth wins, in which one correct member is necessary and sufficient for a correct group response, is the best-fitting social combination process on insight or "Eureka" puzzles (Shaw, 1932, as reanalyzed by Lorge & Solomon, 1955;

Marquart, 1955), creativity tasks (Laughlin et al., 1976), and mathematical problems (Laughlin & Ellis, 1986; Stasson et al., 1991). These tasks fit conditions a and b of Postulate 4, and have correct answers that are either intuitively and immediately obvious to the incorrect members (condition c) or demonstrable by a single correct member (condition d).

Stasser and Stewart (1992) directly tested Postulates 3, 4, and 5. They predicted and found that fewer group members are necessary for a group solution when they believe that a correct answer exists in solving a murder mystery (intellective task) than when they believe that a correct answer does not exist and they are gathering evidence for a possible indictment by a grand jury (judgmental task). More generally, we may conjecture that the well-established finding that groups predominantly discuss shared information supporting a less optimal decision rather than discuss and integrate distributed information supporting a more optimal decision (e.g., Stasser, Taylor, & Hanna, 1989; Stasser & Titus, 1987) may apply relatively more to tasks near the judgmental end of the continuum of Postulate 3 than to tasks near the intellective end. Tindale (1993) applied the ideas of Postulates 3, 4, and 5 to decision errors made by individuals and groups, and Tindale, Smith, Thomas, Filkins, and Sheffey (chapter 5 of this volume) have applied them to asymmetric social influence processes in small groups.

In summary, previous research on social combination processes on a wide range of group tasks supports the generalization of Postulate 5 that the number of group members that is necessary and sufficient for a group response is inversely proportional to the demonstrability of the response. The conditions of demonstrability are specified by Postulate 4. Tasks at the intellective end of the continuum of Postulate 3 require the fewest members for a (correct) group response, and tasks at the judgmental end of the continuum require the most members for a (consensual) group response. Within the context of this general social combination theory of group decision making we now specifically consider collective induction.

A THEORY OF COLLECTIVE INDUCTION

Postulate 6. Inductive tasks are both intellective and judgmental.

On an inductive task such as rule learning, analogies, number series, or statistical inference a proposed hypothesis is plausible or nonplausible to some degree. Plausible hypotheses are consistent with available evidence, whereas nonplausible hypotheses are inconsistent with available evidence. One of the plausible hypotheses may be *arbitrarily* designated as correct by social consensus outside of an experiment or by a researcher in an experiment, thus imposing certitude on plausibility for the purposes of living in society or research. A proposed nonplausible hypothesis may be demonstrated to be nonplausible by failure to correspond to the available evidence, so this aspect of an inductive task is intellective. A proposed plausible hypothesis (including the correct hypothesis) may not be demonstrated to be uniquely correct relative to any other plausible hypothesis that is also consistent with the available evidence, so this aspect of an inductive task is judgmental.

Postulate 7. If at least two group members propose correct and/or plausible hypotheses, the group selects among those hypotheses only (demonstration); otherwise, the group selects among all proposed hypotheses.

Postulate 8. If a majority of members propose the same hypothesis, the group follows a majority social combination process (voting); otherwise, the group follows a proportionality process (turn taking) and proposes an emergent hypothesis with probability $1/(H + 1)$, where H is the number of proposed hypotheses (group members).

Postulate 7 specifies the set of hypotheses among which the group selects, and Postulate 8 specifies the selection process. Postulate 7 considers the demonstration of nonplausibility analogous to a truth-supported wins process, so that two correct and/or plausible members are able to persuade the other members to reject nonplausible hypotheses but one correct or plausible member is not. Postulate 8 proposes that the social combination process in collective induction involves all of voting, turn taking, and emergent hypotheses, rather than any one of these processes of resolution of disagreement alone. Groups with a majority follow the majority hypothesis, whereas groups without a majority follow a proportionality process (turn taking) and propose an emergent hypothesis with the same probability as the hypothesis proposed by each group member, hence $1/(H + 1)$.

Postulates 7 and 8 formalize the particular social combination process in collective induction. They were first proposed by Laughlin, VanderStoep, and Hollingshead (1991) as a parsimonious a posteriori explanation of the obtained social combination process for 200 four-person groups in two previous experiments on rule learning (Laughlin, 1988; Laughlin & McGlynn, 1986). Kerr, Stasser, and Davis (1979) called this inductive procedure of searching for an explanation of obtained group responses *model fitting*. Once proposed, the model may then be tested as an a priori theory on new data, which Kerr et al. called *model testing*. Hastie et al. (1983) gave a lucid explanation of the two procedures in the context of jury decision making.

Following this model-fitting and model-testing approach, the predictions of Postulates 7 and 8 were first tested against four other plausible models for the 200 groups from which they were derived. Postulates 7 and 8 had the lowest rank of the five models for a Friedman analysis of variance by ranks, and differed significantly from each of the other four models by Wilcoxon tests. The predictions of Postulates 7 and 8 and these other four models were then tested as a priori theories (model testing) on 200 new groups (78 from Laughlin, 1992, and 128 previously unreported). Postulates 7 and 8 again had the lowest rank of the five models for a Friedman analysis of variance by ranks, and differed significantly from each of the other four models by Wilcoxon tests. Accordingly, the present chapter presents the results over all 400 groups in order to increase both power and generality, but it is important at the outset to emphasize that Postulates 7 and 8 were derived a posteriori on one set of 200 groups, and then tested a priori on a new set of 200 groups. The subjects over these 400 groups were 1,376 college students at the University of Illinois, Urbana-Champaign, and 224 at Texas Tech University.

A RULE INDUCTION PARADIGM

The problems required the induction of a rule that partitioned a standard deck of 52 playing cards with four suits (clubs = C, diamonds = D, hearts = H, spades = S) of 13 cards (ace = 1, two = 2, three = 3, ..., king = 13) into cards that were examples or nonexamples of the rule. Instructions explained that the rule could be based on suit (e.g., "diamonds"), number (e.g., "eights"), or any combination of numerical and logical operations on suit and number (e.g., "even diamonds alternate with odd spades"). The problem began with a card that was known to be an example of the rule (e.g., the eight of diamonds for the rule "two diamonds and two clubs alternate").

Each trial consisted of three stages. First, each group member recorded his or her own hypothesis (proposed correct rule). Second, the members discussed to consensus on a group hypothesis. Third, the group selected one of the 52 cards and was informed whether the selected card was an example or nonexample of the rule. Examples were displayed to the right of the initial card, and nonexamples were displayed below the last card played. The experimenter did not indicate whether or not any of the member or group hypotheses were correct or incorrect until after the final group hypothesis.

The basic instructions were as follows:

This is an experiment in problem solving. The objective is to figure out an arbitrary rule that divides an ordinary deck of 52 playing cards into cards that fit or do not fit the rule. Aces have the value 1, deuces 2, and so on to tens 10, jacks 11, queens 12, and kings 13. The rule may be based on any characteristics of the cards, including suit, number, numerical and logical operations, alternation, and so on. For example, if the rule were "diamonds," all diamonds would fit the rule, and all hearts, clubs, and spades would not fit the rule. I will start you with one card that does fit the rule. The first step will be for each of you to write your first hypothesis on your individual hypothesis sheet. Then the four of you will decide on a group hypothesis, which one of you will write on this group hypothesis sheet (the group recorder was designated by a roll of a die). Then you will play any one of the 52 cards you choose. If the card you play also fits the rule, I will place it to the right of the first card. If the card does not fit the rule, I will place it below the first card. Then you will each make your second individual hypothesis, make your second group hypothesis, and play a second card. If this second card fits the rule, I will place it to the right of the last card that fits the rule and if it does not fit the rule, I will place it below the last card played. This procedure will continue for 10 trials of individual hypotheses, group hypothesis, and group card play. After the 10 trials you will make your final individual hypotheses and your final group hypothesis. I will not say whether or not your hypotheses are correct until the end of the problem.

The experimenter then demonstrated this procedure with four sample cards for each of four illustrative rules ("diamonds," "even diamonds," "even diamonds or clubs above the six," and "odd spades alternate with even hearts"). Discussion was completely free within the groups. No group decision rule (e.g., unanimity, majority) for either hypotheses or card plays was imposed or implied by the instructions (if the subjects asked what decision rule to use they were told it was up to them to decide). Several decks of cards, sorted by suits in ascending order from ace to king, were available, so the same card could be played more than once. The correct rules involved patterns of alternation over three, four, or five cards (e.g., "two red and one black alternate," "two clubs and two diamonds alternate," "two spades and three clubs alternate").

Figure 4.1 gives a diagram of the three stages of member hypotheses, group hypothesis, and group card choice. Table 4.1 gives an illustration for the correct rule "two diamonds and two clubs alternate."

Predicted Group Hypotheses From Postulates 7 and 8

Denote the single correct hypothesis as C, plausible hypotheses as P, and nonplausible hypotheses as N. Follow each C, P, or N by the number of group members proposing the hypothesis. For example, C3P1 indicates that three members proposed the correct hypothesis and one member proposed a plausible hypothesis; P2P2 indicates that two members proposed one plausible hypothesis (say, "diamonds") and two members proposed a second plausible hypothesis (say, "even diamonds"). There are 38 possible distributions of member hypotheses on each trial. The group hypothesis may be P4, P3, P2, P1, N4, N3, N2, or N1 for a given distribution of member hypotheses (say, P2, P1, or N1 for P2P1N1). In addition, for all 38 distributions the group hypothesis may be correct (C), an emergent plausible hypothesis not proposed by any member on that trial (P0), or an emergent nonplausible hypothesis not proposed by any member on that trial (N0).

Table 4.2 gives the predicted probabilities of the 11 possible types of group hypotheses for the 38 possible distributions of member hypotheses.

Obtained Group Hypotheses

Table 4.3 gives the obtained probabilities of each of the 11 possible types of group hypotheses (C, P4, ..., N0) for each of the 38 possible types of distributions of member hypotheses (C4, C3P1, ..., N1N1N1N1) over all group problems.

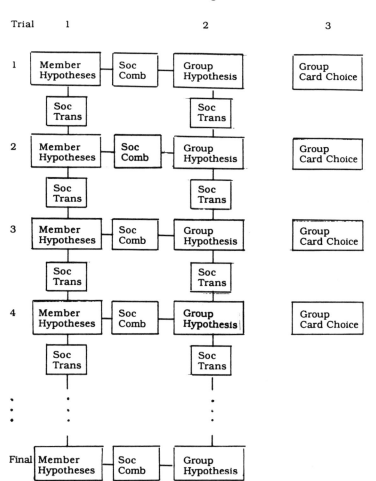

FIG. 4.1. Three stages of collective induction, indicating social combination (Soc Comb) and social transition (Soc Trans) processes.

The predictions of the theory (POST) were then tested against the predictions of four other plausible models: (a) Equiprobability (EQUI); (b) Majority, Plurality Otherwise, Proportionality Otherwise (MPP), (c) Proportionality (PROP), (d) Correct-Supported Wins, Majority Otherwise, Plurality Otherwise, Proportionality Otherwise (CSW). The predicted proportions of each group hypothesis for each distribution of member hypotheses were determined for each of POST, EQUI, MPP, PROP, and CSW by multiplying the predicted probabilities of each group hypothesis by the respective row sum and dividing by the total number of group hypotheses (4,821). The absolute deviations between predicted and

TABLE 4.1
Illustration of Card Plays and Hypotheses

Given Example	Card Plays		
8D	2D 2C		8C
	AH		8H
	QH		2S
	10H		9S
	8S		

Hypotheses:

1. even diamonds (after known given example of 8D)
2. even diamonds and odd hearts (after first card play of 2D)
3. even diamonds and even hearts (after second card play of AH)
4. even diamonds below jack
5. two red alternate with two black
6. eights and twos of diamonds
7. eights and twos of diamonds and clubs
8. two red eights or twos alternate with two club eights or twos
9. diamonds and clubs
10. two even diamonds alternate with two even clubs
11. two diamonds alternate with two clubs (after 10th card play of 9S

Note. C = clubs, D = diamonds, H = hearts, S = spades. Correct rule is "two diamonds alternate with two clubs." Cards that are examples of the rule are placed to right of last example; nonexamples are placed below last card played.

obtained proportions were then summed for each of the 34 distributions for each model, excluding 1 distribution that did not occur (C2N2) and 3 distributions for which all five models make the same prediction (C4, P4, N4). A Friedman two-way analysis of variance by ranks for these 34 distributions (rows) for the five models (columns) was significant, $\chi^2(4) = 25.04$, $p < .001$. The ranks for the five models were 2.53 for POST, 2.78 for MPP, 2.82 for PROP, 2.87 for CSW, and 4.0 for EQUI. These ranks indicated that Postulates 7 and 8 provided the best relative fit of the five models.

Wilcoxon signed-rank comparisons were then conducted for POST versus each of the four other models. There was a significantly lower mean rank for POST than each of MPP, PROP, CSW, and EQUI, $z = 1.74$, $p < .05$; $z = 1.74$, $p < .05$; $z = 1.97$, $p < .05$; $z = 3.31$, $p < .001$, respectively. Thus, POST provided a significantly better fit than each of the four other models, all of which have been supported on other types of group tasks.

TESTS OF TWO FURTHER PREDICTIONS
FROM THE THEORY

Prediction I. If the correct hypothesis is proposed by at least one group member on some trial, the final group hypothesis will be correct.

TABLE 4.2
Predicted Probabilities of Group Hypotheses for Distributions of Member Hypotheses From
Postulates 7 and 8

	Group Hypothesis										
Distribution	C	P4	P3	P2	P1	P0	N4	N3	N2	N1	N0
C4	1.00	–	–	–	–	.00	–	–	–	–	.00
CP31	1.00	–	–	–	.00	.00	–	–	–	–	.00
C3N1	1.00	–	–	–	–	.00	–	–	–	.00	.00
C1P2	.40	–	–	.40	–	.20	–	–	–	–	.00
C2P1P1	.40	–	–	–	.40	.20	–	–	–	–	.00
C2P1N1	.53	–	–	–	.27	.20	–	–	–	.00	.00
C2N2	.80	–	–	–	–	.20	–	–	.00	.00	.00
C2N1N1	.80	–	–	–	–	.20	–	–	–	.00	.00
C1P3	.00	–	1.00	–	–	.00	–	–	–	–	.00
C1P2P1	.20	–	–	.40	.20	.20	–	–	–	–	.00
C1P2N1	.27	–	–	.53	–	.20	–	–	–	.00	.00
C1P1P1P1	.20	–	–	–	.60	.20	–	–	–	–	.00
C1P1P1N1	.27	–	–	–	.53	.20	–	–	–	.00	.00
C1P1N2	.40	–	–	–	.40	.20	–	–	.00	–	.00
C1P1N1N1	.40	–	–	–	.40	.20	–	–	–	.00	.00
C1N3	.00	–	–	–	–	.00	–	1.00	–	–	.00
C1N2N1	.20	–	–	–	–	.05	–	.—	.40	.20	.15
C1N1N1N1	.20	–	–	–	–	.05	–	–	–	.60	.15
P4	.00	1.00	–	–	–	.00	–	–	–	–	.00
P3P1	.00	–	1.00	–	.00	.00	–	–	–	–	.00
P3N1	.00	–	1.00	–	–	.00	–	–	–	.00	.00
P2P2	.00	–	–	.80	–	.20	–	–	–	–	.00
P2P1P1	.00	–	–	.40	.40	.20	–	–	–	–	.00
P2P1N1	.00	–	–	.53	.27	.20	–	–	–	.00	.00
P2N2	.00	–	–	.80	–	.20	–	–	.00	–	.00
P2N1N1	.00	–	–	.80	–	.20	–	–	–	.00	.00
P1P1P1P1	.00	–	–	–	.80	.20	–	–	–	–	.00
P1P1P1N1	.00	–	–	–	.80	.20	–	–	–	.00	.00
P1P1N2	.00	–	–	–	.80	.20	–	–	.00	–	.00
P1P1N1N1	.00	–	–	–	.80	.20	–	–	–	.00	.00
P1N3	.00	–	–	–	.00	.00	–	1.00	–	–	.00
P1N2N1	.00	–	–	–	.20	.05	–	–	.40	.20	.15
P1N1N1N1	.00	–	–	–	.20	.05	–	–	–	.60	.15
N4	.00	–	–	–	–	.00	1.00	–	–	–	.00
N3N1	.00	–	–	–	–	.00	–	1.00	–	–	.00
N2N2	.00	–	–	–	–	.00	–	–	.80	–	.20
N2N1N1	.00	–	–	–	–	.00	–	–	.40	.40	.20
N1N1N1N1	.00	–	–	–	–	.00	–	–	–	.80	.20

Once proposed, the correct hypothesis will necessarily be consistent with all
further evidence, whereas this evidence may make other previously plausible
hypotheses nonplausible. The correct hypothesis should therefore remain under
consideration by the proposer on the subsequent trial and is likely to gain
another adherent whose hypothesis is disconfirmed by subsequent evidence.

TABLE 4.3
Obtained Probabilities of Group Hypotheses for Distributions of Member Hypotheses for 400 Groups

					Group Hypothesis							
Distribution	*C*	*P4*	*P3*	*P2*	*P1*	*P0*	*N4*	*N3*	*N2*	*N1*	*N0*	*Sum*
C4	1.00	–	–	–	–	.00	–	–	–	–	.00	673
C3P1	.88	–	–	–	.09	.03	–	–	–	–	.00	106
C3N1	.91	–	–	–	–	.02	–	–	–	.07	.00	44
C2P2	.59	–	–	.37	–	.00	–	–	–	–	.04	27
C2P1P1	.79	–	–	–	.13	.06	–	–	–	–	.02	53
C2P1N1	.76	–	–	–	.14	.05	–	–	–	.00	.05	21
C2N2	x	–	–	–	–	x	–	–	x	–	x	0
C2N1N1	.67	–	–	–	–	.00	–	–	–	.33	.00	6
C1P3	.20	–	.77	–	–	.03	–	–	–	–	.00	30
C1P2P1	.21	–	–	.62	.09	.09	–	–	–	–	.00	34
C1P2N1	.33	–	–	.67	–	.00	–	–	–	.00	.00	15
C1P1P1P1	.39	–	–	–	.33	.26	–	–	–	–	.02	54
C1P1P1N1	.48	–	–	–	.22	.26	–	–	–	.04	.00	27
C1P1N2	.00	–	–	–	.00	.00	–	–	.50	–	.50	2
C1P1N1N1	.40	–	–	–	.33	.20	–	–	–	.00	.07	15
C1N3	.00	–	–	–	–	.00	–	1.00	–	–	.00	1
C1N2N1	.00	–	–	–	–	.00	–	—	1.00	.00	.00	2
C1N1N1N1	.75	–	–	–	–	.00	–	–	–	.25	.00	4
P4	.00	.99	–	–	–	.01	–	–	–	–	.00	913
P3P1	.00	–	.90	–	.07	.03	–	–	–	–	.00	698
P3N1	.01	–	.89	–	–	.03	–	–	–	.04	.02	169
P2P2	.00	–	–	.95	–	.05	–	–	–	–	.00	198
P2P1P1	.00	–	–	.62	.28	.09	–	–	–	–	.01	540
P2P1N1	.01	–	–	.63	.17	.10	–	–	–	.06	.04	196
P2N2	.00	–	–	.57	–	.04	–	–	.39	–	.00	28
P2N1N1	.00	–	–	.74	–	.08	–	–	–	.05	.13	39
P1P1P1P1	.01	–	–	–	.72	.26	–	–	–	–	.01	310
P1P1P1N1	.00	–	–	–	.64	.25	–	–	–	.04	.07	226
P1P1N2	.00	–	–	–	.46	.12	–	–	.36	–	.06	33
P1P1N1N1	.01	–	–	–	.45	.22	–	–	–	.23	.10	123
P1N3	.00	–	–	–	.03	.07	–	.90	–	–	.00	31
P1N2N1	.00	–	–	–	.22	.08	–	–	.46	.11	.14	37
P1N1N1N1	.02	–	–	–	.37	.21	–	–	–	.29	.11	62
N4	.02	–	–	–	–	.00	.98	–	–	–	.00	45
N3N1	.00	–	–	–	–	.00	–	.94	–	.06	.00	16
N2N2	.00	–	–	–	–	.00	–	–	1.00	–	.00	2
N2N1N1	.00	–	–	–	–	.00	–	–	.82	.18	.00	17
N1N1N1N1	.00	–	–	–	–	.13	–	–	–	.63	.25	24
Sum	959	900	804	734	753	341	44	44	59	104	79	4821
Proportion	.20	.19	.17	.15	.16	.07	.01	.01	.01	.02	.02	

Given these two correct members, only the correct and any plausible hypotheses will be considered by the group (Postulate 7). If the correct hypothesis gains a third adherent it will be the majority hypothesis and adopted by the group by the first part of Postulate 8. If the correct hypothesis does not gain a third adherent it will eventually become the group hypothesis by the proportionality (turn-taking) process of the second part of Postulate 8. Once proposed as the group hypothesis, the correct hypothesis will be consistent with all further evidence, so it will continue to be proposed. Hence, if the correct hypothesis is proposed by at least one group member on some trial, the final group hypothesis should be correct.

At least one group member proposed the correct hypothesis on some trial on 225 of the 400 problems. The final group hypothesis was correct on 201 of these 225 problems, for a conditional probability of .89. This is strong support for the first prediction that if the correct hypothesis is proposed by at least one group member on some trial the final group hypothesis will be correct.

Prediction 2. If the correct hypothesis is not proposed by at least one group member on some trial the final group hypothesis will be incorrect.

If no group member has proposed the correct hypothesis the group will follow a majority process for either a plausible or nonplausible hypothesis if there is a majority, and a proportionality process with a probability of .20 of an emergent hypothesis if there is no majority. However, the theory does not predict that these emergent hypotheses will be correct. Thus, if the correct hypothesis is not proposed by at least one group member on some trial the final group hypothesis should be incorrect.

There were 175 of 400 problems on which no group member proposed the correct hypothesis on any trial. The final group hypothesis was incorrect for 174 of these 175 problems, for a conditional probability of .994, strongly supporting the second prediction that if the correct hypothesis is not proposed by at least one group member on some trial the final group hypothesis will be incorrect.

CONCLUSIONS

Support for the Theory

The predictions of Postulates 7 and 8 fit the obtained distributions of group hypotheses for distributions of member hypotheses better than each of four other plausible social combination models, each of which has had strong support in previous research on various group tasks. The social combination process in collective induction is more complex than that of both tasks closer to the intellective end of the intellective-judgmental task continuum of Postulate 3, where a truth-wins or truth-supported-wins process typically prevails, and tasks closer to the judgmental end of the continuum, where a majority, plurality otherwise, process typically prevails (Postulate 5). Consistent with the position that induction is both intellective and judgmental (Postulate 6), the social combination process depends on the distribution of correct, plausible, and nonplausible hypotheses group member hypotheses (Postulate 7) and includes four processes of resolution of disagreement—voting, turn taking, demonstration, and generation of a new emergent hypothesis—rather than any one of them alone (Postulate 8).

Thus, the social combination process in collective induction is complex but orderly, and may be formalized by Postulates 6, 7, and 8 within the more general social combination approach to group decision making of Postulates 1 through 5. Predictions 1 and 2 were derived from the theory and were clearly supported: The groups recognized and adopted the correct hypothesis if it was proposed by some member on some trial, but they did not form correct emergent group hypotheses that no group member had previously proposed.

Generality of the Theory

We believe that the eight postulates of the current theory organize a large amount of previous theory and research on group decision making in general (Postulates 1 through 5) and collective induction in rule learning in particular (Postulates 6, 7, and 8), and that the rule induction task abstracts the essential features of collective induction. Each hypothesis corresponds to a proposed generalization or theory, and each card play corresponds to an experiment or observation designed to test predictions from the proposed generalization. The set of possible hypotheses is indeterminate rather than determinate at the outset, corresponding to the large number of initially indeterminate hypotheses in a typical real-world inductive domain (and hence differing from much traditional research on concept attainment with a fixed set of initial hypotheses). The progressive array of examples and nonexamples corresponds to the progressive growth of evidence and the concomitant reduction in the number of plausible hypotheses. Thus, because of these abstractions of the essential aspects of collective induction, the theory and results should have implications in domains of collective induction beyond the rule induction paradigm of this research.

ACKNOWLEDGMENTS

This research was supported by Office of Naval Research Contract N00014-86-K-0322 (Patrick R. Laughlin, principal investigator) and National Science Foundation Grant SES-9121690 (Patrick R. Laughlin and John S. Chandler, principal investigators).

REFERENCES

Black, D. (1958). *The theory of committees and elections*. Cambridge, England: Cambridge University Press.

Bottger, P. C., & Yetton, P. W. (1988). An integration of process and decision scheme explanations of group problem solving performance. *Organizational Behavior and Human Decision Processes, 42*, 234–249.

Burnstein, E. (1982). Persuasion as argument processing. In H. Brandstatter, J. H. Davis, & G. Stocker-Kreichgauer (Eds.), *Group decision making* (pp. 103–124). London: Academic Press.

Crott, H. W., Szilvas, K., & Zuber, J. A. (1991). Group decision, choice shift, and polarization in consulting, political, and local political scenarios: An experimental investigation and theoretical analysis. *Organizational Behavior and Human Decision Processes, 49*, 22–41.

Crott, H. W., & Werner, J. (1994). The norm-information-distance model: A stochastic approach to preference change in group interaction. *Journal of Experimental Social Psychology, 30*, 68–95.

Crott, H. W., Zuber, J. A., & Schermer, T. (1986). Social decision schemes and choice shift: An analysis of group decisions among bets. *Journal of Experimental Social Psychology, 22*, 1–21.

Cvetkovich, G., & Baumgardner, S. R. (1973). Attitude polarization: The relative influence of discussion group structure and reference group norms. *Journal of Personality and Social Psychology, 26*, 159–165.

Davis, J. H. (1973). Group decision and social interaction: A theory of social decision schemes. *Psychological Review, 80*, 97–125.

Davis, J. H. (1980). Group decision and procedural justice. In M. Fishbein (Ed.), *Progress in social psychology* (Vol. 1, pp. 157–229). Hillsdale, NJ: Lawrence Erlbaum Associates.

Davis, J. H. (1982). Social interaction as a combinatorial process in group decision. In H. Brandstatter, J. H. Davis, & G. Stocker-Kreichgauer (Eds.), *Group decision making* (pp. 27–58). London: Academic Press.

Davis, J. H. (1992). Some compelling intuitions about group consensus decisions, theoretical and empirical research, and interpersonal aggregation phenomena: Selected examples, 1950–1990. *Organizational Behavior and Human Decision Processes, 52*, 3–38.

Davis, J. H., Hornik, J. A., & Hornseth, J. P. (1970). Group decision schemes and strategy preferences on a sequential response task. *Journal of Personality and Social Psychology, 15*, 397–408.

Davis, J. H., Kerr, N. L., Atkin, R. S., Holt, R., & Meek, D. (1975). The decision processes of 6- and 12-person juries assigned unanimous and 2/3 majority rules. *Journal of Personality and Social Psychology, 32*, 1–14.

Davis, J. H., Kerr, N. L., Stasser, G., Meek, D., & Holt, R. (1977). Victim consequences, sentence severity, and decision processes in mock juries. *Organizational Behavior and Human Performance, 18*, 346–365.

Davis, J. H., Kerr, N. L., Sussmann, R., & Rissman, A. K. (1974). Social decision schemes under risk. *Journal of Personality and Social Psychology, 30*, 248–271.

Davis, J. H., & Restle, F. (1963). The analysis of problems and prediction of group problem solving. *Journal of Abnormal and Social Psychology, 66*, 103–116.

Einhorn, H. J., Hogarth, R. M., & Klempner, E. (1977). Quality of group judgment. *Psychological Bulletin, 84*, 158–172.

Faust, W. L. (1959). Group versus individual problem solving. *Journal of Abnormal and Social Psychology, 59*, 68–72.

Hackman, J. R., & Morris, C. G. (1975). Group tasks, group interaction process, and group performance effectiveness: A review and proposed integration. In L. Berkowitz (Ed.), *Advances in experimental social psychology* (Vol. 8, pp. 45–99). New York: Academic Press.

Hastie, R. (1986). Review essay: Experimental evidence on group accuracy. In G. Owen & B. Grofman (Eds.), *Information pooling and group accuracy* (pp. 129–157). Westport, CT: JAI.

Hastie, R., Penrod, S., & Pennington, N. (1983). *Inside the jury*. Cambridge, MA: Harvard University Press.

Hill, G. W. (1982). Group versus individual performance: Are N + 1 heads better than one? *Psychological Bulletin, 91*, 517–539.

Kaplan, M. F., & Miller, C. E. (1987). Group decision making and normative versus informational influence: Effects of type of issue and assigned decision rule. *Journal of Personality and Social Psychology, 53*, 306–313.

Kelley, H. H., & Thibaut, J. W. (1969). Group problem solving. In G. Lindzey & E. Aronson (Eds.), *The handbook of social psychology* (Vol. 4, pp. 1–101). Reading, MA: Addison-Wesley.

Kerr, N. L., Atkin, R. S., Stasser, G., Meek, D., Holt, R. W., & Davis, J. H. (1976). Guilt beyond a reasonable doubt: Effects of concept definition and assigned decision rule on the judgments of mock jurors. *Journal of Personality and Social Psychology, 31*, 574–593.

Kerr, N. L., Davis, J. H., Meek, D., & Rissman, A. K. (1975). Group position as a function of member attitudes: Choice shift effects from the perspective of social decision scheme theory. *Journal of Personality and Social Psychology, 31*, 574–593.

Kerr, N. L., & MacCoun, R. J. (1985). The effects of jury size and polling method on the process and product of jury deliberation. *Journal of Personality and Social Psychology, 48*, 349–363.

Kerr, N. L., Stasser, G., & Davis, J. H. (1979). Model-testing, model-fitting, and social decision schemes. *Organizational Behavior and Human Performance, 23*, 399–410.

Lambert, R., (1978). Situations of uncertainty: Social influence and decision processes. In H. Brandstatter, J. H. Davis, & H. Schuler (Eds.), *Dynamics of group decisions* (pp. 53–66). Beverly Hills, CA: Sage.

Lamm, H., & Myers, D. G. (1978). Group-induced polarization of attitudes and behavior. In L. Berkowitz (Ed.), *Advances in experimental social psychology* (Vol. 11, pp. 145–195). New York: Academic Press.

Laughlin, P. R. (1980). Social combination processes of cooperative problem-solving groups on verbal intellective tasks. In M. Fishbein (Ed.), *Progress in social psychology* (Vol. 1, pp. 127–155). Hillsdale, NJ: Lawrence Erlbaum Associates.

Laughlin, P. R. (1988). Collective induction: Group performance, social combination processes, and mutual majority and minority influence. *Journal of Personality and Social Psychology, 54*, 254–267.

Laughlin, P. R. (1992). Performance and influence in simultaneous collective and individual induction. *Organizational Behavior and Human Decision Processes, 51*, 447–470.

Laughlin, P. R., & Adamopoulos, J. (1980). Social combination processes and individual learning for six-person cooperative groups on an intellective task. *Journal of Personality and Social Psychology, 38*, 941–947.

Laughlin, P. R., & Adamopoulos, J. (1982). Social decision schemes on intellective tasks. In H. Brandstatter, J. H. Davis, & G. Stocker-Kreichgauer (Eds.), *Group decision making* (pp. 81–102). London: Academic Press.

Laughlin, P. R., & Ellis, A. L. (1986). Demonstrability and social combination processes on mathematical intellective tasks. *Journal of Experimental Social Psychology, 22*, 177–189.

Laughlin, P. R., Kerr, N. L., Davis, J. H., Halff, H. M., & Marciniak, K. A. (1975). Group size, member ability, and social decision schemes on an intellective task. *Journal of Personality and Social Psychology, 33*, 80–88.

Laughlin, P. R., Kerr, N. L., Munch, M. M., & Haggarty, C. A. (1976). Social decision schemes of the same four-person groups on two different intellective tasks. *Journal of Personality and Social Psychology, 33*, 80–88.

Laughlin, P. R., & McGlynn, R. P. (1986). Collective induction: Mutual group and individual influence by exchange of hypotheses and evidence. *Journal of Experimental Social Psychology, 22*, 567–589.

Laughlin, P. R., VanderStoep, S. W., & Hollingshead, A. B. (1991). Collective versus individual induction: Recognition of truth, rejection of error, and collective information processing. *Journal of Personality and Social Psychology, 61*, 50–67.

Lorge, I., Fox, D., Davitz, J., & Brenner, M. (1958). A survey of studies contrasting the quality of group performance and individual performance: 1920–1957. *Psychological Bulletin, 55*, 337–372.

Lorge, I., & Solomon, H. (1955). Two models of group behavior in the solution of Eureka-type problems. *Psychometrika, 29,* 139–148.

MacCoun, R. J., & Kerr, N. L. (1988). Asymmetric influence in mock jury deliberation: Jurors' bias for leniency. *Journal of Personality and Social Psychology, 54,* 21–33.

Marquart, D. I. (1955). Group problem solving. *Journal of Social Psychology, 41,* 103–113.

McGrath, J. E. (1984). *Groups: Interaction and performance.* Englewood Cliffs, NJ: Prentice-Hall.

Miller, C. E. (1989). The social psychological effects of group decision rules. In P. Paulus (Ed.), *Psychology of group influence* (2nd ed., pp. 327–356). Hillsdale, NJ: Lawrence Erlbaum Associates.

Moreland, R. L., & Levine, J. M. (1992). The composition of small groups. In E. L. Lawler, B. Markovsky, C. Ridgeway, & H. Walker (Eds.), *Advances in group processes* (Vol. 9, pp. 237–280). Greenwich, CT: JAI.

Myers, D. G. (1982). Polarizing effects of social interaction. In H. Brandstatter, J. H. Davis, & G. Stocker-Kreichgauer (Eds.), *Group decision making* (pp. 125–161). London: Academic Press.

Myers, D. G., & Lamm, H. (1976). The group polarization phenomenon. *Psychological Bulletin, 83,* 602–627.

Penrod, S., & Hastie, R. (1979). Models of jury decision making: A critical review. *Psychological Review, 86,* 462–492.

Platt, J. R. (1964). Strong inference. *Science, 146,* 347–353.

Shaw, M. E. (1932). Comparison of individuals and small groups in the rational solution of complex problems. *American Journal of Psychology, 44,* 491–504.

Shiflett, S. (1979). Toward a general model of small group productivity. *Psychological Bulletin, 86,* 67–79.

Smoke, W. H., & Zajonc, R. B. (1962). On the reliability of group judgments and decisions. In J. H. Criswell, H. Solomon, & P. Suppes (Eds.), *Mathematical methods in small group process* (pp. 279–290). Stanford, CA: Stanford University Press.

Stasser, G., Kerr, N. L., & Davis, J. H. (1989). Influence models and consensus processes in decision making groups. In P. B. Paulus (Ed.), *Psychology of group influence* (2nd ed., pp. 279–326). Hillsdale, NJ: Lawrence Erlbaum Associates.

Stasser, G., & Stewart, D. (1992). Discovery of hidden profiles by decision-making groups: Solving a problem versus making a judgment. *Journal of Personality and Social Psychology, 63,* 426–434.

Stasser, G., Taylor, L. A., & Hanna, C. (1989). Information sampling in structured and unstructured discussion of three- and six-person groups. *Journal of Personality and Social Psychology, 57,* 67–78.

Stasser, G., & Titus, W. (1987). Effects of information load and percentage of shared information on the disseminating of unshared information during group discussion. *Journal of Personality and Social Psychology, 53,* 81–93.

Stasson, M. F., Kameda, T., Parks, C. D., Zimmerman, S. K., & Davis, J. H. (1991). Effects of assigned group consensus requirement on group problem solving and group members' learning. *Social Psychology Quarterly, 54,* 25–35.

Steiner, I. D. (1966). Models for inferring relationships between group size and potential group productivity. *Behavioral Science, 11,* 273–283.

Steiner, I. D. (1972). *Group process and productivity.* New York: Academic Press.

Thomas, E. J., & Fink, C. F. (1961). Models of group problem solving. *Journal of Abnormal and Social Psychology, 63,* 53–63.

Tindale, R. S. (1993). Decision errors made by individuals and groups. In N. J. Castellan, Jr. (Ed.), *Individual and group decision making: Current Issues* (pp. 109–124). Hillsdale, NJ: Lawrence Erlbaum Associates.

Tuckman, B. W. (1967). Group composition and group performance of structured and unstructured tasks. *Journal of Experimental Social Psychology, 3,* 25–40.

Tuckman, B. W., & Lorge, I. (1962). Individual ability as a determinant of group superiority. *Human Relations, 15,* 45–51.

Zajonc, R. B., Wolosin, R. J., Wolosin, M. A., & Sherman, S. J. (1968). Individual and group risk taking in a two-choice situation. *Journal of Experimental Social Psychology, 4*, 89–106.

Zaleska, M. (1978). Some experimental results: Majority influence on group decisions. In H. Brandstatter, J. H. Davis, & H. Schuler (Eds.), *Dynamics of group decisions* (pp. 67–74). Beverly Hills, CA: Sage.

Zuber, J. A., Crott, H. W., & Werner, J. (1992). Choice shift and group polarization: An analysis of the status of arguments and social decision schemes. *Journal of Personality and Social Psychology, 62*, 50–61.

5

SHARED REPRESENTATIONS AND ASYMMETRIC SOCIAL INFLUENCE PROCESSES IN SMALL GROUPS

R. Scott Tindale
Christine M. Smith
Linda S. Thomas
Joseph Filkins
Susan Sheffey
Loyola University of Chicago

There are two basic theoretical assumptions that guide the interpretations of the various findings discussed in this chapter. The first serves as the cornerstone of Davis' (1973) social decision scheme theory and has played an important role in small-group research since the early work of Lorge and Solomon (1955) and Taylor (1954). Social decision scheme theory starts with the assumption that small-group interaction can be seen as a *combinatorial process,* where task elements (be they ideas, task responses or preferences, resources, etc.) must be combined in such a way as to allow a group to reach consensus on a particular task (Davis, 1982). The theory then goes on to represent such processes in terms of a social decision scheme matrix, the elements of which represent conditional probabilities linking distinguishable preference distributions among the group members to particular group-level outcomes. (See Davis, 1973, 1982, or Stasser, Kerr, & Davis, 1989, for more complete descriptions of the theory.)

Combinatorial processes in ad hoc, task-oriented groups (i.e., groups not constrained by rules of order or leader veto powers, etc.) can often be seen as mainly a function of social influence (either normative or informational—often both), where members with opposing preferences try to convince each other of the merits of their preferred alternatives. A common theme in social influence research has been the power of large versus small factions (though for counterexamples, see Moscovici, 1976; Nemeth, 1986). Many recent models of social influence, such as social impact theory (Latané, 1981; Latané & Wolfe, 1981), the other-total ratio (Mullen, 1983), and the social influence model (Tanford & Penrod, 1984) all use faction size as the central component. Research specifically focused on influence in small groups has demonstrated the power of larger versus smaller factions (e.g., Tindale, Davis, Vollrath, Nagao, & Hinsz, 1990), and majority/plurality and related faction-size models have often been found to provide excellent fits to empirical data (e.g., Davis, 1982; Hastie, Penrod, & Pennington, 1983; Tindale & Davis, 1983, 1985). Recent theories of self-categorization in groups (Turner & Oakes, 1989), and self-attention as it relates to groups (Mullen, 1987) also provide compelling reasons why members of larger factions within groups, as compared to members of smaller faction, would be less easily influenced and more likely to define themselves as members of the faction. In addition, in societies based on democracy, majority-wins rules are often mandated by law, probably leading to general perceptions that majorities are most fair, right most of the time, and so forth. Thus, for many small decision-making groups, a majority or faction-size model of social influence in groups should provide a good baseline prediction.

Table 5.1 shows the social decision scheme representation of a majority-wins/ equiprobability-otherwise decision process for a six-person group deciding between two alternatives. (Equiprobability otherwise assumes that anytime a majority is not defined—e.g., a 3-3 split in this case—either alternative is equally likely to be chosen by the group.) As the table indicates, a majority model predicts that influence will be symmetrical across decision alternatives (i.e., a majority favoring alternative A is just as likely to win as a majority favoring alternative B). Figure 5.1 shows the predictions of a majority-wins/equiprobability-otherwise model over all possible probabilities of any given individual (in the population of potential group members) preferring A for six-person groups. As indicated in the figure, compared to a proportionality model (which simply predicts that the probability of a group choosing A is equal to the probability that any given individual will choose A), a majority model exacerbates in the group decision distribution those

TABLE 5.1
Majority-Wins Equiprobability-Otherwise Social Decision Scheme

Individual Distribution	Social Decision Scheme	
A B	A	B
6 - 0	1.00	0.00
5 - 1	1.00	0.00
4 - 2	1.00	0.00
3 - 3	0.50	0.50
2 - 4	0.00	1.00
1 - 5	0.00	1.00
0 - 6	0.00	1.00

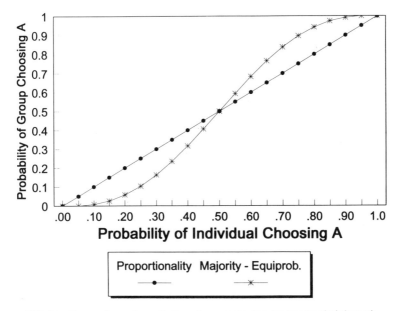

FIG. 5.1. Comparison of predictions from majority-wins/equiprobability-otherwise and proportionality social decision scheme models for six-person groups.

tendencies found in the population of individuals.[1] When the probability of any given individual choosing A is less than .50, a majority model predicts that the probability a group will choose A is lower than the individual probability. However, when the individual choice probability for A is greater than .50, the group probability is greater than the individual probability. In addition, the relative increase in group over individual choice probabilities for individual values greater than .50 are symmetric to the relative decrease in group, as compared to individual choice probabilities when individual choice probabilities are less than .50. Thus, a simple majority model assumes that majorities are equally powerful, regardless of which alternative they support.

Although majority/plurality models have fared well as predictors of group decision outcomes, there are a number of studies that show consistent and often striking asymmetric deviations from majority-type processes. In particular, work by Laughlin (1980; Laughlin & Ellis, 1986) on problem-solving groups, and by Davis (1980), Kerr and MacCoun (1985), and others on mock jury verdicts have shown that majorities favoring certain alternatives (correct solutions and not-

[1]It should be noted that group size has a substantial impact on the degree to which majority models (and other social decision scheme models, such as truth wins and truth-supported wins—see Fig. 5.2) create deviations from strict proportionality. As group size increases, the deviations become larger. For groups as small as three members, the deviations tend to be slight.

guilty verdicts, respectively) have considerably more influence than majorities favoring other alternatives, and that minorities favoring those same alternatives can sometimes overpower majorities. Such asymmetric deviations from majority-type processes have typically been explained by concepts specific to the particular task domains of interest (although see Kerr & MacCoun, 1985, for a discussion of the conceptual similarity between the problem-solving and mock jury results). However, in the discussion that follows, we argue that such asymmetric deviations can, to a large extent, be explained by the degree to which group members *share a specific representation of the task.*

In the current context, a *shared representation* is any task/situation-relevant concept, norm, perspective or cognitive process that is shared by most or all of the group members. Task-relevant means that the shared representation will have some implication for the choice alternatives involved, and the degree to which a shared representation will impact on group decision processes will vary as a function of relevance. Its impact should also vary as a function of the degree to which it is shared among the group members, and to the degree to which other conflicting shared representations may be present. If no such task-relevant shared representation exists (or if multiple conflicting representations exist), groups will follow a symmetric majority-type process. However, when one does exist, the group process will tend to take on an asymmetric property favoring a particular decision alternative. Some examples of what is meant by a shared representation are: cultural or societal norms, norms localized within the group, learned rules or axioms, specific instructions or information-processing objectives, perspectives on or ways of framing the problem, and/or cognitive heuristics (e.g., representativeness, availability, etc.; see Kahneman, Slovic, & Tversky, 1982). Group members may or may not be aware of such representations, and are probably not aware of the impact these representations have on group processes.

The notion of shared representations has surfaced recently in the theorizing of a number of social psychologists (e.g., Moscovici, 1984; Witte, 1994). Moscovici used the term "social representations" to delimit the concept "collective representations" proposed by Durkheim (1898, cited in Farr & Moscovici, 1984). Moscovici's notion of social representations involves the cognitive representations that allow for "social reality." These are the cognitive mechanisms, symbolized in language, that allow members of groups, societies, and cultures to communicate and meaningfully behave toward one another. In essence, they make up the shared meanings that represent (or define) the world around us. As such, our use of the term shared representations would define a subset of Moscovici's social representations, delimited by the relevance of the representations to a specific group task.[2]

---

[2]Although we feel that Moscovici would probably consider many of the things we call shared representations as consistent with his ideas on social representations, it is unclear to us whether such things as cognitive heuristics would be considered within that framework. Cognitive heuristics are simplifying strategies rather than concepts, and are often not consciously invoked. Thus, Moscovici may not consider them aspects of social representations.

Witte (1994) used the term shared representation to denote the shared cognitions group members have about "being" a group. Thus, his shared representations involve such things as norms and expectations for appropriate behavior in groups, knowledge of status hierarchies, and so on. In contrast, our use of the term refers to shared cognitions (or cognitive strategies) about the *task*, rather than about the group, or groups in general.

In the following sections, we attempt to show how the concept of shared representations can be used to explain a number of findings concerning small-group processes and performance on cognitive (i.e., decision-making and problem-solving) tasks. We begin with some well-established findings, and then proceed to discuss recent results from our own research.

GROUP PROBLEM-SOLVING RESEARCH

Probably the strongest asymmetries in social influence found in groups have been demonstrated in the problem-solving domain (see Laughlin 1980; Laughlin & Adamopoulos, 1982, for review). Laughlin and his associates have consistently shown that for groups working on certain types of problem-solving or "intellective" tasks, relatively small factions (one or two members) can influence much larger factions as long as the small factions advocate for the "correct" answer. Rather than showing majority-type processes, the data from problem-solving groups tend to be well represented by either "truth-wins" or "truth-supported-wins" social decision schemes (although see Davis, 1982, for a discussion of some exceptions when group member uncertainty is quite high). A truth-wins decision scheme (a more recent name for Lorge & Solomon's, 1955, Model A) predicts that groups containing at least one member with the correct answer will reach consensus on the correct answer, regardless of the size of the incorrect faction. Similarly, truth-supported-wins predicts that groups with at least two correct members will reach the correct answer as a group. Figure 5.2 shows the predictions of both the truth-wins and truth-supported-wins models in comparison to a majority model for six-person groups (see Footnote 1). As shown in the figure, both the truth-wins and truth-supported-wins models predict asymmetric influence toward the correct answer regardless of the probability that any given individual could solve the problem. The figure also shows these asymmetries to be quite strong, especially for the truth-wins model.

Laughlin (1980) argued that group performance on intellective tasks conforms to truth-wins or truth-supported-wins models rather than majority models because such tasks have *demonstrably correct solutions*. More recently, Laughlin and Ellis (1986) defined four criteria for a response alternative having demonstrability. First, there must be a verbal or mathematical system for solving the problem that is *shared* among the group members. Second, there must be sufficient information available to demonstrate the correctness of a response within the system. Third, the group members who do not solve the problem correctly must

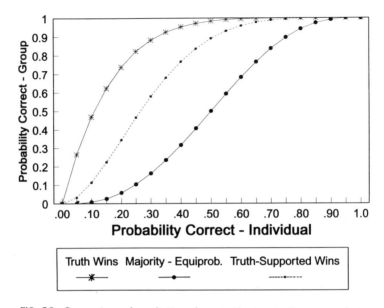

FIG. 5.2. Comparison of predictions from truth-wins, truth-supported-wins, and majority-wins/equiprobability-otherwise social decision scheme models for six-person groups.

have sufficient knowledge of the system to recognize a correct answer when one is proposed. Finally, members who do solve the problem correctly must have sufficient ability, motivation, and time to demonstrate the correct solution to the incorrect members.

Although all four criteria are probably important, the first is central to our concerns in this chapter. A verbal or mathematical system that is shared among the group members is an instance of what we are calling a shared representation. If all the members of a group share a knowledge or belief system that lends credence to a particular alternative, that alternative becomes easier to defend in a group discussion. Thus, minority factions supporting that alternative may gain a level of power or influence greater than that warranted simply by the relative size of their faction because their preferred alternative is more compelling than others in the available set. For problem-solving tasks, the "compellingness" comes from the correctness of the response, given the shared knowledge system in which the problem is embedded. However, as we try to demonstrate in the following sections, a response alternative can be more compelling within a particular shared representation, even for tasks where no actual correct answer exists, or in cases where the alternative is incorrect according to some normative, but less well shared, system. Thus, due to a shared representation that favors a particular alternative, a normatively incorrect alternative may be more compelling, and thus easier to defend, than a normatively correct alternative.

MOCK JURY RESEARCH

One of the main paradigms for studying group processes has been mock jury research (Davis, 1980; Hastie et al., 1983; Stasser, Kerr, & Bray, 1982; Tindale & Davis, 1983). It is also in this context that majority or faction-size models have received their greatest degree of support. In particular, a two-thirds majority, if present, tends to consistently predict the final group verdict (Davis, 1980; Tindale & Davis, 1983). However, a very consistent finding in the mock jury literature is what has been called the "leniency bias" or "defendant protection norm" (Stasser et al., 1982). The basic finding is that initial majorities favoring not guilty are more powerful than majorities favoring guilty (Davis, Kerr, Stasser, Meek, & Holt, 1977; Nemeth, 1977), and that even-split juries tend to render not-guilty verdicts if they do not hang (Davis et al., 1977; Kerr & MacCoun, 1985). For example, Davis et al. found that a two-thirds majority/defendant-protection-otherwise social decision scheme (presented in Table 5.2) provided the best fit to their mock jury verdict data. As can be seen in the table, this model predicts that 12-person juries without an initial two-thirds majority will decide not guilty 75% of the time and hang 25% of the time. This is predicted even for juries with an initial seven-person majority favoring guilty.

Figure 5.3 shows the predictions of the two-thirds majority/defendant-protection-otherwise (labeled "2/3 majority/lenient" in the figure) in comparison to the predictions of a symmetric two-thirds majority/hung-otherwise model for 12-person juries. As indicated, the defendant protection model shifts the verdict distribution toward not guilty, showing a particularly large shift in the middle range of the individual-level probability of guilt distribution. Thus, the group response distribution is pulled toward the more compelling not-guilty response.

TABLE 5.2
Majority-Wins Defendant-Protection-Otherwise Social Decision scheme

Individual Distribution		*Social Decision Scheme*		
Guilty	*Not Guilty*	*Guilty*	*Not Guilty*	*Hung*
12 - 0		1.00	0.00	0.00
11 - 1		1.00	0.00	0.00
10 - 2		1.00	0.00	0.00
9 - 3		1.00	0.00	0.00
8 - 4		1.00	0.00	0.00
7 - 5		0.00	0.75	0.25
6 - 6		0.00	0.75	0.25
5 - 7		0.00	0.75	0.25
4 - 8		0.00	1.00	0.00
3 - 9		0.00	1.00	0.00
2 - 10		0.00	1.00	0.00
1 - 11		0.00	1.00	0.00
0 - 12		0.00	1.00	0.00

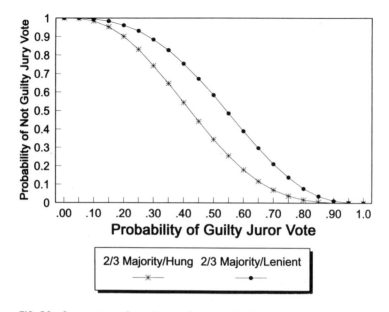

FIG. 5.3. Comparison of predictions from two-thirds majority-wins/hung-otherwise and two-thirds majority-wins/defendant-protection-otherwise (lenient) social decision scheme models for 12-person juries.

A recent study by Tindale, Davis, et al. (1990) also found evidence for the asymmetrical power of not-guilty versus guilty verdicts. Tindale, Davis, et al. composed groups containing various different-size majority and minority factions. Most relevant for our present purposes are the data for different-size majorities facing a single minority member. Majorities of size five, four, three, and two members favoring both guilty and not-guilty verdicts were used. Figure 5.4 presents the percentages of majority members who stayed with their initial verdict preference. For majorities favoring not guilty, the size of the majority was irrelevant—virtually all majority members still preferred not guilty after deliberation. However, size was important for majorities favoring guilty. For guilty majorities of size three or more, relatively few members changed their choice to not guilty (largest absolute number was five). However, over 37% of the two-person majority members originally favoring guilty (12 out of 32) changed to not guilty—a significant divergence from the other three guilty-majority conditions.

Although there is no "demonstrably correct" alternative in mock jury decision making, there is considerable evidence that the not-guilty alternative is more powerful or compelling than the guilty alternative. Recent research by MacCoun and Kerr (1988) indicates that the "reasonable doubt criterion" is an important component, because mock juries using the "preponderance of the evidence" criterion do not show the bias. Such results are quite compatible with the shared representation ideas presented here. Because all jurors receive the same in-

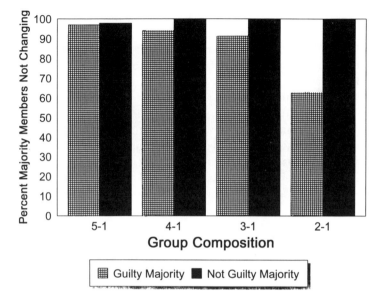

FIG. 5.4. Comparison of degree of majority member change for guilty versus not-guilty majorities. Adapted from Tindale, Davis, et al., 1990. Copyright 1990 by American Psychological Association. Reprinted by permission.

structions from the judge, those instructions set up a shared task representation for the jury. When that shared representation favors a particular response alternative (i.e., not guilty if any reasonable doubts of guilt can be found), that alternative will become easier to defend in the group discussion, even by smaller factions. When the shared representation does not favor one of the alternatives (i.e., preponderance of the evidence), a symmetrical majority-type process should continue to operate. Thus, the asymmetries found for mock juries can be seen as stemming from processes similar to those found for problem-solving groups, only to a much lesser degree.

RISK AND GROUP DECISIONS

Another dominant paradigm in the groups area has been the study of group risk-taking propensities. Group polarization research was largely based on comparisons of individual versus group (or pre- vs. postgroup individual) risk preferences on choice dilemma items (Myers & Lamm, 1976; Vinocur & Burnstein, 1974). The fact that groups polarize or shift in the direction of the initial skewness in individual preferences is quite consistent with a majority process (Stasser et al., 1989). However, Laughlin and Early (1982) showed that the best-fitting social decision schemes for two standard choice dilemma items that produced the largest shifts were not majority models. They found that a "risk-supported-wins" model fit best for the "strong risk" item (i.e., the item producing the largest risky shift) and a "conservative-supported-wins" model fit best for the "strong conservative" item. The group decision results for the two items used that showed weaker shifts were well represented by majority models. Thus, for certain choice dilemma items, asymmetric influence toward a particular pole (either risk or caution) does appear to exist.

A recent study by Tindale, Sheffey, and Scott (1993) that focused on decisions concerning risk in groups shows how two different shared representations can mutually impact on the influence process in groups. The study addressed the notion of shared frames of reference toward a particular decision problem using Tversky and Kahneman's (1981) "Asian disease" problem. The Asian disease problem presents subjects with the hypothetical outbreak of a new Asian disease that if left unchecked will kill 600 people. Subjects are then asked to choose between two alternative courses of action with identical expected values: one that guarantees that 200 people will live (or 400 will die) and a second that specifies a one-third probability that all 600 people will live (or none will die) and a two-thirds probability that none will live (or all will die). Research using this problem has shown that subjects tend to be risk averse (i.e., choose the nonprobabilistic alternative) when the decision alternatives are framed in terms of gains (lives saved) and risk seeking (i.e., choose the probabilistic alternative) when the alternatives are framed in terms of losses (lives lost or deaths). However, both the data obtained in our study and those reported by Tversky and Kahneman overall show a slight preference for the more risky or probabilistic alternative. Thus, a shared representation favoring the risky alternative, regardless of how the alternatives are framed, could potentially exist for this problem.

Tindale et al. (1993) composed groups with differing numbers of members receiving the "gains" versus the "loss" version of the problem. (Surprisingly enough, most of the participants never realized that different group members had different versions of the problem.) Two of the composition conditions are particularly relevant here. In some cases, three of the four group members received the gains problem whereas one member received the loss problem. In other cases, this was reversed with three of the members receiving the loss version and only one member receiving the gains version. The observed social decision scheme matrices for these two conditions are presented in Table 5.3.[3]

The top half of Table 5.3 shows the social decision scheme for the condition where three group members received the gains frame. If we assume that the problem in general favors the risky alternative, but the gains frame shared by a majority of the members favors the nonrisky alternative, we have two shared representations acting in opposite directions. As can be seen in the table, the

---

[3]Observed social decision scheme, as opposed to the theoretical or a priori type previously discussed, are derived after the fact by tabulating the relative frequencies with which groups containing particular distinguishable individual-member distributions chose each of the response alternatives. Thus, these matrices are empirical, rather than theoretical, derivations.

TABLE 5.3
Observed Social Decision Scheme Matrices for the Three Gains-One Loss and the Three Loss-One gain Conditions

3 Gains - 1 Loss Condition

Individual Distribution		*Social Decision Scheme*	
A - B	*N*	*A*	*B*
4 - 0	4	1.00	0.00
3 - 1	5	1.00	0.00
2 - 2	11	0.36	0.64
1 - 3	4	0.00	1.00
0 - 4	0	-	-

1 Gains - 3 Loss Condition

Individual Distribution		*Social Decision Scheme*	
A - B	*N*	*A*	*B*
4 - 0	0	-	-
3 - 1	1	0.00	1.00
2 - 2	5	0.00	1.00
1 - 3	9	0.00	1.00
0 - 4	9	0.00	1.00

Note. Alternatives: A = risk averse; B = risk seekings.
Adapted from Tinsdale, Sheffey, and Scott, 1993. Copyright 1993 by Academic Press. Reprinted by permission.

observed social decision scheme matches quite closely a simple majority-wins/ equiprobability-otherwise decision scheme (which was also the best-fitting model of those tested). Assuming the two different shared representations counteracted one another, we would expect a symmetric majority-type process. The bottom half of Table 5.3 shows the observed social decision scheme matrix for the condition where three members received the loss frame. Here, the two shared representations both favor the same alternative—the risky one. As indicated in the table, even when the majority of group members favored the risk-averse alternative, the group still reached consensus on the risk-seeking alternative. This matrix is identical to a "risk-wins" decision scheme, which obviously was the best-fitting model of those tested, although a majority model could not be rejected as viable on statistical grounds. Thus, using the same problem, but altering the degree to which a particular frame or problem representation was shared among the group members produced seemingly very different types of social influence processes within the groups.

GROUP DECISION ERRORS

Ever since Marjorie Shaw first attributed the superior problem-solving ability of groups to error checking (Shaw, 1932), the field has generally perceived groups as error-correcting entities. Although there is some evidence for groups correcting errors made by individual members (Hastie et al., 1983; Hinsz, 1990: Tindale & Sheffey, 1988), there is also a growing body of evidence showing that groups can also exacerbate individual-level error tendencies (Argote, Seabright, & Dyer, 1986; Tindale, 1993). The fact that groups might accentuate some types of individual errors is predictable from majority process models. For any task where the probability of an individual making an error is greater than .50, a majority model would predict an increase in the error rate at the group level. Such processes can account for at least some of the findings where groups make more errors than do individuals (Tindale, 1993). However, the studies discussed in this section also show that, for certain types of tasks, incorrect or biased alternatives can be chosen by groups even when the initial majority endorses the correct response. We attribute these instances to situations where shared representations among the group members actually favor incorrect, as opposed to correct, alternatives.

In a study by Tindale (1989), individuals and five-person groups were asked to evaluate 48 employee profiles for potential promotion to middle-level management positions. The purpose of the study was to assess whether the limited feedback typical of most employment decision situations (i.e., feedback is only available for candidates hired—or in this case, promoted) could be linked to the continued use of overly conservative decision rules and whether group discussion would alter the use of such biased rules. The employee profiles contained numeric scores on eight equally weighted dimensions (though subjects were not told how to weight the dimensions). Within each block of eight candidates, half of the candidates were defined as promotable (i.e., had composite scores above the mean of the distribution) and half were not promotable. Prior to the actual promotion judgments, subjects were provided with "practice candidates" designed to instill a conservative bias. While evaluating the candidates, both individuals and groups received either no feedback as to the correctness of their decisions (no feedback condition), feedback only after decision to promote (partial feedback condition), or feedback after every decision (total feedback condition).

The promotion decision results basically showed that feedback reduced the conservative bias for both individuals and groups, although the bias attenuated somewhat over trials in all conditions. However, the bias disappeared in the total feedback condition almost immediately. In the partial feedback condition, the bias remained intact until the fourth block of candidates, and in the no feedback condition, the bias was still present even in the sixth and final block of candidates. This pattern is interesting given the results of the social decision scheme analyses for the three different feedback conditions across trial blocks.

Collapsing across trial blocks and conditions, the social decision scheme that provided the best fit to the data was a four-fifths majority–proportionality otherwise model. This model also provided the best fit to the observed decision scheme matrices for all six trial blocks in the total feedback condition. However, this was not the case for certain trial blocks in the no and partial feedback

TABLE 5.4
Observed Social Decision Scheme Matrices for Trial Blocks 2 - 4 for the Total, Partial, and No Feedback Conditions

Total Feedback Condition

Ind. Dist.			Trial Block 2		Trial Block 3		Trial Block 4	
P	NP	P	NP	P	NP	P	NP
5 - 0		1.00	0.00	1.00	0.00	1.00	0.00
4 - 1		1.00	0.00	1.00	0.00	1.00	0.00
3 - 2		0.58	0.42	0.69	0.31	0.55	0.45
1 - 4		0.00	1.00	0.00	1.00	0.05	0.95
0 - 5		0.00	1.00	0.00	1.00	0.00	1.00

Partial Feedback Condition

Ind. Dist.			Trial Block 2		Trial Block 3		Trial Block 4	
P	NP	P	NP	P	NP	P	NP
5 - 0		0.97	0.03	1.00	0.00	1.00	0.00
4 - 1		0.95	0.05	1.00	0.00	0.82	0.18
3 - 2		0.23	0.77	0.50	0.50	0.83	0.17
1 - 4		0.00	1.00	0.00	1.00	0.00	1.00
0 - 5		0.00	1.00	0.00	1.00	0.00	1.00

No Feedback Condition

Ind. Dist.			Trial Block 2		Trial Block 3		Trial Block 4	
P	NP	P	NP	P	NP	P	NP
5 - 0		1.00	0.00	1.00	0.00	0.95	0.05
4 - 1		1.00	0.00	0.93	0.07	1.00	0.00
3 - 2		0.73	0.27	0.50	0.50	0.33	0.67
1 - 4		0.00	1.00	0.00	1.00	0.04	0.96
0 - 5		0.00	1.00	0.01	0.99	0.00	1.00

Note. P - promote; NP = not promote.

conditions. Table 5.4 presents the observed social decision scheme matrices for trial blocks two through four for each feedback condition. As indicated in the table, four-fifths majorities tended to win out virtually all of the time. Similarly, in the total feedback condition, three-person majorities facing two-person minorities defined the group's response more often than not in all three trial blocks (and in fact did so in all six trial blocks). However, this was not always the case for the partial and no feedback condition. For trial blocks two and three in the partial feedback condition, and trial blocks three and four in the no feedback condition, minorities favoring the "not promote" alternative (which is consistent with a conservative bias) were at least as influential (and in two cases, considerably more influential) than the opposing three-person majorities favoring promote. Thus, once again we see an asymmetry in the majority decision process where a particular alternative becomes easier to defend, to the point that a minority faction supporting it can overpower a majority. In addition, the alternative encompassing this added power is the one consistent with the shared task representation—in this case, an experimentally defined one (i.e., the conservative bias). Given that there were an equal number of promotable and nonpromotable candidates, the asymmetries presented here tended to produce erroneous, rather than correct, decisions.

Two more recent studies also show that groups can sometimes make more errors (or nonnormative responses) than individuals, and that the erroneous alternatives can be more compelling or easier to defend. Both studies compared individuals and groups in terms of their propensity to commit conjunction errors (Tversky & Kahneman, 1983). Conjunction errors occur when subjects estimate the probability of a conjunctive event (e.g., Linda is a bank teller and a feminist) to be higher than one or both of the elements that form the conjunction. Conjunction errors are particularly likely when one of the component elements is perceived to be highly likely and the other is perceived to be relatively unlikely. In such cases, the probability estimate for the conjunction tends to fall in between the estimates for the component parts. Tversky and Kahneman argued that this occurs because the conjunction is more representative of the object of judgment than the unlikely component. Thus, the representativeness heuristic is seen as the causal mechanism behind the conjunction fallacy.

Tindale, Sheffey, and Filkins (1990) compared individuals and groups on a series of probability estimation problems involving conjunctions. Although a number of variables were manipulated, we are mainly concerned with the individual–group comparisons, and the social decision scheme results. Figure 5.5 shows the error percentages for individuals and groups across all the conjunction problems used in the study. As indicated, groups tended to exacerbate the tendency for conjunction errors already present in the individual estimates. More interesting, however, are the results concerning the observed social decision schemes for the conjunction judgments. Table 5.5 presents the observed social decision scheme for all of the group conjunction judgments. As indicated, groups

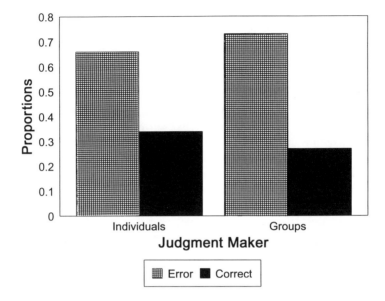

FIG. 5.5. Proportion of conjunction errors by individuals and groups. From Tindale, 1993. Copyright 1993 by Lawrence Erlbaum Associates. Reprinted by permission.

where a majority made errors were quite likely to also make errors. However, groups where the majority of the members were correct were still more likely than not to make errors. Even when all four group members avoided the conjunction error prior to group discussion, groups fell prey to the error 37% of the time.

If we assume that representative thought processes are common in these types of probability judgments, and thus were shared among most of the group members, the pattern of results just discussed fit nicely with the findings presented previously in this chapter. Even if individual group members did not fall

TABLE 5.5
Observed Social Decision Scheme for Conjunction Problems

Individual Distribution		Social Decision Scheme	
Correct - Error	N	Correct	Error
4 - 0	16	0.63	0.37
3 - 1	65	0.42	0.58
2 - 2	166	0.36	0.64
1 - 3	189	0.27	0.73
0 - 4	131	0.10	0.90

Note. From Tindale, 1993. Copyright 1993, Lawrence Erlbaum Associates. Reprinted by permission.

prey to making the conjunction error, it is likely that the conjunctive events did appear more representative to those members. Thus, in group discussion, when trying to assess where the most accurate estimate should fall, if even one subject mentioned that the conjunctive event seemed plausible because of the highly likely element imbedded in the conjunction, this could be enough to allow representativeness to influence the group choice.

This argument seems necessarily conditioned on two assumptions. First, it assumes that subjects were not sufficiently well versed in probability theory to assert and defend a correct response based on the laws of probability. Given the high rate of errors by individuals, and the fact that the subjects were introductory psychology students (meaning they probably had not yet taken a statistics course), this first assumption seems warranted. The second assumption is that, regardless of how subjects made their initial probability estimates for the conjunctive events, they were not very confident in these estimates. Although no firm standard is available to specify a sufficient lack of confidence, subjects' confidence ratings for the conjunctive events averaged 5.73 (range of means across problems: 5.51–5.89) on a 9-point scale, ranging from 1 (not at all) to 9 (extremely) confident, where the anchor for "5" was "moderately confident." Thus, we can say, at least, that subjects were not overly confident in their probability estimates for the conjunctive events.

If we assume that the observed social decision scheme found by Tindale et al. (1990) would remain constant across individual-level error probabilities, then we can compare how group performance would differ under such a decision processes as compared to other processes (e.g., majority). Figure 5.6 presents the results of such a comparison for four-person groups (the group size used in the Tindale et al. study). Predictions based on the observed decision scheme are compared to three different theoretical models: majority-wins/equiprobability-otherwise, proportionality, and strict equiprobability (i.e., any alternative brought up in group discussion is equally likely to be chosen). As indicated in the figure, the observed decision scheme would produce a greater number of errors (i.e., fewer correct responses) than any of the other symmetric models— considerably more as the probability of a correct response by individuals increases. In terms of the shape of the predicted distribution, the observed decision scheme more closely mirrors the equiprobability decision scheme than either of the other two. This may also indicate that subjects were not particularly confident of their judgments for this task, because Davis (1982) showed that the equiprobability model tends to work well for tasks with high levels of uncertainty. In any case, the observed decision scheme definitely shows a strong pull toward the conjunction error response.

Tindale, Filkins, Thomas, and Smith (1993) conducted a study similar to Tindale et al. (1990) that attempted to reduce the number of conjunction errors in groups using two different techniques: a discussion-structuring technique that required all group members to state and justify their estimates prior to any discussion, and

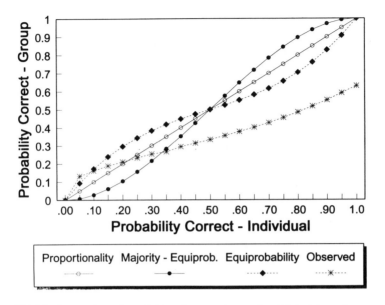

FIG. 5.6. Comparison of predictions from an observed social decision scheme and majority, proportionality, and equiprobability models for four-person groups.

an instructional technique that warned groups to avoid inconsistencies among the various probability estimates. Neither technique showed any impact on the group error rates, but due to the use of a somewhat simpler design, some clear comparisons between different types of conjunctions were possible. Three different types of conjunctions were used: conjunctions of two likely events, conjunctions of two unlikely events, and conjunctions of one likely and one unlikely event (the standard situation used by Tversky & Kahneman, 1983). Figure 5.7 shows the data pattern for a significant individual–group by problem type interaction. The figure shows that for two likely events, and one likely and one unlikely event, groups made a greater number of conjunction errors than did individuals. However, for two unlikely events, individuals were about 50% likely to make conjunction errors, and groups made even fewer errors than individuals. Again, assuming subjects were making these judgments based on the representativeness heuristic, this pattern of results makes sense. The conjunction of two unlikely events would probably seem even less representative than either of the events themselves. This would tend to reduce the number of conjunction errors by individuals. In addition, the shared nature of the use of the heuristic would tend to make arguments for lower probability estimates for these conjunctions more compelling in the group. Thus, as was found, groups should make fewer errors than individuals for these types of conjunctions.

Table 5.6 presents the observed social decision schemes for the likely-likely and likely-unlikely conjunctions combined, and the unlikely-unlikely conjunctions.

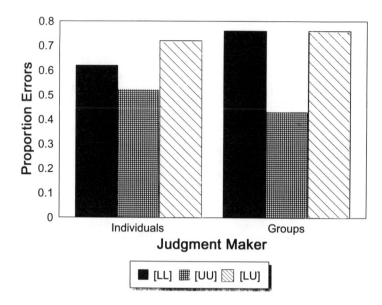

FIG. 5.7. Comparison of individual and group conjunction errors for three types of conjunction problems.

TABLE 5.6
Observed Social Decision Schemes for Different Types of Conjunction Problems

Likely-Likely and Likely-Unlikely Problems

Individual Distribution		*Social Decision Scheme*	
Correct - Error	*N*	*Correct*	*Error*
4 - 0	10	0.80	0.20
3 - 1	35	0.46	0.54
2 - 2	83	0.30	0.70
1 - 3	147	0.22	0.78
0 - 4	109	0.08	0.92

Unlikely-Unlikely Problems

Individual Distribution		*Social Decision Scheme*	
Correct - Error	*N*	*Correct*	*Error*
4 - 0	14	0.86	0.14
3 - 1	32	0.81	0.19
2 - 2	49	0.59	0.41
1 - 3	26	0.31	0.69
0 - 4	5	0.00	1.00

As can be seen, the observed decision scheme for the likely-likely and likely-unlikely conjunctions is quite similar to the one found by Tindale et al. (1990). Minorities that made the conjunction errors are still more influential than majorities that did not. However, for the unlikely-unlikely conjunctions, the error response does not seem to show the same degree of power. In fact, although slight, the asymmetry in the matrix is shifted toward the correct response. However, the data from this condition were modeled quite accurately by a symmetric majority model. Thus, in the conditions where there is a strong, shared heuristic influence toward error, the asymmetry in the observed social decision scheme is present. When the heuristic influence does not lead to error, the asymmetry disappears.

The general position taken here has been that whenever a cognitive process or shared belief system leads to a particular bias or error, and that cognitive process or belief system is shared among the group members, groups should be more error prone than individuals. However, there is some evidence in the literature that groups attenuate some biases generally found at the individual level. In particular, Wright and Wells (1985) found that groups showed less bias due to the "fundamental attribution error" than did individuals. The fundamental attribution error is defined as the tendency for people to ignore situational constraints, and thus emphasize dispositional explanations, when looking for causes of behavior. Wright and Wells assumed that, because not everyone falls prey to this bias, if a minority member (someone who did not make the attribution error) mentioned the importance of considering situational constraints during group discussion, this would convince the other group members to decrease their dispositional emphasis. However, the analyses of the group discussions showed that the reduction in dispositional attributions was not related to mentions of the situational constraints.

A recent study by Wittenbaum and Stasser (1995) provides a potential explanation for these seemingly inconsistent results that is congruent with the position espoused here. Using basically the same procedures as Wright and Wells (1985), Wittenbaum and Stasser compared pre- and postgroup individual attitude judgments about an essay writer who took either a positive or negative stance toward legalizing marijuana in the essay. Subjects were told that the essay writers did not choose which position to take in the essay—a classic situation used to demonstrate the fundamental attribution error. When subjects had no prior expectations concerning the essay writer's attitude toward the issue, group members were less likely to judge the essay writer's attitude as consistent with the essay position after discussion as compared to before discussion. However, Wittenbaum and Stasser found that less extreme attitude judgments after group discussion were related to mentions of the decreased quality of the essay. (It should be noted that, in contrast to the Wright and Wells results, they also found less extreme attitude judgments when the situational constraints were mentioned.) In actuality, the essays remained constant across conditions, so such assertions by group members were not valid. However, these results suggest that there may have been a generally shared belief that essays written by writers assigned to a particular position would not be well written. If such a common belief existed, its effects on individual judgments may have been very slight due to the power of the fundamental attribution error. However, once explicitly mentioned in the group discussion, its general plausibility could have been compelling enough to attenuate the extremity of the group member attitude judgments after group discussion. This is obviously just one of many potential post hoc explanations for their results, but it does show how a belief shared among group members could account for attenuation, as well as exacerbation, of biases and errors in groups.

SUMMARY AND FUTURE DIRECTIONS

The notion of socially shared cognitions has recently become a major focus in a number of disciplines within psychology (Brewer, 1994; Farr & Moscovici, 1984; Resnick, Levine, & Teasley, 1991). This trend has not been ignored in the groups literature. The ideas of distributed cognitions (Hutchins, 1991), transactive memory (Wegner, 1987), and shared mental models (Cannon-Bowers, Salas, & Converse, 1993) are beginning to change the way in which group processes and performance are conceptualized. We see the ideas and the interpretations of the empirical findings presented here as generally congruent with this trend. We have attempted to outline some basic ideas concerning how shared cognitive representations interact with social influence processes in groups engaged in problem-solving and decision-making tasks. However, the empirical findings presented throughout this chapter, although consistent with our ideas, cannot be interpreted as evidence for them. The empirical findings preceded and guided the conceptualizations—not the other way around.

In order for the notion of shared representations to impact positively on the field, interesting research questions derived from such notions need to be rigorously investigated. In addition, research methods oriented toward measuring and identifying shared cognitions need to be developed and employed. A greater emphasis is needed on the cognitive dimensions underlying group discussion and interaction—an emphasis sorely lacking in much of the research discussed here. Empirical investigations similar to the Wittenbaum and Stasser (1995) study would be good places to start. Our own research is currently focused on the cognitive strategies employed by subjects when estimating conjunctive probabilities, and the degree to which these different strategies are deemed generally plausible by group members. In addition to empirical work, more theoretical work is needed, especially in relation to providing tight conceptual definitions for what constitutes a *shared* belief system or cognitive process, and when such shared processes would impact on group performance for various tasks.

In the final analysis, the usefulness of such ideas will also rest on whether they are relevant for addressing important questions and advancing our knowledge of group behavior. One area where shared representations may prove useful is for understanding cultural differences in group functioning. Culture is at least partially defined by the idea of shared beliefs, values, and so on, and groups composed of culturally similar versus dissimilar members may allow for powerful tests of the assertions made throughout the chapter, as well as aid in our understanding of how culture might impact on group performance. Our understanding of how shared cognitions influence groups and their members is still in its infancy and we hope that this chapter may stimulate others to share in its development.

ACKNOWLEDGMENTS

The authors would like to thank James Davis, Robyn Dawes, and Gwen Wittenbaum for comments on an earlier draft of the chapter.

REFERENCES

Argote, L., Seabright, M. A., & Dyer, L. (1986). Individual vs. group use of base rate and individuating information. *Organizational Behavior and Human Decision Processes, 38*, 65–75.

Brewer, M. B. (June, 1994). *The social bases of cognition: Closing the circle.* Invited symposium presented at the American Psychological Society Sixth Annual Convention, Washington, DC.

Cannon-Bowers, J. A., Salas, E., & Converse, S. (1993). Shared mental models in expert team decision making. In N. J. Castellan, Jr. (Ed.), *Individual and group decision making: Current issues* (pp. 221–246). Hillsdale, NJ: Lawrence Erlbaum Associates.

Davis, J. H. (1973). Group decision and social interaction: A theory of social decision schemes. *Psychological Review, 80*, 97–125.

Davis, J. H. (1980). Group decision and procedural justice. In M. Fishbein (Ed.), *Progress in social psychology* (Vol. 1, pp. 157–230). Hillsdale, NJ: Lawrence Erlbaum Associates.

Davis, J. H. (1982). Social interaction as a combinatorial process in group decision. In H. Brandstatter, J. Davis, & G. Stocker-Kreichgauer (Eds.), *Group decision processes* (pp. 27–58). London: Academic Press.

Davis, J. H., Kerr, N. L., Stasser, G., Meek, D., & Holt, R. (1977). Victim consequences, sentence severity, and decision processes in mock juries. *Organizational Behavior and Human Performance, 18*, 346–365.

Farr, R. M., & Moscovici, S. (1984). *Social representations.* Cambridge, England: Cambridge University Press.

Hastie, R., Penrod, S., & Pennington, N. (1983). *Inside the jury.* Cambridge, MA: Harvard University Press.

Hinsz, V. B. (1990). Cognitive and consensus processes in group recognition memory performance. *Journal of Personality and Social Psychology, 59*, 705–718.

Hutchins, E. (1991). The social organization of distributed cognition. In L. B. Resnick, J. M. Levine, & S. D. Teasley (Eds.), *Perspectives on socially shared cognition* (pp. 283–307). Washington, DC: American Psychological Association.

Kahneman, D., Slovic, P., & Tversky, A. (1982). *Judgment under uncertainty: Heuristics and biases.* Cambridge, MA: Cambridge University Press.

Kerr, N. L., & MacCoun, R. J. (1985). The effects of jury size and polling method on the process and product of jury deliberation. *Journal of Personality and Social Psychology, 48,* 349–363.

Latané, B. (1981). The psychology of social impact. *American Psychologist, 36,* 343–355.

Latané, B., & Wolf, S. (1981). The social impact of majorities and minorities. *Psychological Review, 88,* 438–453.

Laughlin, P. R. (1980). Social combination processes of cooperative problem-solving groups on verbal intellective tasks. In M. Fishbein (Ed.), *Progress in social psychology* (Vol. 1, pp. 127–156). Hillsdale, NJ: Lawrence Erlbaum Associates.

Laughlin, P. R., & Adamopoulos, J. (1982). Social decision schemes on intellective tasks. In H. Brandstatter, J. H. Davis, & G. Stocker-Kreichgauer (Eds.), *Group decision making* (pp. 81–94). London: Academic Press.

Laughlin, P. R., & Early, P. C. (1982). Social combination models, persuasive arguments theory, social comparison theory, and choice shift. *Journal of Personality and Social Psychology, 42,* 273–280.

Laughlin, P. R., & Ellis, A. L. (1986). Demonstrability and social combination processes on mathematical intellective tasks. *Journal of Experimental Social Psychology, 22,* 177–189.

Lorge, I., & Solomon, H. (1955). Two models of group behavior in the solution of Eureka-type problems. *Psychometrika, 20,* 139–148.

MacCoun, R. J., & Kerr, N. L. (1988). Asymmetric influence in mock jury deliberations: Jurors' bias for leniency. *Journal of Personality and Social Psychology, 54,* 21–33.

Moscovici, S. (1976). *Social influence and social change.* London: Academic Press.

Moscovici, S. (1984). The phenomenon of social representations. In R. M. Farr & S. Moscovici (Eds.), *Social representations* (pp. 3–69). Cambridge, England: Cambridge University Press.

Mullen, B. (1983). Operationalizing the effect of the group on the individual: A self-attention perspective. *Journal of Experimental Social Psychology, 19,* 295–322.

Mullen, B. (1987). Self attention theory: The effects of group composition on the individual. In B. Mullen & G. Goethals (Eds.), *Theories of group behavior* (pp. 125–146). New York: Springer-Verlag.

Myers, D. G., & Lamm, H. (1976). The group polarization phenomenon. *Psychological Bulletin, 83,* 602–627.

Nemeth, C. J. (1977). Interactions between jurors as a function of majority vs. unanimity decision rules. *Journal of Applied Social Psychology, 7,* 38–56.

Nemeth, C. J. (1986). Differential contributions of majority and minority influence. *Psychological Review, 93,* 23–32.

Resnick, L. B., Levine, J. M., & Teasley, S. D. (Eds.). (1991). *Perspectives on socially shared cognitions.* Washington, DC: American Psychological Association.

Shaw, M. E. (1932). Comparison of individuals and small groups in the rational solution of complex problems. *American Journal of Psychology, 44,* 491–504.

Stasser, G., Kerr, N. L., & Bray, R. M. (1982). The social psychology of jury deliberations: Structure, process & product. In N. Kerr & R. Bray (Eds.), *The psychology of the courtroom* (pp. 221–255). New York: Academic Press.

Stasser, G., Kerr, N. L., & Davis, J. H. (1989). Influence processes and consensus models in decision-making groups. In P. Paulus (Ed.), *Psychology of group influence* (2nd ed., pp. 279–326). Hillsdale, NJ: Lawrence Erlbaum Associates.

Tanford, S., & Penrod, S. (1984). Social influence model: A formal integration of research on majority and minority influence. *Psychological Bulletin, 95,* 189–225.

Taylor, D. W. (1954). Problem solving in groups. In *Proceedings XIV, International Congress of Psychology, 1954.* Amsterdam: North Holland Publishing.

Tindale, R. S. (1989). Group v. individual information processing: The effects of outcome feedback on decision making. *Organizational Behavior and Human Decision Processes, 44,* 454–473.

Tindale, R. S. (1993). Decision errors made by individuals and groups. In N. J. Castellan, Jr. (Ed.), *Individual and group decision making: Current issues* (pp. 109–124). Hillsdale, NJ: Lawrence Erlbaum Associates.

Tindale, R. S., & Davis, J. H. (1983). Group decision making and jury verdicts. In H. H. Blumberg, A. P. Hare, V. Kent, & M. F. Davies (Eds.), *Small groups and social interaction* (Vol. 2, pp. 9–38). Chichester, England: Wiley.

Tindale, R. S., & Davis, J. H. (1985). Individual and group reward allocation decisions in two situational contexts: The effects of relative need and performance. *Journal of Personality and Social Psychology, 48,* 1148–1161.

Tindale, R. S., Davis, J. H., Vollrath, D. A., Nagao, D. H., & Hinsz, V. B. (1990). Asymmetrical social influence in freely interacting groups: A test of three models. *Journal of Personality and Social Psychology, 58,* 438–449.

Tindale, R. S., Filkins, J., Thomas, L. S., & Smith, C. M. (1993, November). *An attempt to reduce conjunction errors in decision-making groups.* Poster presented at the Society for Judgment and Decision Making meeting, Washington, DC.

Tindale, R. S., & Sheffey, S. (1988, August). *Task assignment redundancy and group memory.* Paper presented at the American Psychological Association Annual Convention, Atlanta.

Tindale, R. S., Sheffey, S., & Filkins, J. (1990, November). *Conjunction errors by individuals and groups.* Paper presented at the Society for Judgment and Decision Making meeting, New Orleans.

Tindale, R. S., Sheffey, S., & Scott, L. A. (1993). Framing and group decision-making: Do cognitive changes parallel preference changes? *Organizational Behavior and Human Decision Processes 55,* 470–485.

Turner, J. C., & Oakes, P. J. (1989). Self-categorization theory and social influence. In P. Paulus (Ed.), *Psychology of group influence* (2nd ed., pp. 233–278). Hillsdale, NJ: Lawrence Erlbaum Associates.

Tversky, A., & Kahneman, D. (1981). The framing of decisions and the psychology of choice. *Science, 211,* 453–458.

Tversky, A., & Kahneman, D. (1983). Extensional vs. intuitive reasoning: The conjunction fallacy in probability judgments. *Psychological Review, 90,* 293–315.

Vinocur, A., & Burnstein, E. (1974). Novel argumentation and attitude change: The case of polarization following discussion. *Journal of Personality and Social Psychology, 29,* 305–315.

Wegner, D. M. (1987). Transactive memory: A contemporary analysis of the group mind. In B. Mullen & G. Goethals (Eds.), *Theories of group behavior* (pp. 185–208). New York: Springer-Verlag.

Witte, E. H. (1994, June). *Group performance: The solution of two divergent tasks.* Paper presented at the 16th Annual Nags Head Conference on Groups, Networks, and Organizations, Highland Beach, FL.

Wittenbaum, G. W., & Stasser, G. (1995). The role of prior expectancy and group discussion in the attribution of attitudes. *Journal of Experimental Social Psychology, 31,* 82–105.

Wright, E. F., & Wells, G. L. (1985). Does group discussion attenuate the dispositional bias? *Journal of Applied Social Psychology, 15,* 531–546.

6

"WHEN ARE N HEADS BETTER (OR WORSE) THAN ONE?": BIASED JUDGMENT IN INDIVIDUALS VERSUS GROUPS

Norbert L. Kerr
Michigan State University

Robert J. MacCoun
University of California, Berkeley

Geoffrey P. Kramer
Indiana University, Kokomo

A great deal of research in social and cognitive psychology has been devoted to demonstrating what is probably an uncontroversial proposition—that human judgment is imperfect. What makes this work interesting and useful is that such imperfections often constitute more than random fluctuations around "rational," prescribed, or ideal judgments. Rather, humans consistently exhibit systematic biases in their judgments. Such judgmental biases are not only of theoretical interest; they also can have serious consequences (cf. Dawes, 1988; Thaler, 1985) and identifying means of controlling them is an important challenge.

These questions have largely been the province of investigators in the areas of cognition, social cognition, and judgment and decision making, all of whom have understandably focused primarily on the behavior of the individual judge. However, in many important instances, the judges who are potentially vulnerable to such systematic biases are not individuals but groups. In this chapter, we (as social psychologists) explore the following question: Are decision-making groups any less (or more) subject to judgmental biases than individual decision makers? For example, might we expect deliberating juries to be any less (or more) sensitive than individual jurors to proscribed extralegal information such as the race of a victim? Our goal is to shed light on when groups are more biased than individuals, when individuals are more biased than groups, and most important, whether and why there are patterns in such comparisons. (It is not an objective of the present chapter to provide a review of the empirical literature directly comparing the accuracy of individual and group judgment. See Kerr, MacCoun, & Kramer, 1994, for such a review; see Hastie, 1986; Hill, 1982, for more general reviews of the group performance literature.)

SDS: A PSYCHOLOGICAL MODEL

In exploring these questions, we (like several other chapters in this volume) utilize a *social combination* approach (Davis, 1980; Laughlin, 1980; Stasser, Kerr, & Davis, 1989) in general, and Davis' Social Decision Scheme (SDS) model (e.g., Davis, 1973) in particular. The SDS model suggests that the prediscussion preferences of group members can be related to group decisions through simple functions or rules, termed social decision schemes. A familiar example is a majority-rules social decision scheme, which predicts that the group ultimately settles on the alternative initially favored by a majority of group members. Of course, some groups may not have an absolute majority favoring an alternative at the beginning of deliberation. To deal with such cases not handled by the primary scheme, one must often posit one of various subschemes (e.g., plurality-wins, averaging) along with the primary decision scheme so that all possible initial distributions of preferences are accounted for. Decision schemes need not be deterministic, predicting one particular group decision with certainty. Rather, they can (and usually are) stochastic rules. For example, groups occasionally (e.g., Johnson & Davis, 1972) seem to operate under an equiprobability decision scheme for which all alternatives with at least one advocate have an equal chance of being selected as the group decision.

Social decision schemes have sometimes been described (e.g., Myers & Lamm, 1976) as if they were simple and explicit voting rules governing group decision making and judgment—for example, one way in which a group may reach a decision would be to take a poll of its members at the outset of group discussion and simply endorse whatever alternative achieves a numerical majority. Although such voting rules do exist and have contributed to the formulation of empirically testable social decision schemes (e.g., Davis, Kerr, Atkin, Holt, & Meek, 1975; Kerr et al., 1976), it is a mistake simply to equate social decision schemes with explicit voting rules. Rather, the operative social decision scheme summarizes the totality of *all* modifications to information processing resulting from moving from the individual (as judge or decision maker) to the group (as judge or decision maker). The operative social decision scheme (i.e., the scheme that accounts for the behavior of any particular type of group on any particular type of task) does include the functioning of an effective *decision rule* (i.e., the level of consensus required at the *end* of group deliberation to define a group decision; Miller, 1989). But it also includes much more. For one thing, it includes the availability of resources (e.g., information) to group members that were not available to them as individual judges. In addition, the operative scheme also summarizes any **changes** (relative to functioning as an individual judge) in the way group members retrieve, encode, evaluate, and process task-relevant information (cf. Hinsz, Tindale, & Vollrath, 1991). Given our current state of knowledge, we cannot even anticipate all such possible changes, much less specify a priori which ones may arise and be important for any particular judgmental task. However, what we can do is identify certain generic social decision schemes that are of theoretical interest and/or have been shown to accurately summarize the group decision-making process for a sizable range of interesting tasks. We can then explore theoretically the implications of these social decision schemes for the contrast of bias between individual and group judges.

In this chapter we consider three generic social decision schemes. The generic social decision scheme for which there is the widest empirical support (see Stasser et al., 1989) is the majority-wins social decision scheme, of which the simple-majority-wins scheme is a prototype. It has been shown that such a primary decision scheme (or a close relative like a two-thirds-majority wins; cf. Davis et al., 1975) accurately summarizes the decision-making process of groups at many different tasks, including attitudinal judgments (Kerr, Davis, Meek, & Rissman, 1975), duplex bets (Davis, Kerr, Sussman, & Rissman, 1974), and jury decisions (see Davis, 1980, for a review). Laughlin (e.g., Laughlin & Ellis, 1986) has suggested that such a decision scheme generally applies to group decision making at what he has termed *judgmental tasks,* tasks that possess no clear, universally shared criterion for the "correctness" of decision alternatives. Many aesthetic, political, ethical, and attitudinal judgments are, in this sense, judgmental tasks, as are tasks whose evaluative criteria are complex, vague, or only partially shared (e.g., jury decision making). The unifying feature of this fuzzy set of "majority" social decision schemes is that they all exhibit "strength in numbers." That is, the probability that relatively large initial factions will prevail in the group is disproportionately greater than such factions' relative size (and, conversely, relatively small initial factions will prevail with a probability lower than their relative size). This reflects the underlying logic of Laughlin's hypothesis—when there is no "objective" basis for evaluating the "correctness" or "accuracy" of a judgment (i.e., no widely shared and easily applied evaluative conceptual system), we must rely on social consensus to define a valid response (cf. Festinger, 1954).

If majority-wins decision schemes exhibit disproportionate strength in numbers, then we may also envision decision schemes in which there is little or no strength in numbers. One such decision scheme is an "equiprobability" scheme, mentioned in passing earlier, in which every alternative with at least one advocate is equally likely to become the group's final choice. Johnson and Davis (1972) and Davis, Hornik, and Hornseth (1970) found evidence that such a decision scheme accurately accounted for group probability matching judgments. Davis (1982) speculated that this decision scheme might characterize group decision making under high task uncertainty. Laughlin and Ellis (1986) and Kerr (1983, 1992b) speculated that such a decision process might arise when group members have very little commitment to or investment in their personal preferences and/or maintaining group harmony is crucial. In support of the latter conjectures, Kerr (1992b) reported that as the importance of the issue being discussed by group members declined, so did initial factions' apparent strength in numbers.

Laughlin (1980; Laughlin & Ellis, 1986) also suggested that for many tasks there *is* a widely shared consensus on the criteria for the evaluating group decisions. Simple mathematics problems nicely illustrate such *intellective tasks*; basic mathematical rules provide an objective basis for arguing that one solution is better than another. Laughlin and Ellis suggested that particular alternatives are *demonstrably correct* for a purely intellective task when certain basic conditions are met (e.g., there is enough information available to identify a correct response, advocates of the correct response have the motivation and ability to present and defend it). For such tasks (which may well be fairly rare), Laughlin has shown (e.g., Laughlin & Ellis, 1986; Laughlin, Kerr, Munch, & Haggarty, 1976) that all that is required for the group to choose the "correct" alternative is for there to be a single group member who initially advocates this alternative (a "truth-wins" social decision scheme). (There exists some suggestive evidence—e.g., Laughlin & Early, 1982; Laughlin, Kerr, Davis, Halff, & Marciniak, 1975—that when these demonstrability conditions are not as uniformly met, advocates of the "correct" alternative may require some social support to prevail—a "truth-supported-wins" decision scheme.) The distinctive feature of such decision schemes is their asymmetry—factions favoring the "correct" alternative are more likely to prevail than comparable (i.e., equally large) factions favoring an "incorrect" alternative.[1]

SDS: A PHYSICAL METAPHOR

To simplify our presentation, we have restricted our attention to the simplest possible judgment task—one with only two choice alternatives. Because we sometimes use jury decision making to illustrate our ideas, for convenience we label those two alternatives G and NG (for guilty and not guilty). Although certain interesting and distinctive processes can arise in cases where the response scale is mulitchotomous or continuous (Davis, 1991, and chapter 3 of this volume; Kerr, 1992a), nearly all of the judgmental biases of interest here can be reduced to the simple dichotomous case by collapsing response categories. (See Kerr et al., 1994, for a discussion of the few instances where this simplifying assumption represents a real oversimplification.)

---

[1]Perhaps because of the utility of generic majority decision schemes or because it affords a conceptual simplification, some scholars have presumed that *all* social decision schemes necessarily represent very simple functions (like majority-wins) relating predeliberation preference distributions to group decisions. As the present discussion shows, however, decision schemes can and sometimes do incorporate useful complexities, such as the nonequivalence of advocates of different alternatives (inherent in asymmetries like those discussed in the text) or the nonequivalence of different members of the group (e.g., see Kirchler & Davis, 1986).

There exists a formal mathematical model employing probability theory and matrix algebra (see Davis, 1973, and chapter 3 of this volume; Stasser et al., 1989; and the Appendix), which we might utilize to examine the relative degree of bias by individuals and groups under any particular generic social decision scheme; indeed, elsewhere (Kerr et al., 1994) we did just that. However, in this chapter we employ a physical metaphor to illustrate the effects of our three generic social decision schemes. The starting point for any application of the SDS model is individual, predeliberation preferences. In our simple, two-alternative case, we can simply summarize individual opinion by $p(G)$ = the proportion of individuals favoring the G alternative; of course, $p(NG) = 1 - p(G)$. Now, imagine that we represent this predeliberation individual preference by sliding a metal ball along a smooth rod; the farther to the right we move the ball, the stronger individual preference for the G alternative (see the left half of Fig. 6.1). So, as Case 1 in Fig. 6.1 illustrates, if $p(G) = 0$, such that *no* individuals prefer the G alternative (e.g., all jurors begin deliberation convinced that the defendant is not guilty), the ball would be at the extreme left end of the bar. (Note that the scale at the bottom of the figure can be used to gauge the location of the ball.[2]) If $p(G) = 1.0$ (Case 2), the ball would be at the extreme right end. If $p(G) = .5$ (Case 3), then the ball would be at the midpoint of the bar. And so on.

With a few simple assumptions we can use this "ball-on-a-bar" metaphor to summarize how group opinion—which we designate, using uppercase letters, as $P(G)$—would differ from individual opinion—which we have been calling $p(G)$—under any of our generic social decision schemes. First, assume that once individual opinion is determined (i.e., once the ball has been placed at a particular point on the bar), the ball is then tethered to the bar with an elastic cord (e.g., a rubber band or bungee cord). Psychologically, one might simply think of this "tethering" as the commitment of individuals to their original positions—individual opinion can be moved, but it takes a stronger psychological "force" (to use a field theory notion) to move it a great distance than a short distance, just as the greater a distance along the bar one wanted to slide the tethered ball, the greater the physical force that would be required.

Let's begin with a generic majority-wins social decision scheme, for which there is high strength in numbers. We can roughly[3] summarize the net effect of

---

[2]It is worthwhile to remind the reader that these scales do *not* represent individual or group positions on a continuous response scale. Rather, they represent the proportion of individuals or groups favoring the first of the two discrete response alternatives.

[3]The reader should note that this physical metaphor is presented as a heuristic or didactic tool. Although the simple version presented here captures most of the essential qualitative and quantitative features of the generic decision schemes of interest, readers should not take the metaphor too literally. For example, the physical laws governing magnetic forces stretching metal balls tethered with springs are not mathematically isomorphic with the SDS model mathematics. And, as we soon note, modifying the metaphor to make it a more precise analogue of the SDS model can easily undermine the methaphor's simplicity and, hence, its utility as a heuristic device.

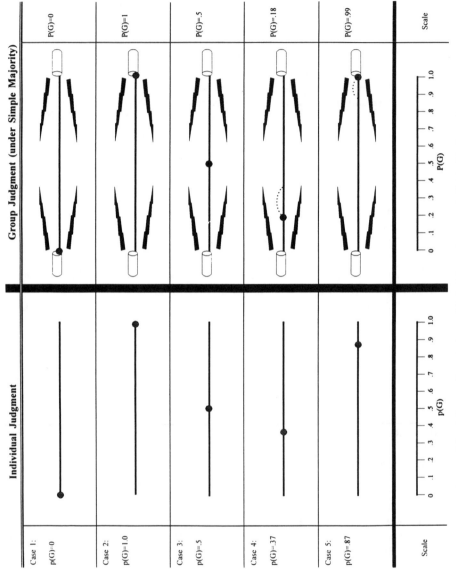

FIG. 6.1. Effect of a simple-majority social decision scheme on individual judgment.

such a group decision-making process by imagining flipping a switch that turned on two identical electromagnets, one at each end of the bar (see the right panels in Fig. 6.1). How would the resultant magnetic fields (graphically represented by the jagged lines in Fig. 6.1) created by such a pair of magnets affect the location of a tethered metal ball? Consider Case 1 when the ball "began" (i.e., prior to group deliberation) at the left end of the bar, that is, $p(G) = 0$. The magnet at the left end of the bar, being much closer, would exert a much stronger magnetic force than the magnet at the distant other end. The net result of these two opposing forces would be a net force strongly pulling the ball to the left. But, of course, the ball is already as far to the left as possible, so it would simply remain where it is, that is, $P(G) = 0$. That is, when *no* individuals prefer the G alternative, all groups will begin deliberation unanimously favoring the NG alternative. Under a majority-wins (and practically any other) decision scheme, the group should *always* end up choosing NG under such assumptions. Similarly, in Case 2—that is, $p(G) = 1.0$—the net effect of the magnets would be a strong force pulling the ball to the right, but because it is already as far right as possible, the ball does not move and $p(G) = P(G) = 1.0$. In Case 3, where the ball begins in the middle of the bar—that is, $p(G) = .5$—the two magnets exert equal and opposing forces on the ball, and once again the ball does not move; that is, $p(G) = P(G) = .5$.

We have purposely begun with three special cases where the magnetic forces would not move the ball. But in every other imaginable case, there would be both a net force pulling on the ball and some room for the ball to move. Consider hypothetical Case 4, where $p(G) = .37$. Because the ball is closer to the left magnet than to the right magnet, the net force pulls the ball to the left. But because the ball is tethered (represented graphically by the dashed arc connecting the ball to its original, pregroup deliberation position), the amount of movement is limited. In Fig. 6.1, the amount of movement indicated for Case 4 is equal to what would occur under a simple-majority decision scheme in an 11-person group, namely, $P(G) = .18$. (The effect would be weaker [stronger] if the group size were smaller [larger]. You could imagine that group size represents how much current is sent to the electromagnets [note that this "group size as current" metaphor applies equally well to the other generic social decision schemes to be discussed later]. The larger the group, the greater the current, the stronger the magnetic forces created at each end of the bar, the stronger the resultant force on the ball at any point [except the middle of the bar where the two forces would cancel each other out exactly], and hence, the farther the tethered ball should move. So, for example, for Case 4 [$p(G) = .37$], a 3-person group would be much like a weaker pair of magnets, producing less movement of the ball; namely, for a 3-person group, a simple-majority process would only move the ball from $p(G) = .37$ to $P(G) = .31$ [vs. .18 for an 11-person group]. In all of the figures employing our ball-on-a-bar metaphor, group size is assumed to be 11.)

Likewise, in Case 5, where $p(G) = .87$, the nearby right magnet is much stronger than the rather distant left magnet, and so there should be a strong force pulling the tethered ball to the right; here, assuming an 11-person group, $P(G) = .99$. [Actually, our ball-on-the-bar metaphor is a bit too oversimplified. With a real elastic tethering cord, there would be some starting $p(G)$ point close enough to the right end such that the net force resulting from turning on the two magnets would be great enough to pull the ball all the rest of the way to the closer end of the bar. But in groups, as long as there is *some* disagreement—that is, $p(G) \neq 1.0,0.0$—there remains some nonzero probability that a randomly composed group could end up with an initial majority favoring the less popular alternative, and hence, prevailing in the group (under a simple-majority decision scheme). Of course, if $p(G)$ is extreme and the group is large, this probability may be very small indeed: For example, if $p(G) = .95$, the probability of a randomly composed 11-person group having an initial majority favoring the unpopular NG alternative is only .000006. Thus, our physical ball-on-a-bar metaphor would be more accurate if it included some mechanism to keep the tethered ball from moving "too" close to either end of the bar (e.g., "cushioning" springs attached to each end of the bar). However, our metaphor is complex enough as it is. Just keep in mind that balls near one end of the bar prior to group discussion (i.e., to turning on the electricity) can only move close to that nearby end of the bar, but can never actually touch it.]

It should not surprise us that a group decision-making process characterized by strength in numbers tends to exaggerate in groups whatever preferences are evident among individuals (cf. Davis, 1973; Kerr et al., 1975). And, to reverse the logic, we might expect a social decision-making process with scant strength in numbers, such as the equiprobability scheme, to have precisely the opposite effect—namely, to attenuate in groups whatever preferences are evident among individuals. And indeed, this is the case (cf. Davis, 1973). In terms of our metaphor, we can summarize the net effect of the equiprobability scheme by imagining flipping a switch that turned on a single electromagnet at the middle of the bar (see Fig. 6.2). Here, let's begin with Cases 5 and 4. In each of these cases, the tethered ball is pulled back toward the middle of the bar, qualitatively the opposite effect of a majority scheme (compare with Fig. 6.1).[4] Of course, when the ball begins at the middle (Case 3), it would simply remain there after the magnet was turned on. Our simple physical metaphor also suggests that when the ball begins at either end (Cases 1 and 2), it will also be pulled toward the middle (although perhaps not very far given the distance to the magnet). However, the equiprobability decision scheme requires that *someone* in the group advocate an alternative before it has *any* chance of prevailing in the group.

---

[4]Once again, a strictly accurate metaphor would require some kind of mechanism to prevent balls not actually beginning at the middle of the bar from being pulled all the way to the middle. But, again, we opt for our simpler, if slightly less accurate, version of the metaphor.

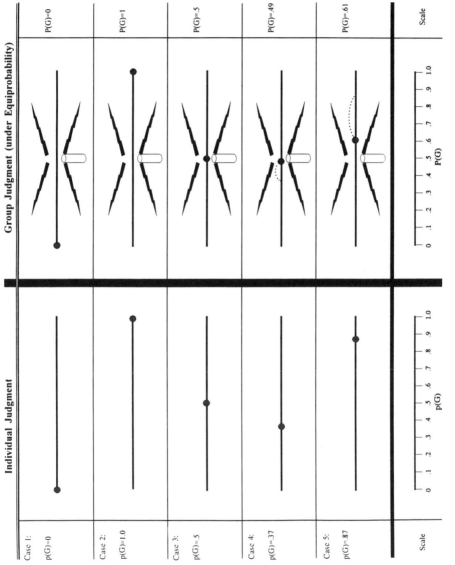

FIG. 6.2. Effect of an equiprobability social decision scheme on individual judgment.

113

When $p(G) = 1.0$ or 0.0, only one alternative has any advocates and hence, only it can prevail. So, we must further assume that if the ball begins at the very end of the bar, there it must remain (see Fig. 6.2, Cases 1 & 2).

Our third class of generic social decision schemes are those with an asymmetry, giving factions advocating certain "correct" positions relatively greater influence than comparably large factions advocating other, "incorrect" positions. For our discussion, let's assume that it is the NG alternative that is the "correct" one. (Incidentally, much research has shown just such an asymmetry in jury decision making; cf. MacCoun & Kerr, 1988.) The net effect of such an asymmetry can be simply represented in our ball-on-a-bar metaphor through a modification of the majority-wins version. Recall that version had two *equally strong* magnets at each end of the bar. We can vary the relative "correctness" of the two decision alternatives simply by varying the relative strength of the two magnets. So, in our present discussion, the magnet at the NG end is stronger than at the other end (see Fig. 6.3, where this is represented by a larger magnet with a stronger magnetic field at the left end of the bar).[5] As noted earlier, Case 1 [i.e., $p(G) = 0$] and Case 2 [i.e., $p(G) = 1.0$] do not permit any movement—balls initially touching the end of the bar are stuck there. But because of the asymmetry of forces, Case 3 does result in a net movement toward the NG end of the bar (see Fig. 6.3). As with the simple-majority case, there should be a point somewhere along the bar where the forces of the two magnets cancel one another out, but because the left magnet is stronger here, that point must be closer to the right end of the bar than the left end [e.g., for the strongly asymmetric decision scheme represented in Fig. 6.3,[6] that point is at $p(G) = .77$]. The location of this point and the relative strengths of the two magnets should make the effect of the unequal magnets in Cases 4 and 5 fathomable.

To review, we have used the ball-on-the-bar metaphor to represent the net effect of groups operating under a majority-wins, an equiprobability, and an asymmetric (favoring the NG alternative as more "truthful" than the G alternative) social decision scheme.[7] With this metaphor in mind, we can now return to explore our primary question: When are groups are more biased than individuals? But first, we need to clarify what we could and do mean when we speak of "bias."

---

[5]One might think about this in terms of the "Balance" knob on one's stereo. When it is placed in the middle position, both left and right stereo speakers have equal volume. As one turns that knob counterclockwise, the volume on the right speaker goes down as the volume on the left speaker simultaneously goes up. Similarly, one could imagine using a rheostat to vary how much electricity went to each of the two end-of-bar magnets.

[6]See the Appendix for more detail on the particular asymmetric decision scheme utilized here.

[7]For the reader who would like to examine the SDS mathematics that precisely describes the movement of the balls-on-the-bar in our figures, the Appendix provides a general description as well as some specific, illustrative calculations represented in our figures.

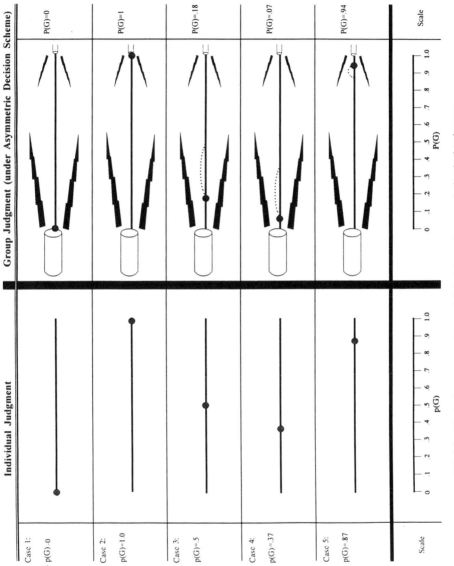

FIG. 6.3. Effect of an asymmetric social decision scheme on individual judgment.

VARIETIES OF BIAS

Just as there are different plausible social processes, there are also different ways of thinking about the concept of "biased judgment." Although bias implies departure from a normative model of "correct" judgment, that departure can take different forms, and, it turns out, which form of bias is being considered has different implications for the comparison of individual and group bias.

Hastie and Rasinski (1988) suggested several distinctive "logics" for establishing a systematic bias in judgment. In this chapter, we consider three of their logics or types of bias. The first and most straightforward type of bias is a direct comparison between judgment and a normatively defined criterion (e.g., Davis, Spitzer, Nagao, & Stasser, 1978). For example, Kahneman and Tversky (1979) asked Ss to choose between two courses of action with identical expected values, one with a certain outcome (which, in our notation, could be labeled as alternative G) and a second with an uncertain outcome (which we could call the NG alternative). Unbiased judgment should result in indifference between the two choices; that is, the normative model of expected utility theory prescribes that $p(G) = .50$. However, Kahneman and Tversky showed that this choice is biased by the way in which the choices were described or "framed"—for example, subjects generally preferred Choice NG with uncertain loss to Choice G with a certain loss (or, to use the usual terminology, subjects seem to be risk seeking when the outcomes are framed as losses; conversely, they were risk averse when the outcomes were framed as gains). Unbiased judgment in this example prescribes a specific and precise use of available information (namely, computation and comparison of objective-expected utilities); biased judgment reflects systematic departure from this prescribed and precise use of information. For this reason, we have termed this type of bias a "sin of imprecision" of judgment (cf. Kerr et al., 1994).

A key feature of such a sin of imprecision is that the no-bias criterion is defined theoretically, and the magnitude of bias is defined by the discrepancy between that criterion and a human judgment. The other two types of bias we consider utilize an empirical rather than a theoretical no-bias criterion. In one such type of bias, which we have termed a "sin of commission," the model of ideal, unbiased judgment holds that certain information is irrelevant or nondiagnostic for the required judgment. For example, the rules of evidence usually require that an unbiased juror pay no attention to a victim's race or a defendant's physical attractiveness in deciding whether or not the defendant is guilty. Bias is manifest by the use of such information. This typically involves comparison of a condition in which the potentially biasing information is provided (e.g., jurors considering a stimulus trial with a physically unattractive defendant) with a control condition in which either this information is missing (e.g., no information provided on defendant attractiveness) or qualitatively different information is provided (e.g., the defendant is physically attractive). We might call the former the High-bias condition and the latter the Low-bias condition. A sin of commission has occurred when the judgments in these two conditions differ significantly.

We term the third and final type of bias a "sin of omission." This occurs when the judge *fails* to use information held to be diagnostic by the idealized model of judgment. For example, many studies (e.g., Hamill, Wilson, & Nisbett, 1980) have shown that judges frequently fail to utilize diagnostic base-rate information. A sin of omission has occurred when conditions differing on the availability of such information *fail* to produce reliably different judgments (e.g., no difference in judgment between subjects given different levels of base-rate information).

EXPLORING THE RELATIVE BIAS OF INDIVIDUAL AND GROUP JUDGES (UNDER A "SINGLE-GROUP-PROCESS" ASSUMPTION)

With three generic social decision schemes and three different types of bias (i.e., the sins of imprecision, commission, and omission), one could imagine nine unique combinations of group process and bias type that we might explore. Considering all these (and still other) combinations is beyond the scope of the present chapter (see Kerr et al., 1994, for a more thorough analysis). Rather, here we examine just a few interesting and informative combinations. To begin with, we focus on the effects of our three generic decision schemes on sins of commission.

As noted previously, a sin of commission requires the contrast of two conditions that differ in the availability or strength of normatively proscribed information. These we have termed the High-bias and Low-bias conditions. For example, jurors are not supposed to pay any attention to a criminal defendant's physical attractiveness; nevertheless, they sometimes do so (e.g., Efran, 1974). Imagine a Low-bias condition in which jurors had no information about the defendant's attractiveness. Based on their consideration of the evidence, individual jurors would come to verdict preferences—that is, an overall conviction rate, $p_L(G)$. We can represent this Low-bias condition in our ball-on-a-bar metaphor with a metal ball labeled L (see the left half of Fig. 6.4). For a case with fairly weak evidence against a defendant, that conviction rate might be low and the L ball would be nearer the left end of the bar (e.g., see Case 1 for individuals in Fig. 6.4); if the evidence of guilt was very strong, then the L ball would lie near the right end of the bar (e.g., see Case 4); and so forth. If physical unattractiveness biases individual jurors, then jurors in a High-bias condition, in which the defendant was very physically unattractive, should convict at a higher rate [i.e., $p_H(G) > p_L(G)$]. By analogy, we would represent the High-bias condition by a second ball, labeled H, which would lie to the right of the L ball. The magnitude of the individual bias, which we call b for bias, is simply the distance between the balls: For example, in Case 1 in Fig. 6.4, $b = p_H(G) - p_L(G) = .6 - .4$

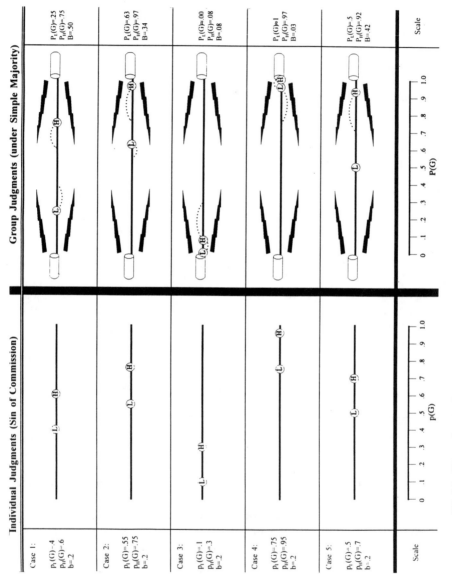

FIG. 6.4. Effect of a simple-majority social decision scheme on hypothetical sins of commission.

= .2. Now, what we would like to know is, what if juries (i.e., groups) rather than individuals had been the decision makers in our hypothetical experiment—how far apart would the balls be? But our metaphor allows us to say where the balls should be under any of our three generic social decision schemes. All we have to do is "turn on the magnets."

But before hitting any switches, we need to make an important point. For the moment, we are assuming that all groups (both Low-bias *and* High-bias groups) operate under the same social decision scheme. What this means psychologically is that although information that gives rise to a judgmental sin of commission may alter the distribution of individual preference, it does *not* alter the process whereby groups achieve consensus. So, for example, the fact that the defendant was physically unattractive might increase the probability that I judge him guilty, but having such information would not, for example, make me any more or less a persuasive advocate for conviction in jury deliberation. In terms of our metaphor, this means that the two balls lie on the same bar and when the magnets are turned on, the behavior of the two balls depends only on their location on the bar, and not on the type (High- or Low-bias) of ball. So, for example, the magnets would affect the H ball sitting at, say, $p(G) = .30$ in exactly the same way that they would affect the L ball if it happened to be sitting at that same location (e.g., compare the H ball in Case 2 vs. the L ball in Case 4). We call this the "single-group-process" assumption. As we soon see, this is an important simplifying assumption. Very different conclusions must be drawn if this assumption is violated.

Sins of Commission Under a Majority-Wins Decision Scheme

Now, let's turn on the identical-twin magnets of the majority decision scheme. In Fig. 6.4, the results are pictured for five illustrative cases. In Case 1, each ball is attracted toward the nearer magnet, causing the two balls to separate. That is, for this particular situation—namely, $p_L(G) = .4$, $p_H(G) = .6$, and b = individual bias = $.6 - .4 = .2$—under a simple-majority-rules process, groups should exhibit an even stronger bias effect [in Fig. 6.4, like all the figures, group size is assumed to be 11; here, $P_L(G) = .25$, $P_H(G) = .75$, and B = group bias = $.75 - .25 = .50 > .20$, and relative bias = $B - b = .30$]. The same result can occur when both balls begin on the same side of the midpoint. For example, consider Case 2 in Fig. 6.4. The magnitude of the individual bias is the same as in Case 1 [viz., $p_H(G) - p_L(G) = .75 - .55 = .20$]; however, the conviction rate is uniformly higher (by .15) for both conditions. For the majority-wins scheme, the *direction* of movement depends on which side of the midpoint a ball is located, but the *magnitude* of movement depends on the exact location of the ball—the closer a ball gets to either end, the stronger the force exerted on it, and the farther it should move (barring floor and ceiling effects). So, in Case 2, even though the Low-bias ball does move to the right [from $p_L(G) = .55$ to $P_L(G) = .63$], the High-bias ball, being closer to the right end to begin with, moves even farther [from $p_H(G) = .75$ to $P_H(G) = .97$] and hence, bias is again relatively greater among groups (.34) than among individuals (.20). Case 5 provides another, similar example, where $p_L(G) = .5$ and $p_H(G) = .70$. Here, the L ball, being right in the middle, does not move at all, whereas the H ball is pulled to the right, thereby accentuating the magnitude of bias among groups. The examples considered thus far illustrate one important point—the relative magnitude of bias exhibited by individuals versus groups depends on where the individuals begin. For example, by simply varying the strength of the case against a defendant, the magnitude of bias among juries should vary, even though biasing information had an identical effects on individual jurors' judgment for each of the cases ($b = .2$ in Cases 1, 2, and 5).

The cases considered thus far suggest that group operating under a majority decision scheme will exaggerate (to some degree) the magnitude of bias evident among individuals. Thus, whatever its merits as a means of determining a just or acceptable group decision, under a wide range of conditions, a majority-wins process will exaggerate whatever preferences individuals exhibit (Kerr et al., 1975), including preferences for biased use of information. However, such a conclusion would be too sweeping. Sometimes the reverse will be true—sometimes a majority-wins group process will attenuate biased judgment. When? Whenever both balls are already "close" to the same end of the bar before the magnets are turned on. Consider Case 3 in Fig. 6.4. Here, the magnitude of bias among individuals is again the same as in the previous two cases (viz., .20); the only difference is in the overall rate of conviction [in Case 3, conviction rates are fairly low in *both* conditions, viz., $p_L(G) = .1$, $p_H(G) = .3$]. When we turn on the magnets, the L ball will have a very strong pull to the left and the H ball will have a weaker pull to the left. But, because the L ball began quite close to the left end, its range of possible movement in that direction is quite limited (with a maximum of .1), whereas the H ball is less restricted. Functionally, this is very much like a floor effect. The net effect is to *reduce* the distance between the two balls—that is, to *attenuate* the bias. Of course, given the symmetry of this majority-wins process, the same result would occur at the other end of the bar (e.g., see Case 4).

One might dismiss such "floor" or "ceiling" effects as rare and easily recognized exceptions to the general rule, but this would be a mistake. This is most strikingly illustrated by the clearest empirical exception to the general rule that juries exaggerate juror bias—Kaplan and Miller (1978). Kaplan and Miller (Study 3) examined the biasing effect of the nonevidentiary behavioral style of various people involved in presenting the case to jurors. In the part of the design of most direct interest to us, Kaplan and Miller contrasted a condition in which the defense attorney acted in an obnoxious manner versus a second condition in which it was the prosecutor who acted obnoxiously. The legally relevant, material evidence presented to the mock jurors was identical in both conditions. The normative model of judgment would prescribe that the jurors ignore the legally irrelevant factor of attorney obnoxiousness when making the central judgment of guilt or innocence. However, Kaplan and Miller confirmed a judgmental sin of commission by jurors—prior to jury deliberation, the defendant was judged to be guiltier when his attorney acted obnoxiously than when it was the prosecutor who acted obnoxiously. Kaplan and Miller also manipulated the overall strength of evidence against the defendant and, as one would expect, jurors were more likely to convict when the evidence against the defendant was stronger. Jurors then deliberated the case for 10 minutes in 12-person juries and then provided postdeliberation guilt judgments (which are typically very highly correlated with jury verdict; e.g., Kerr, 1981). The differences between individual (i.e., predeliberation) and group (i.e., postdeliberation) judgments are presented in Fig. 6.5. As the figure shows, following deliberation there was a significant polarization effect involving a shift toward greater guiltiness in the high guilt-appearance conditions, and toward innocence in the low guilt-appearance conditions. However, there were no significant postdeliberation attorney obnoxiousness biases in postdeliberation judgments; that is, juries were less biased than jurors.

Reasoning from information integration theory (e.g., Anderson, 1974), Kaplan has argued (1982; Kaplan & Miller, 1978; Kaplan & Schersching, 1980) that individual jurors' judgments are reached through the integration of many sources of information—personal predispositions (e.g., authoritarianism, general lack of

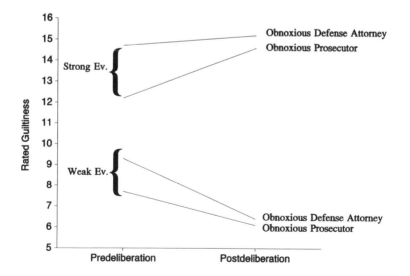

FIG. 6.5. Comparison of individual and group bias in Kaplan and Miller (1978, Exp. 3). Adapted from Figure 3 of Kaplan and Miller (1978). Reproduced with permission.

sympathy for criminals, etc.), biasing extralegal factors (e.g., liking for defendant or victim, attitudes toward parties identified with them [like their counsel]), and, most important, evidentiary factors. Furthermore, he argued that jurors recognize, either without reminder or through judicial instructions, that the biased, extralegal material should not actually be considered. This recognition, he implied, results in the content of jury deliberation being dominated by valid, acceptable information (viz., evidentiary material). Because most of the new information to which a juror is exposed during deliberation would not be biasing, Kaplan suggested that deliberating jurors should attach greater weight to the evidence and less weight to personal biases during than before deliberation.

This line of argument suggests qualitative differences in the process of individual and group judgment. However, our present analysis predicts exactly the pattern of results observed by Kaplan and Miller (1978). We know from much research that juries tend to follow one or another variation on a majority-rules decision scheme (Davis, 1973; Kalven & Zeisel, 1966; Stasser, Kerr, & Bray, 1982; Zeisel & Diamond, 1978). And our metaphor shows (see Fig. 6.4, Cases 3 & 4) that if all subjects (in both the High- and Low-bias conditions) are near a response pole (a result produced in Kaplan & Miller by the strength-of-evidence manipulation), that mean group judgment should be polarized and the error of commission bias in individuals should be attenuated in groups. All our analysis requires to account for this pattern of results is that juries follow a majority-wins decision scheme (a well-established result). Kaplan and Miller's theoretical assumption that jury deliberation successfully debiases juror thinking is not necessary to account for their data.

Let's summarize what we have shown so far about the effects of a simple-majority-wins decision process on the relative degree of bias in individuals versus groups. It depends on (a) (quantitatively) the size of the group, (b) the magnitude of the individual bias, and (c) the extremity of individual judgment. This last point deserves emphasis—it suggests, for example, that Kaplan and Miller (1978) would have reached *precisely the opposite conclusion* about the biasing effect of jury deliberation had they examined the effect of the biasing information (viz., counsel obnoxiousness) with a stimulus trial producing less extreme guilt judgments among individual jurors.

Sins of Commission Under an Equiprobability Decision Scheme

We saw earlier that a decision scheme with little strength in numbers (e.g., equiprobability) tended qualitatively to have exactly the opposite effect on group judgment as one with considerable strength in numbers (e.g., majority wins) (i.e., the contrast of the "magnet-in-the-middle" vs. the "magnets-at-the-ends"). Thus, it should not surprise us that all the patterns revealed by the preceding discussion of a majority-wins process tend to be reversed under an equiprobability decision scheme (see Fig. 6.6). That is, such a decision-making process will attenuate the

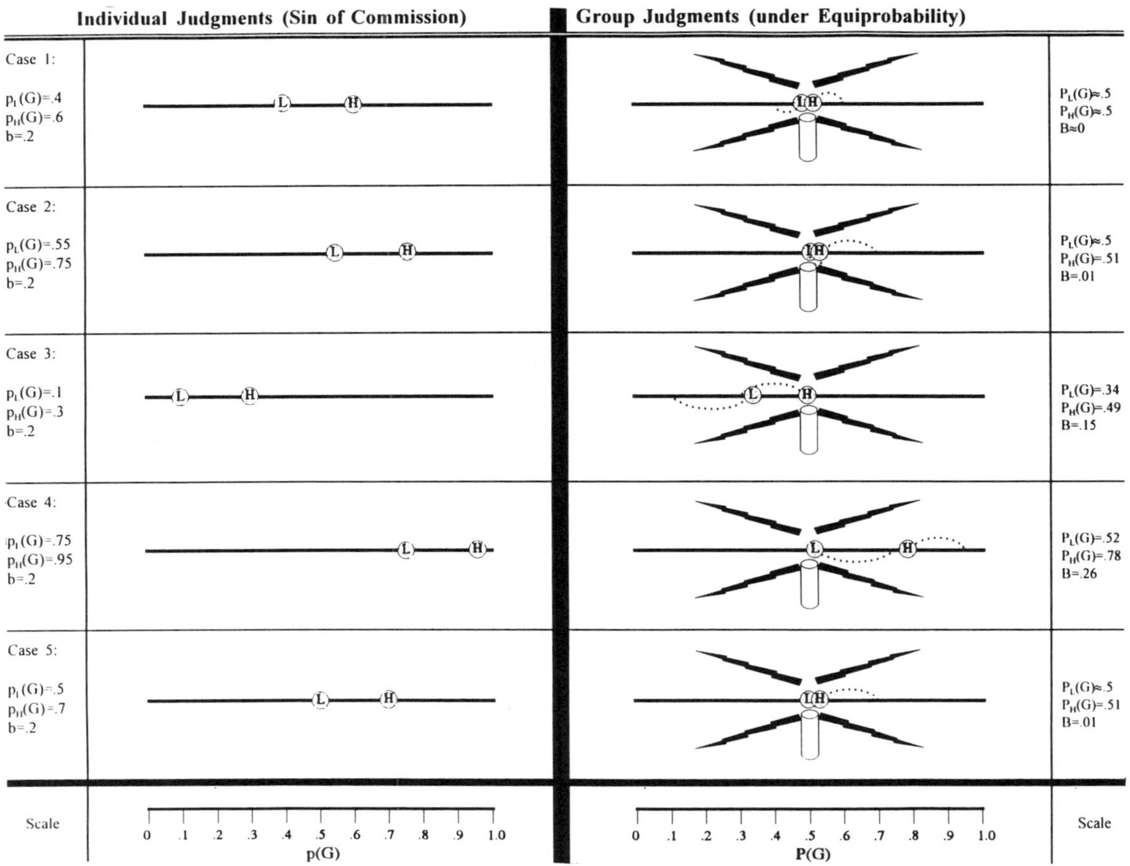

FIG. 6.6. Effect of an equiprobability social decision scheme on hypothetical sins of commission.

123

magnitude of a sin of commission bias observed among individuals *unless* individual judgments in the two conditions being contrasted are both fairly extreme (in which case bias tends to be greater among group than among individual judges; see Case 4).

It is not the widespread applicability of the equiprobability process that makes these results interesting. Indeed, as noted previously, this generic type of group decision-making process has only been empirically confirmed for a few, rather unusual judgment tasks. What these analyses do demonstrate, though, is that even if many other important features of the judgment setting are held constant (such as judgment task, magnitude and location of individual bias, group size), one can reach exactly the opposite conclusions about the relative degree of bias of groups and individuals under different group decision-making processes. So, for example, if group members tenaciously defend their initial preferences and finally wear down opposing minority views (one type of social process consistent with "majority wins"), a juridic sin of commission would generally be stronger in groups than individuals (Fig. 6.4). But if group members were for any good reason uncommonly eager to accommodate opposing viewpoints (Kerr, 1992b), even to the point of disregarding entirely which viewpoints had many and which had few advocates (consistent with the equiprobability scheme), then groups should generally show a weaker bias than individuals (Fig. 6.6). The clear point is that no conclusion about the relative bias of individuals and groups can be reached without careful specification of the operative group decision-making process. This point is underscored by the following consideration of asymmetric decision processes.

Sins of Commission Under an Asymmetric Social Decision Scheme

Suppose one alternative was, to some degree, "demonstrably correct" (in Laughlin's terms), giving factions advocating that alternative relatively greater likelihood of prevailing than comparably sized factions advocating the other alternative. In terms of our metaphor, one of the end magnets is stronger than the other. The consequences of such an asymmetry are depicted in Fig. 6.7. Inspection of these illustrations shows that such an asymmetry tends to expand the region within which the functional floor effect occurs (and, in the present, strongly asymmetric example, shrink the region within which anything else occurs). Thus, when one alternative is demonstrably correct (or very nearly so), judgmental sins of commission will usually be less pronounced among groups than among individuals. The only exceptions occur when the H and L balls bracket the point where the magnetic forces cancel one another out (e.g., see Case 4) or where they very nearly do so (e.g., Case 5). The stronger the asymmetry, the smaller this area will be. One point of the previous section is markedly underscored—the relative degree of individual versus group bias can be exqui-

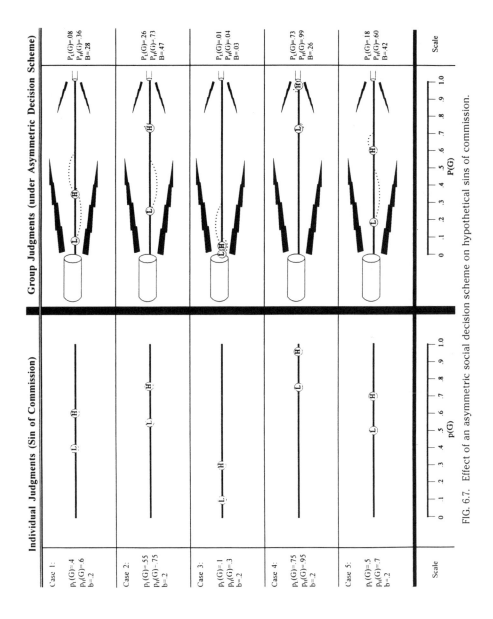

FIG. 6.7. Effect of an asymmetric social decision scheme on hypothetical sins of commission.

sitely sensitive to the precise location of individual preference prior to group discussion.

Sins of Imprecision and Omission Under the Assumption of a Single Group Process

We do not attempt here a thorough, illustrative case-by-case analysis of judgmental sins of imprecision under the single-group-process assumption (again, see Kerr et al., 1994, for such an analysis). We do, though, note a couple of important points. First, the effect on relative bias of moving from individual to group decision makers for this type of judgmental bias depends not only on the "location on the bar" (i.e., the judgments) of individuals, but also on where the theoretically defined, no-bias criterion is located. So, for example, consider Case 4 [$p(G) = .37$] in Fig. 6.1. Under a simple-majority decision scheme, groups would shift to the left: to $P(G) = .18$. Now, if "Ideal" judgment, $p_I(G) = P_I(G)$, had been the NG alternative—that is, $p_I(G) = P_I(G) = 0$—the polarizing effect of the simple-majority process would have attenuated bias: from $b = |\ p(G) - p_I(G)\ | = .37$ to $B = |\ P(G) - P_I(G)\ | = .18$. On the other hand, had the "ideal" judgment been the G alternative [i.e., $p_I(G) = P_I(G) = 1.0$], the same majority-wins social process would have had exactly the opposite effect, exaggerating the degree of bias [from $b = |\ p(G) - p_I(G)\ | = |\ .37 - 1.0\ | = .63$ to $B = |\ P(G) - P_I(G)\ | = |\ .18 - 1.0\ | = .82$]. Other patterns (sometimes even more complex) can arise when the ideal point is not at the extreme [e.g., if G is a certain gain and NG is an equivalent but uncertain gain in a framing experiment, subjects *should* be indifferent between the choices and hence $p_I(G) = P_I(G) = .5$]. The key point is that for this particular type of judgmental bias, one can get diametrically opposite conclusions depending on what the "ideal" is.

Second, it is sometimes possible to examine a particular judgmental bias either as a sin of imprecision or as a sin of commission. For example, as we just discussed, one could show the biasing effect of decision framing by simply demonstrating that more Ss preferred a certain gain to an uncertain gain [i.e., that p(certain gain) > .50]; this conceptualizes and operationalizes framing effects as sins of imprecision. Alternatively, one could hypothesize no difference in preference for the "certain" alternative between subjects in a gain frame condition from those in a loss frame condition (cf. McGuire, Kiesler, & Siegel, 1987); that is, that $p_{\text{loss frame}}$(certain alternative) = $p_{\text{gain frame}}$(certain alternative). The latter approach operationalizes the framing effect as a sin of commission (i.e., b > 0 implies that frame, which should not matter, in fact does matter). Under a simple-majority rule, the former sin of imprecision will generally be *stronger* in a group than among individuals [see Fig. 6.1 to see why this would be true unless $p(G) = 0.0$ or 1.0]. However, the latter sin of commission could sometimes be stronger and sometimes be weaker (depending on whether the "floor" and "ceiling" effects came into play; see Fig. 6.4). Thus, under certain conditions, one could reach exactly the opposite conclusion about the relative susceptibility of individuals and groups to framing biases depending on how one chose to operationalize the framing bias in the first place (i.e., as a sin of imprecision vs. as a sin of commission).

Having shown just how many factors affect relative bias for sins of imprecision and commission, it is gratifying to be able to say that the third type of judgmental sin, the sin of omission, cannot occur under the single-group-process assumption. Recall that sins of omission meant that judges failed to use valid information. That is, subjects with the information (e.g., in a H-bias condition) do *not* make different judgments from subjects without this information or with a different amount or kind of such information (e.g., in a L-bias condition), whereas the normative model of unbiased judgment prescribes that they should differ. But if bias requires that $p_H(G) = p_L(G)$, then, to use our metaphor, the two balls start at the same place. Under the single-group-process assumption they would necessarily end up at the same place, and hence, precisely the same bias (i.e., null effect) would be manifest among groups that had been manifest among individuals.

EXPLORING THE RELATIVE BIAS OF INDIVIDUAL AND GROUP JUDGES (UNDER A "DUAL-GROUP-PROCESS" ASSUMPTION)

There is evidence, however, of differences between individuals and groups in their susceptibility to sins of omission. For example, Wright, Luus, and Christie (1990) examined the tendency of attributors to underutilize consensus information. Subjects received a description of one of the classic Latané and Darley (1970) bystander intervention experiments, and were told that Greg, 1 of 15 participants in the experiment, was either 1 of 6 who did not help (high consensus), or was the only one who did not help (low consensus). Subjects were then asked to rate the extent to which Greg's personality and/or the particular situation were responsible for his behavior. These judgments were made either by three- or four-person groups or by individuals. Wright et al. found no effect of the consensus information on attributions among individuals (a sin of omission), but this information did significantly affect groups' consensual attribution judgments—groups used the prescribed consensus information that the individuals ignored.

As noted previously, this pattern cannot occur under the single-group-process assumption. Because these and similar results undoubtedly do occur (see Kerr et al., 1994), the only possibility is that the single-group-process assumption is sometimes violated. For the Wright et al. (1990) study, for example, different group decision-making processes had to apply to the two consensus information conditions. The simplest way to represent this with our balls-on-a-bar metaphor is to assume that a *different* set of magnetic forces apply to the H- and L-bias

balls. In Fig. 6.8, we assume that the G alternative represents making a dispositional attribution ("Greg acted as he did because of his personality") and the
NG alternative represents a wholly situational attribution ("Greg acted as he did
because of the particular situation he found himself in"). On the left panel of
Fig. 6.8 we assume that among individuals a relatively more dispositional attribution is equally popular with subjects in both consensus-information conditions [for purposes of illustration, we assume that $p_H(G) = p_L(G) = .40$]. We place
the L ball on one bar and the H ball on a second bar. Now, suppose that
consensus information available in the H-bias condition is highly potent ("demonstrably correct" in Laughlin's terminology) although relatively few subjects
individually recognize its diagnostic value for making attributions. Group discussion gives the opportunity for those who do recognize its relevance to share
it with others. This suggests that some advocates of the G (i.e., situational
attribution) alternative will be particularly able to sway advocates of the NG
(dispositional attribution) faction. This is represented in Fig. 6.8 by assuming
that there is a strong asymmetry in the H condition favoring the G alternative.
In the L-bias (i.e., low-consensus) condition, no advocates of alternative G would
have this potent information. Rather, the available low-consensus information
might well make the NG alternative "demonstrably correct" ("if he's the only
one who acted this way, it must be something unique about his personality that
caused his behavior"). This would be equivalent to an asymmetric set of forces
favoring the NG alternative. As the figure shows, the net effect of these assumptions would be to result in individuals showing a bias, but groups not doing so
(i.e., groups using the prescribed consensus information).

Under such a dual-group-process assumption, it is particularly difficult to
predict relative bias. Not only must all the preceding factors be considered (e.g.,
group size, absolute and relative positions of the H and L groups, etc.), but the
precise nature of the two group processes must also be specified. Entirely
different results can follow from different pairs of group processes, and the
possible pairing of such different decision schemes are theoretically limitless (e.g.,
the strength and favored direction of two asymmetric decision schemes could
vary in an infinite number of ways). Our present purpose is not to specify when
and how such dual processes do, in fact, occur (although this is a very important
theoretical question). Rather, here we are simply attempting (a) to demonstrate
that availability of certain information can indeed alter the nature of the group
decision-making process, (b) to illustrate how such dual processes can affect the
relative susceptibility of individuals and groups to such biases, and (c) to suggest
that an adequate analysis of the bases of relative bias effects needs to include
empirical evidence on whether a single-group-process assumption is justified.

This latter point deserves some attention. It is possible to provide such
empirical evidence indirectly. For example, Wright et al. (1990) showed that
prescribed use of consensus information could be produced not only by group
discussion but also by reading a transcript of another group's discussion or a

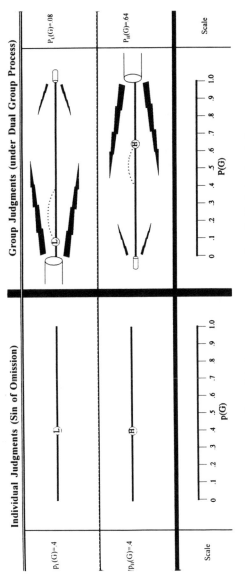

FIG. 6.8. Effect of dual group processes on a hypothetical sin of omission.

set of arguments generated by an individual. Such findings suggest that simply hearing arguments explaining the utility of consensus information reveals the "correctness" of certain alternatives.

But it is also possible to provide such evidence *directly* by estimating the operative social decision scheme separately in H-bias and L-bias groups. This has been done in several studies (e.g., see chapter 5 of this volume; also see Kerr et al.'s, 1994, review). A good illustration is provided by Kramer, Kerr, and Carroll's (1990) study of the biasing effects of pretrial publicity. Kramer et al. examined the biasing effects of prejudicial pretrial publicity; because such information should not be considered by the jury, its use represents a sin of commission. In juries reaching verdicts, there is usually a legally prescribed, prodefendant leniency preference (cf. Davis, Stasser, Spitzer, & Holt, 1976; Mac-Coun & Kerr, 1988)—jurors are supposed to give a criminal defendant the benefit of any doubts. This manifests itself as a prescribed asymmetry favoring acquittal (in addition to the basic majority-wins process that generally characterizes jury decision making). However, Kramer et al. found that this legally prescribed, prodefendant tilt was eliminated if juries had first been exposed to prejudicial pretrial publicity. For example, in L-bias juries (i.e., never exposed to prejudicial emotion-laden pretrial publicity), all six-person juries that began deliberation with an even 3G-3NG split and that reached a verdict ended up acquitting the defendant. However, an unusual trend in the opposite direction occurred in the H-bias juries (exposed to such publicity)—60% were convictions. Negative publicity about a defendant led juries to no longer give him the benefit of the doubt—a real change in the jury decision-making process. Similarly, MacCoun (1990) also found that juries were more biased than individual jurors in their response to a defendant attractiveness manipulation. Like Kramer et al. (1990), he found suggestive evidence that juries were less likely to give an unattractive defendant the benefit of the doubt; that is, the social decision scheme was not asymmetric in the unattractive defendant condition.

SUMMARY AND CONCLUSIONS

The history of research on group processes has been repeatedly characterized by investigators posing oversimple questions. Examples include such questions as "Do individuals perform better or worse in the presence of others?" or "Which is more productive, groups or individuals?" or "Which is more prone to make risky decisions, groups or individuals?" In every case, it was eventually shown that there were no simple and direct answers to such questions—rather, the answer depended strongly on a host of factors, particularly the precise nature of the task. Likewise, in the present chapter we have tried to show that there is no simple answer to the oversimple question: Which is more biased, individuals or groups? On the other hand, under reasonable assumptions about the group decision-making process, we can provide useful partial answers. We have shown that the direction and size of relative bias depends on a number of factors, including group size, how the bias is defined (i.e., the type of bias), the magnitude of individual bias, and the "location" of the biased individual judgment (e.g., the extremity of judgment; the proximity of individual judgment to an ideal judgment or to the more popular pole or to the midpoint of the judgmental dimension). Most important, we have shown how relative bias depends crucially on the nature of the group decision-making process itself, which, in turn, appears to depend strongly on certain features of the judgment/decision task (e.g., whether there is a demonstrably correct alternative).

Furthermore, we have described a physical metaphor that captures many essential features of several generic social decision-making processes. We have used this metaphor to present several special cases that illustrate the qualitative effects of such group processes. The interested reader can use the same metaphor to explore other imaginable cases of personal interest.

The SDS model offers a powerful conceptual framework with which to identify, classify, and analyze bases for individual–group differences in utilization of normatively significant information (or, for that matter, any information). With it, we can begin to distinguish between situations where a single group decision-making process affects relative bias (effects explicated earlier under a single-group-process assumption) and situations where one must concede that certain information alters that process (requiring a dual-group-process assumption). The latter situations seem to us to represent potentially rich sources of knowledge about both group and individual judgmental and decision-making processes.

Moreover, the SDS model offers a methodology for exploring such issues, either empirically (e.g., via direct estimation of the social decision scheme under various conditions) or via simulation (e.g., with computer simulation [Davis & Kerr, 1986] or using simplifying metaphors, as was done in this chapter). Utilizing the conceptual and methodological tools introduced in this chapter, it is possible not only to show that several factors matter when comparing the relative bias of individual versus group decision makers, but also to begin to understand where they matter, how much they matter, and why they matter.

ACKNOWLEDGMENTS

This chapter represents an overview of an article that comprehensively reviews the empirical literature and provides a detailed theoretical analysis of the contrast of judgmental bias in individuals and groups (Kerr, MacCoun, & Kramer, 1994).

REFERENCES

Anderson, N. H. (1974). Cognitive algebra: Integration theory applied to social attribution. In L. Berkowitz (Ed.), *Advances in experimental social psychology* (Vol. 7, pp. 1–101). New York: Academic Press.

132

Davis, J. H. (1973). Group decision and social interaction: A theory of social decision schemes. *Psychological Review, 80*, 97–125.

Davis, J. H. (1980). Group decision and procedural justice. In M. Fishbein (Ed.), *Progress in social psychology* (pp. 157–229). Hillsdale, NJ: Lawrence Erlbaum Associates.

Davis, J. H. (1982). Social interaction as a combinatorial process in group decision. In H. Brandstätter, J. H. Davis, & G. Stocker-Kreichgauer (Eds.), *Group decision making* (pp. 27–58). Orlando/London: Academic Press.

Davis, J. H. (1991, June). *Continuous social decision schemes.* Paper presented at the Nags Head International Conference on Groups, Networks, and Organizations, Highland Beach, FL.

Davis, J. H., Hornik, H., & Hornseth, J. (1970). Group decision schemes and strategy preferences in a sequential response task. *Journal of Personality and Social Psychology, 15*, 397–408.

Davis, J. H., & Kerr, N. L. (1986). Thought experiments and the problem of sparse data in small-group performance research. In P. Goodman (Ed.), *Designing effective work groups* (pp. 305–349). New York: Jossey-Bass.

Davis, J. H., Kerr, N. L., Atkin, R., Holt, R., & Meek, D. (1975). The decision processes of 6- and 12-person mock juries assigned unanimous and ⅔ majority rules. *Journal of Personality and Social Psychology, 32*, 1–14.

Davis, J. H., Kerr, N. L., Sussmann, M., & Rissman, A. K. (1974). Social decision schemes under risk. *Journal of Personality and Social Psychology, 30*, 248–271.

Davis, J. H., Spitzer, C. E., Nagao, D. H., & Stasser, G. (1978). Bias in social decisions by individuals and groups. In H. Brandstätter, J. H. Davis, & H. Schuler (Eds.), *Dynamics of group decisions* (pp. 33–52). Beverly Hills, CA: Sage.

Davis, J. H., Stasser, G., Spitzer, C. E., & Holt, R. W. (1976). Changes in group members' decision preferences during discussion: An illustration with mock juries. *Journal of Personality and Social Psychology, 34*, 1117–1187.

Dawes, R. M. (1988). *Rational choice in an uncertain world.* San Diego: Harcourt Brace.

Efran, M. G. (1974). The effect of physical appearance on the judgment of guilt, interpersonal attraction, and severity of recommended punishment on a simulated jury task. *Journal of Research in Personality, 8*, 45–54.

Festinger, L. (1954). A theory of social comparison processes. *Human Relations, 1*, 117–140.

Hamill, R., Wilson, T. D., & Nisbett, R. E. (1980). Insensitivity to sample bias: Generalizing from atypical cases. *Journal of Personality and Social Psychology, 39*, 578–589.

Hastie, R. (1986). Experimental evidence on group accuracy. In B. Grofman & G. Owen (Eds.), *Decision research* (Vol. 2, pp. 129–157). Greenwich, CT: JAI.

Hastie, R., & Rasinski, K. A. (1988). The concept of accuracy in social judgment. In D. Bar-Tal & A. W. Kruglanski (Eds.), *The social psychology of knowledge* (pp. ??–??). Cambridge, England: Cambridge University Press.

Hill, G. W. (1982). Group versus individual performance: Are N+1 heads better than one? *Psychological Bulletin, 91*, 517–539.

Hinsz, V. B., Tindale, R. S., & Vollrath, D. A. (1991, June). *The emerging conception of groups as information processors.* Paper presented at the Nags Head Conference on Groups, Networks, and Organizations, Boca Raton, FL.

Johnson, C., & Davis, J. H. (1972). An equiprobability model of risk taking. *Organizational Behavior and Human Performance, 8*, 159–175.

Kahneman, D., & Tversky, A. (1979). Prospect theory: An analysis of decision under risk. *Econometrica, 47*, 263–291.

Kalven, H., & Zeisel, H. (1966). *The American jury.* Boston: Little, Brown.

Kaplan, M. F. (1982). Cognitive processes in the individual juror. In N. Kerr & R. Bray (Eds.), *The psychology of the courtroom* (pp. 197–220). New York: Academic Press.

Kaplan, M. F., & Miller, L. E. (1978). Reducing the effects of juror bias. *Journal of Personality and Social Psychology, 36*, 1443–1445.

Kaplan, M. F., & Schersching, C. (1980). Reducing juror bias: An experimental approach. In P. Lipsitt & B. Sales (Eds.), *New directions in psycholegal research* (pp. ??–??). New York: Van Nostrand-Reinhold.

Kerr, N. L. (1981). Social transition schemes: Charting the group's road to agreement. *Journal of Personality and Social Psychology, 41*, 684–702.

Kerr, N. L. (1983, August). Issue importance, group polarization, and social decision schemes. In D. Nagao & D. Vollrath, Chairs, *Social decision schemes and opinion change.* Symposium conducted at the 1983 American Psychological Association Convention, Los Angeles.

Kerr, N. L. (1992a). Group decision making at a multialternative task: Extremity, interfaction distance, pluralities, and issue importance. *Organizational Behavior and Human Decision Processes, 52*, 64–95.

Kerr, N. L. (1992b). Issue importance and group decision making. In S. Worchel, W. Wood, & J. Simpson (Eds.), *Group process and productivity* (pp. 68–88). Newbury Park, CA: Sage.

Kerr, N. L., Atkin, R., Stasser, G., Meek, D., Holt, R., & Davis, J. H. (1976). Guilt beyond a reasonable doubt: Effects of concept definition and assigned decision rule on the judgments of mock jurors. *Journal of Personality and Social Psychology, 34*, 282–294.

Kerr, N. L., Davis, J. H., Meek, D., & Rissman, A. (1975). The group position as a function of member attitudes—Polarization effects from the perspective of social decision scheme theory. *Journal of Personality and Social Psychology, 31*, 574–593.

Kerr, N. L., MacCoun, R. J., & Kramer, G. P. (1994). *Bias in judgment: Comparing individuals and groups.* Unpublished manuscript, Michigan State University, East Lansing.

Kirchler, E., & Davis, J. H. (1986). The influence of member status differences and task type on group consensus and member position change. *Journal of Personality and Social Psychology, 51*, 83–91.

Kramer, G. P., Kerr, N. L., & Carroll, J. S. (1990). Pretrial publicity, judicial remedies, and jury bias. *Law and Human Behavior, 14*, 409–438.

Latané, B., & Darley, J. M. (1970). *The unresponsive bystander: Why doesn't he help?* New York: Appleton-Crofts.

Laughlin, P. R. (1980). Social combination processes of cooperative problem-solving groups on verbal intellective tasks. In M. L. Fishbein (Ed.), *Progress in social psychology* (Vol. 1, pp. 127–155). Hillsdale, NJ: Lawrence Erlbaum Associates.

Laughlin, P. R., & Early, P. C. (1982). Social combination models, persuasive arguments theory, social comparison theory, and choice shift. *Journal of Personality and Social Psychology, 42*, 273–280.

Laughlin, P. R., & Ellis, A. L. (1986). Demonstrability and social combination processes on mathematical intellective tasks. *Journal of Experimental Social Psychology, 22*, 177–189.

Laughlin, P. R., Kerr, N. L., Davis, J. H., Halff, H. M., & Marciniak, K. A. (1975). Group size, member ability, and social decision schemes on an intellective task. *Journal of Personality and Social Psychology, 31*, 522–535.

Laughlin, P. R., Kerr, N. L., Munch, M., & Haggarty, C. (1976). Social decision schemes of the same four-person groups on two different intellective tasks. *Journal of Personality and Social Psychology, 33*, 80–88.

MacCoun, R. J. (1990). The emergence of extralegal bias during jury deliberation. *Criminal Justice and Behavior, 17*, 303–314.

MacCoun, R. J., & Kerr, N. L. (1988). Asymmetric influence in mock jury deliberation: Jurors' bias for leniency. *Journal of Personality and Social Psychology, 54*, 21–33.

McGuire, T. W., Kiesler, S., & Siegel, J. (1987). Group and computer-mediated discussion effects in risk decision making. *Journal of Personality and Social Psychology, 52*, 917–930.

Miller, C. E. (1989). The social psychological effects of group decision rules. In P. Paulus (Ed.), *Psychology of group influence* (2nd ed., pp. 327–356). Hillsdale, NJ: Lawrence Erlbaum Associates.

Myers, D., & Lamm, H. (1976). The group polarization phenomenon. *Psychological Bulletin, 83,* 602–627.

Stasser, G., Kerr, N. L., & Bray, R. (1982). The social psychology of jury deliberation: Structure, process, and product. In N. Kerr & R. Bray (Eds.), *The psychology of the courtroom* (pp. 221–256). New York: Academic Press.

Stasser, G., Kerr, N. L., & Davis, J. H. (1989). Influence processes and consensus models in decision-making groups. In P. Paulus (Ed.), *Psychology of group influence* (2nd ed., pp. 279–326). Hillsdale, NJ: Lawrence Erlbaum Associates.

Thaler, R. (1985). Mental accounting and consumer choice. *Marketing Science, 4,* 199–214.

Wright, E. F., Luus, C. E., & Christie, S. D. (1990). Does group discussion facilitate the use of consensus information in making causal attributions? *Journal of Personality and Social Psychology, 59,* 261–269.

Zeisel, H., & Diamond, S. S. (1978). The effect of peremptory challenges on jury verdicts: An experiment in federal district court. *Stanford Law Review, 30,* 491–531.

APPENDIX

In the text, we use the "magnets and ball-on-a-bar" metaphor to summarize the effect of three generic social decision schemes. Some readers may desire to supplement the understanding of the SDS model afforded by this metaphor with a more explicit presentation of the formal model itself. In this Appendix, we provide a brief introduction to that formal model (see Davis, 1973, or Stasser et al., 1989, for more detailed treatments), present the specific social decision schemes used in calculating the predicted $P(G)$ values in Figs. 6.1–6.4 and 6.6–6.8, and also provide an illustration of the calculations underlying those predictions.

The basic unit of analysis of the SDS model is the distribution of individual predeliberation preferences. Two parameters are fixed in the simplest version of the model: (a) the group size $= r$, and (b) the number of response alternatives $= n$. Given these parameters, there are $m = (n + r - 1)!/(r!(n - 1)!)$ such possible splits or "distinguishable distributions," where response alternatives are distinguishable but individual group members are not. For example, in the situation usually considered in the text where an 11-person group must choose between two alternatives (e.g., guilty, not guilty), there are $(2 + 11 - 1)!/11!(1!) = 12$ such possible splits of predeliberation opinion; these are listed in the leftmost panel of Table 6.1.

To make its predictions, the model then requires only two additional pieces of information: (a) the overall distribution of *individual* preferences and (b) a social decision scheme. The latter is a rule that specifies $d_{ij} =$ the probability that the group will adopt the *j*th decision alternative when it begins discussion with the *i*th possible initial split of member opinion. It is convenient, both for presentational and computational purposes, to arrange the d_{ij} in matrix form, creating an mxn stochastic matrix D. This "social decision scheme matrix" specifies the likelihood that each available alternative is chosen for every possible initial distribution of member preference. The column headings at the top

TABLE 6.1
Illustrative Social Decision Scheme Matrices

Possible Splits			Generic Social Decision Schemes					
			Majority		Equiprobability		Asymmetric	
G	NG	Π	G	NG	G	NG	G	NG
11	0	Π_1	1.0	0.0	1.0	0.0	1.0	0.0
10	1	Π_2	1.0	0.0	.50	.50	.99	.01
9	2	Π_3	1.0	0.0	.50	.50	.98	.02
8	3	Π_4	1.0	0.0	.50	.50	.96	.04
7	4	Π_5	1.0	0.0	.50	.50	.19	.80
6	5	Π_6	1.0	0.0	.50	.50	.10	.90
5	6	Π_7	0.0	1.0	.50	.50	.07	.93
4	7	Π_8	0.0	1.0	.50	.50	.05	.95
3	8	Π_9	0.0	1,0	.50	.50	.03	.97
2	9	Π_{10}	0.0	1.0	.50	.50	.02	.98
1	10	Π_{11}	0.0	1.0	.50	.50	.01	.99
0	11	Π_{12}	0.0	1.0	0.0	1.0	0.0	1.0

of the table are the generic majority-wins, equiprobability, and strongly asymmetric decision schemes that are used to compute P(G) values throughout the text of this chapter.

Making those computations is quite straightforward. First, if we know the distribution of individual preference (p(G),p(NG)) and we can assume that groups are randomly composed of such individuals, then we can estimate π_i = the probability that a group would begin deliberation with the ith possible initial split using the binomial expansion. For example, if the fourth possible initial split is (8G,3NG), then $\pi_4 = (11!)/(8!)(3!) p(G)^8 (1 - p(G))^3$. The vector of such π values, π, summarizes how groups are likely to begin deliberation. Second, if π is expressed as a row vector, then the distribution of group decisions, P = (P(G),P(NG), predicted under any particular social decision scheme, D, is obtained by postmultiplying π by D, that is, $P = \pi \times D$.

To illustrate, suppose p(G) = .37, which is just Case 4 in Figs. 6.1–6.3. In this case, using the binomial distribution would produce a π vector of $(\pi_1, \pi_2, \ldots, \pi_{12})$ = (.000018,.0003,.0028,.0145,.0494,.1176,.2003,.2436,.2074,.1177,.0401,.0062). Then, postmultiplying this vector by the generic majority social decision scheme results in P(G) = 1.0 × .000018 + 1.0 × .0003 + ... + 0.0 × .0062 = .185, which is just the proportion of groups predicted to favor the G alternative in Fig. 6.1 (Case 4). Similarly, using the equiprobabilty D results in P(G) = (1 × .000018 + .5 × .0003 + .5 × .0028 + ... + .5 × .0401 + 0 × .0062 = .497, which (within rounding error) is the proportion of groups predicted to favor the G alternative in Fig. 6.2 (Case 4). And to complete this illustration, under the asymmetric D, P(G) = 1 × .000018 + .99 x .0003 + .98 x .0028 . . . + 0 x .0062) = .072, which the reader will find is the predicted value given in Fig. 6.3 (Case 4). Using similar calculations, all of the predicted distributions of group decisions under the three generic decision schemes in the text were computed.

PROCEDURAL INFLUENCE IN CONSENSUS FORMATION: EVALUATING GROUP DECISION MAKING FROM A SOCIAL CHOICE PERSPECTIVE

Tatsuya Kameda
Hokkaido University

Today's proliferation of committee duties, board meetings, and so on, and the inefficiencies occasionally experienced in those meetings pose a rather basic question to one of the "truisms" in our society: Why do we use groups when deciding important issues? What is wrong with entrusting those decisions to a *benevolent* leader who is very competent? There seem to be at least two causes or assumptions behind our inclination to decision making by groups. The first is a belief in the ultimate superiority of group problem-solving ability to individual ability: Although groups may sometimes be inefficient, they are regarded to be *on average* or *in the long run* superior to, or at least more stable than individuals acting alone on a decision task (see the other chapters in this volume for social-psychological assessments of the validity of this assumption). The second cause for the use of groups is concerned with social values that seem to be widely accepted in modern society. People tend to reject the notion of decisions being imposed by a single authority, because they sense some kind of "dictatorship" in such a system. Jury decision making provides a good example of this point. Although the "accuracy" of jury verdicts is sometimes in serious doubt (e.g., civil cases containing highly technological material), people still seem to reject the notion that a professional and competent authority should solely decide the case (cf. Hastie, Penrod, & Pennington, 1983; Kalven & Zeisel, 1966). Related to this point is public acceptance of a decision. The literature on participative decision making in organizational contexts has repeatedly shown that employees' participation in a decision process increases the acceptability of the ensuing decision and eases its subsequent implementation (Kotter &

Schlesinger, 1981; Locke & Schweiger, 1979). Along with the findings from the research on procedural justice (cf. Lind & Tyler, 1988; Thibaut & Walker, 1975), these notions indicate that people generally value a participative or collective form of decision making; a decision process that is monopolized by a single authority tends to be suspected or even criticized as "undemocratic," even though the ensuing decision may be objectively superb and fair.

This chapter focuses on the latter cause (i.e., rejection of a potential dictatorship) for group decision making. Behind this cause, there seems to be an implicit assumption that a consensus achieved by an *interactive* group will represent members' preferences reasonably well. Although this assumption may seem self-evident on the surface, we believe such appearances are sometimes deceptive. In the following, we examine several studies indicating that group decisions can in principle be biased to a certain individual's or a faction's advantage through a tactical manipulation of consensus procedures.

CONSENSUS PROCEDURES

We can regard collective decision making as a *mapping* between microlevel individual preferences and a macrolevel group decision; a set of individual preferences are transformed into a group choice by a certain social procedure. Thus, the focal issue of how well the collective choice represents individual opinions can essentially be captured as a problem concerning "goodness" of the transformation function or the aggregation procedure in the mapping process.

Public Choice Contexts

In the context of public choice (e.g., election), such a transformation function is usually defined explicitly. Election rules (e.g., plurality principle, majority rule), voting procedures (e.g., approval voting, one-vote-per-person-rule), and so on are formally specified. Social choice theorists have evaluated the functioning of these aggregation procedures, pointing out that even intuitively appealing rules can in principle yield a collective decision that is sometimes counterintuitive or even unacceptable in terms of democratic values (e.g., Black, 1958; Farquharson, 1969; Fishburn, 1973). A simple but appealing example of such "misbehavior" of decision procedures can be found with a familiar majority rule. Suppose that an assembly is composed of three parties that divide the whole seats evenly. Deciding on a foreign trade policy, three bills have been proposed. Among the three bills, Party X prefers bill x most that has been drafted by the party, bill y next, and bill z the last (i.e., its preference order is $x > y > z$). Likewise, suppose that the preference orders of the other two parties are $y > z > x$, $z > x > y$, respectively. Suppose also that the chairperson of the assembly is from Party X and naturally hopes bill x to be the assembly's choice. The chair's power is restricted to the management of voting procedure and cannot vote him- or herself except for under special circumstances (e.g., when a tie occurs). The chairperson conceives the "binary procedure" (Ordeshook, 1986) according to the following agenda (voting sequence): first calling for a vote between bills y and z, then a vote between the previous winner and bill x. Given the ordinary *majority* principle, the first vote yields y as a winner, then the second vote between y and x favors x—the chairperson's personally preferred alternative. Notice that, if the chair is from Party Y, the personally preferred outcome, y, can be obtained by the agenda, x versus z first, then the winner z versus y. The trick with this binary procedure is to delay the appearance of the personally preferred alternative in the voting sequence as late as possible. This paradox, called the Condorcet paradox, implies that collective choice is sometimes dependent on a particular path by which voting is conducted and can be biased to a particular individual's or a faction's advantage. Actually, this result has been extended in a general manner. Arrow's (1963) famous general possibility theorem indicates that, when two or more members decide among three or more alternatives, *any* nondictatorial decision rule can in principle yield mutually contradictory (more specifically, intransitive) results (see, e.g., Ordeshook, 1986, for more details about these procedural phenomena).

Interactive Groups

We can find a conceptually parallel issue in decision making by interactive groups (e.g., committees, panels, juries). As in social or public choice, *procedural influence* can potentially be a serious problem in the interactive, face-to-face group context. The situation can even be worse there, because consensus procedures in such a context are occasionally fuzzy or seemingly innocent; although decision rules are defined formally in some cases (e.g., quorum rules, official agenda), it is often the case that discussion procedures are selected somewhat discretionarily by a chairperson or a vague social convention. Therefore, it is essential to explore potentially biasing effects accruing from common consensus procedures used in committees, panels, and so forth.

In considering the issue of procedural influence in such interactive group decision-making contexts, two conceptually different approaches are conceivable: the *aggregation approach* and the *interaction approach*. The aggregation approach is similar to the traditional approach taken by social choice theorists. Recall that the "biasing" effects of the binary procedure described earlier is attributed *solely* to the aggregation process itself; people vote according to their original preferences,[1] and the aggregation functions (i.e., the specific agenda by which voting is conducted and the majority rule) determine the outcome of collective choice. Likewise, in the interactive group decision-making context, some of the procedural effects may accrue from the aggregation procedure itself.

---

[1]If the agenda and the distribution of opinions in the assembly are known in advance, it is theoretically possible to take a counteraction against the agenda effects by strategically misrepresenting ones' original preferences in the voting sequence. This is called a strategic voting. However, in most actual cases (especially when the number of alternatives and voters are large), it is hard to prespecify the chairperson's agenda and the opinion distribution, making the adoption of strategic voting extremely difficult (cf. C. R. Plott & M. E. Levine, 1978).

Even though members' initial preferences are essentially *unchanged* during the group interaction, totally different outcomes might emerge due to a tactical manipulation of the consensus procedure by a chairperson, and so on. In contrast, the interaction approach takes a somewhat different view. This approach presumes that changes in members' cognition or behavioral patterns due to a consensus procedure essentially will underlie procedural effects; a chairperson's strategic manipulation of a procedure may affect members' participation rates in group discussion, confidence levels in their opinions, and so forth, while in the process of guiding a consensual outcome in a certain direction. Therefore, the two approaches put a different emphasis on the origins of procedural effects: the aggregation mechanisms per se (although they are likely to be less formal in an interactive setting than in a public choice context) or members' cognitive or behavioral changes during group interaction. In the following, we examine research pertinent to each of these approaches and show that both types of influences are indeed functioning in an interactive, face-to-face consensus formation.

ILLUSTRATIONS OF THE AGGREGATION APPROACH

Agenda Influence

An early example of this approach is Levine and Plott's pioneer work on *agenda influence* (M. E. Levine & C. R. Plott, 1977; C. R. Plott & M. E. Levine, 1978). An agenda is a series of alternative choices on which the group votes. As shown in the Condorcet paradox described earlier, the imposition of a particular voting sequence can sometimes determine a group outcome in a predictable way. Actually, what Levine and Plott showed in their work is an empirical demonstration of the Condorcet paradox in an *interactive* group decision-making context. In their experiment, these researchers induced individual members' preference orders among several alternatives by providing different incentives to each of the options if it becomes a final group choice. The incentive structure was different among members, and thus an intragroup conflict existed regarding a desirable group decision. Group members *discussed* the issue and conducted a series of votes. Plott and Levine imposed majority rule and a particular agenda by which voting is conducted; the set of alternatives was divided into two subsets at each round of the voting sequence, and the winning (by majority rule) subset was further divided into two subsets and voted on, until a single alternative was finally selected. (Notice that the series of divisions follows the binary procedure; see the aforementioned example of a hypothetical assembly.)[2]

---

[2]Notice also that the researchers functionally played the role of a "manipulative" chairperson in this study; they imposed a decision procedure on groups that was theoretically expected to guide the final group choice in a particular direction. Members discussed the issue under this procedure, and the ensuing group decisions were contrasted to the model's prediction. This research strategy is common in other studies to be examined later.

C. R. Plott and M. E. Levine (1978) administered four different agendas in their experiment. Given the differences in the monetary incentive structure among members and the absence of a clear "common goal," it is unlikely that group discussion changed members' personal preferences. Furthermore, the alternatives were identified by abstract symbols (i.e., A, B, C, etc.) and lacked any substantive content, thus making group discussion likely to be informationally and normatively barren. Plott and Levine developed a probabilistic group-choice model (later in this chapter, similar models based on a binomial property are introduced) that assumes *no* changes in individuals' original preference orders. Based on this model, they set up each agenda to yield a certain alternative as a group choice with probability near one. Indeed, the results showed that most of the actual group choices were in accordance with the predicted outcomes. Because no cognitive or behavioral changes of members were assumed in their model, the agenda effects observed there are most likely to have originated from the aggregation process itself. Interestingly, they observed similar agenda effects in an actual flying club meeting in which group discussion and interaction should have far richer (and therefore potentially disturbing to the emergence of the predicted procedural effects) contents than in their experiment. (Another demonstration of the agenda influence has been observed in a jury decision-making context; cf. Davis, Tindale, Nagao, Hinsz, & Robertson, 1984.)

Deliberation Style: Verdict Driven Versus Evidence Driven

More recently, we examined procedural influence similar to agenda effects from a somewhat different perspective (Kameda, 1991). We used a mock jury situation for the experiments, which was supposed to contain rich and involving material for discussion; deliberation subsequently ranged from disputes over factual matters to highly value-laden arguments that reflected individuals' personal beliefs.

"Compound" or "Elemental" Procedure. This study investigated two representative discussion procedures, both of which seem to be intuitively plausible and generally applicable to a decision-making context that involves *factual* considerations. The focal task situation requires assessments of several key conditions or criteria to yield a final decision. Jury decision making provides abundant examples of such a decision structure. For instance, in a trial in which a defendant is charged with first-degree murder, proof of premeditation is one of the key elements to render a guilty verdict in U.S. law. Thus, a jury working on this case is required to discuss the presence or absence of this element, in conjunction with other criteria constituting the charge of first-degree murder.[3]

---

[3]In some cases, criteria relevant for rendering a final decision can themselves be disputed. However, in this context, we assume that these criteria are already fixed by law, social convention, and the like, and that their legitimacy is not to be debated. It should be noted that the law, social convention, and so on, also specifies the logical relation between the conditions

In those decision contexts involving several key criteria, a chairperson can conceive two distinct discussion procedures. In the first procedure, which we named the *elemental* procedure, the chair solicits members' judgments of each of the relevant conditions, one by one, in order to establish a collective evaluation for each of the criteria. When the collective judgments of the relevant conditions are completed, the chairperson combines these evaluations into a final group decision according to the aggregation requirement (e.g., conjunctive or disjunctive combination—see Footnote 3) provided by the law, social convention, and so forth. In the second procedure (the *compound* procedure), the chair asks each member's overall conclusion from the beginning. Instead of collectively examining the relevant conditions one by one, group members are asked to express their personal conclusions (e.g., to convict or to acquit, to hire or not to hire) at the outset, and then to discuss the issue until they reach a final group decision. In other words, the two procedures switch the focus of group interaction substantially: The elemental procedure should facilitate exchanges of members' views on each of the criteria (e.g., factual issues), whereas the compound procedure should promote exchanges of their conclusions or overall preferences.

Actually, Hastie et al. (1983) reported discussion styles parallel to the afore-mentioned distinction in mock jury deliberations. They observed that some juries focus on reviewing evidence closely and constructing a plausible story of the case. Similar to the elemental procedure defined earlier, this type of jury (called *evidence-driven* juries by Hastie et al.) starts deliberation by exchanging their views of the key facts; the first task set by these juries is thus to establish plausible facts in the case, and the final verdict follows this stage almost automatically. On the other hand, some juries open their deliberations with a public expression (e.g., polling) of individual verdict preferences. In this type of jury (*verdict-driven* juries), deliberation centers on exchanging overall verdict preferences that jurors formed individually before the initiation of deliberation. This is parallel to those group processes created by the compound procedure.

Although both of these procedures seem innocent and easy to implement in a decision setting, they are expected to affect final group outcomes substantially. A simple example illustrates this point. Suppose that a three-person committee is to decide whether or not to hire a candidate for an opening. There are two key criteria for this decision, both of which must be met to hire the candidate

---

and a final decision. The conceptually most basic relation is a *conjunctive* or a *disjunctive* combination: To render a final affirmative decision (e.g., conviction, promotion, employment), *all* conditions must be satisfied (conjunctive combination), or satisfying *at least one* of the conditions is sufficient (disjunctive combination). See, for example, Carrington and Babcock (1977) for concrete instances of these requirements in U.S. legal contexts. Also, note that our usage of *conjunctive/disjunctive* is not the same as that of Steiner (1972). Whereas Steiner classified relationship of group performance and member resource using these terms, our usage here is strictly limited to their meanings as logical connectives.

(i.e., conjunctive requirement). Suppose also that the three members have formed personal judgments of the issue prior to the meeting as follows:

	Criteria		Conclusion
	(1)	(2)	
Person A	Yes	Yes	Hire
Person B	Yes	No	Not hire
Person C	No	Yes	Not hire

Person A, personally hoping this candidate will be hired, serves as a chairperson of this meeting. Given an ordinary majority rule, the chair is likely to lose by one to two, if calling for an immediate polling about each member's *conclusion* (i.e., the compound procedure). However, the chairperson can also use the elemental procedure, asking for members' evaluations of the key *criteria* one by one. Again assuming the same majority rule, both criteria should be judged positively. Therefore, the chairperson combines these two positive elemental judgments according to the conjunctive requirement and can "legitimately" conclude that the candidate be hired—the opposite conclusion reached by the compound procedure.

The preceding results can be extended in a general manner by a simple probabilistic model. Assuming that group decisions are essentially governed by majority process (e.g., Davis, Kameda, & Stasson, 1992; Kameda & Davis, 1990; Kameda & Sugimori, 1993; Laughlin, 1980) and that members' assessments of the key criteria are mutually independent, it can be shown that the compound and elemental procedures will significantly affect the chance of an affirmative alternative (e.g., to convict, to hire, to promote) becoming the final group decision. More concretely, when the task requirement is *conjunctive*, the elemental procedure will be more likely to yield an affirmative group decision than the compound procedure; however, this relation will be reversed when the task requirement is *disjunctive*.[4] In other words, the task requirement is expected to interact

---

[4]For the purpose of illustration, suppose that a group is composed of six members and that there are two key criteria to consider. Let us denote the probability of an individual initially inclined to affirm criterion i as p_i $(0 < p_i < 1)$. Suppose also that the law, social convention, and so on, provide the conjunctive requirement in this decision. When a chairperson uses the *compound* procedure, the probability that an individual is initially inclined to conclude affirmatively (i.e., to convict, to hire) is given by $p_1 p_2$, provided that judgments of the two conditions are mutually independent. Assuming a majority process in consensus formation (i.e., an initial majority finally prevails in determining a group decision), the probability that the group decides in the affirmative is given by:

$$P = \sum_{n=4}^{6} \binom{6}{n} (p_1 p_2)^n (1 - p_1 p_2)^{6-n} \tag{1}$$
$$= 15(p_1 p_2)^4 - 24(p_1 p_2)^5 + 10(p_1 p_2)^6.$$

with the discussion procedure in determining the final group outcome. This implies that the chairperson can in principle heighten the chance that the personally preferred alternative is chosen as a final group decision, by carefully selecting one of the two discussion procedures depending on the task requirement at hand.

Experimental Test. We tested these predictions using two mock jury trials in which the law requires conjunctive or disjunctive assessments of key conditions, respectively. In this study, six-person mock juries were randomly formed and discussed the issue until reaching a final group verdict. The discussion was unconstrained except for the general "guideline" that groups were instructed to follow; in addition to the critical distinction between the compound and the elemental procedure, either majority or unanimity rule was assigned as a consensus requirement to assess the robustness of the predicted procedural effects. These discussion procedures were imposed by an experimenter at the outset of group deliberation, and there was no interruption thereafter.

The results supported the model's prediction. Figure 7.1 displays the proportions that groups decided in the affirmative (i.e., judging the defendant to be liable) in the eight conditions. As predicted, the elemental procedure yielded a higher rate of affirmative decision than the compound procedure in the conjunctive case, but this relation was just reversed in the disjunctive case.

Just like C. R. Plott and M. E. Levine's (1978) group-choice model, the model as examined here (see Footnote 4) assumed *no* changes in individuals' original judgments about the issue due to group interaction; the "aggregation mechanisms" (i.e., the compound or elemental procedures) per se were predicted to produce the different affirmative-decision rates. Indeed, the results indicated that the actual decision rates accorded reasonably well with the model's predictions; none of the four observed decision rates in Fig. 7.1 (the rates were collapsed over

---

When the chairperson uses the *elemental* procedure, the corresponding group probability is given by:

$$P = (15p_1^4 - 24p_1^5 + 10p_1^6)(15p_2^4 - 24p_2^5 + 10p_2^6). \tag{2}$$

It can be shown that group probability, P, given by Equation 2 is larger than that from Equation 1 for *any* combination of p_1 and p_2. That is, the preceding binomial model implies that the elemental procedure will be *more* likely to yield an affirmative group choice than the compound procedure. (Notice also that this assertion holds for the entire range of p_i; the chairperson does not need to know the judgment/opinion configuration among members in advance, and thus can in principle *always* enhance the chance of the personally preferred alternative being chosen as a final group decision.) The prediction about the *disjunctive* case can be derived in the same manner. However, in this case, the direction of inequality becomes just opposite to the conjunctive case: The elemental procedure will be *less* likely to produce an affirmative group decision than the compound procedure (cf. Grofman, 1985; Kameda, 1991, for more details).

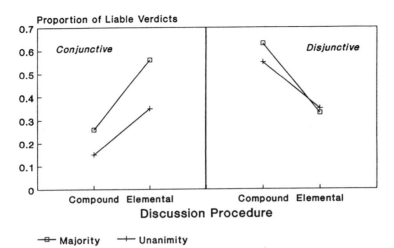

FIG. 7.1. Proportion of affirmative group decisions (liable verdicts) as a function of discussion procedure, assigned decision rule, and task requirement. From Kameda (1991). Copyright 1991 by American Psychological Association. Reprinted by permission.

the majority and unanimity rule conditions) showed significant deviations at the .20 level from the model's predictions.[5] These quantitative successes of the model indicate that the observed procedural effects essentially result from the aggregation mechanisms themselves, even though the decision circumstance allows face-to-face, full-fledged communication opportunities among members.

Consensus Requirements: Majority or Unanimity. Interestingly, the focal procedural phenomenon was robust across different consensus requirements (i.e., majority or unanimity rule). This result is consistent with the previous finding that whether majority or unanimity rule is assigned as an official consensus requirement, group decision is essentially determined by a majority process at least in a dichotomous choice setting (e.g., Davis, Kerr, Atkin, Holt, & Meek, 1975; Kameda & Sugimori, 1993; Kerr, Atkin, Stasser, Meek, Holt, & Davis, 1976; see Miller, 1989 for a comprehensive review). However, the results on members' personal reactions to the discussion procedures showed a somewhat different picture. Figure 7.2 displays members' acceptance of group decisions. We made a distinction between members whose personal conclusions (i.e., to

---

[5]We calculated the proportion of subjects who made a positive judgment for each of the two conditions *individually prior to* group interaction, and used these proportions as parameter estimates for p_1 and p_2 in the model (cf. Footnote 4). The predicted group decision rates were thus based on individuals' *original* probability of judging each condition affirmatively, and did not incorporate the potential effects accruing from group interaction (e.g., members' opinion changes). As is evident in the example of the three-person recruiting committee, the model takes the aggregation approach defined earlier.

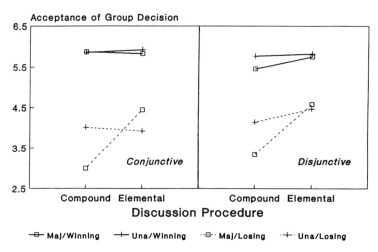

FIG. 7.2. Acceptance of group decision as a function of discussion procedure, assigned decision rule, and consistency between individual and group decisions (Maj = majority rule, Una = unanimity rule). From Kameda (1991). Copyright 1991 by American Psychological Association. Reprinted by permission.

find the defendant liable or not) were consistent with their group's final verdict ("winning" members) and members who "lost" in the deliberation. As can be seen, the winning members generally showed a high acceptance of the group outcomes, irrespective of particular procedures assigned to the deliberation (see the upper portion of the graphs). However, the distinction in procedures was critical for the losing members. The compound procedure was unpopular when combined with majority rule (see the lower left corner of each graph), whereas not so when combined with unanimity rule. This result implies that members' criticisms against a certain procedure might be circumvented through a tactical combination with other popular procedures. Given the finding that assigning either majority or unanimity rule results in essentially the same consensus pattern, the manipulative chairperson who wishes to use the compound procedure for his or her personal advantage may be wise to combine it with unanimity rule.

ILLUSTRATIONS OF THE INTERACTION APPROACH

The preceding examples indicate that some of the procedural influences in an interactive group context are essentially products of the aggregation mechanisms per se; members' personal reactions to the procedures may be important in their own right (e.g., acceptability of final group outcomes), but are not directly responsible for producing the procedural phenomena themselves. In this section, we focus on a different avenue in procedural influence. We examine several studies indicating that a chairperson's strategic use of procedures affects members' participation rates in discussion, confidence levels in their opinions, and so on, and then causes procedural effects; members' cognitive or behavioral changes during group interaction function as *moderators* for these effects.

Straw Polling

In a series of studies, Davis and his colleagues examined effects of *straw polling* in consensus formation (Davis, Kameda, Parks, Stasson, & Zimmerman, 1989; Davis, Stasson, Ono, & Zimmerman, 1988; Davis et al., 1993). The straw poll refers to a "nonbinding" polling procedure to publicize members' preferences and facilitate consensus processes. Davis and others demonstrated that this seemingly neutral procedure can sometimes affect positions that members officially take during group interaction. One of the key aspects that these researchers addressed with straw polling was a particular *sequence* by which a chairperson solicited each member to express personal preference. Davis et al. (1989) noted: "While vocal expression or a show of hands can be simultaneous, it is also possible to carry out a sequential, member-by-member poll (sometimes called a "roll-call" vote) ... A poll can be taken by name, order of seating, seniority, or something else" (p. 1000).

Notice that members' seating positions, ages, and so on, based on which roll-call votes may be taken, are sometimes correlated with the opinions that those members hold. People who have similar opinions may tend to sit closely, or policy preferences might differ across ages. If so, soliciting members' opinions in a particular sequence (based on seating order, seniority, etc.) can produce an actually unrepresentative appearance of unanimity regarding the opinion distribution in a group. That is, a particular preference expressed unanimously by preceding members might be perceived as a dominant opinion by members to follow, and may facilitate conformity among the latter members. A chairperson can thus use such Asch-type effects (Asch, 1956) intentionally, by starting a member-by-member poll from a "faction" that holds preferences similar to the chair's preference.

Davis et al. (1988) tested these notions by manipulating a polling sequence in six-person mock juries that were composed of three members initially inclined to vote guilty and three members inclined to vote not guilty. The polling sequence took one of the two forms in which guilty sayers were solicited to poll first or not-guilty sayers first. The results indicated that the critical fourth voters were indeed influenced by the preceding "local majorities." (Notice that there were no actual majorities in these groups at the outset, because they were evenly divided between the guilty and not-guilty factions). Interestingly, despite the fairly significant Asch-type effects observed at the individual opinion level, the manipulation of sequence in straw polling did not have sizable effects on final group verdicts. Davis et al. (1989) conducted "thought experiments" (numerical simulations) on this issue and concluded that the group-level effects that are expected to emerge from sequential straw polling may be too small to detect empirically with regular sample sizes. However, given the numerous opportunities (i.e., "replications" in the real world) in which straw polling can be taken by committees, panels, and so forth, the small effect-size may not necessarily negate the potential side effects of straw polling on actual consensus formation (cf. Davis & Kerr, 1986).

Hierarchy and Local Consensus Formation

More recently, we revisited the notion of *local majority* from a different perspective. We focused on a majority–minority relation defined in *hierarchical* decision-making processes (Kameda & Sugimori, 1995). Decision-making bodies occasionally have a hierarchical, multi-subgroup structure. This is especially common in organizational or administrative contexts, in which consensus must be made within and across several departments or divisions (Likert, 1967). In this structure, each member often has two roles, one defined at the *local*, subgroup level that the person belongs to primarily, and the other defined at the *global*, upper group level. These roles are sometimes in conflict (as exemplified in the conflict between individual and societal rationality in social dilemmas; cf. Dawes, 1980), and members experience some cross-pressure emanating from different levels. Besides these role dilemmas, the issue of locality and globality is also relevant for a member's "opinion status" in a group. For instance, when a consensus must be made between dichotomous alternatives, we can define a theoretically distinct majority–minority status, one at the local level and the other at the global level. Figure 7.3 illustrates this situation. In this case, members endorsing alternative A constitute the majority if viewed from the global level. We thus call these members *global majorities*. However, the majority–minority relation is reversed regionally in the second section: members endorsing alternative B (members 5 & 6) constitute *local majorities*. Therefore,

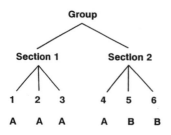

FIG. 7.3. An illustration of the global and local majority–minority status.

a multi-subgroup situation occasionally allows this type of local "irregularity," posing a potential dilemma especially for local minorities.

"Single-Stage" or "Two-Stage" Consensus Procedure. Suppose that, in this context, a cross-sectional, final consensus is achieved through a joint discussion by *all* members. In other words, due to social convention and the like, this group adopts a form of participative decision making, resembling "direct democracy" (cf. Rousseau, 1984).[6] It is possible to define two types of consensus procedures in such hierarchical, multi-subgroup contexts. The first type, which we named *single-stage procedure*, is much like the case in which there is no divisioning. Members participate in the joint discussion immediately, before the divisional differences are emphasized. When there emerges a need for consensus formation in the group, a chairperson calls for the joint meeting quickly so that opportunities for opinion coordination at the local level are minimized. The second type, *two-stage procedure*, reflects the opposite perspective. In this procedure, the chairperson encourages discussion at the section level prior to the entire joint conference; the deliberation thus proceeds in a hierarchical manner, first at the division level and then at the global level. In other words, the chair intentionally delays the joint meeting as late as possible so that local-level consensus in each division emerges on the issue.

It seems possible to introduce the notion of "partisan voting" in politics (cf. Ordeshook, 1986) in considering the effects of the latter, two-stage procedure. Partisan voting refers to political behavior whereby assemblypersons poll at a conference based on the consensus in their party; their voting behavior at the assembly does not necessarily reflect personal preferences, but rather conforms to the local decision that was established within the party beforehand. The two-stage procedure that emphasizes opinion coordination at the division level prior to the entire conference may thus facilitate social processes analogous to partisan voting.

The substantive literature indicates that consensus formation on judgmental tasks (Laughlin, 1980) is typically governed by majority processes (cf. Davis et al., 1992; J. M. Levine & Moreland, 1991; Stasser, Kerr, & Davis, 1989), although it has also been pointed out that minorities can sometimes exert covert and enduring influences on majorities (cf. Maass & Clark, 1984; Moscovici, 1980; Nemeth, 1986). The single-stage and two-stage procedures previously defined may switch the foci of such majority-influence processes. When the consensus formation is conducted in a *single* step, the global majorities may essentially

---

[6]The participative decision making of this type assumes that the number of relevant members is not large. In this sense, it may be more realistic in some cases to assume that only representatives from subdivisions participate in the collective decision. However, the distinction between direct and representative methods in the focal context does *not* yield different conclusions to be described later (cf. Galam, 1991; Kameda & Sugimori, 1995; Ono, Tindale, Hulin, & Davis, 1988, for detailed discussions of this point).

determine group outcomes. In contrast, when the *two-stage* procedure is used, the local majorities can exert direct and exclusive influence over the local minorities prior to the entire meeting. To the extent that those local influences promote cognitive and behavioral changes for the regional minorities, the local majorities can expand their power. As shown in the simple example explained earlier (cf. Fig. 7.3), the global and the local majorities are not necessarily in agreement in all divisions. If so, the two-stage procedure may function to the advantages of those members who constitute *local majorities* in particular sections but are *minorities if viewed from the global level*. A chairperson can in principle select one of the two procedures for the personal advantage, depending on his or her perception that the personal preference is shared by either the majorities or the minorities in the entire (i.e., global) group.

Preliminary Study.   To test these notions, we first conducted a preliminary experiment using a particular group composition as shown in Fig. 7.3. Six-person groups discussed a social issue (i.e., adequacy of capital punishment in a criminal trial publicized in Japan at the time) following one of the two discussion procedures. A pilot survey indicated that majorities (about two thirds) in the student population thought that capital punishment was an appropriate sentence in this case. Thus, alternative A in Fig. 7.3 was defined as pro death penalty, and alternative B was defined as con death penalty. When the two-stage procedure was used, three-person subgroups were provided 10 minutes as an "opportunity to exchange information and reach a tentative consensus," prior to the joint discussion by all members. Groups under the single-stage procedure started deliberation right away without subgroup discussions. In both conditions, 45 minutes were given for the *joint* discussion by all members. The major focus of this experiment was to examine if the two-stage procedure causes conformity effects for member 4 (cf. Fig. 7.3; a member belonging to the global majority but locally in the minority) that endures even at the entire discussion by all six members. Table 7.1 indicates proportions of members who converted their opinions to the opposite (i.e., pro to con, con to pro) between pre- and postgroup interaction under each of the two procedures.

As can be seen, such members who experienced the local minority status under the two-stage procedure showed a much higher opinion change rate (.429; see the third row) than the members who held the same initial preference but never had a minority experience under the single-stage procedure (.136), $\chi^2(1, N = 58) = 5.53$, $p < .025$. Note that this is a social process quite similar to the "partisan voting effect" described earlier. Notice also that the local majorities (members 5 & 6 in Fig. 7.3) held their opinions tightly (.000) under the two-stage procedure, compared with the corresponding members under the single-stage procedure (.318), $p < .005$ by Fisher's exact test. A similar pattern was also observed with the members' participation rates in the entire group discussion; the local minorities tended to be silent at the joint conference. Furthermore, these individual-level changes resulted in a substantive difference in the final

TABLE 7.1
TABLE 7.1
Proportions of Members Who Converted Their Opinions to the Opposite Between Pre- and
Postgroup Interaction

Type of Members (Condition)	Initial Opinion	Proportion
Majority (Single-Stage)	pro	.136 (6 of 44)
Minority (Single-Stage)	con	.328 (7 of 22)
Local Minority (Two-Stage)	pro	.429 (6 of 14)
Local Majority (Two-Stage)	con	.000 (0 of 28)

Note. This is a contrast between member's initial opinion and post-group opinion that was assessed after the entire discussion was all over. The numbers in parentheses refer to the observed frequencies. From Kameda and Sugimori (1995). Copyright 1995 by the American Psychological Association. Adapted by permission.

group decisions. Sixty-four percent of the group decisions under the single-step procedure were the majority supporting, pro death penalty. However, *no* groups under the two-stage procedure yielded the pro death-penalty decision; this decrease in the pro-decision rate was compensated by the high hung rate (79%). It should be noted that, given the general majority-prevailing tendency in group decision making, such deadlock can be regarded as a kind of "victory" for the local majorities (*minorities* if viewed from the global level); stalemating the group discussion might increase the possibility of obtaining some compromise from the global majorities. Therefore, in the case of two three-person subgroups, the chairperson whose personal preference is shared by global *minorities* is actually better off if using the two-stage procedure, at least when the opinion split in the group happens to be the one in Fig. 7.3.

Study 2: Random Group Composition. We developed a probabilistic group-choice model based on parameter estimates obtained in Study 1 and tested this model in Study 2. The second study did *not* use a particular group composition (e.g., 4–2 split as used in Study 1) and compared the two procedures generally; six-person groups were formed *randomly* and were assigned one of the discussion procedures. Notice that this is theoretically comparable to a situation in which a chairperson wishing to guide group consensus to the personal advantage has *no* knowledge about the specific opinion configuration in the group; the chair applies one of the two consensus procedures with *no exact information* about the opinion split within the decision-making committee.[7] In contrast, Study

---

[7]This situation is mathematically equal to the case where several members are sampled from the population to form a decision-making committee. Although the chairperson has a general idea about which of the alternatives is preferred by the majority in the population, there is no way to know in advance the specific opinion configuration among the sampled committee members. Therefore, the chairperson's choice of the procedure to make the situation personally advantageous must be made on a probabilistic basis, without the knowledge (or guarantee) that the opinion split in the committee coincides with the special pattern as illustrated in Fig. 7.3.

1 that presumed a particular opinion configuration (i.e., 4–2 split) is analogous
to the case in which the chairperson *must* have this information in order to
manipulate consensus procedure. Extending the generality of decision setting
this way, the results again showed that the pro alternative that was supported
by the *majorities* in the subject population was selected 62.5% under the single-
stage procedure, whereas this proportion dropped to 34.7% under the two-stage
procedure, $\chi^2(1, N = 73) = 5.06$, $p < .025$. As in Study 1, the decrease in the
pro-decision rate under the latter procedure was paralleled by the increase in
the hung rate. Furthermore, the pro-decision rates observed in the two procedural conditions were consistent with the probabilistic model's predictions
reasonably well. In Footnote 8, we sketched basic features of the model.[8]

Thought Experiment.   Given the success of the model, we can further extend
the decision setting into different-size groups. Our focal concerns are: By strategically switching a consensus procedure from one to the other, to what extent can
the manipulative chairperson theoretically enhance the probability of guiding
group outcome to the personally preferred alternative? How are these effects
related to the size of a decision-making group? To assess the change in probability,
we calculated theoretical *differences in group decision rates* between the two
discussion procedures, based on the choice models as illustrated in Footnote 8.

Suppose that, in a dichotomous decision making, an individual is initially
inclined to prefer an alternative, say policy A, with probability, p. (Put differently,
policy A is supported by p% of people in the population.) Figure 7.4 depicts

---

[8]For an illustration, suppose a six-person group is composed of two three-person subgroups
as examined in Studies 1 and 2. Let us denote the individual probability of preferring a given
alternative as p. Put differently, p% of the population prefer the alternative in a dichotomous
decision setting (e.g., to approve or disapprove the policy). Then, if the chairperson uses the
single-stage procedure, the group probability, P, that the group selects the alternative is given
by (assuming a strict majority process):

$$P = \sum_{i=4}^{6} \binom{6}{i} p^i (1-p)^{6-i}. \tag{3}$$

On the other hand, if the chairperson uses the *two-stage* procedure, P is given by:

$$P = \left[\sum_{i=2}^{3} \binom{3}{i} p^i (1-p)^{3-i} \right]^2, \tag{4}$$

because the group can decide on the alternative only if both of the two subgroups support it.
Other models for different-size groups can be constructed in the same way. (Actually, these
models were slightly different from the model tested in Study 2, although both were essentially
characterized by binomial properties. See Kameda and Sugimori [1995] for details. In the
original article, we also conducted a numerical simulation for the case in which the committee
is composed of *three* subgroups.)

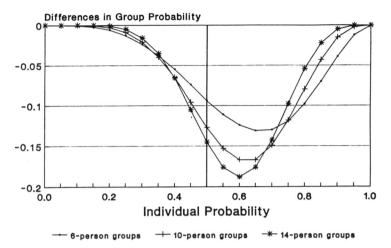

FIG. 7.4. Theoretical differences in group decision rates (the probability for the two-stage method minus the probability for the single-stage method), as a function of group size and the individual probability of initially preferring the alternative. From Kameda and Sugimori (1995). Copyright 1995 by American Psychological Association. Reprinted by permission.

differences in group decision rates (the probability that a group finally selects policy A under the two-stage procedure *minus* the corresponding probability of choosing policy A under the single-stage procedure: cf. *P* given by Equation 4 – *P* given by Equation 3 in Footnote 8), when the group is composed of *two* subgroups. The abscissa of the figure represents the individual probability of preferring policy A (or the proportion of A supporters in the population), and we consider 6-, 10-, and 14-person groups with two equal-size subdivisions.

First, notice that the difference in group decision rates is *negative* for the entire range of individual probability. That is, in the case of *two* subgroups, whether the focal alternative (policy A) is supported by the majority (the proportion is larger than 50%, viz., $p > .5$) or the minority ($p < .5$) in the population, the group is *always* less likely to decide on the alternative under the two-stage procedure than under the one-stage procedure—the difference is always negative. The hung rate becomes generally high in the two-stage case.

However, this does *not* mean that the two methods are impartial for the majority and the minority sides. For example, suppose that 65% of the population are inclined to prefer policy A, whereas the remaining 35% prefer the other alternative, policy B. Thus, the majority-endorsing alternative in this case is policy A. If the group size is *six* and the chairperson uses the two-stage method rather than the single-stage procedure, the chance that the group adopts the majority-supporting policy A is cut by 13.1% (see the graph of six-person groups in Fig. 7.4 at $p = .65$), whereas the comparable loss for the minority-supporting policy B is 3.8% (see the graph at $p = .35$). Thus, the loss in the probability of winning that accrues from the two-stage procedure is potentially larger for the majority than the minority sides. Actually, the "relative loss" becomes more serious for the majority side with the increase in group size, 16.7% (vs. 4% for the minority side) for 10-person groups, and 17.6% (vs. 3.5%) for 14-person groups. In the case of two subgroups, the two-stage method is more advantageous for the minority than for the majority side in a sense that it "damages" the latter severely while demanding little sacrifice from the former. Thus, consensus formation in a multi-subgroup context can potentially be manipulated to an individual's or a faction's advantage. A chairperson who senses (but is ignorant of the *exact* opinion configuration among members; see Footnote 7) that the personally preferred alternative is *not* supported by majorities will be better off if selecting the two-stage procedure; if the personal preference seems to be shared by majorities, the use of single-stage procedure will be strategically better for the chair's personal purpose.

Nemawashi: A Japanese-Style Consensus Formation

Thus far, we have discussed decision procedures that assume *simultaneous* exchanges of opinions, information, and so on, among members. However, in some cases, group consensus might be essentially achieved without having the simultaneous, joint discussion phase. Although the joint discussion is certainly the most important and straightforward medium for consensus formation, consensus building that is mainly based on a *series of person-to-person negotiations* is also found, especially in some of the non-Western cultures (cf. Takahashi & Takayanagi, 1985). A consensus technique, called *Nemawashi* in Japanese, is a typical example. Heller and Misumi (1987) described *Nemawashi* as follows:

> *Nemawashi* is an informal preliminary sounding out of opinions. It gives minority views an adequate hearing and prepares the group for consensus or formal vote. The method allows everybody, even dissenters, to come out of the decision process without public humiliation or shame ... *Nemawashi* in Japanese means to prepare for transplanting a large tree by cutting off most of the main roots a year or two before it is transplanted. Transplanted into the sphere of decision making, it means that before putting an important formal proposal to a board or committee meeting, the initiator tries informally discover who might oppose the suggestion so that, *through discussion and persuasion*, the opposition can be cut off, reduced, or eliminated. *Nemawashi* tries to achieve consent before major decisions have to be reached. In western countries a similar procedure is something called "lobbying," but it is less ritualized because *unanimous agreement* is not a requirement in the same way that it is in Japan where *Nemawashi* has become the standard procedure preceding formal meetings. As a consequence, formal meetings may degenerate into stylized predictable patterns.... (p. 216; emphasis added)

We examined effects of the *Nemawashi* procedure on group consensus through a computer simulation employing several social psychological notions (Kameda

& Nidaira, 1993). Our focal concern was to examine the degree that a consensual outcome by the *Nemawashi* procedure reflects members' original preferences (i.e., "collective welfare"), in comparison to a group outcome through the simultaneous, joint discussion procedure. In contrast to *Nemawashi*, the latter type of procedure basically attempts to achieve consensus without coordinating or negotiating preferences/opinions among members beforehand; rather it emphasizes public exchanges of opinions in the presence of *all* other members. Jury decision making is a typical example of this sort.

Many-to-One Influence. We focused on the *sequential* aspect of the *Nemawashi* procedure (cf. Davis et al., 1988, 1989, 1993) given that it is essentially characterized as a series of person-to-person negotiation/persuasion processes. Of course, if successful, one gradually obtains social power as one's "faction" grows in the negotiation processes; although each negotiation is conducted on an individual-to-individual basis, the persuader carries faction support (i.e., people who have been persuaded to that point) in each negotiation. Conceptualizing basic social processes in *Nemawashi* this way, it seems plausible to apply the notions of Latané's social impact theory (Latané & Wolf, 1981) here; a most typical social influence in *Nemawashi* may essentially be viewed as a "many(faction)-to-one" influence.

Parameters Determining the Results of Each Negotiation. In the simulation, we conceptualized that success or failure of each negotiation in *Nemawashi* is probabilistically determined by the following parameters: (a) *original* social power that the persuader holds over a target in a hierarchical system (as typical in an organizational context, a hierarchical power structure among members was assumed), (b) *acquired* social power due to the accumulated success of the preceding persuasions (i.e., growth of own faction), (c) discrepancy between the persuader's position and the target's preference, and (d) individual differences in targets' latitude of acceptance (cf. Hovland, Harvey, & Sherif, 1957).

***Completion of* Nemawashi.** It was also assumed that, when a negotiation is successful, the persuader must make a compromise to accommodate the target's preference; the size of compromise is determined as a function of the power relation between the persuader and the target (i.e., when the persuader is strong in relation to the target, the compromise is small; cf. Hunter, Danes, & Cohen, 1984). The persuader then proceeds to a next target and starts a new negotiation with the "consensual" outcome to that point (i.e., a policy incorporating the preceding members' preferences in the sequential manner as described previously) as the persuader's proposal. The persuader repeats such negotiation process with *every* member in the group. (Recall that "unanimous agreement" is emphasized in *Nemawashi*. See excerpts from Heller & Misumi, 1987.) If and only if such individual-to-individual negotiation is completed through *all* members, *Nemawashi* is successful, and the final consensual outcome is regarded as the group's policy. In the simulation, a person who was located at the bottom in the power hierarchy (i.e., the least powerful person) was selected as an initiator of the *Nemawashi* processes. That person conducted a series of negotiations through the hierarchical social network.

Comparison of "Collective Welfare." Conceptualizing *Nemawashi* this way, we compared the extent to which a consensual outcome reflects members' original preferences between *Nemawashi* and other decision procedures. In the simulation, individual members' original preferences were generated randomly as points in a two-dimensional "policy space" (cf. Ordeshook, 1986). A point assigned to a member can be regarded as the ideal point for the member; as the distance between a given policy (also represented as a point in the two-dimensional space) and the member's ideal point becomes larger, the policy's "utility" for the member diminishes.[9] Therefore, it is possible to judge the relative merit of two policies, say A and B, for the group as follows: If the number of members who prefer policy A to policy B (i.e., the number of members whose original ideal points are closer to policy A than to policy B) exceeds half of the group members, then policy A can be regarded as the majority-supporting policy. In this sense, policy A achieves higher "collective welfare" than policy B.

Group Outcome Through the Simultaneous Procedure. In the focal comparisons, one group policy was a consensual outcome achieved by the *Nemawashi* procedure. As another group policy, we considered a consensual outcome achieved by the *simultaneous, joint discussion* procedure. As pointed out by Davis (chapter 3 of this volume), it is often the case that a *quantitative* group decision under the joint discussion procedure may be approximated as a linear combination of members' initial preferences. Because the exact weightings for the linear combination may vary depending on a decision task and context, we examined several plausible weighting models. Linear models approximating a group decision by the *mean* or the *median* of the members' original preferences are the most straightforward examples of this sort. Besides the mean and median models, we also examined several weighting models based on other properties. For example, members' original preferences were weighted by their relative power in the group ("power model"), or by the distance between a member's preference and the other members' preferences ("distance model"—the more central a member's preference in the configuration of group members' preferences, the more weight it carries; cf. Davis, chapter 3 of this volume), or by the combination of the power and distance ("power-distance model").

---

[9]This approach, called the spatial models of election and committees, is widely used in political science to represent the preference structure among members in a collective. For more details, see, e.g., Ordeshook (1986) and Grofman (1993).

TABLE 7.2
Comparison of Degree of "Collective Welfare" Achieved by *Nemawashi* and Other
Consensus Procedures

Comparison	Nemawashi Better[a]	Nemawashi Worse
Simultaneous Decision Making		
Mean Model	12.4%	87.6%
Median Model	11.3%	88.7%
Power Model	32.2%	67.8%
Distance Model	23.2%	76.8%
Power-Distance Model	34.5%	65.5%
Dictatorial Decision Making	76.8%	23.2%

Note. From Kameda and Nidaira (1993).
[a]Cases in which a consensual outcome by the *Nemawashi* procedure acquired *more* supporters (i.e., majority of the members) than a group decision predicted for another consensus procedure.

To make a baseline comparison, a decision procedure that always selects the top person's preference (i.e., the position of one located at the top of the hierarchical structure) as a group's choice was defined as *dictatorial decision making.*

Results. Table 7.2 displays the results of these comparisons for the 177 simulation trials in which *Nemawashi* was successful.[10] Surprisingly, the consensual outcome by *Nemawashi* generally attains *lower* collective welfare than the simultaneous discussion procedure. All of the simultaneous decision models yield "better" (i.e., majority-supporting) outcomes more often than the *Nemawashi* procedure, although *Nemawashi* is obviously superior to the dictatorship. This result seems to be counterintuitive, given the *unanimous* aspect emphasized in *Nemawashi;* if everyone is consulted "equally" in the *Nemawashi* process, why does it yield inferior outcomes as compared with the simultaneous procedure weighting members' preferences even *unequally* based on status in the group (i.e., power model)? Actually, the comparison may work against *Nemawashi* even more severely, if we consider tactical planning for the negotiation sequence in *Nemawashi.* In the present simulation, the order of negotiations was predetermined by the imposed network irrespective of the targets' preferences. However, in actual cases, it seems conceivable that the initiator of *Nemawashi* may start negotiation with the targets who hold preferences close to one's own in order

---

[10]The simulation was run for 3,600 trials, changing the parameters systematically. Of those trials, *Nemawashi* was successful in 177 (4.92%) cases. Although this success rate may seem to be small, it is mainly due to the rather stringent criterion for success; if a single person disagrees in the negotiation sequence even once, the entire *Nemawashi* is assumed to fail. That is, no chance for making a new proposal, reformulation, and so on, was assumed in the simulation.

to build up his or her "faction" quickly, and then proceed to the targets having dissimilar preferences. If so, *Nemawashi* may bias the consensual processes even more severely. Although the simulation is still tentative and much remains to be studied, these results indicate that uncritical reliance on seemingly plausible and conventionally accepted procedures may sometimes be hazardous.

CONCLUSION

This chapter has focused on social-value aspects of group decision making. Although interactive group decision making is generally believed to be better than a dictatorial decision process and to represent the "will" of individual members (i.e., their preferences, opinions, etc.) reasonably well, the empirical and theoretical results reviewed in this chapter indicate that such a view may be overly optimistic, and perhaps seriously misleading in some cases. As in collective choice, procedural mechanisms intervening between individual preferences as inputs and a group decision as an output are also quite critical in the interactive decision-making context. Seemingly neutral procedures that are set arbitrarily by a chairperson, vague social custom, and so forth, can in principle yield a group decision that is counterintuitive or even unacceptable in terms of democratic values. Of course, many decision situations have formal rules of procedure, a set of bylaws, and the like, which may limit the chair's or leader's discretion in selecting a procedure. However, this does not guarantee that the institutionalized procedure is free from a systematic bias. As such, uncritical reliance on it could be sometimes equally dangerous. The recognition of procedural influence in group decision making and empirical research on the related issues are fairly recent developments in social psychology. However, the importance of the issue has been long recognized in other areas of social science (e.g., economics, political science), and sophisticated *analytical* developments have been made in the literature. Given the theoretical and practical importance of the issue, it seems an urgent task to narrow the gap that exists between our analytical and empirical knowledge about procedural influence in consensus formation.

ACKNOWLEDGMENTS

Portions of this chapter were presented at the Conference on Theoretical Developments in Small Group Research; Hamburg, Germany, November 17–22, 1992. I am grateful to James H. Davis, Erich Witte, Scott Tindale, and Bernard Grofman for their helpful comments on drafts of this article. Thanks are extended to the participants of the conference for the supportive discussions. Financial support from the Japanese Ministry of Education, Science and Culture (Grant 05710094) is also gratefully acknowledged.

REFERENCES

Arrow, K. J. (1963). *Social choice and individual values* (2nd ed.). New Haven, CT: Yale University Press.

Asch, S. E. (1956). Studies of independence and conformity: A minority of one against a unanimous majority. *Psychological Monographs, 70* (Whole No. 416).

Black, D. (1958). *The theory of committees and elections.* Cambridge, England: Cambridge University Press.

Carrington, P. D., & Babcock, B. A. (1977). *Civil procedure: Cases and comments on the process of adjudication* (2nd ed.). Boston: Little, Brown.

Davis, J. H., Kameda, T., Parks, C., Stasson, M., & Zimmerman, S. (1989). Some social mechanics of group decision making: The distribution of opinion, polling sequence, and implications for consensus. *Journal of Personality and Social Psychology, 57,* 1000–1012.

Davis, J. H., Kameda, T., & Stasson, M. F. (1992). Group risk taking: Selected topics. In F. Yates (Ed.), *Risk-taking behavior* (pp. 163–199). Chichester, England: Wiley.

Davis, J. H., & Kerr, N. (1986). Thought experiments and the problem of sparse data in small group research. In P. S. Goodman (Ed.), *Designing effective work groups* (pp. 305–349). San Francisco: Jossey-Bass.

Davis, J. H., Kerr, N. L., Atkin, R. S., Holt, R., & Meek, D. (1975). The decision processes of 6- and 12-person mock juries assigned unanimous and two-thirds majority rules. *Journal of Personality and Social Psychology, 32,* 1–14.

Davis, J. H., Stasson, M., Ono, K., & Zimmerman, S. (1988). Effects of straw polls on group decision making: Sequential voting pattern, timing, and local majorities. *Journal of Personality and Social Psychology, 55,* 918–926.

Davis, J. H., Stasson, M. F., Parks, C. D., Hulbert, L., Kameda, T., Zimmerman, S. K., & Ono, K. (1993). Quantitative decisions by groups and individuals: Voting procedures and monetary awards by mock civil juries. *Journal of Experimental Social Psychology, 29,* 326–346.

Davis, J. H., Tindale, R. S., Nagao, D. H., Hinsz, V. B., & Robertson, B. (1984). Order effects in multiple decisions by groups: A demonstration with mock juries and trial procedures. *Journal of Personality and Social Psychology, 47,* 1003–1012.

Dawes, R. (1980). Social dilemmas. *Annual Review of Psychology, 31,* 169–193.

Farquharson, R. (1969). *Theory of voting.* New Haven, CT: Yale University Press.

Fishburn, P. (1973). *The theory of social choice.* Princeton, NJ: Princeton University Press.

Galam, S. (1991). Political paradoxes of majority rule voting and hierarchical systems. *International Journal of General Systems, 18,* 191–200.

Grofman, B. (1985). The accuracy of majorities for disjunctive and conjunctive decision tasks. *Organizational Behavior and Human Decision Processes, 35,* 119–123.

Grofman, B. (Ed.). (1993). *Information, participation, and choice: An economic theory of democracy in perspective.* Ann Arbor, MI: University of Michigan Press.

Hastie, R., Penrod, S., & Pennington, N. (1983). *Inside the jury.* Cambridge, MA: Harvard University Press.

Heller, F. A., & Misumi, J. (1987). Decision making. In B. M. Bass, P. J. D. Drenth, & P. Weissenberg (Eds.), *Advances in organizational psychology* (Vol. 1, pp. 207–219). Beverly Hills, CA: Sage.

Hovland, C. I., Harvey, O., & Sherif, M. (1957). Communication discrepancy as determinants of opinion change. *Journal of Abnormal and Social Psychology, 55,* 242–252.

Hunter, J. E., Danes, J. E., & Cohen, S. H. (1984). *Mathematical models of attitude change* (Vol. 1). New York: Academic Press.

Kalven, H., & Zeisel, H. (1966). *The American jury.* Boston: Little, Brown.

Kameda, T. (1991). Procedural influence in small-group decision making: Deliberation style and assigned decision rule. *Journal of Personality and Social Psychology, 61,* 245–256.

Kameda, T., & Davis, J. H. (1990). The function of the reference point in individual and group risk decision making. *Organizational Behavior and Human Decision Processes, 46,* 55–76.

Kameda, T., & Nidaira, I. (1993). *An analysis of sequential consensus formation processes: A computer simulation of the* Nemawashi *procedure* [in Japanese]. Paper presented at the 41st annual meeting of the Japanese Group Dynamics Association, Kumamoto, Japan.

Kameda, T., & Sugimori, S. (1993). Psychological entrapment in group decision making: An assigned decision rule and a groupthink phenomenon. *Journal of Personality and Social Psychology, 65,* 282–292.

Kameda, T., & Sugimori, S. (1995). Procedural influence in two-step group decision making: Power of local majorities in consensus formation. *Journal of Personality and Social Psychology, 69,* 865–876.

Kerr, N. L., Atkin, R., Stasser, G., Meek, D., Holt, R., & Davis, J. (1976). Guilt beyond a reasonable doubt: Effects of concept definition and assigned decision rule on the judgments of mock jurors. *Journal of Personality and Social Psychology, 34,* 282–294.

Kotter, J. P., & Schlesinger, L. A. (1981). Choosing strategies for change. *Harvard Business Review, 57,* 106–114.

Latané, B., & Wolf, S. (1981). The social impact of majorities and minorities. *Psychological Review, 88,* 438–453.

Laughlin, P. R. (1980). Social combination processes of cooperative, problem-solving groups on verbal intellective tasks. In M. Fishbein (Ed.), *Progress in social psychology* (Vol. 1, pp. 127–155). Hillsdale, NJ: Lawrence Erlbaum Associates.

Levine, J. M., & Moreland, R. L. (1991). Progress in small group research. *Annual Review of Psychology, 41,* 585–634.

Levine, M. E., & Plott, C. R. (1977). Agenda influence and its implications. *Virginia Law Review, 63,* 561–604.

Likert, R. (1967). *The human organization.* New York: McGraw-Hill.

Lind, A. E., & Tyler, T. R. (1988). *The social psychology of procedural justice.* New York: Plenum.

Locke, E. A., & Schweiger, D. M. (1979). Participation in decision making: One more look. In B. M. Staw (Ed.), *Research in organizational behavior* (Vol. 1, pp. 265–340). Greenwich, CT: JAI.

Maass, A., & Clark, R. D. III (1984). Hidden impact of minorities: Fifteen years of minority influence research. *Psychological Bulletin, 95,* 428–450.

Miller, C. E. (1989). The social psychological effects of group decision rules. In P. Paulus (Ed.), *Psychology of group influence* (2nd ed., pp. 327–355). Hillsdale, NJ: Lawrence Erlbaum Associates.

Moscovici, S. (1980). Toward a theory of conversion behavior. In L. Berkowitz (Ed.), *Advances in experimental social psychology* (Vol. 13, pp. 209–239). New York: Academic Press.

Nemeth, C. (1986). Differential contributions of majority and minority influence. *Psychological Review, 93,* 23–32.

Ono, K., Tindale, R. S., Hulin, C. L., & Davis, J. H. (1988). Intuition vs. deduction: Some thought experiments concerning Likert's linking-pin theory of organization. *Organizational Behavior and Human Decision Processes, 42,* 135–154.

Ordeshook, P. C. (1986). *Game theory and political theory: An introduction.* New York: Cambridge University Press.

Plott, C. R., & Levine, M. E. (1978). A model of agenda influence on committee decisions. *American Economic Review, 68,* 146–160.

Rousseau, J. J. (1984). *Of the social contract* (C. M. Sherover, Trans.). New York: Harper & Row.

Stasser, G., Kerr, N. L., & Davis, J. H. (1989). Influence processes and consensus models in decision-making groups. In P. Paulus (Ed.), *Psychology of group influence* (2nd ed., pp. 279–326). Hillsdale, NJ: Lawrence Erlbaum Associates.

Steiner, I. D. (1972). *Group processes and productivity.* San Diego, CA: Academic Press.

Takahashi, N., & Takayanagi, S. (1985). Decision procedure models and empirical research: The Japanese experience. *Human Relations, 38,* 767–780.

Thibaut, J., & Walker, L. (1975). *Procedural justice.* Hillsdale, NJ: Lawrence Erlbaum Associates.

SOCIAL INFORMATION-PROCESSING MODELS

8

MODELS OF PARTICIPATION DURING FACE-TO-FACE UNSTRUCTURED DISCUSSION

Garold Stasser
Sandra I. Vaughan
Miami University

Four decades ago, Bales and his colleagues (Bales, 1953; Bales, Strodtbeck, Mills, & Roseborough, 1951) observed the conversations of male groups who were discussing human relations problems. Two notable lines of inquiry emanated from this early work. One line of inquiry is built on Bales' (1950) interaction process analysis, which captures the task-oriented and socioemotional content of speech acts. Among other things, this work explores the problem of maintaining a functional balance between task and social activities. This chapter focuses on the other line of inquiry, which is the modeling of participation rates among group members. Bales (1953) noted several striking regularities in the frequencies of initiating and receiving communications during face-to-face discussions. First and foremost, members of a group typically formed a hierarchy of participation. Second, this hierarchy was evident in speakers' communications to specific individuals in the group but was even more pronounced for communications directed to the group as a whole. Third, the number of communications received by a member was highly correlated with the number of communications that he initiated.

Following the lead of Bales and his colleagues, Stephan and Mishler (1952) obtained speaking-turn data from the weekly meetings of classroom discussion groups. Each group had an instructor (leader) whose primary role was to facilitate discussion. Figure 8.1 gives the percentage of speaking turns taken by students when ordered by their overall participation in class sizes of five to

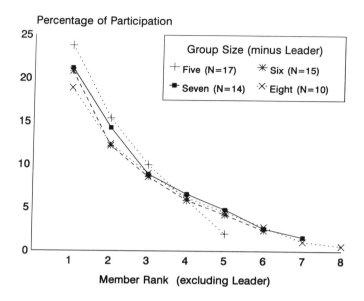

FIG. 8.1. Percentage of speaking turns by member rank and group size. Data from Stephan and Mischler (1952).

eight. (Turns taken by the instructor are not included in Fig. 8.1; instructors' contributions accounted for 39% to 45% of speaking turns for the group sizes included in the graph.) Stephan and Mishler noted that the difference in speaking rates is relatively large between the first- and second-ranked members and that this difference between adjacent ranks becomes decreasingly smaller at the lower ranks.

The emergence of speaking hierarchies has intrigued several social scientists since this early work. A substantial portion of the ensuing work has attempted to capture the regularities of speaking frequencies with formal models (e.g., Burke, 1974; Goetsch & McFarland, 1980; Horvath, 1965; Kadane & Lewis, 1969; Stephan & Mishler, 1952). Recently, there has been a revival of such modeling efforts (e.g., Balkwell, 1991; Fisek, Berger, & Norman, 1991; Parker, 1988; Skvoretz, 1988; Stasser & Taylor, 1991). Some of this recent work (Dabbs & Ruback, 1987; Parker, 1988; Stasser & Taylor, 1991) has noted another feature of speaking patterns: Individual members do not distribute their participation evenly throughout discussion. Instead, much of an individual's contributions is concentrated in periods of high activity (called megaturns by Dabbs & Ruback, 1987).

This chapter reviews models of participation in small-group discussion by considering first models of speaking hierarchies and then models that also incorporate intermittent patterns of speaking. One criticism of attempts to model speaking patterns has been the concentration on model fitting without much consideration of the processes that generate these characteristic patterns (e.g., Kadane & Lewis, 1969; Leik, 1969). Whereas this criticism is generally appropriate, some of the models reviewed herein are built on assumptions about process. Moreover, there is a fairly extensive body of research that has examined antecedents of participation rates including such variables as status cues (Fisek et al., 1991), seating arrangements and visibility (Baker, 1984), speaking latencies (Willard & Strodtbeck, 1972), and trait measures such as dominance (Watson, 1971).

Formal models of participation rates have not directly addressed the link between patterns of participation and group productivity. For example, the models do not address outcome questions such as, "Does, or under what conditions does, the degree of participation inequality affect the decisions that groups are likely to reach?" Speaking turns are opportunities to contribute informational resources to the group and to influence the course of group action. Nonetheless, formal models have not explicitly represented speaking as the conduit for funneling member resources into a group product.

After reviewing the formal models of speaking turns, we describe a computational model that uses speaking turns as the primary process by which groups fashion collective decisions. This model incorporates the SPEAK model of Stasser and Taylor (1991) into the DISCUSS model of group decision making (Stasser, 1988). After exploring some illustrative questions using this revised DISCUSS model, we outline an agenda for future modeling and empirical work.

Participation Hierarchies

Bales et al. (1951) proposed that the distribution of speaking turns in a group could be approximated by a harmonic function of the form:

$$P_i = 1/[i \sum_{j=1}^{N} 1/j], \tag{1}$$

where P_i is the proportion of turns taken by the ith ranked member in the speaking hierarchy and N is group size. This function captures the diminishing differences in speaking rates between ranks as one moves through the speaking hierarchy and is relatively simple. Nonetheless, Bales et al. (1951) were not entirely satisfied with its descriptive precision.

Stephan and Mishler (1952) concluded that an exponential function is descriptively superior to the harmonic function:[1]

$$P_i = [ar^{i-1}]/100, \tag{2}$$

[1]Technically, an exponential function is a function of e, the base of the natural logarithm, raised to a power whereas Equation 2 would usually be called a power function. However, the literature that is reviewed in this chapter has traditionally referred to the formulation proposed by Stephan and Mishler (1952) and variants of that formulation as exponential functions. We maintain this practice.

where P_i is the proportion of turns taken by the member occupying the ith rank in the speaking hierarchy ($i = 1, 2, \ldots, N$; where N is group size), a an estimate of the proportion for the first-ranked member, and r is the proportional change in speaking rates between adjacent ranks ($0 < r < 1$). Because Stephan and Mishler's groups included a leader (actually, an instructor in a classroom setting) and they wanted to exclude leaders' contributions from the distribution to be modeled, the a parameter was useful in their application. However, if one is simply interested in describing the distribution of speaking turns in groups without a clearly designated leader (i.e., without excluding any member from the emergent hierarchy of participation), then defining

$$a = 100/[\Sigma_{j=1}^{N} r^{j-1}], \tag{3}$$

and substituting for a in Equation 2 yields:

$$P_i = [r^{i-1}]/[\Sigma_{j=1}^{N} r^{j-1}]. \tag{4}$$

Generally, an exponential function of the form of equation 4 has been regarded as providing a better description of the distribution of speaking turns in a group than the original harmonic function (Equation 1) proposed by Bales and his colleagues (Burke, 1974; Kadane & Lewis, 1969; Stephan, 1952; Stephan & Mishler, 1952). However, Kadane and Lewis concluded that there is not compelling empirical evidence to prefer one formulation over the other based on their reanalysis of data obtained from Bales et al. (1951) and Stephan and Mishler (1952). This lack of resolution is not surprising given the paucity of empirical data and the fact that both models generate a negative decelerating function between speaking frequency and participation rank similar to the empirical relationship observed in many, freely interacting discussion groups (as in Fig. 8.1).

Nonetheless, the exponential model has received the most attention. Kadane and Lewis (1969) and Kadane, Lewis, and Ramage (1969) reviewed two classes of explanations for the exponential patterns in speaking-turn data: methodological artifact (Coleman, 1960; Leik, 1965) and speaking queues (Horvath, 1965).

Methodological Artifact.   Coleman (1960) proposed that the exponential relationship might arise because participation rates are, first, ordered by members within a group (to obtain the hierarchy), and then, aggregated across groups of a given size. He proposed that the process of sampling speech acts from a parent distribution in which all members are equally likely to speak would, due to sampling variations, produce unequal speaking frequencies within any one discussion. Then, when observed speaking frequencies are ordered within groups and aggregated across groups by participation ranks, something akin to an exponential relationship between rank and speaking frequency would emerge. Kadane and Lewis (1969) dismissed this explanation by noting that, whereas the ordering and aggregation process might produce an approximate exponential relationship when generating small samples of speech acts, it would not when the number of speech acts sampled approached those numbers observed in the typical empirical study.

Leik (1967) proposed a similar idea suggesting that, if the distribution of speaking tendencies were unimodal but skewed, the ordering within groups and aggregating across groups could produce an exponential relationship. Whereas Kadane and Lewis (1969) granted that it is theoretically possible to find a parent distribution of speaking tendencies that would yield exponentially distributed participation rates for any given group size, the parent distribution would necessarily be different for groups of different sizes. Nonetheless, they showed that sampling members from a highly positively skewed distribution of speaking propensities would yield an *approximate* exponential distribution of participation rates by rank for group sizes 3 to 12. Specifically, the distribution that they examined had a density given by the reciprocal of $X\ln(15)$, $1 \leq X \leq 15$, where X can be interpreted as a measure of speaking propensity or rate and ln is the natural logarithm function. The skew in this distribution is dramatic with an expectation that 39% of the cases sampled would have the lowest value of 1, 68% of the cases would fall at or below 3, and the remaining 32% distributed over the long "tail" stretching from 4 to 15.

In sum, the plausibility of the methodological artifact explanation rests on the plausibility of the corollary assertion that distributions of speaking propensities are highly and positively skewed in the populations from which groups are formed. This idea is not preposterous, but it does contradict the prevailing and conventional notion that complex psychological predispositions, such as talkativeness, are determined by many factors acting more or less independently, and, thus by the central limit theorem, tend to be distributed unimodally and symmetrically (Lowry, 1989).

In the end, however, we have two reservations about this class of explanations. First, we are uncomfortable with the connotation of *methodological artifact* (although we have also used this terminology for convenience). The implication is that the notion of exponentially distributed participation hierarchies is either uninteresting or of limited value in understanding group process. To the contrary, this view suggests that the emergence of speaking hierarchies is a natural consequence of combining individuals with differing speaking propensities and, whereas the exponential model may not describe accurately what happens in any one group, it potentially provides a useful baseline expectation for how speech acts are distributed among members.

Our second reservation is that this class of explanations attributes the origins of speaking hierarchies to member predispositions that are imported into the group and presumably not affected by the dynamics of discussion. Parenthetically, we should note that these reservations are not equally applicable to all of the work that is tagged with the methodological artifact label. For example,

Leik (1965, 1967, 1969) did portray the distributional consequences of combining people with different speaking propensities as interesting, and he explicitly considered the possibility that speaking propensities are determined partly by the social context.

Speaking Queues. Horvath (1965) argued that the exponential relationship between speaking frequencies and participation rank could arise from the process of allocating speaking turns during discussion. He suggested that there may be an implicit or explicit queue for claiming each speaking opportunity such that a person will speak with a probability of p only if each preceding person in the queue failed to speak. He showed that, under the assumption that all members are equally likely to speak when given the opportunity (p equal for all members), a queuing process would yield exponentially distributed speaking frequencies when members' contributions are ordered by their location in the queue.

Without reviewing Horvath's (1965) formal proof, one can illustrate the process that he envisioned by analogy. Imagine a basketball team taking turns shooting free throws; player A goes first, player B second, player C third, and so forth. The process continues until one player is successful; if none is successful on the first round, the process cycles through the players again and continues to recycle until one player is successful. Claiming a turn in Horvath's model is like making a basket in this contrived game of basketball. If all players are equally good (or poor) shooters, then a player higher in the order (e.g., A) will be more likely than a player lower in the order (e.g., B) to make the successful terminating shot. Moreover, if the process is repeated many times with the same order of shooting and each player receives a score equal to the number of times he or she makes the successful terminating shot, the distribution of player scores will be an exponential function of the form proposed by Stephan and Mishler (1952).

One appealing feature of this queuing explanation, beyond its cleverness, is that it does not rest on the assumption of a complex distribution of speaking tendencies in the population from which groups are formed. Indeed, it assumes that all members are equally likely to claim a turn when it is offered. Unfortunately, this gain in parsimony may be offset by a loss in generalizability. Horvath (1969) admitted that this equality assumption may be untenable for some groups, especially groups whose members differ markedly in status, ability, or talkativeness.

Kadane et al. (1969) raised concerns about the empirical adequacy of Horvath's (1965) model by showing that other models with less restrictive assumptions fit better speaking-turn data obtained from a number of sources. Nonetheless, as Horvath (1969) noted, the speaking queue model (and, thus, the more general Stephan and Mishler, 1952, exponential model) provided a reasonably good approximation to the data analyzed by Kadane et al. Given that the assumption that all are equally likely to claim a turn is probably violated to some degree in many groups, Horvath was impressed by the fit of the queuing model rather than its failure to fit as well as more general models.

Perhaps a more serious concern than the question of empirical fit is the plausibility of the round-robin process proposed by Horvath (1965). At least three questions deserve consideration. First, how are the speaking queues established within groups (origin of queues)? Second, is there a social or psychological mechanism by which the group could efficiently and quickly cycle through the queue after every speech to determine the next speaker (economy of queue maintenance)? Casual reflection on the experience of participating in discussions suggests that such a mechanism would have to operate with little or no deliberate attention to, or even awareness of, the queuing process. Third, is it reasonable to suppose that the same queuing order is operative after every speech (constancy of queue)? Two implications of a constant queuing order are that turn taking in discussion is not affected by who has spoken recently and that each member's participation is distributed more or less evenly throughout discussion.

Horvath (1965) provided a possible answer for both the origin and economy questions. He suggested that a speaking queue might originate from differential speaking latencies among members. Members slower to respond at the termination of one turn would get an opportunity to speak only if their faster peers choose not to speak. Moreover, queues originating from speaking latencies would not require monitoring by members and could plausibly emerge without member awareness. Willard and Strodtbeck (1972) proposed a similar role for speaking latency and found that a measure of verbal response latency (obtained from a sentence completion task) accounted for about 35% of the variability in participation rates among members of four-person groups.

Nonetheless, Horvath's (1965) speaking latency mechanism is, by his own admission, merely a suggestion, and one could imagine other mechanisms for establishing and maintaining queues. For example, queuing might be partly a by-product of the physical arrangement of members (e.g., seating locations and distances). Speaking opportunities may be awarded first to highly visible members via subtle cues such as a glance from the foregoing speaker (Baker, 1984; Burke, 1974; Duncan, 1972; Steinzor, 1950). For another example, expectation states theorists (Berger, Conner, & Fisek, 1974; Ridgeway, 1984) suggest that status hierarchies in a group form quickly based on mutually shared performance expectations derived from limited information such as social cues and behavioral exchanges that occur early in the interaction. Furthermore, one's standing in a status hierarchy is thought to mediate influence, participation, and access to other valued social commodities (Fisek et al., 1991; Fisek & Ofshe, 1970; Ridgeway & Berger, 1986). The point is that the formation and operation of speaking queues in discussion groups is not such an incredible idea; there are psychological (speaking latencies), ecological (seating arrangements), and social (shared performance expectations) processes that could produce queuelike behavior in allocating speaking opportunities.

More problematic for the queuing model is that speaking queues are implicitly viewed as invariant throughout a group's interaction (i.e., one's place in the queue is constant). Dabbs and Ruback (1987) summarized compelling empirical evidence showing that individuals' vocalizations are not distributed evenly throughout a group's interaction. Similarly, Stasser and Taylor (1991) found that members of six-person mock juries were more likely to speak if they had spoken recently. Parker (1988) also found that the pattern of recent speakers changed the likelihood that particular members would speak on the next turn. These observations suggest that the same speaking queue is not operative throughout a group's interaction unless one supposes that the probabilities of members taking a turn fluctuate over time. This supposition, of course, contradicts a fundamental assumption of the model—namely, that the probability of speaking when offered an opportunity is constant across people (and, by implication, across time).

Summary. The Stephan and Mishler (1952) exponential model provides a working, although imperfect, model of how speaking turns are distributed among a group's members over the course of face-to-face, unstructured discussions. Its modest descriptive success makes questions regarding possible underlying mechanisms worth considering. One class of explanations is based on the process of sampling members from a population in which speaking propensities are markedly skewed and then defining participation ranks within groups and aggregating speaking frequencies across groups by rank. As Kadane and Lewis (1969) showed, such an explanation works reasonably well if the world of potential group members is inhabited by mostly quiet people with a few verbose to very verbose ones. Another explanation is based on a queuing model of speaking-turn allocation. This model views the world of potential group members as being homogeneous in speaking propensities but having unequal opportunities to speak as dictated by a "pecking order" within a group once it is formed.

An inherent limitation in these models is that they implicitly view participation rates as stable across time. Of course, this deficiency is understandable because the data that they were designed to model obscure variations in members' participation rates because the speaking frequencies are aggregated both across groups and across time.

Intermittent Speaking

Dabbs and Ruback (1987) noted that speaking turns are clustered such that individuals are more likely to speak if they have spoken recently. Parker (1988) and Stasser and Taylor (1991) observed similar clustering in their sequential analyses of speaking turns. Parker accounted for temporally uneven patterns in turn taking by viewing conversation in groups as characterized primarily by dyadic exchanges.

Floors. Parker (1988) described turn taking by defining four group states as diagrammed in Fig. 8.2: floor, broken floor, regain, and nonfloor. A *floor* is defined by two members exchanging turns, and the group moves to a *broken floor* when a third member interrupts the dyadic exchange by usurping one of the floor holders' turns. For example, suppose that persons A, B, C, and D were engaged in a discussion. The speaking sequence ABABC would define a floor state until C took A's turn at which point the group would be in a broken floor state. Parker observed that floors occurred frequently in the conversations of his four-person groups; groups were in a floor state 61% of the time. Moreover, when in a floor state, they stayed in the floor state (i.e., next turn was taken by a floor holder) 63% of the time and moved to the broken floor (i.e., next turn taken by an intruder) only 37% of the time. Note that, if the three available members were equally likely to take the next turn in a four-person group, these transition frequencies would be essentially reversed: From an existing floor, groups would stay in the floor state only 33% of the time and move to a broken floor 67% of the time.

Broken floors are transient states in that the next speaking turn will move the group into one of the other three states. First, if B takes the next turn in the foregoing sequence (ABABCB), the floor state is reestablished with B and C being the new floor holders. Second, if D takes the next turn (ABABCD), the group moves to a *nonfloor* state and continues there until any two members start alternating turns to establish a new floor. Third, if the displaced member (A in the foregoing example) takes the next turn (ABABCA), the group moves to a *regain* state (that

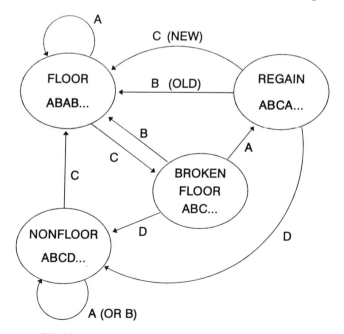

FIG. 8.2. Parker's (1988) context model of speaking turns.

is, the displaced member attempts to regain his or her place in the speaking sequence). Again, the attraction of the floor state was evident in Parker's (1988) groups. If the three available members were equally likely to take the next turn, each of the three transitions out of a broken floor would occur equally often (i.e., 33% of the time for a four-person group). The most frequent transition from a broken floor was to a new floor (56% of the time) and the least likely transition was to a nonfloor (12% of the time). About a third of the time, the displaced member took the next turn and moved the group to the regain state.

The regain state, like the broken floor, is transient and is resolved in one of three ways. Two of the ways reestablish the floor state: The old floor can be reestablished if the old floor holders resume exchanges after the intrusion (e.g., ABABCAB, where the AB alternation resumes after the intrusion by C in the foregoing example), or a new floor can emerge if the intruder and the "regaining" member start alternating turns (e.g., ABABCBC). The third possibility moves the group to a nonfloor state (e.g., ABABCBD). Again, each of these transitions (new floor, old floor, and nonfloor) out of the regain state would occur equally often if each of the three available members were equally likely to take the next turn when a four-person group is in the regain state. However, in Parker's (1988) groups, the transitions from regain to new floor (.46) and to old floor (.42) were prevalent.

In summary, the floor state was predominant in Parker's (1988) groups. Once established, the floor was maintained by the next speaking turn more often than the baseline expectation for a random sequence of turns by equally talkative members. Moreover, once the floor state was disrupted, movements to reestablish a floor occurred much more often than predicted by such a baseline expectation. Of course, floorlike patterns could emerge if two members were especially talkative so that they took most of the turns. However, Parker demonstrated that the maintenance of a floor and movements toward a floor occurred more often than would be expected by random switches that were constrained by the marginal rates of participation of members.

Stasser and Taylor (1991) observed similar patterns in their six-person mock juries. These juries were in a floor state 49% of the time. Once in a floor state, they remained there on the next turn 52% of the time (compared to a chance expectation of 20% for six persons). Moreover, when not in a floor, juries moved toward a floor state more frequently than predicted by a random switch baseline. For example, juries in a broken floor state moved immediately back to a floor 46% of the time (20% chance expectation). On the one hand, movement of these six-person juries among the group states deviated even more from the random baseline expectations than did the movements of Parker's (1988) four-person groups. On the other hand, it is clear that floors were less prevalent in the six-person juries. That is, the increased competition for speaking time in the six-person juries, as compared to the four-person groups, seemingly made it more difficult to maintain a floor and to reestablish a floor once it was disrupted.

Parker's (1988) floor model captures some intricate sequential patterns in speaking turn allocation during face-to-face discussions. The prevalence of floor states is consistent with Dabbs and Ruback's (1987) observation that each member's contributions to discussion tend to be clustered. By definition, the two members who hold the floor will speak frequently and other members will be silent as long as the floor is maintained.

As a descriptive framework, the floor model does not explicitly address the psychological or social mechanisms that guide the sequential allocation of turns. In our presentation of the model, we have emphasized the notion of dyadic exchange. This characterization suggests that floor holders not only hold the floor but direct their contributions to one another. Although floors may arise because two members engage in an extended dialogue, the floor model does not necessarily imply that floor holders are talking to one another while the remainder of the group is a passive audience to their interaction. Indeed, Parker (1988) viewed the orchestration of turns during unstructured, face-to-face interaction as a group-level phenomenon involving a mosaic of verbal and nonverbal signals (Duncan, 1972; Duncan & Fiske, 1977). He speculated that group states (floors, nonfloors, broken floors, regain) represent different social contexts that affect the rules of interaction. For example, group members may be particularly responsive to "back-channel" requests for the next turn from floor holders or recently displaced floor holders (in the broken floor state). Additionally, a speaker may terminate his or her turn by awarding the first opportunity to speak (e.g., by eye contact) to either the other floor holder or a recent floor holder (Burke, 1974). In terms of Horvath's (1965) queuing model, such context-sensitive rules of interaction would essentially rearrange the queue depending on the recent history of speaking in the group.

It is likely that such implicit rules of interaction guide the allocation of speaking turns, but it is also likely that psychological variables are operative. At some times, a member may be distracted, daydreaming, deep in thought, or simply uninterested in the current topic of conversation and, thus, relatively unlikely to speak unless a turn remains unclaimed for an extended period of time. At other times, the same member may be alert, ready to articulate an idea, or particularly invested in the current topic and, thus, primed to speak as soon as social conventions permit. Such psychological states probably change from moment to moment during the course of discussion and collectively determine one's momentary disposition or desire to speak at the next opportunity. Thus, rules of social discourse may grant some members first or more opportunity to speak at the end of a turn whereas psychological states may determine the likelihood that a member will speak when given the opportunity.

Whereas the floor model highlights orderliness in the progression of speakers and provides a convenient descriptive framework, it does not lend itself to prediction. To apply the model to new groups, one can either assume that the transition parameters (of which six are structurally unconstrained) are invariant from one application to another or simply reestimate the parameters. In particular, there is no obvious way to relate transition rates among states to group size, although Stasser and Taylor's (1991) results suggest, not surprisingly, that floors are less stable and more difficult to establish in larger groups.

SPEAK Model. Stasser and Taylor (1991) proposed that speaking-turn allocation in unstructured, face-to-face discussions are the manifestation of (a) stable differences in speaking rates (speaking hierarchies), (b) momentary increases in speaking likelihood following a turn ("megaturns"; Dabbs & Ruback, 1987), and (c) the inherent competition among members for a turn. More specifically, they proposed that the probability that member i will take a turn, p_i, is given by:

$$p_i = S_i / \Sigma_{j=1}^{N} S_j, \tag{5}$$

where S_i and S_j are the propensities of the ith and jth members to speak, and N is group size. By the nature of speaking turns, S_i is zero if member i has just spoken; otherwise it depends the individual's overall speaking rate, P_i, and any momentary increment in speaking likelihood due to having spoken recently, I_i:

$$S_i = \begin{vmatrix} 0, \text{ if } i \text{ just spoke} \\ P_i + I_i, \text{ otherwise.} \end{vmatrix} \tag{6}$$

The distribution of stable rates within a group were modeled as an exponential function following Stephan and Mishler's (1952) lead:

$$P_i = r^i / [\Sigma_{j=1}^{N} r^j], \tag{7}$$

where the subscripts, i and j, designate members as they are ordered by rank in the speaking hierarchy, and r is the proportional change in speaking rate from one rank to the next.

The increment in speaking likelihood due to having spoken recently was given by an exponential decay function:

$$I_i = de^{-bt}, \tag{8}$$

where t is the number of turns since member i spoke, e is the base of the natural logarithm, and d and b are free parameters. The parameter d determines the immediate increment in speaking propensity due to having just spoken, and b determines how quickly the increment decays over subsequent turns if the member fails to speak again.

SPEAK is a computational model that generates a sequence of speaking turns. For each turn, SPEAK computes the probability of each member speaking (using

Equations 5 through 8) and samples a speaker at random using the resulting vector of probabilities.

In addition to the "raw" sequence of turns, SPEAK outputs the proportion of turns that simulated groups were in each of the four states defined by Parker's (1988) floor model and the relative frequencies of transitions among states. Stasser and Taylor (1991) found that the state and transition frequencies for simulated groups matched closely those observed in their six-person juries when the following parameter values were used: $r = .7$ in Equation 7; and $d = .79$ and $b = 1$ in Equation 8. Additionally, they competitively tested the full model with the foregoing parameter values (*Full* with unequal overall participation among members and variable participation across time for each member) with three special case models: (a) equal overall participation among members but variable participation across time (*Variable*), (b) unequal overall participation but constant participation across time (*Unequal*), and (c) equal participation distributed evenly across time (*Random*). Only the full model fit closely the observed state and transition frequencies. As Fig. 8.3 shows, submodels of SPEAK that assume equal participation among members or constant participation across time fail to produce the dominance of the floor state that was observed in the six-person juries.

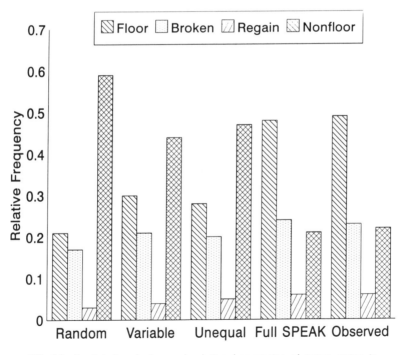

FIG. 8.3. Predicted and observed relative frequencies of group states in six-person juries. Data from Stasser and Taylor (1991).

Stasser and Taylor (1991) also found that the full SPEAK model with essentially the same parameter values as given previously was able to reproduce the state and transition frequencies that Parker (1988) observed in his four-person, conversational groups. The results for predicted and observed state frequencies are given in Fig. 8.4. This initial success raises the attractive possibility that the formulations in SPEAK may be nearly invariant over a range of group sizes and tasks. Parker's four-person groups were simply instructed to converse for an hour whereas Stasser and Taylor's six-person groups played the role of a jury in a criminal trial. Important common elements, however, were face-to-face discussion and the absence of any imposed structure or role assignment (e.g., assigned or elected leader). Thus, in both cases, we suspect that turn taking was governed by some mix of momentary fluctuations in psychological readiness to speak and generalized norms of interaction for minimally constrained conversation in small groups.

The selection of the decay function (Equation 8) to model transient readiness to speak was based primarily on mathematical tractability and fit to empirical data (e.g., see Fig. 2, p. 679, in Stasser & Taylor, 1991). Nonetheless, there is an interesting feature of the decay function. It predicts that the tendency to speak decreases by a constant ratio for each missed turn after the last speech, approaching a base-rate speaking propensity. This feature suggests the operation

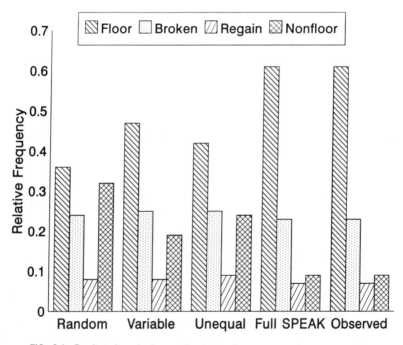

FIG. 8.4. Predicted and observed relative frequencies of group states in four-person conversational groups. Data from Stasser and Taylor (1991).

of something akin to the queue mechanism proposed by Horvath (1965) to explain the exponential function relating participation frequency to overall rank in participation. That is, speaking may momentarily move one up in the queue for the next turn, but each failure to take a subsequent turn may move one down a notch until the usual place in the queue is reached.

Whereas it is an interesting possibility that a queuing mechanism could account for both overall and momentary differences in speaking rates, we suspected that the requeuing process necessary to maintain the floor patterns in the data would disrupt the hierarchical patterns in overall participation. We do not know of any tractable mathematical way of representing the sequential requeuing process imposed on an overall queue. Thus, we resorted to computer simulation of the queue/requeue process. The queue/requeue simulation model was able to produce state frequencies similar to those observed in Parker's (1988) four-person and Stasser and Taylor's (1991) six-person groups but, in doing so, produced highly irregular patterns of overall participation rates. For example, successful production of the state frequencies for the six-person juries resulted in overall participation being concentrated among, and about equally distributed across, the top three participators. Thus, it seems unlikely that queuing alone can account for both the overall and the sequential patterns of turn taking.

Summary. Both Parker (1988) and Stasser and Taylor (1991) observed distinctive sequential patterns of speaking turns during unstructured, face-to-face discussion. In both cases, sequences that alternated between two members (floors) occurred more often than expected if members' contributions were spread evenly throughout discussion. Parker suggested that social norms that are sensitive to recent group history may guide the allocation and claiming of turns in a way that favors the establishment and maintenance of floors. Stasser and Taylor represented the turn-taking process as a competition for speaking time and proposed that individuals who are ready to speak are more likely to win the competition. Readiness to speak was viewed as a combination of stable (for the duration of the interaction) individual differences in speaking propensity and momentary increments in speaking readiness if one has recently spoken. However, Stasser and Taylor admitted that speaking readiness is probably not entirely due to covert psychological states but is also affected by the social management of speaking turns and by conversational conventions that maintain the topical coherence of discussion (see, e.g., Tracy, 1985).

Thus, there are no compelling conceptual or theoretical reasons to prefer one model over the other, and both models capture essentially the same sequential patterns that have been observed in the limited empirical record of sequential speaking turns during group discussion. However, from a modeling perspective, SPEAK offers some advantageous over Parker's (1988) group state model. First, it is more parsimonious in that SPEAK has three free parameters (r in Equation 7 and d and b in Equation 8) whereas the floor model has six free transition parameters. Second, SPEAK explicitly includes group size in its formulations whereas the floor model does not. Finally, SPEAK maintains the identity of members and can elaborate these identities by associating with speakers other attributes such as access to information, preferences, and certainty of opinion. Because of these features, SPEAK provides a vehicle for moving from representations of discussion process to questions about group product.

Group Decisions and Speaking Turns

We have identified two trademarks of unstructured, face-to-face discussion: unequal participation among members and variable participation across time for each member. In spite of the regularities that emerge when discussion is viewed from afar through the lens of formal models, unequal and variable participation can produce rather chaotic episodes. A low participator may speak frequently near the beginning of discussion and then fall silent (perhaps strangely silent to his peers) for the rest of discussion. In contrast, a high participator may frequently exchange turns with first one person and then another during the early and late stages of the interaction, but she may make no contributions to debates that occur between these flurries of activity. For any one group, the pattern of participation that emerges during discussion may have a substantial impact on the group's action. Early and frequent contributors are likely have a disproportionate amount of influence by winning early converts and by shaping the shared knowledge pool upon which group action is based (Hoffman, 1979; Kerr, 1981; Stasser & Taylor, 1991). Nonetheless, as one moves away from particular cases and considers how process relates to product at a more global level, such irregularities may simply appear to be random noise.

DISCUSS Model. In order to explore more systematically how, and under what conditions, speaking patterns may relate to group product, we built the SPEAK model into DISCUSS, a more general computer model of group decision making (Stasser, 1988). Figure 8.5 presents an abbreviated flow chart of this updated version of DISCUSS. Input to the model includes group size, the distribution of access to information among members, and a specification of a participation submodel. The participation submodels include the range of possibilities permitted by selecting parameter values in the SPEAK model (r, in Equation 7, and d and b, in Equation 8). Among these possibilities is a *random* model with equal probabilities of participation among members distributed equally across time (i.e., $r = 1$, in Equation 7, and $d = 0$ and $b = 0$, in Equation 8). DISCUSS also offers a *round-robin* participation model, which forces a highly regulated and egalitarian pattern of turn taking.

The information distribution input specifies who among the members has access to what information about the decision alternatives. Information about an alternative is represented as having directional valence ("−" and "+" denoting

DISCUSS MODEL

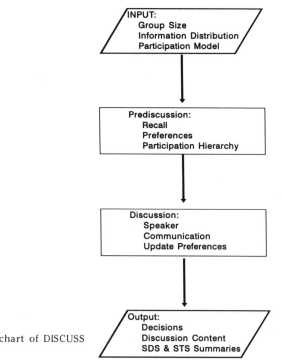

FIG. 8.5. Flow chart of DISCUSS model.

opposing and supporting information, respectively) and weight ("0" denoting irrelevant or neutral information and higher values indicating more importance or relevance).

The prediscussion phase involves members sampling items from the information pool to which they have access. Sampling and recall of information is presumed to be imperfect with a decreasing probability of permanently storing individual items as the size of the accessible information pool increases. Having formed the contents of members' memories, DISCUSS computes the prediscussion preferences by averaging the evaluative valences of the items recalled about each decision option; a member tentatively prefers the decision option with highest positive (or least negative) summary evaluation. During the prediscussion phase, DISCUSS also distributes members over the speaking hierarchy if the selected participation model specifies unequal overall participation (i.e., $r \neq 1$, in Equation 7). In the current version of DISCUSS, this assignment of members to ranks in the hierarchy can be random or based on the amount of retained information (i.e., members who know more at the onset of discussion tend to talk more).

Discussion is simulated as a cycle of speaker selections. Once a speaker is selected for a turn, the content of the speech is sampled from the speaker's permanent memory and other members reassess their preferences if the sampled item was not currently in their memory. Figure 8.6 gives a more detailed representation of the discussion phase. The discussion continues until a required consensus is reached (levels of required consensus can be varied as an input parameter) or until a stalemate is reached. Stalemate occurs if a consensus fails to emerge and a specified number of contiguous speakers are unable to add anything new to discussion (usually, this stalemate number equals group size although this choice can be changed as an input option).

DISCUSS also models different styles of discussion. A *nonadvocacy* model samples items at random from a speaker's memory whereas an *advocacy* model samples only items that do not oppose the speaker's current preference. That is, in the advocacy version, a speaker will not contribute an item that opposes his or her current preference or supports a currently nonpreferred option, but may contribute neutral items about any option. DISCUSS also permits graduations between these two extremes by biasing contributions in favor of preferred options but not excluding preference-inconsistent contributions. However, we consider only purely nonadvocacy or advocacy versions here.

The simulation of discussion forms the core of the DISCUSS model, and the succession of speakers generated by the selected participation model is the primary mechanism that controls the content of discussion and the emergence of a consensus. That is, the stream of speaking turns is the conduit through which available information is funneled and transformed into a group decision.

DISCUSSION PHASE

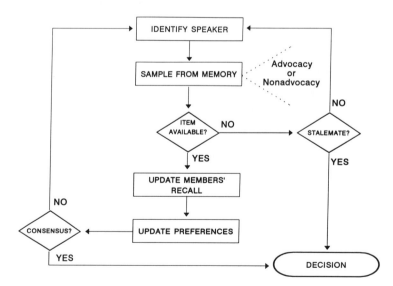

FIG. 8.6.   Expanded flow chart of discussion phase in DISCUSS.

Output includes group decisions, members' postdiscussion preferences, and the content of discussion (i.e., what items were discussed). Additionally, DIS-CUSS computes group-level summaries of process: Observed social decision scheme matrices give the relative frequencies of each decision for every distinguishable array of members' prediscussion preferences, and observed social transition schemes given the relative frequencies of transition among the possible alignments of preference from one speaking turn to the next (see Davis, 1973; Kerr, 1981; Stasser, Kerr, & Davis, 1989, for more detailed accounts of social decision and social transition schemes).

A Simulation Study. For the pattern of speaking turns to affect, systematically and substantially, the distribution of group decisions, two conditions seem to be necessary. First, at least some members must have access to different sets of information. If members were sampling from identical sets of information, it would seemingly matter little who talked more or when they talked. Second, individuals' participation rates would need to be related to other task-relevant characteristics of members such as preference or knowledge. For example, if some members knew more than others but speaking was unrelated to amount of knowledge, then groups would benefit when knowledgeable members were, by chance, high participators but other groups would suffer when the knowledgeable members happened to be low participators. Thus, in the long run, the distribution of group decisions produced by unequal participation would probably be barely distinguishable from those produced by equal participation models.

In order to explore the effect of participation patterns, we examined three participation models via DISCUSS simulations: random (equally likely participation by all members at all times), round-robin, and a full SPEAK version using the parameter estimates obtained from Stasser and Taylor (1991). Two variants of the SPEAK model were investigated: In one case, members were assigned to the speaking hierarchy at random and, in the other case, members who remembered more at the onset of discussion were ranked higher than members who remembered less. We also varied group size (4, 6, or 12), style of discussion (advocacy or nonadvocacy), and prediscussion access to information (all shared or hidden profile distribution).

We constructed a test decision task for which groups were to decide between two alternatives, A and B. There were 24 items of information pertaining to A: 12 were positive, 8 were neutral, and 4 were negative. There were also 24 items of information about B: 8 positive, 8 neutral, and 8 negative. Because all items of information were equally weighted, A was the better option due to its having more positive and fewer negative items than B. In the all-shared distribution, all group members had access to all 48 items before discussion. In the hidden profile condition (Stasser, 1988), only two of the members (an informed minority) had access to all information. The other members (an ill-informed majority) in the hidden profile case had access to a biased set of information before discussion. They could not access six of the positive items about A and six of the negative items about B. Because of this restricted access to the information pool, the ill-informed majority would tend to prefer B before discussion. Of interest was the degree to which the informed minority could prevail against the misled majority in the hidden profile conditions. Five hundred discussions were simulated in each of the conditions defined by the design of the study, and simulated discussions continued until a unanimous consensus emerged (or a stalemate occurred).

Two conclusions were clear. First, as we suspected, choice of participation model had little effect on the distribution of group decisions when all members had access to all information before discussion, and the results that are presented here are aggregated across models in the all-shared conditions. Second, when members' participation rates were not associated with the amount of information recalled before discussion, SPEAK predictions were nearly identical to the predictions for the equal participation (random) model regardless of group size or style of discussion. Therefore, we present only the results for the SPEAK model in which amount of information recalled determined the location of a member in the speaking hierarchy.

Figure 8.7 displays the distributions of group decisions (A, B, or H, where *H* denotes "hung" or stalemate) for simulated four-person groups. Four-person groups with the hidden profile distribution of information decided A more than

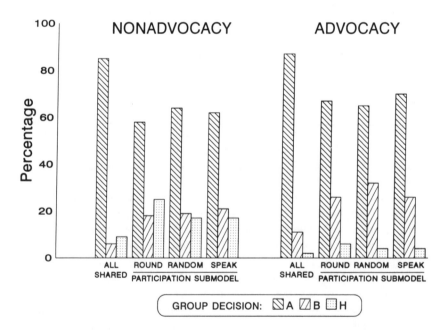

FIG. 8.7. Predicted distributions of decisions for four-person groups as a function of DISCUSS participation submodel.

60% of the time, and neither style of discussion (nonadvocacy vs. advocacy) nor participation model had much effect. We should note that the "informed minority" of two in these four-person groups was not really a numerical minority (i.e., two members had access to all information and two had restricted access). As a result, the two completely informed members were able to prevail more often than not over the two less-informed members regardless of the participation model.

For six-person groups (Fig. 8.8), the advocacy style resulted in the informed, two-person minority prevailing more often than did the nonadvocacy style, and the nonadvocacy style produced many stalemates. This pattern was particularly evident when speaking turns were determined by a round-robin procedure. Moreover, there was a trend for the minority to benefit from the unequal, intermittent pattern of participation simulated by the SPEAK model. This trend was most pronounced for nonadvocacy discussions.

These patterns were even more evident for 12-person groups (Fig. 8.9). For these larger groups, round-robin and nonadvocacy discussions produced very few A decisions when only a minority of two was fully informed. In contrast, the unequal, intermittent patterns of speaking generated by SPEAK produced nearly 50% A decisions under an advocacy style. These simulation results suggest that the most egalitarian, fair-minded model of discussion (nonadvocacy, round-robin) resulted in the fewest groups discovering the superiority of A when only a minority was fully informed.

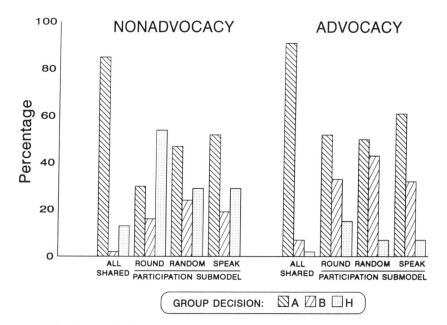

FIG. 8.8. Predicted distributions of decisions for six-person groups as a function of DISCUSS participation submodel.

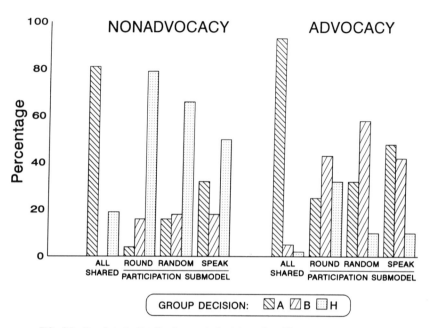

FIG. 8.9. Predicted distributions of decisions for 12-person groups as a function of DISCUSS participation submodel.

Summary. Under a wide range of conditions, the complex patterns of speaking generated by the full SPEAK model produced distributions of group decisions that were barely distinguishable from those produced by a random or round-robin model: small groups (namely, four-person), equal access to information (all shared), and speaking hierarchies that were unrelated to access to information. Under these conditions, the sequential patterns of speaking that characterize face-to-face, unstructured discussion were essentially background noise. However, the simulation study also identified noteworthy exceptions for which the assumptions about speaking patterns did matter. In particular, when a fully informed minority could potentially compensate for the ill-informed preferences of a majority, they were more successful when: participation rank was associated with the amount of information recalled at the onset of discussion, and members were advocates. These conclusions are contrary to the conventional wisdom that minority viewpoints are most likely to survive when equal participation and fair-minded discussion are encouraged. In none of our simulated conditions did a round-robin procedure or a nonadvocacy style facilitate the adoption of the minority position.

However, the conventional wisdom that minorities benefit from egalitarian procedures is probably not entirely wrong. From the vantage point of the DISCUSS model, it is easy to see how our results could have come out differently. The assumptions one makes about what drives participation rates are critical. For example, if proponents of the initially more popular position were more likely to talk, then minorities would likely not prevail under unequal participation models and may benefit from a round-robin procedure. Or, if participation were correlated with preference certainty rather than amount of information recalled, then the fully informed minorities might have enjoyed less of an advantage in constructing the participation hierarchies. Finally, our test case was constructed so that minorities had access to more information. One can imagine a case in which the minority has unique access to critical information that is necessary to identify a superior option but has access to less information overall than a majority. For this kind of case, participation rates driven by amount of knowledge would work against the airing of the critical information and, thus, against the group's using the information to reach a better informed decision. In summary, the answers to two critical questions are central to constructing realistic simulations of group decision making: How is access to informational resources distributed among a group's members, and how is this access related to participation, if at all?

A Theoretical Agenda

Formal models not only summarize efficiently and precisely what we think we know about a process, but their development and implementation also make us very aware of what we do not know (Abelson, 1968; Davis & Kerr, 1986; Ostrom, 1988; Stasser, 1990). What we know is that people who are engaged in unstructured, face-to-face discussion typically form a hierarchy of overall participation and alternate between periods of high and low activity. Additionally, who participates, and when and how often they participate, have important consequences for group productivity when access to task-relevant resources is related to patterns of participation. Finally, there is a growing body of empirical work that documents effects of participation that may go beyond any one episode of group interaction. Most notably, high participators are frequently granted leadership status by fellow group members (see Mullen, Salas, & Driskell, 1989, for a recent review).

What do we not know about participation in small-group discussions? Our review suggests that the most important unanswered questions are concerned with the factors that predict and the processes that mediate talking in groups. Some theorists have focused on social (interpersonal) variables and processes (e.g., Horvath, 1965; Parker, 1988) whereas others have emphasized psychological (cognitive and emotional) states (Leik, 1965; Stasser & Taylor, 1991). However, the dichotomy between social and psychological explanations is somewhat forced, and the most promising approach to understanding participation patterns is to consider how psychological and social processes meld to shape the flow of verbal interaction.

For example, it is tempting to view talkativeness as an enduring psychological trait that an individual carries from one group interaction to another. A characteristic level of talkativeness may be a derivative of other stable traits such as intelligence, verbal quickness (Horvath, 1965; Willard & Strodtbeck, 1972;), or social dominance (Rosa & Mazur, 1979). However, such stable personality characteristics and abilities are probably best viewed as a backdrop against which social interaction is staged. It seems more fruitful to consider proximal psychological variables that are, to some degree, situation specific and responsive to the social demands in a given group and interaction.

Work on status hierarchies in sociology provides one framework for understanding how speaking hierarchies might emerge during group discussion (Berger, Fisek, Norman, & Zelditch 1977; Fisek & Ofshe, 1970; Ridgeway, 1984; Skvoretz, 1988; Smith-Lovin, Skvoretz, & Hudson, 1986). For example, expectation states theory (Berger et al., 1977) proposes that members of a group develop shared expectations about one another's potential contributions to the realization of group goals. These expectations can be based on imported social characteristics (diffuse status cues: gender, age, occupation, etc.), prior experience, or emergent impressions derived from behaviors displayed early in the interaction. Once established, these shared performance expectations define a status hierarchy that controls allocation of valued commodities such as speaking time and influence.

Although expectation states theory does not elaborate in detail on the psychological and social mechanisms that underlie the establishment and maintenance of expectations and the accompanying status hierarchy, it has the appealing feature of representing hierarchies as an emergent aspect of a group's interaction. Some enduring traits may give one an advantage in the implicit negotiation of status in a group. However, the development of shared performance expectations may be responsive to cues that are quite specific to the current social and task environment. Additionally, this perspective emphasizes the importance of *shared* representations of members' performance capabilities. One's own self-perceptions can lead to assertive behavior, but, if self-perceptions are not congruent with others' perceptions, these behaviors may be rejected as valid claims to status (Ridgeway, 1984). Finally, expectation states theory allows for the possibility that expectations are multidetermined. Shared expectations can be based on an array of personal attributes: knowledge, confidence, personal investment in the group's task, and so forth. Moreover, the impact of such attributes may vary from situation to situation. For example, gender is viewed as a diffuse status characteristic in this tradition, and being female is presumed to be associated with lower status (see, e.g., Skvoretz, 1988). Nonetheless, the theory does not preclude that possibility that, for some kinds of tasks or groups, females may be granted higher status, have more influence, and receive more opportunities to participate (Dovidio, Brown, Heltman, Ellyson, & Keating, 1988; Eagly & Johnson, 1990). For these reasons, expectation states theory seems to provide a general conceptual framework for formulating more detailed and dynamic models of how individual, group, and environmental (task) factors combine to shape group interaction in general and to orchestrate speaking turns in particular (Hackman & Morris, 1975).

Whereas expectation states theory may provide some insights to how speaking hierarchies are established and maintained, it does not directly address a fundamental question posed by our DISCUSS simulation. Namely, how is access to informational resources related to participation, if at all? Moreover, the empirical literature addressing such a question is sparse. We suggest several suppositions as seed for future modeling and empirical efforts. The first supposition is that members who know more participate more. The second supposition is a variant of the first: Members who *think* that they know more than others participate more. Whereas knowing more provides the fuel to sustain high participation, the perception that one knows more may provide the motivation to participate (e.g., by making one's efforts seem indispensable to the group endeavor; Kerr & Bruun, 1983; Williams & Karau, 1991). A third supposition is that certainty of preference leads to more participation (Hastie, 1986; Hinsz, 1990; Sniezek, 1992). If so, members who have information that predominantly favors one decision alternative over others would participate more. A fourth, and overarching supposition, is that the relationship between access to informational resources and participation is stronger if tasks are viewed as intellective rather than judgmental (Laughlin & Ellis, 1986; Stasser & Stewart, 1991). That is, to the degree that discussants expect that information will lead to a defensibly correct (or superior) answer, their propensity to participate may be driven by their perceptions of being relatively knowledgeable and certain. Surprisingly, we know of no direct empirical evidence that addresses the foregoing suppositions about relationships among prior access to information, perceptions of task demands, and participation rates.

We have suggested that expectation states theory provides a general framework for formulating ideas about how participation hierarchies form. However, this framework does not offer as much promise for understanding sequential patterns of participation (Dabbs & Ruback, 1987; Parker, 1988; Stasser & Taylor, 1991). Whereas a status hierarchy may be malleable in the early stages of interaction, it is viewed as almost immutable once it is established. At the moment, we are inclined to entertain the possibility that the mechanisms that establish speaking hierarchies are quite different in nature than those that govern the moment-to-moment changes in speaking likelihood. Stasser and Taylor observed that increments in speaking likelihood stemming from recent participation appeared to be unrelated to one's overall speaking rate. Similarly, the rate of decay in speaking likelihood over missed turns was similar for both high and low participators. One possibility is that a speaking (or status) hierarchy provides a speaking queue as envisioned by Horvath (1965), but that context-specific rules of interaction (Parker, 1988) and transient psychological states (Stasser & Taylor, 1991) determine the likelihood that a member will claim a turn when it is available.

Models of speaking in social and performance groups have produced a rich array of ideas about the nature of group interaction. Nonetheless, existing models have barely begun to articulate fully the social and psychological mechanisms that orchestrate the sequence of speaking turns during unstructured, face-to-face interactions. This microcosm of social behavior may be as challenging to model as are the dynamical systems of societal evolution, planetary movement, and weather.

ACKNOWLEDGMENTS

This work was supported partly by National Science Foundation Grant SBR-9410584 and partly by Office of Naval Research Grant N00012-90-J-1790 to the first author.

REFERENCES

Abelson, R. P. (1968). Simulation and social behavior. In G. Lindzey & E. Aronson (Eds.), *Handbook of social psychology* (Vol. 2, pp. 274–356). Reading, MA: Addison-Wesley.

Baker, P. (1984). Seeing is behaving: Visibility and participation in small groups. *Environment and Behavior, 16*, 159–184.

Bales, R. F. (1950). *Interaction process analysis*. Cambridge, MA: Addison-Wesley.

Bales, R. F. (1953). The equilibrium problem in small groups. In T. Parsons, R. F. Bales, & E. A. Shils (Eds.), *Working papers in the theory of action* (pp. 444–476). Glencoe, IL: The Free Press.

Bales, R. F., Strodtbeck, F. L., Mills, T. M., & Roseborough, M. E. (1951). Channels of communication in small groups. *American Sociological Review, 16*, 461–468.

Balkwell, J. (1991). From expectations to behavior: An improved postulate for expectation states theory. *American Sociological Review, 56*, 355–369.

Berger, J., Conner, T. L., & Fisek, M. H. (1974). *Expectation states theory: A theoretical research program*. Cambridge, MA: Winthrop.

Berger, J., Fisek, M. H., Norman, R. Z., & Zelditch, M., Jr. (1977). *Status characteristics and social interaction: An expectation states approach*. New York: Elsevier.

Burke, P. (1974). Participation and leadership in small groups. *American Sociological Review, 39*, 832–843.

Coleman, J. (1960). The mathematical study of small groups. In H. Solomon (Ed.), *Mathematical thinking in the measurement of behavior* (pp. 1–149). Glencoe, IL: The Free Press.

Dabbs, J. M., Jr., & Ruback, R. B. (1987). Dimensions of group process: Amount and structure of vocal interaction. In L. Berkowitz (Ed.), *Advances in experimental social psychology* (Vol. 20, pp. 123–169). San Diego: Academic Press.

Davis, J. H. (1973). Group decisions and social interaction: A theory of social decision schemes. *Psychological Review, 80*, 97–125.

Davis, J. H., & Kerr, N. L. (1986). Thought experiments and the problem of sparse data in small group research. In P. Goodman (Ed.), *Designing effective work groups* (pp. 305–349). San Francisco: Jossey-Bass.

Dovidio, J. F., Brown, C. E., Heltman, K., Ellyson, S. L., & Keating, C. F. (1988). Power displays between women and men in discussions of gender-linked tasks: A multichannel study. *Journal of Personality and Social Psychology, 55*, 580–587.

Duncan, S. (1972). Some signals and rules for taking speaking turns in conversation. *Journal of Personality and Social Psychology, 23*, 283–292.

Duncan, S. D., & Fiske, D. W. (1977). *Face-to-Face Interaction.* Hillsdale, NJ: Lawrence Erlbaum Associates.

Eagly, A. H., & Johnson, B. T. (1990). Gender and leadership style: A meta-analysis. *Psychological Bulletin, 108*, 233–256.

Fisek, M., Berger, J., & Norman, R. (1991). Participation in heterogeneous and homogeneous groups: A theoretical integration. *American Journal of Sociology, 97*, 114–142.

Fisek, M., & Ofshe, R. (1970). The process of status evolution. *Sociometry, 33*, 327–346.

Goetsch, G., & McFarland, D. (1980). Models of the distribution of acts in small discussion groups. *Social Psychological Quarterly, 43*, 173–183.

Hackman, J. R., & Morris, C. G. (1975). Group tasks, group interaction process, and group performance effectiveness: A review and proposed integration. In L. Berkowitz (Ed.), *Advances in experimental social psychology* (Vol. 8, pp. 45–59). New York: Academic Press.

Hastie, R. (1986). Experimental evidence on group accuracy. In B. Grofman & G. Owen (Eds.), *Information pooling and group decision making* (pp. 129–157). Greenwich, CT: JAI.

Hinsz, V. B. (1990). Cognitive and consensus processes in group recognition memory performance. *Journal of Personality and Social Psychology, 59*, 705–718.

Hoffman, R. L. (Ed.). (1979). *The group problem solving process: Studies of a valence model.* New York: Praeger.

Horvath, W. (1965). A mathematical model of participation in small group discussions. *Behavioral Science, 10*, 164–166.

Horvath, W. (1965). Comment on the paper by Kadane, Lewis, and Ramage "Horvath's theory of participation in group discussions." *Sociometry, 32*, 362–364.

Kadane, J. B., & Lewis, G. H. (1969). The distribution of participation in group discussions: An empirical and theoretical reappraisal. *American Sociological Review, 34*, 710–723.

Kadane, J. B., Lewis, G. H., & Ramage, J. G. (1969). Horvath's theory of participation in group discussions. *Sociometry, 32*, 348–361.

Kerr, N. L. (1981). Social transition schemes: Charting the road the agreement. *Journal of Personality and Social Psychology, 41*, 684–702.

Kerr, N. L., & Bruun, S. E. (1983). The dispensability of member effort and group motivation losses: Free-rider effects. *Journal of Personality and Social Psychology, 44*, 78–94.

Laughlin, P. R., & Ellis, A. L. (1986). Demonstrability and social combination processes on mathematical intellective tasks. *Journal of Experimental Social Psychology, 22*, 177–189.

Leik, R. K. (1965). Type of group and the probability of initiating acts. *Sociometry, 28*, 57–65.

Leik, R. K. (1967). The distribution of acts in small groups. *Sociometry, 30*, 280–299.

Leik, R. K. (1969). Comment on Kadane and Lewis. *American Sociological Review, 34*, 723–724.

Lowry, R. (1989). *The architecture of chance.* New York: Oxford University Press.

Mullen, B., Salas, E., & Driskell, J. E. (1987). Salience, motivation, and artifact as contributions to the relationship between participation rate and leadership. *Journal of Experimental Social Psychology, 25*, 545–559.

Ostrom, T. M. (1988). Computer simulation: The third symbol system. *Journal of Experimental Social Psychology, 24*, 381–392.

Parker, K. (1988). Speaking turns in small group interaction: A context-sensitive event sequence model. *Journal of Personality and Social Psychology, 54*, 965–971.

Ridgeway, C. L. (1984). Dominance, performance and status in groups: A theoretical analysis. In E. J. Lawler (Ed.), *Advances in group processes* (Vol. 1, pp. 59–93). Greenwich, CT: JAI.

Rosa, E., & Mazur, A. (1979). Incipient status in small groups. *Social Forces, 58*, 12–37.

Skvoretz, J. (1988). Models of participation in status-differentiated groups. *Social Psychology Quarterly, 51*, 43–57.

Smith-Lovin, L., Skvoretz, J. V., & Hudson, C. G. (1986). Status and participation in six-person groups: A test of Skvoretz's comparative status model. *Social Forces, 64*, 992–1005.

Sniezek, J. A. (1992). Groups under uncertainty: An examination of confidence in group decision making. *Organizational Behavior and Human Decision Processes, 52*, 124–155.

Stasser, G. (1988). Computer simulation as a research tool: The DISCUSS model of group decision making. *Journal of Personality and Social Psychology, 24*, 393–422.

Stasser, G. (1990). Computer simulation of social interaction. In C. Hendrick & M. S. Clark (Eds.), *Review of personalty and social psychology: Research methods in personality and social psychology* (Vol. 11, pp. 120–141). Beverly Hills, CA: Sage.

Stasser, G., Kerr, N. L., & Davis, J. H. (1989). Models of influence in decision-making groups. In P. B. Paulus (Ed.), *Psychology of group influence* (2nd ed., pp. 279–326). Hillsdale, NJ: Lawrence Erlbaum Associates.

Stasser, G., & Stewart, D. (1992). The discovery of hidden profiles by decision-making groups: Solving a problem versus making a judgment. *Journal of Personality and Social Psychology, 63*, 426–434.

Stasser, G., & Taylor, L. (1991). Speaking turns in face-to-face discussions. *Journal of Personality and Social Psychology, 60*, 675–684.

Steinzor, B. (1950). The spatial factor in face-to-face discussion groups. *Journal of Abnormal Social Psychology, 45*, 552–555.

Stephan, F. F. (1952). The relative rate of communication between members of small groups. *American Sociological Review, 17*, 482–486.

Stephan, F. F., & Mishler, E. G. (1952). The distribution of participation in small groups: An exponential approximation. *American Sociological Review, 17*, 598–608.

Tracy, K. (1985). Conversational coherence: A cognitively grounded rules approach. In R. L. Street, Jr., & J. N. Cappella (Eds.), *Sequence and pattern in communicative behavior* (pp. 30–49). London: Edward Arnold.

Watson, D. (1971). Reinforcement theory of personality and social systems: Dominance and position in a group power structure. *Journal of Personality and Social Psychology, 20*, 180–185.

Willard, D., & Strodtbeck, F. (1972). Latency of verbal response and participation in small groups. *Sociometry, 35*, 161–175.

Williams, K. D., & Karau, S. J. (1991). Social loafing and social compensation: The effects of expectancy and co-worker performance. *Journal of Personality and Social Psychology, 61*, 570–581.

9

STRENGTH FROM WEAKNESS: THE FATE OF OPINION MINORITIES IN SPATIALLY DISTRIBUTED GROUPS

Bibb Latané
Florida Atlantic University

Minority influence theory has become remarkably popular over the past 15 years in part because it solves the seeming contradiction of social psychology by history. I argue that the concept of minority influence is muddled and prejudicial in its terminology, and propose the language of social impact theory as a substitute for expressing core hypotheses for the paradox of strength from weakness. I use this language to describe six ways in which minorities can gain such strength, including procedural effects and changes in actors' behavior, as well as through observers' attributions. In addition, I show that majorities in faction-size models necessarily include more distant and therefore less influential members; natural selection will weed out weaker minority members; and the very power of majorities may lead them to persist in outdated positions, allowing minorities to have truth on their side. Finally, I present recent computer simulations of dynamic social impact to show that self-limiting properties of influence in self-organizing social systems can protect the diversity of opinion through the formation of local clusters, eliminating the so-called contradiction by history of social psychology. This language and approach, faithful to Moscovici's original insights, provides new techniques for understanding the negotiation of social reality.

Over the past 15 years, a powerful idea has captured the attention of social psychologists—first in Europe, and now in the rest of the world. Since 1976, Serge Moscovici has personally shown how much influence a single individual can have by imposing a new idea, *minority influence,* on the consciousness of our discipline (Moscovici, 1976, 1980, 1985). With a growing number of colleagues and collaborators, he has opened our eyes to a variety of new and paradoxical phenomena that seem to show that when it comes to social influence, there can be strength from weakness, thereby challenging the foundational assumptions of social psychology. The phrase minority influence has become pervasive in the attitude change literature, framing the way we talk and think about these fascinating questions and stimulating a recent outpouring of summaries, extensions, reviews, and critiques (e.g., Kruglanski & Mackie, 1990; Levine & Russo, 1987; Maass, West, & Cialdini, 1987; Mugny & Perez, 1991).

WHY IS THE MINORITY INFLUENCE CONCEPT SO APPEALING?

Although a number of empirical studies show minority influence effects, the results have often proved difficult to replicate, confusing, and/or interpretable in more conventional theoretical terms (Turner, 1991). I do not here review the provocative but controversial theoretical and empirical arguments for and against this concept, but merely cite three powerful (if not entirely legitimate) reasons why people may believe in minority influence.

Wishful Thinking. Social scientists, European and American both, have a soft spot in their heart for minorities. In addition to a general tendency to root for the underdog, many of us are members of ethnic minorities and virtually all of us, as academic social scientists who live in a world that undervalues what we do and in a discipline that overvalues originality, are members of opinion minorities. As a result, I suspect, all of us would like to think of minorities as special, perhaps even as heroic, and certainly as ultimately correct.

Personal Experience. A second source of our faith in minorities comes from personal experience, which tells us that we can individually receive more attention arguing for a new rather than an old idea, for an unpopular rather than a popular view, on the side of the few rather than the many, for change rather than the status quo. Granted, some of this attention may be negative, but it gives us the impression that we are having an effect. This impression may not be just an illusion—social impact theory (Latané, 1981) tells us that we have individually more influence as a member of a minority than when part of the majority. This phenomenon results from the marginally decreasing impact of additional members of a group (influence often seems to grow as the square root of the number of people involved) so that the larger the group, the less influential any additional member will be. Thus, we may confuse our greater impact as an individual for a greater total impact of our smaller group. Of course, as with the previous argument, this is not a good reason for assuming special potency for minority influence.

Evidence From History. Perhaps the most compelling reason for belief in the concept of minority influence has been that minorities in the real world persist and occasionally even prevail, despite the common social psychological intuition that simple theories of social influence predict convergence on a common opinion. Moscovici and his collaborators have been entirely correct in claiming that conventional theory in its simplest forms was sometimes taken as inevitably leading to majority domination. And they have been effective in pointing out the contradiction with history, which often shows the submission of stasis to change, of orthodoxy to dissent. Only by positing special powers for minorities, they have claimed, can we resolve this contradiction.

I show in this chapter that the idea that social influence should inevitably lead to consensus is incorrect. There is no problem in explaining the persistence of minorities with conventional social psychological theory if we assume nonlinear attitude change, recognize the spatial distribution of people, and examine the dynamic consequences of their influence on each other.

WHAT IS WRONG WITH THE TERM MINORITY INFLUENCE?

Although more than 15 years of research on minority influence has led to its establishment as a bona fide scientific orthodoxy, I believe its terminology is fundamentally flawed and needs to be restated, if not replaced. Although many of the theoretical ideas associated with the idea of minority influence are excellent and the issues are certainly central to social psychology, I believe the term itself to be flawed and misleading—leading to muddled, prejudicial thinking and deficient research designs.

It Is Muddled. Some of the confusion comes from alternative uses of the term *minority* in lay language. People who by choice or by force maintain strong racial and ethnic identities and elites with the privileges of great ability, wealth, or specialized education are, in fact as well as by definition, in the minority. Neither of these common forms of minority, it seems, is what is meant by *minority influence,* but several other things are. Most of the confusion comes from the fact that researchers lump seemingly quite different phenomena under the same label. For example, in different studies from the same research tradition, majorities have been operationalized as: (a) the numerically larger faction in a small fixed-size group (in this research tradition, the small ad hoc group is often taken as a metaphor for society at large), (b) a powerful, advantaged ingroup (such as a ruling elite), (c) a single expert versus a militant group (e.g., the teacher in an art appreciation class has been called part of the majority, whereas the mass of students is considered the minority), (d) the orthodox, conventional, normative status quo or zeitgeist, and (e) the prevailing attitude in an unspecified population.

These differing operationalizations lead to inconsistent and confusing results. Each of them seems to carry major conceptual difficulties. For example, a common paradigm for studying minority influence is to accompany a statement with information that either 12% or 88% of respondents to a national survey endorse it (e.g., Papastamou, 1990). When does a minority become a majority? If 12% is a minority and 88% a majority, what is 38%? Minority influence researchers seem unable to produce a clear answer, much less a consensus. Thirty-eight percent is too large a group to enjoy the advantages imputed to minorities, too small to be a majority, and the theory, couched in the minority–majority dichotomy, does not seem to have any place for alternatives.

If we hear "12% of Americans like to eat fried chicken" we are likely to think "How few!" When told "12% of Americans like to eat fried cockroaches" our reaction is likely to be astonishment at "So many?" Tying the concept of majority–minority to simple numbers is arbitrary and incomplete. Is it realistic to assume that students will find it credible that as many as 88% of a population will agree on any new issue? Is this equally plausible as the assertion that only 12% agree? The symmetry between 12% and 88% is only superficial, masking the fact that on most issues there is no real majority, but simply several minorities who hold real positions and a large number of people who do not care.

Part of the problem here is that we do not yet have a good theory of how information about the distribution of opinions on a topic is received, encoded, and retrieved. Is it actual size or perceived size that determines minority–majority status, and if the latter, whose perceptions count? Unfortunately, the language of minority influence theory does not seem suited to providing answers to these questions.

Similar conceptual uncertainties can be raised with respect to each of the other operationalizations of minority influence. As I expand later, confounding strength and number is at the root of many of the conceptual difficulties with the concept of minority influence. Although both the lack of power and the lack of numbers are aspects of weakness, they may have very different consequences and should not be conflated.

If there is a core meaning to these differing kinds of minority, it would seem to be their common ability to wrest advantage from disadvantage, influence from powerlessness, strength from weakness. If this is the intended core meaning, however, it would be better to revise our terminology to say so.

These uncertainties document the degree to which the concept of minority is muddled. The lack of clear meaning is not the only problem, however. Even worse, the concept prejudges unresolved issues.

The Term Is Prejudicial. It seems to assume that the critical aspect of social influence is the relative balance of proponents and opponents of a point of view. There is at least as much reason to believe that often the absolute number of each is the important thing. It is a categorical term—the very concept implies a two-faction system in which the minority is the counterpoint of the majority as figure is to ground. Such cases do exist in the world, but they by no means predominate. The concept has little room for situations when there is no majority and many minorities, and when most people have neither an opinion nor any knowledge about a topic. It has an inherent problem with respect to the issue of reference point—the majority with respect to one population (say, university students) is a minority with respect to a larger population (say, Greek citizens). Almost every conceivable group or identity becomes a minority when viewed in the context of the whole world.

To a university student seeking meaning and identity and aspiring to be a member of an intellectual, financial, or moral elite, what is the appropriate reference group for which one would like to know the majority opinion? Is it Greek students, all students, all Greeks, all people? The answer probably depends on the issue and the person, among other things, but unless we have a theoretical basis for how people identify relevant comparison groups, the issue of minority versus majority is misleading and premature.

Social influence may sometimes be determined primarily by the balance of categorical factions espousing different positions. Indeed, Davis' (chapter 3 of this volume) SDS model is explicitly based on this assumption. Often, however, the boundaries between factions are not clearly drawn and people know only what their neighbors think, lacking global information about the popularity of various positions. In such cases the minority–majority distinction becomes particularly problematic. We should not prejudge the question of how people represent differences of opinion by using a theoretical language that admits of no possibility other than a faction-size account.

It Leads to Deficient Research Designs. There is an overreliance on two-by-two designs pitting majority against minority rather than on more complex parametric designs in which the number and strength of one or more factions are varied continuously and independently. Generally, in both small- and large-group applications, the number of supporters and the number of opponents are confounded with each other, often with other characteristics as well. There is an artificially imposed inverse relation between the size of the majority and the size of the minority, which makes it impossible to disentangle the independent effects of either. A richer theoretical language might encourage more representative and fruitful experimental designs.

SOCIAL IMPACT THEORY AS A LANGUAGE FOR DESCRIBING MINORITY INFLUENCE EFFECTS

If the language of minority influence is to be regarded as flawed and ready for retirement, with what shall we replace it? I suggest that the language of social impact theory (Latané, 1981) provides a better alternative for stating hypotheses and describing results.

Social impact theory was conceived as a meta-theory, incorporating the whole body of already identified and yet-to-be-discovered processes whereby people influence one another. Often characterized erroneously as a single-process theory in contrast to Moscovici's dual-process model, Kelman's three-process theory, or Raven's six-process categorization, social impact theory recognizes the existence of a multitude of influence processes, ranging from imitation to conformity. For example, the principles can be applied to such diverse social influence processes as coercion, in which threat or actual physical force is used to obtain compliance, persuasion, in which facts and logical argumentation are marshaled to reorient thinking, contagion, in which simply seeing other people engage in a forbidden behavior may reduce restraints against acting similarly, and obedience, in which individuals subject themselves to authorities.

As a theoretical language, social impact theory distinguishes sources from targets of influence, and identifies three critical aspects of the sources—their *strength,* their *immediacy,* and their *number.* Strength can be taken as referring to the net power, status, expertise, commitment, and so forth, of the sources, immediacy to their closeness in space or time, visual as well as vocal contact, and so on, and number simply to how many individuals are the source of impact. As a theory, I claimed that whichever specific social processes are operating, the impact of a group of people on an individual will generally be a multiplicative function of their strength, immediacy, and number. Further, I specified that with respect to number, a power function should hold, such that there is a decreasing marginal effect of additional people, with total impact being proportional to the square root of the number of people present (Latané, 1981).

Social impact theory represents a summary and integration of much of what we know about social influence, including common sense, lab lore, and well-established empirical results, and is not intended to be in any way counterintuitive or controversial. I believe the theory, in identifying critical dimensions of social influence and their relations, has an almost Kantian necessity about it.

Social impact theory has been applied to such domains as evaluation apprehension (Latané & Harkins, 1976) and obedience (Brown, 1985) and explicitly to problems of majority and minority influence (Latané & Wolf, 1981; Wolf, 1985, 1987; Wolf & Latané, 1983). On balance, empirical research has been favorable, although there is a paucity of research on some aspects of the theory (Jackson, 1986; Mullen, 1985). Here, however, the issue is not the correctness of the theory (e.g., whether multiplicative power functions predominate) but the utility of its language for describing "strength from weakness" effects. I believe the language provides a richer and more precise way of exploring the possibility of strength from weakness than does the minority–majority phraseology.

This theoretical language is compatible with the basic ideas of minority influence—but allows its hypotheses and findings to be stated more clearly. As a meta-theory, it specifically allows for a variety of social influence processes, although it does not itself address the mechanisms that lead to each. Thus, one can use the language to describe both normative and informational influence, social comparison and validation, compliance and conversion, as well as contagion, diffusion of responsibility, evaluation apprehension, imitation, and so forth.

In each case, some aspect(s) of the *strength* of the source(s) of influence can be identified as relevant. However, the specific aspect may differ according to the type of influence. Thus, for informational influence, strength may consist of expertise. If the question at issue is the relative popularity of Bach or the Beatles in their lifetimes, a college student may be more influenced by a professor of music history than by a classmate, but this will not be the case if the question is which kind of music is more fun to listen to. For normative influence, the relevant dimension of strength may often be attractiveness or similarity to self. Thus in deciding what kinds of clothes are "cool," an adolescent is more likely to be influenced by another teen than an adult.

Some aspects of strength are more or less absolute. They derive from enduring characteristics of the source—his or her expertise, attractiveness, intelligence, education, energy. One interesting enduring characteristic may be handicap or dependency, which may confer sympathy or credibility on some issues due to "knowing what it's like." This is a special case of strength from weakness. Other aspects of strength may be contingent on the position taken. Thus a source arguing against her vested interest may be seen as more trustworthy than one arguing for, and a person taking an unpopular position may be seen as more courageous than one who argues for the obvious. Still other aspects of strength are affected by the relationship of the source to the target. Thus, we may be more likely to comply with our friends than with strangers, more likely to pay attention to our own mother than someone else's, more likely to obey our employer than the head of another department.

The strength of a source may be a function of the intensity of his attitude or her commitment to a position, affecting the degree to which he or she devotes energy or other resources to advocating the point of view. People who are unusually high in any given strength attribute are in the minority—an elite minority to be sure. One problem with the language of minority influence is that it confuses the number and status of people who hold a position. Different theoreticians and researchers may have different ideas as to what constitutes strength in a given application, and the theoretical language I propose provides a good framework for stating them.

Immediacy means closeness in space or time, or lack of intervening filters or barriers to influence. According to social impact theory, people are positioned in a social space largely determined by the physical locations where they live and work, and distances between people in this space greatly affect the degree of influence they have on each other. Immediacy is the forgotten factor in most studies of social influence. As we see later, distance (the inverse of immediacy) protects minorities from being overwhelmed and allows them to form spatially coherent clusters.

Immediacy does not itself mean "psychological closeness," which instead seems to refer to some combination of strength and immediacy. I suspect that one of the major reasons for the failure of sociometry to provide good maps of social life is its tendency to confound these attributes.

Number refers to how many sources of influence there are. A major problem with the minority influence concept is that it has conceptually confounded the number of sources with their strength. As we see later, there may be some theoretical and empirical reasons to think that numerically disadvantaged groups may gain some strength from their situation, but it is important to describe these phenomena in clear and theoretically neutral terms. To do so it is necessary to distinguish strength from number.

Sometimes information as to the number of people who favor a position arrives all at once, as when we are told that 50 million Frenchmen favor Brand X (absolute), or that 12% of Greeks want to ban smoking in the workplace (relative). Sometimes, however, it comes in sequentially, as when day by day on our travels in France we observe which brands Frenchmen actually do smoke, or talk with friends and acquaintances about passive exposure to other people's smoke. The former case represents immediate global information about the factions existing in the system as a whole, the latter an accumulation of local information about our own particular region of social space. As we see later, different models may be necessary to account for these different cases.

Strength, immediacy, and number are conceptually independent aspects of influence. However, there are some interesting connections among them that may develop in practice in the real world:

1. *Immediacy and number:* The physical geometry of the world we live in imposes the constraint that only a certain number of people can fit within any given distance. Furthermore, given the largely two-dimensional character of social space (imposed by the predominantly two-dimensional surface of the earth), the number of people within a given distance from us grows as the square of that distance.

2. *Immediacy and strength:* A major source of relational strength may be shared experiences in the past, present, and/or future—and the possibility of these is certainly a function of past, present, or future immediacy.

3. *Strength and number:* Especially interesting in the present context are ways in which the strength of a given source of impact may be affected by the number of sources. The next section introduces three such ways that have been studied in the literature, and I conclude this chapter by adding three more. Each of these processes may lead members of numerically disadvantaged minorities to be individually more influential, and can be taken as explanations for strength from weakness.

In summary, let me state some advantages of social impact theory as a language: It clearly differentiates sources and targets of influence. It allows us to distinguish influence from one's own and from other groups(s). It can be applied to both simultaneous and cumulative influence situations and to cases where global or only local information is available. It unconfounds conceptually distinct attributes of influence—the strength, immediacy, and number of sources. And, as I show later, it provides a useful framework for describing at least six different ways in which members of numerical minorities may gain disproportionate strength.

Social impact theory is a conventional theory, more easily damned for being trite and obvious than for being incorrect (although it certainly has the potential to be so proven). Whether or not it is right, it provides some conceptual distinctions that are greatly needed in talking about phenomena involving the numbers of people advocating a position, relative faction size, power, and influence.

The language of minority influence has ignored the useful and important dimension of immediacy and confounded strength with number. It does not deal satisfactorily with the issue of what reference population should be used to determine whether someone is in a majority or minority. It has prejudged the unsettled questions of when global, faction-size versus local, cumulative influence models apply, whether relative or absolute numbers of people are more important, and what are the relevant reference populations. I believe work in this important area could progress much more rapidly with the help of a clearer language. Social impact theory provides that language.

SOME EXPLANATIONS FOR STRENGTH FROM WEAKNESS

How does social impact theory deal with so-called minority influence? Clearly through the concept of strength. Recasting minority influence hypotheses in terms of social impact theory, we can say that being a member of a numerical or disadvantaged minority can, under certain circumstances, give you higher strength than being a member of a majority, particularly with respect to certain kinds of influence (e.g., validational vs. comparative). The language allows us to distinguish three general ways to explain cases where there seems to be a paradoxical strength in weakness (I add three more at the conclusion of this chapter):

Effects on Observers. The currently most popular explanation for the hypothesis of disproportionate minority influence is that onlookers are especially impressed by the courage, consistency, and conviction of the minority faction and led unconsciously to emulate their thinking style or adopt their perceptual frame, even if not consciously to adopt their conclusions. In this category I place all the hypothesized attributions to deviates of courage, inside knowledge, and so on, that have been suggested by workers in this field (e.g., Nemeth & Wachtler, 1974). According to this class of explanation, the behaviors of the actors are not affected by their minority status, but the interpretations placed on those behaviors by their observers are.

Effects on Actors. Of course, members of minorities may be led by their situation to advance different arguments and adopt different influence strategies than majority members. In particular, they may need to concentrate on novel arguments or attempt to reframe the question if they are to have any influence, and this strategic necessity may lead to a greater ability to open people's eyes to new possibilities. In addition, Levine and Russo (1990) suggested that members of a minority may have extra motivation—worrying about the effects of their deviant status and compensating by trying to appear more confident, be more ingratiating, and/or use better arguments.

In general, people who espouse an unpopular position may act differently than those who defend the status quo. Because there is less diffusion of responsibility, they may prepare more thoroughly than members of the larger group, and thus have better arguments. Having fewer others to coordinate their arguments with, they may have more opportunities to tailor them to the occasion, and thus be more convincing. There may be less chance of internal conflict within the group, which would distract attention and reduce effectiveness. These examples show ways in which being a member of a numerically disadvantaged group can motivate or allow actors to exert greater influence, thus adding to their strength. Strength becomes an achieved attribute of the influence source rather than one ascribed by observers.

Procedural Effects. In both formal and informal groups, the minority may have better access to the floor than the majority. In informal groups, there is more communication to deviates, at least at first, as they seem to have something different to say (Schachter, 1951). Formal groups often cannot wrap up their work until minority views have been disposed of. Equal time rules on TV exemplify the concern for fairness and open-mindedness that may drive these phenomena. These procedural effects mean that minority views often receive disproportionately more time and attention than majority views and add to the strength of the numerically disadvantaged minority. Procedural effects may not be psychologically glamorous, but they are often remarkably powerful (Davis, Hulbert, & Au, in press).

In some sense, all of the processes just described may be considered artifactual—the effects of minority status are in each case mediated by some other, more fundamental variable. Instead, I believe they all may represent the way things are organized in the real world. They all represent hypotheses as to how being a deviate may confer strength on otherwise powerless or isolated individuals or groups.

Each of these hypotheses is cast in the framework of social impact theory. They increase our confidence in the power of the theoretical language to describe a variety of sometimes subtle phenomena. Specific ideas as to the differing sources of strength for different social influence processes (i.e., conversion vs. compliance, persuasion vs. contagion, etc.) can easily be expressed in this language.

IS THE GROUP AN ADEQUATE METAPHOR FOR SOCIETY?

Each of these hypotheses is well suited to the prevailing metaphor for society as operating like a small ad hoc group. However, that metaphor, although it has proven very useful to minority influence researchers, may be limiting and ultimately misleading. The metaphor is appealing precisely because it avoids some of the complications of considering that within a larger society, people are members of more than one group, the boundaries of a group from the vantage point of one person may differ from those as seen by another, and there is a flow of people in and out of groups. Unlike the social networks and complex interconnections of the larger society, small ad hoc groups are bounded and fixed in size. Everybody in such a group is equidistant from each other and usually has equal access to the same information.

We need some way of representing the more continuous and variable field of social forces as they exist in social life. We need some way of representing the space in which social interaction takes place. With few exceptions (e.g., electronic networks), almost all social groups have a spatial structure that mediates the flow of influence in them. Even in small face-to-face groups, one sits closer to some people than others, and as we consider society in larger and larger scale, space takes on increasing importance. Both theory (Latané & Liu, in press) and empirical data (Latané, Liu, Nowak, Bonevento, & Zheng, 1995) suggest that social space has a two-dimensional character, with influence decreasing as a function of the square of the distance. As I show later, it is this spatial structure that permits opinion minorities to survive—through the process of clustering they can protect themselves from the global majority by creating a local majority and maintaining regional dominance.

In the remainder of this chapter, I suggest three more ways in which we can expect strength from weakness, applicable to larger scale conceptions of society, in addition to the three group-level processes identified earlier. Before doing so, however, I must digress to introduce the dynamic version of social impact theory and show how it resolves the problem of the apparent contradiction of social psychology by history.

THE CONTRADICTION(?) OF SOCIAL PSYCHOLOGY BY HISTORY

One of the best reasons to believe that minorities have something special going for them is that minorities persist and occasionally prevail, despite the fact that social psychology seems to predict their demise. Couching their theories in terms of "pressures to uniformity," bandwagon effects, contagion, and conformity, social psychologists of the 1950s and 1960s worried about how to preserve independence and maintain diversity in a melting-pot world and sought out special mechanisms to explain why agreement had not yet been reached. But they seemed united by the intuition that social influence should lead to convergence on the mean attitudinal position of the group.

In fact, Robert Abelson (1964) was able to prove, with the aid of linear differential equations, that "universal ultimate agreement is an ubiquitous outcome of a very broad class of mathematical models" (p. 153) of social influence that assume that people are predisposed to be persuaded positively by each other. Abelson showed that in fully connected social networks (i.e., when there is at least one path between any two people) all models that assume that pairs of people exhibit at least some degree of incremental positive adjustment to each other in reaction to discrepancies of opinion will lead eventually to unanimity, with the group as a whole converging on a single position. This proof still stands—if we accept its seemingly reasonable assumptions.

Abelson (1964) was quick to recognize, as most of us do, that such agreement does not seem all that common, and he pointed out the possibility of countervailing processes, such as the existence of conflicting external sources of influence, boomerang and other processes leading to extremification of opinion, and rejection of people with opposing positions. Nevertheless, his work, in the prevailing climate of opinion, was widely taken as showing that convergence was generally to be expected of normal social influence processes, and the usual expectation was that convergence should be at or near the mean of the original distribution, perhaps weighted by such factors as centrality in a social network.

There have been two major embarrassments to the idea of attitudinal convergence to uniformity at the mean, both articulated by Moscovici. On the one hand, the tradition of research and theory on minority influence shows that groups do not completely converge, and the resistance to consensus can be in part attributed to the minority's ability to get the majority to expand its awareness and reconceptualize problems (Moscovici, 1976). On the other hand, to the extent that groups do converge, it is not on the mean prediscussion opinion— rather there seems to be a consistent shift in the direction of the majority point of view (Moscovici & Zavalloni, 1969). Both of these exceptions to Abelson's (1964) "ubiquitous result" would seem to need explanation, and in fact they have elicited many attempts.

What If Attitudes Are Nonlinear? Abelson's (1964) model was based on the prevailing consensus that attitudes are continuous—points on an evaluative continuum—and that attitude change is likely to be a linear shift of location on such a continuum in incremental proportion to the amount of influence exerted. However, the assumption that attitudes are continuous and attitude change incremental may not always hold. Although the analytic simplification afforded by the assumption of linearity is very appealing, this assumption may not stand on very strong empirical ground—under many conditions (some noted by Abelson), attitudes seem to take on a bipolar, categorical quality (Latané & Nowak, 1994; Liu & Latané, in press). Further, as is becoming well known in the study of chaos, nonlinear systems often lead to complex and surprising dynamics, fundamentally different from those of linear systems and best studied through computer simulation.

DYNAMIC SOCIAL IMPACT: THE FATE OF OPINION MINORITIES IN SPATIALLY DISTRIBUTED GROUPS

Social impact theory, as presented in 1981 and in the previous discussion, is a static theory. It describes the effects on an individual of his or her social environment. What happens when we consider the reciprocal effects of the individual on that environment? Recently, Nowak, Szamrej, and Latané (1990) used computer simulation methods to extend the theory to a dynamic representation of the process whereby the individuals in a spatially distributed population interactively and iteratively create the social environment for each other.

For our simulation, Nowak et al. (1990) arranged 1,600 people varying in both persuasive and supportive "strength" in a two-dimensional Euclidean space, randomly assigned 70% as "pro" and 30% "con" on an unspecified issue, and simulated the process of group discussion and negotiation of a new social reality. The computer calculated for each person the total persuasive impact toward change of all the people who held the opposing view as the average force (persuasive strength divided by the square of the distance) exerted by each opposition member, multiplied by the square root of the number of group members. Likewise, for each person, the computer calculated the total support for opinion maintenance from people who held the same position including themselves, as a function of their supportive strength, immediacy, and number. Finally, the computer determined whether each person would keep the same attitude or switch to the opposing view, by seeing which source of impact was greater.

This, then, is a spatially distributed model of nonlinear dynamics, bearing some similarity to physical models of ferromagnets and other such systems (Lewenstein, Nowak, & Latané, 1992). It differs, however, in assuming individual differences. Variations in strength within a population allow for the existence of persuasive leaders who can anchor the borders of clusters. One of the ways that social psychology is unlike physics is that, unlike atoms, people are not interchangeable.

What will be the emergent, cumulative result of the iterative, interactive, recursive operation of these individual processes on the group as a whole as they begin to talk? Figure 9.1, modified from Nowak et al. (1990) shows the final

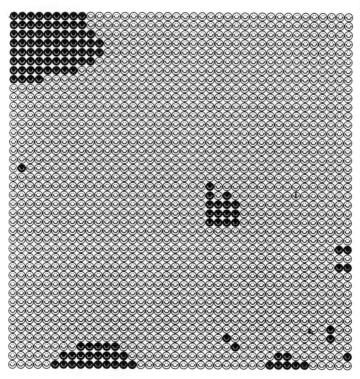

FIG. 9.1. The equilibrium distribution of attitudes in a spatially arrayed group
after 18 rounds of discussion. The group has polarized (the 30% minority has
dwindled to 8%) and clustered.

equilibrium distribution of attitudes among these 1,600 people. The placement
of their faces represents their location in space: "Open" faces represent people
holding the majority view, and "closed" faces the remaining minority.

The first surprise is that groups achieve stable equilibria without unifying or
coming to consensus. That is, even with further social interaction, one should
expect no further movement to consensus, contrary to Abelson's (1964) proof.
However, reminiscent of and perhaps akin to the small-group phenomenon first
labeled "polarization" by Moscovici and Zavalloni (1969), the group has shifted
toward the majority position, with the initial 30% minority now reduced to only 8%.

Most notably, the group has "clustered" into coherent subgroups, with minority members located near each other, often near the border. Clustering
results from people changing, not their locations in space, but their positions
on an issue, bringing them into conformity with their neighbors. It is this clustering that prevents the group from moving to complete uniformity. Increased
clustering decreases the extent to which individuals are exposed to opposing
viewpoints. People within coherent clusters are not exposed to divergent opinions because everyone around them shares their opinion. Only those on the
edges of clusters are exposed to the social pressure of contrary viewpoints.

When clustering results in a stable equilibrium (which is a robust consequence of a wide variety of theoretical circumstances), everybody is in (at least the local) majority. Each of us, comfortable in our majority position (at least of those people who are close and important to us) may wonder how members of other minorities survive, and admire their courage, without realizing that each of them is also likely to be in a local majority. Likewise, each of us, isolated by distance from opposing views, may be a victim of pluralistic ignorance (Noelle-Neumann, 1984) and think we are in the majority.

From a large-scale systematic program of simulations that factorially varied theoretical assumptions, procedures, and parameters (Latané & Nowak, in press), we can draw the following conclusions:

1. Polarization and clustering reminiscent of known real-world phenomena seem to be common predictions from a computer model of dynamic social impact. They are robust consequences of social influence, occurring under a wide range of theoretical circumstances, and not dependent on special assumptions or peculiar parameters.

2. Clustering is caused by the fact that people are more influenced by their neighbors in social space than by people at a distance, and is an argument for the importance of space in social processes.

3. Clustering is facilitated by individual differences in persuasiveness and supportiveness, with individuals high in these attributes able to anchor the borders.

4. Clusters protect minorities from being absorbed into the majority, preventing the group from sliding into uniformity.

5. Social influence processes contain within themselves self-limiting features that protect minorities and prevent the majority from prevailing. To the extent they assume linearity, old intuitions and proofs to the contrary are simply inapplicable. However, although clustering may protect minorities, it also limits their potential influence.

6. Finally, the theory and simulations continue to suggest that so-called "minority" phenomena result from the same processes as majority phenomena, although there may certainly be more than one process operating at a time. At the individual level, minorities are influential in proportion to their strength, immediacy, and the square root of their number—but there are reasons to believe that, under some circumstances, being a member of a minority can add to one's strength.

The results of these computer simulations represent theoretical derivations rather than empirical results. Only the actual collection of data will allow us to see whether these models actually predict real-world phenomena. However, recent empirical work seems to provide strong support for the theory. For example, Latané and L'Herrou (in press) studied 36 cases where 24-person groups discussed an issue over an e-mail network organized into one of three different social geometries. They found that clustering was characteristic of every single group with an initial minority greater than one third (smaller minorities were always eliminated or reduced to a single holdout). Although social space may not be so simple as an equal-density, two-dimensional representation would suggest, the consistency of their results with differing geometries suggests that the qualitative phenomenon of clustering may not be dependent on such simplifying assumptions.

The computer simulation just presented and the thousands we have conducted since show that convergence is not the inexorable consequence of social influence. Over a broad range of assumptions under a wide variety of conditions, dynamic social impact based on simple principles of individual influence leads to polarization and clustering, not unification—without the need to invoke special mechanisms. This demonstration does not, of course, mean that there are no special mechanisms, merely that they are not necessary. These same simulations also suggest some new ways in which minorities may achieve strength from their numerical weakness, which I illustrate later with three further sets of simulations.

FACTION SIZE VERSUS ACCUMULATIVE INFLUENCE MODELS OF SOCIAL INFLUENCE

It is possible to distinguish two very general approaches to how individuals react to their social environment—that individuals respond to the global division of populations into majority and minority factions (Hastie, 1990), and that they respond only to local influence. These two approaches represent fundamentally different conceptions of how people encode information about the beliefs of others.

Global, Faction-Size Models of Social Influence. In general, faction-size models calculate the average strength and immediacy of all the people with opposite views to a target individual, and then multiply by some function of the number of people holding that opinion to estimate the pressure to change. Thus, N is explicitly introduced into the equation. For example, persuasive impact for the particular faction-size model tested here is calculated as the product of the average impact of opposing individuals and the square root of their number, with each individual's impact assumed to equal their strength divided by the square of their distance. In other words,

$$\hat{\imath}_p = \frac{\sum S_i / d_i^2}{N_o} \sqrt{N_o}, \tag{1}$$

where $\hat{i}_p$ represents persuasive impact, or pressure to change, N_o the number of individuals with an opposing view, S_i the strength of source i, and d_i the Euclidean distance from source i. Supportive impact, or pressure to stay, $\hat{i}_s$, is calculated with similar formulas based on the strength and immediacy of those people who hold the same position as the target individual, including the target individual him or herself. The computer then determines whether each person will keep the same attitude or switch to the opposing view by seeing which source of impact, $\hat{i}_p$ or $\hat{i}_s$, is greater. The process is repeated until no further changes in attitude occur.

As we see, due to the averaging process, faction-size models have the property of decreasing total impact as distant or low-strength members are added to a group (they increase N in the denominator, while only marginally increasing the value of the numerator). This effect can be interpreted as resulting from decreased group cohesiveness with increased group size. Results consistent with this prediction were reported by Seta, Crisson, Seta, and Wang (1989) with respect to the impact of an audience on performance apprehension.

Such models are appropriate to situations where the number of people on each side of an issue is known. Obviously, they are most suitable for cases, such as in small groups, or when participants in a Delphi procedure are told the distribution of opinions of their panel, or when news media present the results of public opinion polls, where such information is readily available. Such models seem most compatible with most of the research on minority influence, which explicitly distinguishes minorities from majorities as factions of different sizes, as well as with models in the synergetics tradition (Troitzsch, 1990; Weidlich & Haag, 1983). The simulation reported previously and in Nowak et al. (1990) was done with a global-feedback faction-size model.

Local, Cumulative Influence Models of Social Influence. In many cases, however, especially as group size gets large, it may be unrealistic to assume that people are able to find out the state of the entire system, including the attitudes of people at a distance. Cumulative influence models merely allow individual influences to cumulate in proportion to their strength and some function of their distance, and do not require knowledge of the opinions of the entire group. The specific model introduced here, appropriate when an individual is influenced only by the opinions of those in her vicinity, sets impact equal to the square root of the sum of the squared individual impacts, or

$$\hat{i}_p = \sqrt{\sum (S_i/d_i^2)^2}. \tag{2}$$

Notice that N is not even in the formula, so that it is not necessary for the target to know the total distribution of opinions in the population. Unlike faction-size models, cumulative influence models always predict that adding new members to a group will increase its impact, if only marginally. At the individual level, both models tested here are equivalent to Latané's (1981) social impact formulae when strength and immediacy are constant, or when $N = 1$, but they lead to different results otherwise. For the present simulations, both models also assume that with respect to immediacy, the impact of another person should be an inverse function of the square of the distance from that person.

SIMULATION 1: DYNAMIC CONSEQUENCES OF INDIVIDUAL INTERACTION

To model the individual and group-level changes in attitude over time resulting from social interaction, a computer calculates for each person on each of a series of "days" the total impact toward change of all the people who hold the opposing view and compares it to the total supportive impact of those who share one's own view.

Simulation Details. For the present simulations, strength is represented by a single parameter randomly assigned in a uniform distribution over the range 0–100 and remaining constant throughout the simulation (Nowak et al., 1990, separated strength into two components labeled *persuasiveness* and *supportiveness* and reassigned them randomly after each change in attitude). Immediacy is calculated as the Euclidean distance between people located on a uniform density two-dimensional toroidal surface (the right and left, and upper and lower, edges are wrapped around to eliminate borders and corners). The self is counted as a source of supportive impact, and the distance to the self is arbitrarily set at .84, resulting in the self being 1.5–2 times as influential as the nearest neighbor. Finally, rather than use a strictly parallel computing procedure (which could lead to some synchronous oscillations as opposing neighbors each repeatedly succeed in influencing the other), we adopted a "Knight's Tour" algorithm in which non-neighboring individuals were successively evaluated and changed in turn, with no duplications, until everyone in the village had been assessed. Many of these details do make a difference, at least quantitatively, and the consequences of varying them, alone and in combination, are explored in Latané and Nowak (in press). However, the qualitative behavior of the models is robust with respect to such variations.

Simulation 1 also included a variation of "window" size to determine the effect of varying the size of the reference population. Window size refers to how large a set of neighbors is assumed to influence an individual. Presumably, people may be unaware of or ignore the opinions of others located beyond some distance specified by the window radius. With a radius of 1, only the eight nearest neighbors are considered, whereas with windows of radius 4 and 8, the attitudes of the 80 and 288 nearest people respectively are assessed. Finally, with a full window, everyone in the population has an influence, each in proportion to their strength and immediacy. This window size manipulation allows us to determine whether the size of an individual's reference group affects the predictions of the model. Thus, Simulation 1 consisted of 20 replications of a 2 × 4 design using each model (formula) and 1, 4, 8, and full windows, measuring both polarization and clustering. Because this simulation was done on a PC rather than a mainframe, a population of 400 rather than 1,600 was used, and unless otherwise noted, the initial minority was set at 30%.

Quantitative indices of polarization (P) and clustering (¢) were calculated according to procedures developed by Latané, Nowak, and Liu (1994). Polarization can be measured simply as 1 minus the ratio of the proportion of minority members after influence to the proportion before. This index will be zero if there is no change, one if the minority is completely eliminated, and negative if the minority actually increases. Clustering can be indexed by the probability that neighbors in social space share a common view as compared to individuals spaced farther apart, normalized so that the value of the index will be zero if the system is randomly ordered and approaches one as the system approaches its maximum possible order. In a nonclustered, randomly intermixed, population, the probability of any two individuals sharing a common attitude is independent of the distance between their locations in social space and depends solely on the proportion of people holding one attitude versus the other. In a clustered population, on the other hand, the probability that two individuals share the same opinion is greater if they occupy contiguous locations in social space than if they live far away from each other.

The simulations reported in this chapter were conducted using SITSIM, a program for deriving theoretical expectations from dynamic social impact theory factorially varying assumptions and parameter values. SITSIM is described more fully in Nowak and Latané (1994) and many results are presented in Latané and Nowak (in press).

Results. Despite their different assumptions about the nature of the influence process for individuals, both the faction-size and cumulative influence models had many similar consequences—simulations always reached a stable equilibrium with an entrenched minority, and there was pronounced polarization and clustering with all window sizes.

However, there were strong quantitative effects. Specifically, clustering with the faction-size model is very much affected by the size of the window over which influence is calculated (¢ = .48, .71, .84, .94 for window sizes 1, 4, 8, and full respectively), whereas the cumulative influence model is not much affected by window size. Overall, the faction-size model leads to more clustering (¢ = .74) and less polarization (P = .31) than the cumulative influence model (¢ = .48, P = .51).

The low degree of polarization in the faction-size model results from a curious phenomenon. Always on the first trial, a high proportion of the minority is wiped out, with the smaller minorities suffering the worst. The remaining one or two tight clusters will then start to grow, converting nearby members of the majority. This rebound effect is strongest for the smaller minorities, with the initial 10% minority, after being reduced to less than 2% on the first trial, being able to grow to an average of 25% before stabilizing. This process, like social influence in general, is self-limiting, and minorities rarely become majorities, nor do smaller initial minorities have an advantage over larger. The phenomenon, limited to the faction-size model, presumably results from the fact that a larger majority necessarily includes more distant members, who reduce the average impact of the group.

Discussion. Local influence models assume that influence is direct and un-calculated, with individual impacts simply cumulating. Therefore, the addition of another person to the set of those agreeing or disagreeing with you will always result in an increase in impact. However, because impact decreases as a power of distance, individuals beyond the immediate neighborhood can be disregarded without much error—the impact of people at greater distances is only marginal. There is no need for an individual even to know how many people agree or disagree with him (N does not appear in the model at all), as he or she simply responds to people in proportion to their strength and immediacy, with weak or far-away people having very little influence.

Faction-size models, in contrast, assume that individuals have access to the size, strength, and spatial distribution of the competing opinion groups or fac-tions. This is not entirely unreasonable, because global feedback can often be provided by such political mechanisms as public opinion polls and elections, and cultural feedback comes from educational, institutional, news, and enter-tainment media.

Faction-size models have the interesting property that as weak people or distant members convert to your point of view, they reduce the average strength and immediacy of your supporters, and this effect may be strong enough to overcome the increase in numbers, leading you to become more likely to change. As the size of a cluster grows, its impact on its own members at first increases—but because only so many people can be in the same area at the same time, the addition of more people to your group makes the average group member further away, reducing the group's compactness or cohesiveness. The fourth explana-tion of strength from weakness, then, is that the greater average impact on its members of a small compact group may overcome the numerical advantage of a larger but spatially diffuse group.

Which Model When? Global faction-size models seem especially applicable for groups with a clear self-definition, such as political parties and other clearly defined interest groups with specified positions on well-defined controversial issues. They may be most appropriate when it is possible to gain information about the state of the system as a whole as by polling the jury or counting the ballots.

Minority influence researchers seem to make the strong assumption that it is not the absolute, but the relative size of factions that is critical. The faction-size model is particularly affected by the size of the window. This variation corresponds loosely to the choice of a relevant population against which to compare oneself—Greek students, all Greeks, all people—and suggests a major problem with the minority influence formulation: determining the relevant reference population.

The more usual case would seem to be when people gain information piece-meal, over a period of time, and only about their own region of social space. In these cases, the cumulative influence model seems more plausible. Cumulative impact models may be especially applicable when dealing with issues that have not yet become defined, and groups have not yet become self-conscious of their identity or structure. A major direction for future theoretical and empirical development will be to determine when each model is most appropriate.

It is important to remember, however, that although there are some interesting differences between these approaches, they lead to remarkably similar qualitative results—in both cases, groups generally polarize without unifying, while developing coherent regional opinion clusters.

SIMULATION 2: WHAT IS THE EFFECT OF MINORITY SIZE ON SELECTION FOR STRENGTH?

Our image of the heroic holdout voting his conscience has been shaped by such popular staples as *Twelve Angry Men* and *Profiles in Courage,* which show how embattled minorities can acquire the strength of character to eventually convince the rest of us. Perhaps, however, it is not being in a minority that confers strength, but strength that allows one to survive in the minority. Here I suggest a process of natural selection—only those minority members who are high in strength are likely to survive with their opinions intact, and these selection pressures will be greater the smaller the initial minority. Simulation 2 was designed to determine the effect of different initial minority sizes, ranging from 10% to 50%, on the degree of polarization, clustering, and minority strength. Although simulations were done with both models, minority size had no effect with the faction-size model, in part because of the ability of minorities in that situation to rebound from their initial decline when exposed to a strong majority. Table 9.1 shows the degree of polarization, clustering, and strength according to the initial minority size for the cumulative influence model.

Clearly, the smaller the initial minority, the less the clustering and the more the polarization at the end. With random initial distributions of opinion, smaller initial minorities mean a smaller chance that several sufficiently strong minority

TABLE 9.1
Effect of Initial Minority Proportion on Clustering (¢), Polarization (P), and Majority and Minority Strength (S_{maj} and S_{min})

Initial Minority	¢	P	S_{mai}	S_{min}
50/50 split	.60	.03	51	50
40% minority	.59	.22	51	53
30% minority	.53	.49	51	57
20% minority	.47	.80	51	71
10% minority	.41	.80	51	71

members will be located close enough together to form the nucleus of a cluster, and reduced clustering allows polarization to proceed unchecked.

Finally, we calculated the average strength of individual holders of majority and minority opinions, after the exercise of dynamic social influence (at the start, the mean levels of each were set at an identical 50). The results can be seen in Table 9.1: Surviving minority members ended up stronger than majorities, and this effect was stronger the smaller the size of the initial minority. As discussed previously, I attribute this to a process of natural selection—any surviving minority member must have had sufficient strength to survive, but this process may result in holders of minority opinions not only seeming, but being more courageous, strong, and true. This, then, is a fifth way in which there may be strength in weakness.

SIMULATION 3: CAN MINORITIES EVER PREVAIL? THE ROLE OF TRUTH

I have argued elsewhere (Latané & Wolf, 1981) that minorities often do have access to a special kind of strength. As a result of their pervasive social influence, majorities are often wrong. Majorities can perpetuate solutions that worked in the past but are no longer effective, and they can overwhelm the contrary experience of individuals by a form of pluralistic ignorance. When everyone is complimenting the emperor on his new clothes, it may take the eyes of a child to see through to the naked reality beneath. Minorities, on the other hand, have the advantage of being able to take a fresh look at a changing world and come up with a better idea, unencumbered by the shackles of convention, giving them a potent source of strength—correctness. With truth as your sword, you can win many arguments against numerically superior opposition.

The final simulation to be reported here explored the role of truth in assisting social influence. *Truth* is represented here as a bias toward one position or the other. It is a number (0, 25, or 50) added to either $î_p$ or $î_s$ according to whether

TABLE 9.2
The Effect of Truth (Bias) on Clustering (¢) and Polarization (P)

Bias Favoring Minority	¢	P	Final Size of Minority
-50	.43	.97	1%
-25	.51	.83	5%
0	.54	.38	19%
+25	.58	-.15	41%
+50	.63	-.59	71%

one is a member of the initial minority or majority under the assumption that truth or underlying reality strengthens the arguments of those who side with it, while weakening those who oppose it.

Results—Truth Helps. With a strong bias favoring the majority (+50 and +25), the beleaguered minority suffers even more, being reduced to a mere 1% to 5% of the population. However, it was rarely wiped out (even with the most intense bias in favor of the majority, the minority perished only 25% of the time). When truth favored the minority, it did better, at the highest level allowing the minority to cross over and become the majority. However, the polarization indices are not symmetric (Table 9.2). Even with truth on its side, the initial minority retains a disadvantage, due to the fact that as it increases in numbers, it has already clustered, diminishing its impact and providing some protection for the former majority.

GENERAL DISCUSSION

As promised, these simulations have shown that majority domination—complete convergence on the most prevalent position with the utter demise of all deviates—is not the inevitable result of simple social influence. There is no contradiction between social psychology and history, and no reason from that quarter to suggest special mechanisms protecting minorities.

However, there are several ways, expressible in the language of social impact theory, that members of opinion minorities may acquire special strength. In addition to procedural effects and the effects on the behavior of actors and the attributions of observers noted earlier these simulations have revealed three more: First, the faction-size model reveals a special weakness of the majority—the addition of low-strength or distant members may actually reduce its hold on individuals. Second, there is a natural selection process whereby only those minority members high in supportive strength are likely to survive. Finally, minorities have a special opportunity, caused by the ability of the majority to override reality, to rely on truth. Even with all these advantages and with truth at their side, the models indicate that minorities will remain at a disadvantage, limited to preserving diversity rather than themselves achieving complete domination. These models, at their present state of development, suggest that eventual minority dominance will be the exception rather than the rule.

According to the present view, then, minorities and majorities both have recourse to the same strategies and techniques of influence, and both will generally be successful in proportion to their strength, immediacy, and number. People will, of course, choose their strategies according to their circumstances, and the minority and majority will certainly differ in this respect, with minorities especially needing to appeal to novel arguments and reframe issues. There are at least six mechanisms by which minorities may gain strength from weakness. Some of these mechanisms may seem illusory or artifactual in their causes, but they have real effects. In addition, these simulations show that social influence processes have a self-limiting character that can protect minorities by turning them into local majorities.

In fact, such clustering allows the existence of "hidden diversity" with respect to opinions. As members of a majority, we may be completely unaware of substantial opinion minorities, simply because they are not located near us in social space. As minority members, we may actually believe we are in the majority, because most of those we talk to share our views.

Dynamic social impact theory demonstrates possible mechanisms for the self-organization of society. Recent developments in the theory promise to extend the scale of such organization, as social influence leads to clustering of attitudes, which in turn causes them to become correlated, providing the basis for the emergence of ideology, social categorization, social stereotypes, and social identities (Latané, in press-b; Latané & Nowak, 1992; Lavine & Latané, in press; Schaller & Latané, in press).

In further theoretical developments, I extend the theory to encompass any socially influenceable attribute of an individual and claim that it can provide an account of the regional diversity and historical continuity of culture (Latané, in press-a), and Huguet and Latané (in press) explicitly identify the spatially clustered bundles of cognitive elements arising from dynamic social impact with Moscovici's (1961, 1984) concept of *social representations*, socially derived sets of beliefs, values, and practices that help people make sense of the world.

Thus, although superficially, the present critique of the terminology of minority influence may seem unfriendly, its intention is quite the contrary, for dynamic social impact theory is actually most sympathetic to Moscovici's approach. It is a bottom-up, genetic (Moscovici, 1976) theory, showing how people not only adapt to society but produce, reorganize, and change it. It is based on a process more akin to negotiation and conflict resolution than to power or dependence. Influence is reciprocal, not unilateral, with everyone, both in the majority and the minority, influenced by and influencing each other, creating social reality in the process.

CONCLUSIONS

1. We should not worry about the contradiction between social psychology and history, because none exists. Despite prior intuitions, social influence processes do not, even in theory, inexorably lead to majority domination.

2. We should continue our interest in strength from weakness, without trying to lump disparate phenomena under a single rubric.

3. The minority influence terminology is muddled and misleading—we should replace it with other language, such as that available from social impact theory. It is probably unreasonable to expect us to completely jettison the words *minority* and *majority*, but it is reasonable to ask that we specify the source and target of influence and what aspect of strength is being affected.

4. Specifically, it is important to keep distinct the strength and number of sources, as well as representing their location in social space. In discussing theoretical predictions or experimental results, we should always specify whether we are talking about effects on sources or targets, and whether they are mediated by strength, immediacy, or number.

5. We need more parametric research, especially research that independently varies the size and strength of majorities and minorities.

6. Finally, I encourage us all to attack with renewed interest the fascinating but conceptually difficult problems of the dynamics of social influence. We need to know, not just how an individual responds to social information, but how the actions of many individual actors, responding interactively to each other, lead both to social problems and their solution through social change.

ACKNOWLEDGMENTS

A preliminary version of this chapter was presented at a conference on The Roots of Persuasion held in Valencia, Spain, June 16–18, 1990. Many of the ideas and all of the computer simulations reported in this chapter were achieved in collaboration with Andrzej Nowak of the University of Warsaw who also helped design and develop the simulation program. Responsibility for the critique of the "minority influence" rubric is solely mine. This research was funded by National Science Foundation Grant BNS9009198 and SBR9411603. I thank John Levine, James Liu, and Charlan Nemeth for their comments on an earlier draft.

REFERENCES

Abelson, R. P. (1964). Mathematical models of the distribution of attitudes under controversy. In N. Fredericksen & H. Gullicksen (Eds.), *Contributions to mathematical psychology* (pp. 141–160). New York: Holt, Rinehart & Winston.

Brown, R. (1985). *Social psychology* (2nd ed.). New York: The Free Press.

Davis, J. H., Hulbert, L., & Au, W. T. (in press). Procedural influence on group decision making: The case of straw polls. In R. Y. Hirokawa & M. S. Poole (Eds.), *Communication and group decision making* (2nd ed.). Beverly Hills, CA: Sage.

Hastie, R. (1990, June). *Simulation model of consensus-seeking in small groups.* Paper presented at Nags Head Conference on Formal Models of Social Processes, Kill Devil Hills, NC.

Huguet, P., & Latané, B. (in press). Social representations as dynamic social impact. *Journal of Communication.*

Jackson, J. (1986). Reply to Mullen. *Journal of Personality and Social Psychology, 50,* 508–513.

Kruglanski, A. W., & Mackie, D. M. (1990). Majority and minority influence: A judgmental process analysis. In W. Stroebe & M. Hewstone (Eds.), *European review of social psychology* (Vol. 1, pp. 229–261). Chichester, England: Wiley.

Latané, B. (1981). The psychology of social impact. *American Psychologist, 36,* 343–356.

Latané, B. (in press-a). Dynamic social impact: The creation of culture by communication. *Journal of Communication.*

Latané, B. (in press-b). The emergence of clustering and correlation from social interaction. In R. Hegselmann & H. O. Peitgen (Eds.), *Order and chaos in nature and society.* Vienna: Hölder-Pichler.

Latané, B., & Harkins, S. (1976). Cross-modality matches suggest anticipated stage fright a multiplicative power function of audience size and status. *Perception and Psychophysics, 20,* 482–488.

Latané, B., & L'Herrou, T. (in press). Social clustering in the Conformity Game: Dynamic social impact in electronic groups. *Journal of Personality and Social Psychology.*

Latané, B., & Liu, J. H. (in press). The intersubjective geometry of social space. *Journal of Communication.*

Latané, B., Liu, J., Nowak, A., Bonevento, M., & Zheng, L. (1995). Distance matters: Physical space and social interaction. *Personality and Social Psychology Bulletin, 21,* 795–805.

Latané, B., & Nowak, A. (1992, July). *The emergence of ideology in groups.* Paper presented at the joint meeting of the Society for Experimental Social Psychology and the European Association of Experimental Social Psychology, Leuven, Belgium.

Latané, B., & Nowak, A. (1994). Attitudes as catastrophes: From dimensions to categories with increasing involvement. In R. Vallacher & A. Nowak (Eds.), *Dynamical systems in social psychology* (pp. 219–249). New York: Academic Press.

Latané, B., & Nowak, A. (in press). Self-organizing social systems: Necessary and sufficient conditions for the emergence of consolidation and clustering. In G. Barnett & F. Boster (Eds.), *Progress in communication sciences: Persuasion.* Norwood, NJ: Ablex.

Latané, B., Nowak, A., & Liu, J. (1994). Measuring emergent social phenomena: Dynamism, polarization, and clustering as order parameters of social systems. *Behavioral Science, 39,* 1–24.

Latané, B., & Wolf, S. (1981). The social impact of majorities and minorities. *Psychological Review, 88,* 438–453.

Lavine, H., & Latané, B. (in press). A cognitive-social theory of public opinion: Dynamic impact and cognitive structure. *Journal of Communication.*

Levine, J. M., & Russo, E. M. (1990, June). *Anticipated discussion with majorities and minorities: Impact on cognition processes.* Paper presented at Valencia Conference on the Roots of Persuasion, Valencia, Spain.

Levine, J. M., & Russo, E. M. (1987). Majority and minority influence. In C. Hendrick (Ed.), *Review of personality and social psychology* (Vol. 8, pp. 13–54). Newbury Park, CA: Sage.

Lewenstein, M., Nowak, A., & Latané, B. (1992). Statistical mechanics of social impact. *Physical Review A, 45,* 1–14.

Liu, J. H., & Latané, B. (in press). The catastrophic link between the importance and extremity of political attitudes. *Political Behavior.*

Maass, A., West, S. G., & Cialdini, R. B. (1987). Minority influence and conversion. In C. Hendrick (Ed.), *Review of personality and social psychology* (Vol. 8, pp. 55–79). Newbury Park, CA: Sage.

Moscovici, S. (1961). *La psychanalyse: Son image et son public.* Paris: Presses Universitaires de France.

Moscovici, S. (1976). *Social influence and social change.* London: Academic Press.

Moscovici, S. (1980). Toward a theory of conversion behavior. In L. Berkowitz (Ed.), *Advances in experimental social psychology* (Vol. 13, pp. 209–239). New York: Academic Press.

Moscovici, S. (1984). The phenomenon of social representations. In R. M. Farr & S. Moscovici (Eds.), *Social representations* (pp. 3–69). Cambridge, England: Cambridge University Press.

Moscovici, S. (1985). Innovation and minority influence. In S. Moscovici, G. Mugny, & E. van Avermaet (Eds.), *Perspectives on minority influence* (pp. 9–51). Cambridge, England: Cambridge University Press.

Moscovici, S., & Zavalloni, M. (1969). The group as a polarizer of attitudes. *Journal of Personality and Social Psychology, 12,* 125–135.

Mugny, G., & Perez, J. A. (1991). *The social psychology of minority influence.* Cambridge, England: Cambridge University Press.

Mullen, B. (1985). Strength and immediacy of sources: A meta-analytic evaluation of the forgotten elements of social impact theory. *Journal of Personality and Social Psychology, 48,* 1458–1466.

Nemeth, C., & Wachtler, J. (1974). Creating the perceptions of consistency and confidence: A necessary condition for minority influence. *Sociometry, 37,* 529–540.

Noelle-Neumann, E. (1984). *The spiral of silence: Public opinion—our social skin.* Chicago: University of Chicago Press.

Nowak, A., & Latané, B. (1994). Simulating the emergence of social order from individual behavior. In N. Gilbert & J. Doran (Eds.), *Simulating societies: The computer simulation of social processes* (pp. 63–84). London: University College London Press.

Nowak, A., Szamrej, J., & Latané, B. (1990). From private attitude to public opinion: A dynamic theory of social impact. *Psychological Review, 97,* 362–376.

Papastamou, S. (1990, June). *The role of psychologization in minority influence.* Paper presented at Valencia Conference on the Roots of Persuasion, Valencia, Spain.

Schachter, S. (1951). Deviation, rejection, and communication. *Journal of Abnormal and Social Psychology, 46,* 190–207.

Schaller, M., & Latané, B. (in press). Dynamic social impact and the evolution of culture: A natural history of stereotypes. *Journal of Communication.*

Seta, J., Crisson, J., Seta, C., & Wang, M. (1989). Task performance and perceptions of anxiety: Averaging and summation in an evaluative setting. *Journal of Personality and Social Psychology, 56,* 387–396.

Troitzsch, K. G. (1990). Self-organization in social systems. In J. Gladitz & K. G. Troitzsch (Eds.), *Computer-aided sociological research* (pp. 93–107). Berlin: Akademie-Verlag.

Turner, J. C. (1991). *Social influence.* Milton Keynes: Open University Press.

Weidlich, W., & Haag, G. (1983). *Concepts and models of a quantitative sociology: The dynamics of interacting populations.* Berlin: Springer.

Wolf, S. (1985). The manifest and latent influence of majorities and minorities. *Journal of Personality and Social Psychology, 48,* 899–908.

Wolf, S. (1987). Majority and minority influence: A social impact analysis. In M. P. Zanna, J. M. Olson, & C. P. Herman (Eds.), *Social influence: The Ontario Symposium on Personality and Social Psychology* (Vol. 5, pp. 207–235). Hillsdale, NJ: Lawrence Erlbaum Associates.

Wolf, S., & Latané, B. (1983). Minority and majority influences on restaurant preferences. *Journal of Personality and Social Psychology, 45,* 282–292.

10

THE IMPACT OF INFORMATION ON GROUP JUDGMENT: A MODEL AND COMPUTER SIMULATION

Daniel Gigone
Reid Hastie
University of Colorado

There are many reasons why almost all human societies rely on small groups to make important decisions. Groups, in comparison to individuals, are better able to represent a diversity of goals and values, they distribute the responsibility for consequential decisions, and they elicit commitment to a course of action from many actors at once. It is also hoped that, under some circumstances, groups can make more accurate and more reliable decisions than individuals. One commonly cited condition for the superiority of group decisions is the situation where different members of the group bring relevant, unshared, independent, and valid information to the group decision process. Under such conditions, it is hard not to believe that "several heads are better than one."

At present, there are several excellent studies of the unshared information situation and at least one comprehensive model of the information-sharing process (e.g., Stasser, 1988; Stasser & Titus, 1985). However, there are still many loose theoretical ends and the central question—What is the effect of group discussion on the group decision?—has not been directly addressed empirically. The present empirical research and theoretical model were designed to explicate the role of group discussion of unshared information in group judgment tasks. In the future, the present model may prove to be a step in the direction of a comprehensive theory of group judgment that specifies the role of the group discussion process more explicitly than previous proposals.

The model is based on Brunswikian concepts that have previously been used to describe the judgments of an individual judge (Brunswik, 1956; Hammond, 1966). By extending these concepts to the group judgment, the present model provides a concise description of important aspects of the group judgment process. In addition, the model leads directly to a set of statistical analyses. These analyses, in turn, can be used to test hypotheses about influences on the group judgment process.

THE GROUP JUDGMENT PROCESS MODEL

The Judgment Task

The specific behavior to be modeled consists of a group making a quantitative judgment, based on information that is known to some, but not necessarily all of the group's members. For example, members of a budget committee might possess different items of information concerning the financial needs of a particular government program. As a group, their task is to judge how much money should be allocated to that program, based on the information that they have. In order to fit the statistical model, the available information must itself be scalable. It must be measurable on some dimension or dimensions, whether nominal or ordered. With additional assumptions, the model could be extended to encompass a wider range of phenomena, such as categorical judgments.

The "Lens Model"

The present group judgment model derives from the Brunswikian conception of an individual judgment, as developed by social judgment theory (SJT; Brehmer & Joyce, 1988; Hammond, Stewart, Brehmer, & Steinmann, 1986). The Brunswikian idea of an individual judgment is described by the "lens model." Figure 10.1 diagrams the relationships described by the lens model. In the lens model, the to-be-judged entity takes on some *true value* (Y_e) in the environment. That true value may simply be unknown to the judge, or it may be a future state that must be predicted. Although that true value cannot itself be known to the judge, at least at the time of the judgment, relevant information is available in the form of multiple, redundant *cues* $(X_1, X_2, \ldots, X_n)$. Each of these cues has some true relationship to the true value, which is known as its *cue validity* $(r_{e,1}, r_{e,2} \ldots, r_{e,n})$. Thus, the to-be-judged environment may be described by the true value of a criterion and the set of true relationships between that criterion and a set of observable cues.

Because the judge cannot observe the criterion directly, he or she must make a *judgment* (Y_s). That judgment will be based on the information that is provided by the cues. As with the environment side of the "lens," each of the cues has some relationship with the judgment, which is the judge's *cue utilization* $(r_{s,1}, r_{s,2} \ldots, r_{s,n})$. The set of cue utilizations make up the judge's *judgment policy*. To the extent that the judgment policy matches the set of cue validities, the judgment will be accurate and the judge's *achievement* (r_a) will be high. Across multiple

Environment   Cues   Subject

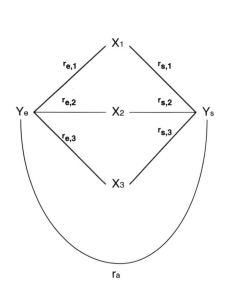

FIG. 10.1. The "lens model" of judgment.

judgments, unreliability is likely to be introduced into both the cue validity and
cue utilization relationships.

Over multiple criteria, the lens model provides a means for describing the
task environment. The environment is described as the best linear model relating the true value of the criterion to the values of the relevant observable cues,

$$Y'_e = \sum_{i=1}^{n} b_{ei} X_i,$$ (1)

where n is the total number of observable cues. The set of coefficients relating
cue values to predicted true values of the criterion ($b_{e1}, b_{e2}, \ldots, b_{en}$) are known
as the *ecological weights*. The predictability of the criterion depends on the fit
of this best linear model.

Similarly, the lens model also suggests how to describe the judgments of an
individual judge. The individual makes judgments of a number of cases sampled
from the environment, each of which is composed of the true values of the set
of relevant cues. Over all k cases, the individual's judgments can be described
by the best linear model relating the judgments to the set of cue values,

$$Y'_s = \sum_{i=1}^{n} b_{si} X_i,$$ (2)

where X_i is the cue value, Y_s is the judgment, b_{ei} is the coefficient estimate for
the relationship between a cue and the judgment, and n is the number of cues

making up each case. The fit of this model indicates the consistency of the individual's judgment policy across cases. The similarity of the coefficient estimates in Equations 1 and 2 and the fits of the two models will be determining factors of the accuracy of the individual's judgments across the multiple cases.

The lens model thus relates the judgments of an individual to the true values of the criterion through the "lens" of the observable cues. However, the same Brunswikian concepts have not been applied to the judgments made by groups.

The Group Judgment

The task environment should not depend on whether the judge is an individual or a group. The true values of the criterion, the true values of the cues, and the relationships between them will all be unchanged. Thus, the best linear model in Equation 1 still describes the relationships between the criterion and the set of cues in the context of group judgments.

The judgment side of the lens, on the other hand, is assumed to be more complex in the case of a group than in the case of an individual judge. The group judgment model equations that follow use slightly different terminology than did Equations 1 and 2, because the terms in model of group judgment will come to have a somewhat different meaning than they have in the classic lens model.

A group is assumed to be made up of a number of individual members (A, B, ..., m), where m is the nominal tag of the "last" member. Each of those members has a memory, which may contain items of information that are relevant to the judgment being made. These items again are known as *cues* (c_1, c_2, ..., c_n), where n is the total number of judgment-relevant cues that are held in a particular member's memory. The set of cues that are known may vary from member to member.

Each member may also hold in memory an opinion about the true value of the to-be-judged entity (M_A, M_B, ..., M_m). Each of these member opinions is assumed to be based on the cues that are available in memory to that member.

Figure 10.2 provides a representation of the group judgment of a three-member group. The small circles represent the individual group members; the central "cloud" represents the group judgment; arrows represent impacts on the group judgment. Thus, Fig. 10.2 shows both cues and member opinions affecting the group judgment.

A member's opinion can be thought of as an individual judgment made by that member from the available cues. It follows that a member's opinion can be summarized as a linear, additive combination of the available cues,

$$M_j = \sum_{i=1}^{n} w_i c_i, \tag{3}$$

where w_i is the weight that the member places on each cue c_i, n is the total number of cues available to the member, and j refers to the particular member.

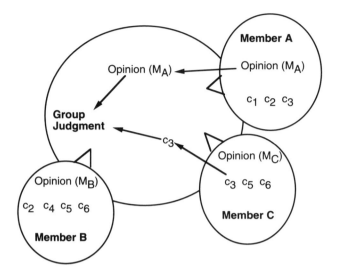

FIG. 10.2. Diagram of group judgment. Arrows indicate impact on the group judgment.

Because information is not necessarily fully distributed among members, the particular set of cues and corresponding weights may differ between members.

Expressing the individual judgment as a linear combination of information follows from various theoretical approaches (Slovic & Lichtenstein, 1971). It can be found in Brunswikian theory and in subsequent work in social judgment theory (Brehmer & Joyce, 1988; Hammond et al., 1986). Information integration theory presents a similar line of thought (Anderson, 1981). In any case, because the nature of the weights is not yet specified, the model could incorporate a number of different information combination rules. For example, the model could be used to describe either a weighted average mechanism, in which case the weights would be scaled to sum to one, or an additive model. The model could also describe an anchor-and-adjustment mechanism (Tversky & Kahneman, 1974), with the magnitude of the weights dependent on the order in which cues are considered by the judge.

The group judgment, then, may be based on two sorts of information. First, the group has available all of the cues that are known to its constituent members. The set of cues available to the group $\{C_1, C_2, \ldots, C_N\}$, where N is the total number of different cues, is the union of all of the sets of cues available to the members (c_i, $i = 1 \ldots n$, for each group member). More than one group member may know the same cue; that shared cue is considered to be a single member of the set of cues available to the group. Thus, we assume that the group has available to it all of the information that is known by one or more group members.

The present model requires that the cues be numerically scaled variables (i.e., "at least" on an ordinal scale). This assumption is not as limiting as it may seem. A nominal variable can easily be represented with one or more numeric cues. For example, a nominal variable with k categories can be expressed with a set of $k - 1$ contrast coded cues (Judd & McClelland, 1989). Scaling functions can be applied to other non-numeric information. Ratings of "good," "fair," and "poor" on some dimension, for example, make up an implicit ordinal scale. However, some judgment-relevant information may not be easily scalable (e.g., "the job candidate has a background in quasi-experimental methods"). Even in cases such as these, on the other hand, the group members likely must use an implicit scaling function (e.g., "fit with faculty interests") to apply that information to the group judgment.

Second, the group has available the members' opinions. Because each member opinion can be represented as linear combinations of the cue values, a member's opinion provides information in the form of a summary of the cues that are known to that member. Although the member opinions are themselves based on the cue values, they may have an influence on the group judgment that is independent of the influence of the cues themselves. The same scaling assumptions apply as for the cues. The usual expectation would be that the member opinions would be on the same scale as the group judgment; however, this is not required by the model.

The aforementioned components all represent aspects of the group judgment that occur at the member level. The communication and sharing of information, on the other hand, do require some amount of actual group process. In the present model, information sharing is assumed to occur through the process of cue pooling. Pooling is defined as a single member's communication of a single cue value to all other group members. After a cue has been pooled, that cue value is assumed to be known by all group members. Various factors might influence the likelihood that a particular cue will be pooled, such as the relevance of the information to the judgment, the salience of the cue, or the number of group members who hold the cue. The model, therefore, includes a term indicating whether or not each cue is pooled $(P_1, P_2, \ldots, P_n)$. In the context of a single group judgment, each cue may only be pooled or not pooled. A cue cannot be partially pooled and cannot be pooled more than once; once a cue is pooled, discussing it again does not change its status. Therefore, each of these pooling terms is represented as a categorical variable indicating whether or not that particular cue has been pooled by one or more group members. Any binary coding of P_i would be consistent with the equations that follow; the choice is arbitrary. However, the most meaningful choice is to define $P_i = 0$ if the corresponding cue (C_i) was not pooled and $P_i = 1$ if the corresponding cue was pooled.

The model assumes that the pooling of cues is the primary group process that is of interest. Other group processes may affect the group judgment by influencing either the tendency of a cue to be pooled or the way in which the cue value and member opinion information is combined into the group judgment.

Like the individual judgment, the group judgment can be summarized as a linear combination. The group judgment might be seen simply as an average or weighted average of the members' opinions. Graesser (1991) proposed such a framework with her "social averaging theorem." The weighted average of members' opinions can be represented as,

$$G = \sum_{j=A}^{m} a_j M_j \qquad (4)$$

where G is the group judgment, M_j is a member's opinion, and m is the last member. Each of the member opinions has a corresponding weight a_j that represents the relationship between that opinion and the group judgment. These weights might be influenced by such factors as the persuasiveness of the members and the leadership roles within the group.

However, the weighted average model does not distinguish between the impact of the discussion of information and other, noninformational influences on the group judgment. A somewhat more complex equation might capture this distinction,

$$G = \sum_{j=A}^{m} a_j M_j + \sum_{i=1}^{n} w_i C_i, \qquad (5)$$

where C_i is a cue value, n is the total number of cues available to the group, and the other terms are the same as in Equation 4. Each of the cues has a corresponding weight w_i that represents the relationship between the value of that cue and the group judgment. Influences on the cue weights might include the relevance of the cues to the judgment or their relative salience.

The present model also assumes that the group judgment will depend on the pooling of cues. Thus, the term that indicates whether or not a cue is pooled must be included in the group judgment summary equation,

$$G = \sum_{j=A}^{m} a_j M_j + \sum_{i=1}^{n} w_i C_i + \sum_{i=1}^{n} f_i P_i, \qquad (6)$$

where P_i is the pooling term and f_i is the weight placed on the pooling term in the group judgment. The weight on each pooling term represents how much the group judgment differs when that cue is pooled, relative to when that cue is not pooled. However, whereas this equation takes cue pooling into effect, it does so in a way that does not pay attention to the value of the cue that is being pooled. Of more relevance is the effect of pooling on the weight that the group places on a cue. That is, does the group place more weight on the value of a cue that is pooled than on one that is not pooled? The product term between each cue value and the matching categorical pooling variable *(CP)* represents this question. These product terms can be added to Equation 6,

$$G = \sum_{j=A}^{m} a_j M_j + \sum_{i=1}^{n} w_i C_i + \sum_{i=1}^{n} f_i P_i + \sum_{i=1}^{n} h_i C_i P_i, \tag{7}$$

with all indexes and other terms the same as Equation 6. The weight corresponding to each of the product terms, h_i, indicates the extent to which the weight for that cue, w_i, depends on whether the cue is pooled. Equation 7 can be summarized schematically as follows, *group judgment = sum of member opinions (weighted) + sum of cue values (weighted) + sum of pooling (pooled = 1, not pooled = 0, weighted) + sum of cue value by pooling products (weighted)*.

Our basic proposal is that the group judgment can be summarized as a linear combination of weighted terms. The group judgment is hypothesized to be a function of the opinions of the group members, the values of the relevant cues, the tendency of the cues to be pooled by the members, and the effect of pooling on the weights that are attached to the cue values. The members' opinions are themselves considered to be linear combinations of the cue values. Thus, the primary influences on group judgment are the information contained in the cue values and the patterns of information pooling. Any other factors influencing the group process are assumed to affect the weights corresponding to the various terms. Hypotheses about group process would thus specify how various factors would influence the model weights.

Analyzing the Group Judgment

Before any such hypotheses can be formulated, however, some method of weight measurement or estimation must be specified. Given a single judgment, based on a single set of cues, a unique set of weights cannot be determined. Instead, the weights must be estimated over a series of judgments, based on different cases. Multiple linear regression can be used to estimate the judgment policy weights. The coefficient estimate associated with each cue can be considered to be an estimate of that cue's weight, scaled to account for the relative magnitudes of the cue values and the judgments. Thus, an individual judge's policy could be estimated by regressing his or her judgments on the full set of cues, across a number of cases. The amount of variance in judgments that is accounted for by the best linear model can be considered a measure of the consistency of the judge's policy, assuming that the residual error is not systematically related to the cue values. In the case of the individual judge, these developments were arrived at by social judgment theory and other regression models of human judgment.

The same logic can be applied to Equation 7, the final result of the analysis of the group judgment process. The resulting coefficient estimates provide the best summary of the group judgment process across judgments, in terms of minimizing squared error between the observed and predicted judgments.

An analysis of a set of group judgments based on Equation 7 would result in an estimated model of the form,

$$\hat{G} = b_0 + \sum_{j=A}^{m} \hat{a}_{Mj} M_j + \sum_{i=1}^{n} \hat{w}_i C_i + \sum_{i=1}^{n} \hat{f}_i P_i + \sum_{i=1}^{n} \hat{h}_i C P_i, \tag{8}$$

where b_0 represents the intercept, the "hat" on each weight indicates that it is a least squares estimate, a_i represents the coefficient estimates for the member opinion terms, w_j represents the coefficient terms for the cue value terms, f_i represents the coefficient estimates for the pooling terms, h_i represents the coefficient estimates for the cue by pooling interaction terms, and all other symbols are the same as those in Equation 7. The intercept term is determined by the magnitude of judgments and of the independent variables, and not by the relationship between the independent variables and the judgments. In a linear model without interaction terms, rescaling the judgments and each of the cues so as to have a mean of zero across all of the cases would result in an intercept of zero. Calculating standardized regression coefficient estimates achieves that end. However, rescaling the values of the product variables would alter the meaning of the corresponding coefficient estimates (Judd & McClelland, 1989).

Each of the coefficients in Equation 8 estimates the independent effect of that particular variable on the judgments. Each member opinion coefficient, w hat_j, estimates the relationship between the opinions of that member and the group judgments, controlling for the opinions of all other members and for the cue values, the pooling values, and their interactions. Each cue value coefficient, a hat_i, estimates the effect of that cue's value on the group judgment when it is not pooled, controlling for all of the other variables. Each pooling coefficient, f hat_i, estimates the effect of pooling that variable on the group judgments when the value of the corresponding cue is zero, controlling for all of the other variables. These weights are not particularly meaningful, then, unless a value of zero is within the typical range of values of that cue. Each of the interaction terms, h hat_i, estimates the difference in the relationship between that cue value and the group judgments when it is pooled compared to when it is not pooled, controlling for all of the other variables. Thus, the interaction term coefficients qualify the interpretation of both the cue value and the cue pooling coefficients.

Factors that influence the group judgment process should affect the corresponding weights in the group judgment process model. As in SJT analyses of individual judgments, the present model intends to describe enduring aspects of group judgment performance, across judgment tasks. The weight on a particular cue, for example, summarizes the effects of all variables, such as perceived judgment relevance and cue salience, that determine that cue's influence on the group judgment. If all of those variables were held constant across judgment tasks, the cue weight would not change.

There are several distinctive (though not unique) characteristics of our approach. First, the theoretical framework we propose assumes that all the opinion change is caused by reception of external information and that information about the solution to a problem or the answer to a judgment question dominates the opinion change process. We do not allow for the occurrence of mere thinking or self-persuasion effects (e.g., Tesser, 1978) and we concentrate on "informational" influence. Second, we assume (and have found some empirical evidence) that individual and group opinion formation and change processes are essentially "linear." This means that when judgment relevant information has been appropriately measured, the individual thinking and social persuasion processes can be validly summarized by linear equations, like those that are basic in elementary statistical regression analyses. Third, we assume that judgments are based on features or attributes of the to-be-judged object and that the judgment relevant dimensions are constant across a set of judgments. As we mention elsewhere, we make the more specific assumption that the cue weights of individuals and groups remain constant (with error) across judgments. The model would not apply to a case in which each judgment was based on a different set of dimensions or on the same set of dimensions weighted differently. Fourth, the statistical models take advantage of chance relationships and therefore should be interpreted with caution. They serve as general descriptions of the policies guiding the individual and group judgments.

The following section describes an experiment in which the previously described regression analyses were used to test a hypothesis concerning the impact of a judgment task, prediscussion information distribution, on the group judgment process.

EXPERIMENT I

This section briefly describes a group judgment study, in order to illustrate the use and interpretation of the regression analysis approach and the value of the model as a description of the group judgment process. The study also provides context for the computer simulation that is described and discussed later in the present chapter. A more detailed discussion of the present experiment can be found in Gigone and Hastie (1993).

The experiment was designed to test the *common knowledge effect* hypothesis. That hypothesis predicts that *the impact of an item of information on a group judgment is directly related to the number of members of the group who know that information prior to group discussion.* The more members who receive an item of information, the more impact that item will have on the group's judgment.

Method

In the study, three-member groups of college subjects made judgments of students' grades in an introductory psychology class. A total of 120 subjects participated as members of 40 groups. Members read information about a particular to-be-judged student, including that student's aptitude test percentile score, attendance in the class, high school grade point average (GPA), enjoyment of the class, workload in other classes during that semester, and anxiety about academic performance. Next, each member judged the student's grade. Then, members met in a group and came to a consensus judgment of the grade. The same task was repeated for 32 judgments of different introductory psychology students.

The study also included an experimental manipulation of cue distribution. In three of the four conditions, each member received only four of the six cues. Within each condition, the cues were distributed so that all three members received two of the cues, two members received two of the cues, and only one member received each of the remaining two cues. A particular cue was given to the same number of members for each of the to-be-judged cases. Between conditions, the number of members with a particular cue varied. The distribution manipulation is summarized in Table 10.1.

Equation 3 provides a summary model that describes the group judgment as a weighted linear combination of the cue values. In that model, the magnitude of a cue weight is a reflection of that cue's impact on the group judgment. Thus, the common knowledge effect hypothesis would predict that the weight for a cue in Equation 3 would depend on the distribution of that cue among group members. Again, these weights can be estimated with a regression analysis, resulting in the estimated equation,

$$\hat{G}' = b'_0 + \sum_{i=1}^{n} \hat{w}'_i C_i, \tag{9}$$

where the prime indicates that the value and meaning of the coefficient estimates are different than in Equation 8. Specifically, the cue weights in Equation 9 (w'_i) subsume all of the impact of the cues into a single term, rather than dividing it among different components.

TABLE 10.1
Experiment 1: Distribution of Information by Experimental Condition: Number of Group Members Sharing Each Cue

	Experimental Condition			
Cue	*I*	*II*	*III*	*Control*
ACT or SAT Percentile	1	3	2	3
Attendance Percentage	2	3	1	3
High School GPA	3	1	2	3
Enjoyment	2	1	3	3
Other Workload	3	2	1	3
Self-Rated Anxiety	1	2	3	3

Recall that two processes were identified through which the value of a cue could affect a group's judgment. The cue could be combined with other cues into one or more of the members' individual opinions (M_j). Subsequently, those member opinions could affect the group judgment. Alternatively, through pooling, the cue could affect the group judgment directly, independent of its influence on the member opinions. The latter influence is represented by the cue value (c_i), pooling (p_i), and cue value by pooling interaction (c_ip_i) terms in Equation 7. Distribution could exert influence through the combined effect of member opinions on the group judgment. On the other hand, the influence could occur independently of member opinions, through the information pooling process.

Equations 8 and 9, therefore, allow cue impact to be decomposed into member-level and group-level effects. To the extent that overall cue impact is mediated by member opinions, the cue value coefficients in Equation 8 will be small. The cues will not have much impact, controlling for the impact of the member opinions. On the other hand, larger weights on any of the cue coefficients would indicate group-level effects.

Stasser, in a number of exemplary studies (Stasser, Taylor, & Hanna, 1989; Stasser & Titus, 1985, 1987), has argued that information distribution affects group judgments through information pooling. The more group members who know an item of information, the more likely that information will be pooled, and therefore the more influence that information will have on the group's judgment. According to Stasser's argument, pooling should have an effect on the group judgment that is independent of member opinions. Such an effect would be indicated by relatively large cue value by pooling interaction coefficient estimates in Equation 8. Moreover, pooling of a cue should be positively related to the number of group members who know the cue prior to the group discussion. If pooling a cue increases its influence on the group judgment, and cue distribution affects pooling, then cue distribution will also affect the cue's total impact on the group judgment.

Results and Discussion

A regression model of the form shown in Equation 9 was computed for each group, across the 32 group judgments. Within each group, the standardized coefficient for each cue was treated as a measure of the impact of that cue on the group's judgments. Figure 10.3 shows the mean coefficients for each cue, as a function of cue distribution. The effect of distribution on the impact of each cue was tested by performing six different one-way analyses of variance, one for each cue, with condition (distribution) as the independent factor. Because regression estimates for all six cues are computed for each group, these analyses are not independent tests. A significant linear simple effect and a nonsignificant quadratic simple effect supports the common knowledge effect hypothesis for a particular cue. The linear effect was significant for four of the six cues, aptitude test percentile [$F(1, 27) = 26.7$, partial $r^2 = .50$, $p < .0001$], attendance percentage

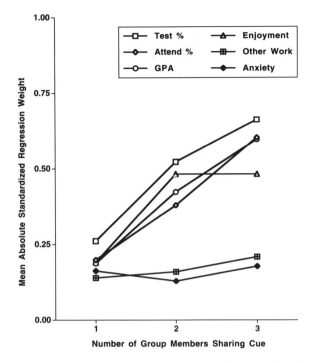

FIG. 10.3. Impact of cues on group judgments as a function of cue distribution—Experiment 1.

$[F(1, 27) = 58.6$, partial $r^2 = .68$, $p < .0001]$, high school GPA $[F(1, 27) = 44.9$, partial $r^2 = .62$, $p < .0001]$, and enjoyment $[F(1, 27) = 23.3$, partial $r^2 = .46$, $p < .0001]$. Each of these cues had more impact on the judgments of groups within which all three members received the cue than in groups within which only one member received the cue. The comparison of the "shared by two" condition to the other two conditions was significant only for the enjoyment cue, $F(1, 27) - 7.81$, partial $r^2 = .22$, $p < .01$. In the condition in which two members received the enjoyment cue, that item of information had more impact on the group judgments than would be expected if the common knowledge effect were linear. Thus, the pattern of results generally supports the common knowledge effect hypothesis.

What about the group process leads to the common knowledge effect? Stasser's explanation requires that cue pooling be positively related to the number of members who know a particular cue. The content of the group discussions was analyzed, providing a record of whether or not each of the cues was pooled during discussion of each of the 32 cases. Figure 10.4 shows the relationship between distribution and pooling for each of the six cues. The linear relationship between distribution and cue pooling was marginally significant for the aptitude test percentile cue $[F(1, 25) = 4.11$, partial $r^2 = .14$, $p = .053]$, and significant for the attendance percentage $[F(1, 25) = 14.9$, partial $r^2 = .37$, $p < .001]$, high school

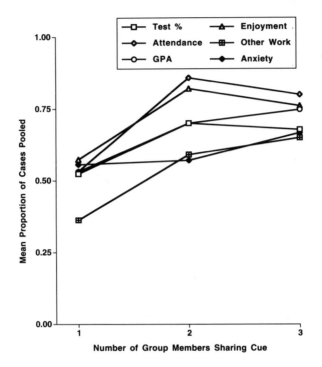

FIG. 10.4. Pooling of cues as a function of cue distribution—Experiment 1.

GPA [$F(1, 25) = 5.97$, partial $r^2 = .19$, $p < .05$], enjoyment [$F(1, 25) = 6.94$, partial $r^2 = .16$, $p < .05$], and other workload cues [$F(1, 25) = 27.8$, partial $r^2 = .53$, $p < .0001$].[1] However, the quadratic test comparing the shared-by-two condition to the average of the unshared and fully shared conditions was significant for attendance percentage [$F(1, 25) = 10.0$, partial $r^2 = .29$, $p < .001$] and enjoyment [$F(1, 25) = 6.05$, partial $r^2 = .19$, $p < .05$], and marginally significant for other workload [$F(1, 25) = 3.10$, partial $r^2 = .11$, $p = .091$]. With the exception of anxiety, all of the cues were discussed more often when fully shared than when known by only one member. However, three of the cues were discussed the most often when they were known by two of the three members.

Within conditions, the frequency of cue pooling was related to cue impact, on average. The relationship between the pooling rate for a cue and that cue's coefficient from Equation 9, controlling for experimental condition, was positive and reliable for test percentile [$F(1, 24) = 6.68$, partial $r^2 = .22$, $p < .05$], attendance percentage [$F(1, 24) = 9.30$, partial $r^2 = .28$, $p < .0001$], and enjoyment [$F(1, 24) = 10.5$, partial $r^2 = .27$, $p < .01$], and marginally reliable for high school GPA [$F(1, 24) = 3.91$, partial $r^2 = .14$, $p = .060$]. Within levels of sharing, a cue had more impact

---

[1]Tapes from two of the groups in the experimental conditions were not analyzable, due to equipment failure.

on a group's judgments when it was pooled more frequently. There are two possible explanations for the preceding finding. More frequent pooling might cause greater cue impact on the group's judgments. On the other hand, a group that considers a cue to be important, and therefore on whose judgments the cue has more impact, might also tend to discuss the cue more often. The same regression analyses shed some light on the issue. Controlling for between-condition differences in pooling rates, cue impact still depended on the number of members who received a cue. The linear effect of sharing was reliable for test percentile [$F(1, 24) = 13.8$, partial $r^2 = .37$, $p < .005$], attendance percentage [$F(1, 24) = 25.9$, partial $r^2 = .52$, $p < .0001$], high school GPA [$F(1, 24) = 23.3$, partial $r^2 = .49$, $p < .0001$], and enjoyment [$F(1, 24) = 10.5$, partial $r^2 = .30$, $p < .005$]. Between-condition differences in cue impact, therefore, cannot be explained by differences in pooling rates. However, within a group, a cue might still have more of an impact on those group judgments prior to which it was pooled.

In order for the effect of distribution on the group judgment to be mediated by pooling, a cue would need to have more of an impact when it was pooled than when it was not pooled. In Equation 8, then, the coefficient estimates for the interactions between cue value and pooling (b_{CPi}) should be significantly different from zero. The mean coefficient estimate for the cue value by pooling interaction was not significantly different from zero for any of the six cues. Above and beyond the member opinions, pooling a cue did not affect the relationship between the cue value and the group judgment. On the other hand, the mean coefficient estimate for a member's opinion (b_{Mk}), controlling for the other members' opinions, the cue values, cue pooling, and the interactions between cue values and pooling, was significantly greater than zero. Thus, even when holding constant the other variables, a single member's prediscussion opinions were significantly related to the group's judgments, on average.

Thus, our analyses of the example study suggest an alternative explanation for the common knowledge effect. The effect of distribution appears to be mediated through the member opinions. Differential cue distribution affects group judgments through the number of member opinions influenced by the cue. The members must be able to learn each other's opinions. In the example study, a mean of 2.93 (out of 3) members pooled their opinions during the discussion of each to-be-judged case. Thus, for the example task, the summary provided by the group judgment process model fits the member opinion pooling explanation for the common knowledge effect better than it does the information pooling explanation.

A second experiment further illustrates the utility of the descriptive model of group judgment and the related regression analyses. It was designed, in part, to systematically replicate the common knowledge effect with larger groups and a larger set of cues. Seven group members received a total of 11 pieces of information about each of the same 32 to-be-judged students. Five new cues were chosen that were not good predictors of course grades, above and beyond the information provided by the other cues. The distribution of 2 of the 11 cues, test percentile and workload in other courses, was varied between groups. Thus, the experiment was designed to test the effect of the differential distribution of those two pieces of information.

EXPERIMENT 2

Method

College student subjects met in seven-member groups. Each group made judgments of the course grades received by the same 32 students. A total of 256 subjects participated as members of 38 groups. Groups were randomly assigned to four conditions (three experimental conditions and a control condition).

In addition to the six cues used in the first study, members received five additional pieces of information about each to-be-judged student: gender, class (year in school), motivation to take the course because it was required, motivation to take the course because of interest in the subject, and need for achievement. In the experimental conditions, each member received either 6 or 7 of the 11 cues prior to the group's discussion of each case. Within a case, each cue was distributed across members according to the design summarized in Table 10.2. Two cues, aptitude test percentile and other workload, were distributed differently between conditions. Either one, four, or seven members received each of those cues. In the control condition, all 11 cues were "fully shared."

The procedure was the same as in the first experiment.

TABLE 10.2
Experiment 2: Distribution of Information by Experimental Condition: Number of Group Members Sharing Each Cue

	Experimental Condition			
Cue	I	II	III	Control
Aptitude %	1	7	4	7
Attendance	2	2	2	7
H.S. GPA	3	3	3	7
Enjoyment	4	4	4	7
Other Work	7	1	4	7
Anxiety	6	6	6	7
Gender	5	5	5	7
Class	7	7	7	7
Motiv./Required	1	1	1	7
Motiv./Interest	3	3	3	7
Need for Achiev.	5	5	5	7

Results and Discussion

Again, the impact of each of the cues on a group's judgments was measured by computing the standardized coefficient estimate for that cue in a regression equation of the form shown in Equation 9. According to the model, each of these coefficients represents the combined impact of the cue, including its impact on the seven members' judgments and any additional impact on the group's judgments that results from pooling of the cue.

The common knowledge effect hypothesis predicts that the impact of a cue on the group's judgments will depend on the number of members who receive that cue. We tested whether the regression weights for the aptitude test percentile and other workload cues varied between conditions, depending on the number of members receiving the cue in question. Again, a significant linear effect and a nonsignificant quadratic effect of the number of group members on cue impact are predicted by the common knowledge effect hypothesis.

In Fig. 10.5, the mean absolute regression weights of both the aptitude test percentile and the other workload cues are plotted as a function of the number of group members who received the cue. For the aptitude test percentile cue, the linear contrast was highly significant [$F(1, 28) = 81.5$, $p < .0001$, partial $r^2 = .75$]. The cue had a much greater impact when it was received by all seven group members prior to every judgment than when it was received by only one member. The quadratic effect was marginally significant and positive [$F(1, 28)$

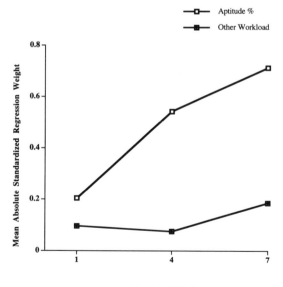

FIG. 10.5. Impact of cues on group judgments as a function of cue distribution—Experiment 2.

= 3.30, $p = .08$, partial $r^2 = .11$]. For the other workload cue, the linear contrast was significant [$F(1, 38) = 4.37, p = .046$, partial $r^2 = .14$]. In addition, the quadratic effect was marginally significant and negative [$F(1, 38) = 3.49, p = .07$, partial $r^2 = .11$]. Both cues had the greatest impact on the group judgments when they were received by all seven group members. However, the magnitude of the effect was much greater for the aptitude test percentile cue than for the other workload cue. In addition, the relative impact of a cue when it was received by four of the seven members was different for the other workload cue than for the aptitude test percentile cue.

Figure 10.6 shows the mean proportion of case discussions during which the aptitude test percentile and other workload cues were pooled, as a function of cue distribution. For the aptitude test percentile cue, only the quadratic contrast was significant [$F(1, 24) = 5.65, p = .03$, partial $r^2 = .20$]. On average, the groups in which four members received the aptitude test percentile cue prior to each discussion pooled that cue more than did groups in the other two conditions. For the other workload cue, only the linear effect of cue distribution was significant [$F(1, 24) = 22.8, p < .0001$, partial $r^2 = .35$]. The more members who received the other workload cue, the more frequently it was pooled.

For the aptitude test percentile and other workload cues, we tested for a relationship between cue pooling and cue impact, within condition. That relationship was not significant for either cue. However, for the aptitude test percentile cue, there was a significant linear effect of cue distribution in the same regression model [$F(1, 23) = 53.5, p < .0001$, partial $r^2 = .71$]. Thus, controlling

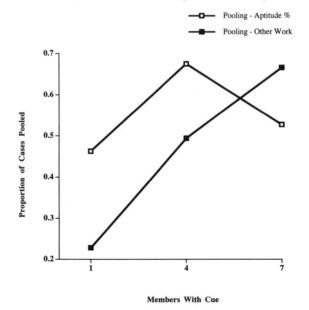

FIG. 10.6. Pooling of cues as a function of cue distribution—Experiment 2.

for the frequency of pooling, the more members who received the aptitude test percentile cue, the more impact that cue had on the group's judgments. Taken together, these results again suggest that the common knowledge effect is not mediated through differences in information pooling between groups.

We also analyzed the effect of cue pooling on cue impact within groups. We performed the analysis for all 11 cues, and for groups in both the three experimental conditions and in the "fully informed" control condition. Within each group, we computed a regression model of the form shown in Equation 8. The interaction term estimates the difference in a cue's impact depending on whether or not it was pooled during the discussion of a case. We then averaged each interaction term coefficient terms across groups and tested for a mean difference from zero. Among the groups in the experimental conditions, none of the mean interaction terms was significantly different from zero. Among the control groups, the coefficient estimates for the aptitude test percentile [$t(6) = 2.80$, $p = .03$], high school GPA [$t(6) = 2.42$, $p = .046$], motivation/required [$t(6) = 2.49$, $p = .04$], and motivation/interest [$t(6) = 3.35$, $p = .01$] cues were significantly different from zero, on average. For groups in the control condition, then, 4 of the 11 cues had more of an impact on a group's judgment when they were pooled. Surprisingly, this effect of pooling occurred even though all seven group members received all of the cues prior to discussion of each case. In those groups, each group member initially received 11 different pieces of information, too much information to recall easily. Perhaps the pooling of a particular cue served as a memory aid or to emphasize the importance of that cue.

A COMPUTER SIMULATION OF GROUP JUDGMENT

The preceding experiments demonstrate the value of the group judgment model that we have developed. With those experiments, we showed the usefulness and meaningfulness of the regression analyses. We were able to show that the effect of unequal information distribution in the grade judgment task was due to the mediation of the members' opinions, rather than due to unequal pooling. Not only are the empirical data consistent with the model, the model provides new insights into the group judgment process.

Despite the success of the model in its encounters with empirical data, the status of the model as theory is somewhat unsatisfying. At its present level of specification, the model serves to describe, but not really to predict. Not that such a descriptive model cannot inform us; that information discussion plays little or no role in at least some group judgment tasks is counterintuitive and surprising. Nevertheless, specifying the model at a smaller grain size should enhance our ability to make testable predictions that go beyond intuitive speculations.

The computer simulation model is one such way to present the model as a concrete, predictive theory. With the aforementioned considerations in mind, we made a "first pass" at translating our verbal model into specific computer algorithms. A description of that attempt follows. Because computer modeling is still rarely employed in theories of social behavior, we first briefly review the area.

The Value of Computer Simulation Modeling

Computer simulation modeling offers a promising approach in the area of social behavior. Early reviews (Abelson, 1968; Hovland, 1960) focused on the advantages of computer simulation for theory development. Since then, computer simulations have proliferated in psychology. However, only a few of those models have focused on social behavior (Hastie, 1988; Hastie, Penrod, & Pennington, 1983; Kalick & Hamilton, 1986; Penrod & Hastie, 1981; Smith, 1988; Stasser, 1988), despite the advantages that computer simulation provides to theorists in social psychology.

A number of authors have commented on the ways in which computer simulation modeling can aid theory development and presentation. For example, the computer simulation serves as an alternative form of expressing a theory of social behavior (Ostrom, 1988). Expressing a theory in a computer language promotes completeness and consistency in reasoning (Hintzman, 1991; Lewandowsky, 1993) and facilitates communication (Hastie, 1988). In addition, the computer model can make clear predictions of social behavior from a complex set of theoretical assertions. However complex the hypothesized system of behavioral causation, the computer can compute predictions (Lewandowsky, 1993). In addition, the computer simulation can model the course of behavior over time. The computer simulation is ideal for making predictions about social behavior, which often involves multiple actors, hypothesized latent variables with several related observable variables, and reciprocal relationships between actors and variables.

However, computer simulation has also been criticized on several grounds. Critics contend that simulations promote overly complex theories (Hintzman, 1991; Loftus, 1985), remove the incentive to do difficult conceptual thinking, and promote the fitting of data over the search for underlying truth (Loftus, 1985). Luce (1989) argued that many important issues in theory construction cannot be embodied in a computer program. Moreover, the development and evaluation of computer models are subject to the same biases as are verbal theories (Hintzman, 1991). In addition, irrelevant aspects of the theory specification as a computer program may have substantial effects on the model's output (Lewandowsky, 1993). Moreover, the output of a computer simulation may be difficult to evaluate (Hintzman, 1991). Hintzman contended that computer models should be evaluated in terms of what we learn from them, rather than by their quantitative output. Despite its many advantages, then, computer modeling is not a panacea for the difficulties involved in the development of verbal theories of social behavior.

Goals of the Present Computer Model

The goals of the present computer simulation are modest. We set out to develop a simple model that is consistent with our intuitions about the group judgment process and with the descriptive model that was presented earlier. As we noted previously, one of the values of computer modeling is its ability to model interacting individuals. Thus, we modeled both individual-level and group-level processes. We determined to keep specific assumptions and parameter fitting to a minimum. By comparing a simple model to the empirical data, we hoped to discover what modifications and what additional assumptions and/or parameters are necessary to adequately model the pooling of unshared information.

Our approach is similar to that advocated by Einhorn, Kleinmutz, and Kleinmutz (1979). They argued that linear regression and (process-tracing) computer simulation models both capture the processes underlying judgment, but at different and complementary levels of generality. In their view, regression models focus on the information combination and learning from feedback subprocesses of judgment, whereas process-tracing models focus on information search. Similarly, our regression models describe the relative importance of cue values, cue pooling, and member opinions across multiple judgments. Our computer model describes in more detail the group's integration of information into a single consensus judgment. Both models describe the same group judgment process, but do so at different levels of analysis.

The Information Processing Model

The computer model simulates groups and group members as information processors. A judgment is made based on the values of a set of cues. A group is composed of some number of individual members. Each member has a judgment policy, which is made up of a set of numerical cue weights. The judgment policy contains a weight for every cue in the cue set. A cue that is irrelevant to a member would be associated with a zero weight in that member's judgment policy. A member's judgment policy is assumed to remain constant during the judgment process. Moreover, in the present simulation, a member's judgment policy does not change across multiple judgments.

Cues are distributed to members at the beginning of the judgment process for each to-be-judged case. A particular cue may be given to any number of the members and a particular member may receive any number of cues. Once a cue is known to a member, either through the initial distribution or through subsequent information pooling, it is not forgotten. Each member forms an initial opinion, which is an additive linear combination of all known cue values, with each cue value weighted (multiplied) by the associated cue weight in that member's judgment policy.

At the beginning of the group discussion, all group members pool their initial opinions. After all of the opinions have been pooled, the members adjust their opinions to reflect the opinions of the other members. The adjustment is a weighted average of the member's own opinion and the opinions of all of the other members. The other members' opinions are all weighted equally.

The case is then discussed for a discrete number of pooling rounds. The total number of pooling rounds depends on the initial disagreement between the members' rounded initial opinions. If all members were in agreement initially, no pooling takes place. Otherwise, the number of pooling rounds is a linear function of the mean absolute difference between each two members. Each pooling round consists of a single member pooling a single cue value. The selection of the pooling member and the pooled cue are random, subject to a member participation parameter (Stephan & Mishler, 1952). Once a cue value has been pooled, it is known by all subjects. A pooled cue only affects a member's opinion if that member did not know the value of that cue prior to the current pooling round. The member's new opinion is a weighted average of the previous opinion and the cue value. The cue value is weighted by the associated weight in that member's judgment policy and the previous opinion is weighted by an opinion weight parameter. The opinion weight parameter is constant across all members and judgments.

After all of the pooling rounds have been completed, the group makes a group judgment. The group judgment is a simple average of all of the members' final opinions. The group judgment is rounded to the nearest whole value. The group then judges the next case, beginning with the information distribution step.

This information processing model was expressed as a computer program in Turbo Pascal, and run on an IBM clone computer under the DOS operating system. A technical description of the computer simulation model can be obtained from the authors.

A SIMULATION OF THE COMMON KNOWLEDGE EFFECT STUDY

Overview

This section describes an attempt to simulate the group judgment study that was discussed earlier. The simulation represents an example of a retrospective simulation (Stasser, 1988), in which the output of the model, with reasonable parameter settings, is compared to the observed data from the empirical study. Part of such a comparison involves choosing the proper dimensions on which to compare the simulated and observed behavior. In the present case, that choice is motivated by the group judgment process model.

Most of the input and the parameter settings used in the simulation were derived from the empirical behavior of the fully shared information control groups in the first example study. Other parameters were set according to past research and our intuitions about the group judgment process.

The design of the simulation was the same as for the three experimental conditions in the example study, with the cue distribution pattern as a between-groups factor.

Model Assessment

In order to test the "behavior" of the model, 100 simulated groups were run in each of the three distribution conditions. Two comparisons between the observed data and the model output are of primary interest. The first question is whether or not the simulation model produces a common knowledge effect of comparable magnitude to the effect observed in the actual groups. The second question is whether or not in the model, the impact of a cue on the group's judgment depends on whether or not it is pooled. In order to answer those questions, the appropriate regression models were computed across the 32 judgments for each simulated group. Those models were of the form shown in Equations 8 and 7, respectively.

Results and Discussion

Figure 10.7 shows the mean absolute standardized regression coefficients, from models regressing the simulated group judgment on the set of six cues (Equation 9), as a function of the number of simulated members who received the cue. Thus, Fig. 10.7 displays the common knowledge effect among the simulated groups. The partial r^2 of the linear effect of cue distribution indicates the percentage of the variation in cue impact that is explained by the mean difference in impact between the "unshared" and "fully shared" conditions. The partial r^2 was equal to .46 for the aptitude test percentile cue, .29 for the attendance percentage cue, .64 for the high school GPA cue, .36 for the enjoyment cue, .05 for the other workload cue, and .09 for the anxiety cue. Thus, the same four cues show a strong common knowledge effect as in the empirical data.

We tested the fit of the model output to the empirical data with multiple single-sample t tests, treating each mean value from the simulation output, averaged across the 100 groups in each condition, as an expected value without any sampling error. Because we are fitting a model to data, rather than testing for an effect that differs from a null hypothesis, we are in effect turning hypothesis testing on its head. We wish to determine whether the predictions of our model are close enough to the empirical results that the difference could have been due to chance—evidence *in support of* our theoretical assumptions. Therefore, the traditional alpha level of 5% may not be appropriate. However, using multiple t

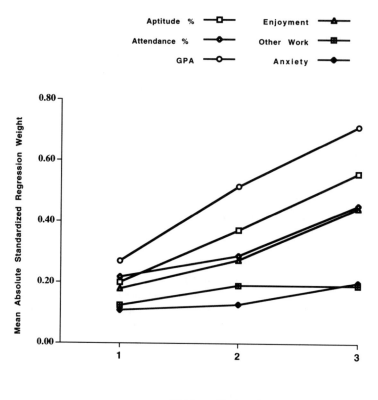

FIG. 10.7. Impact of cues on group judgments as a function of cue distribu-tion—computer simulation model.

tests also inflates the probability of a chance difference on any one of the tests. With those considerations in mind, we report statistics concerning all differences for which the probability of chance occurrence is less than .25. Any such results can be considered to be evidence *against* the good fit of the model output.

We first tested the fit of the mean coefficient estimates from the regression models shown in Equation 9. Among the groups in the experimental conditions, the difference between the empirical groups and the model output was large for four of the six cues, aptitude test percentile [$t(27) = 3.38$, $p = .002$], attendance percentage [$t(27) = 3.01$, $p = .005$], high school GPA [$t(27) = 3.97$, $p = .0004$], and enjoyment [$t(27) = 3.03$, $p = .005$]. For the high school GPA cue, the mean coefficient estimate from the model output was larger than the mean coefficient estimate from the empirical data. For the other three cues, on the other hand, the means from the model output were smaller than the means from the em-pirical data. In the model, then, the magnitude of cue impact failed to fit the empirical data, on average across experimental conditions.

We also tested whether the magnitude of the mean coefficient estimate difference between model output and empirical data depended on experimental condition for any of the six cues. These analyses test whether the common knowledge effect was similar for the empirical groups and the model. A difference was found for the attendance percentage [$F(2, 27) = 5.35$, $p = .01$, $R^2 = .28$] and enjoyment cues [$F(2, 27) = 6.30$, $p = .006$, $R^2 = .32$]. For the attendance percentage cue, the common knowledge effect of information distribution was "steeper" among the empirical groups than in the model output. For the enjoyment cue, the model failed to predict the large impact in the "shared by two" condition. In general, the between-condition differences in cue impact computed from the model's output fit the empirical data, even though the magnitude of the coefficient estimates differed.

We also looked at cue pooling within the computer simulation model. The average number of cues pooled per case, out of six, was lower among the simulated groups than among the empirical groups [$Ms = 3.34$ vs. 3.87, $t(27) = 4.13$, $p = .0003$]. Not surprisingly, then, the pooling rates of four of the six cues were lower for the model output than for the empirical data, including aptitude test percentile [$t(27) = 2.23$, $p = .03$], attendance percentage [$t(27) = 5.19$, $p < .0001$], high school GPA [$t(27) = 2.86$, $p = .008$], and enjoyment [$t(27) = 4.46$, $p < .0001$]. Thus, the model did not predict high enough pooling rates for most of the cues. Moreover, it did not predict the differences in mean pooling rates between cues.

In the computer simulation, cue pooling was much more dependent on information distribution than it was in the empirical data. Figure 10.8 shows the frequency of cue pooling as a function of the number of simulated members who received the cue on each of the 32 trials. The partial r^2 of the linear effect of cue distribution on cue pooling was equal to .77 for the test percentile cue, .81 for the attendance percentage cue, .77 for the high school GPA cue, .83 for the enjoyment cue, .79 for the other workload cue, and .82 for the anxiety cue. Within levels of distribution, then, there was very little variation in the rate of pooling for any of the cues. The strong effect of information distribution on pooling rates in the simulation is reflected in the analyses of between-condition differences in the comparison of pooling rates. Information distribution had an effect on the model-empirical pooling rate difference for all six cues, aptitude test percentile [$F(2, 27) = 4.64$, $p = .02$, $R^2 = .27$], attendance percentage [$F(2, 27) = 5.37$, $p = .01$, $R^2 = .30$], high school GPA [$F(2, 27) = 1.51$, $p = .24$, $R^2 = .11$], enjoyment [$F(2, 27) = 7.11$, $p = .004$, $R^2 = .36$], other workload [$F(2, 27) = 3.00$, $p = .07$, $R^2 = .19$], and anxiety [$F(2, 27) = 6.30$, $p = .006$, $R^2 = .34$]. In every case, the mean pooling rate increased more as a function of the number of group members receiving the cue in the simulation than it did in the empirical data. In addition, the computer model failed to simulate the higher pooling rates of any of the cues when shared by two of the three group members.

We estimated a regression model for each of the simulated groups of the form shown in Equation 8. In those models, the interaction term for each cue

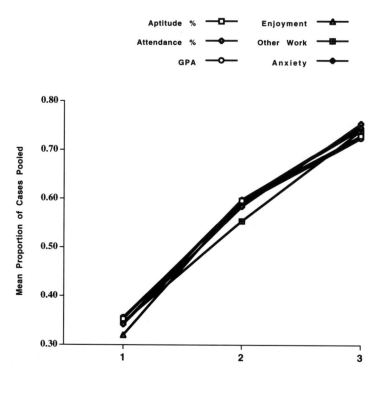

FIG. 10.8. Pooling of cues as a function of cue distribution—computer simulation model.

between pooling and cue value is of primary concern. Only two of the cues showed a notable difference between the empirical and model values, across the three experimental conditions, aptitude test percentile [$t(24) = 1.22$, $p = .24$] and attendance percentage [$t(23) = 1.55$, $p = .13$]. In both cases, the interaction coefficients from the empirical groups were larger, on average, than the mean values from the model output. Between experimental conditions, the size of the model output versus empirical data difference varied for the enjoyment [$F(2, 17) = 2.24$, $p = .14$, $R^2 = .21$] and anxiety cues [$F(2, 17) = 7.09$, $p = .006$, $R^2 = .45$]. In the model, as in the example study, information pooling had little effect on the impact of a particular cue on a particular group judgment.

Thus, our informal analyses show that the model was better at modeling the differences between conditions than the cue-judgment relationships within conditions. In addition, the cue pooling frequencies point out a notable shortcoming of the current computer model. In the model, pooling frequency was highly dependent on the number of group members who had the cue. Pooling by the empirical groups, on the other hand, was not nearly so dependent on cue distribution. In fact, three of the six cues were discussed most often when they were shared by only two of the three members. A better fitting model would therefore require modifications in the cue-pooling mechanism. In the first example experiment, cue pooling and cue impact were related even when controlling for information distribution. This result suggests that a particular cue is pooled more often within groups that consider that cue to be important. In the simulation, perhaps the likelihood that a particular member pools a particular cue should be dependent, in part, on the member judgment policy weight that corresponds to the cue.

In general, the example simulation shows that a group judgment process model like the one instantiated in the computer model is consistent with our more general algebraic model.

CONCLUSIONS

This is a report of the early stages of our effort to construct a comprehensive model of small group judgment from ingredients provided by Brunswik and Hammond, Anderson, and Stasser. We began by laying out a general, descriptive model of quantitative group judgment. That model, based on the Brunswikian "lens model" (Brunswik, 1956; Hammond, 1966) and social judgment theory (Brehmer & Joyce, 1988; Hammond et al., 1986), breaks down the group judgment into a number of components. The group judgment is seen as a weighted linear combination of the values of the relevant informational cues, the opinions of the group members, and the pooling of information. Each member's opinion is hypothesized to be a weighted linear combination of the cues in that member's memory. The various weights in the model equations might be affected by a number of factors, including differences in member roles, differences in cue importance or salience, and the distribution of information among group members.

Our model is distinctive in that it integrates the individual level and the group level of judgment into a single theoretical system. We have fit the SJT approach to individual judgment into an expanded model that applies a similar approach to group judgment. In doing so, we have focused on the pooling of unshared information, the process that is unique to the group level of consensus judgment. As a whole, the model emphasizes that group judgment cannot be set apart from the judgments of the constituent members. Neither can group judgment be understood without considering group-level judgment processes.

From the equations suggested by the model, we developed a set of regression analyses that assess the impact of the various components of the model over multiple group judgments. Similar regression analyses to study group judgment have been used within the framework of information integration theory (Anderson, 1981). Our approach is not unique in its use of regression techniques, but instead in the particular parameters that are estimated.

We believe that the model and analyses allow us to more effectively explore the role of information and discussion in group judgment than do existing approaches. Stasser (Stasser et al., 1989; Stasser & Titus, 1985, 1987) has concluded that the effect of information distribution is mediated by the content of discussion. We do not doubt the validity of his findings. However, with his method, Stasser was unable to completely rule out the mediation of member opinions on his groups' judgments or to estimate the magnitude of the effect of discussion content. Both are possible with our approach.

In our own empirical studies, summarized in the present chapter, we have failed to find significant effects of discussion content on group judgment. We do not believe that the lack of an effect of discussion content can be generalized to all group judgment tasks. Our groups had little incentive to pay close attention to pooled information and it was not clear that they could significantly improve their judgments over simply averaging the judgments of their constituent members. A number of factors might influence the impact of discussion content, such as incentives for accuracy, the transparency of cue meaning, accountability, and the provision of accuracy feedback. Our method should be able to assess the effects of manipulating those and other independent variables.

The regression analysis approach is not without limitations. It requires that groups make quantitative judgments, based on cues that are scalable. On the other hand, this limitation has a corresponding advantage. We have presented one of the few quantitative models of group judgment, in which quantitative judgments can be predicted directly from cue values. However, so that weights may be estimated, a group must also make several judgments from the same set of cues. Moreover, the regression analyses will only pick up relationships that are constant across judgments (consistent with our assumption that the weights represent enduring qualities of the judgment process). Member opinions must also be measured; doing so may cause those opinions to have more weight in the group's judgment. Despite its many advantages, the present approach will not be amenable to the study of all group judgment tasks.

We have also presented a theoretical computer simulation of the small group judgment processes that we have studied empirically. Many forms of such a simulation are possible in the theory development enterprise. In our case, the simulation is a straightforward and rough implementation of the verbal assumptions that surround our proposed algebraic models of the individual and group judgment processes. But surprisingly, many additional assumptions must be explicitly stated to provide a complete summary of our thinking about the group judgment process. Some of these "nonalgebraic" assumptions are methodological (e.g., the parts of the model that simulate the experimental design of information distribution), some are stochastic (e.g., assumptions about the probabilities that group members will share information), and some are structural (e.g., assumptions about when members will update their opinions). The development of the computer simulation model required that these underlying assumptions be specified in concrete, unambiguous form.

In addition, computer simulation modeling is extremely useful in theory testing. We have attempted to state our theoretical assumptions in sufficient detail that computer language instructions can be created to perform a skeletal version of the experimental task given to our human subjects. The performance of such a model can then be compared to the behavior of the human subjects. The simulation model's achievements and failures provide a clear and sobering evaluation of just how much we really know about the processes we are studying and even provide a few clues as to which of our assumptions need to be changed or elaborated. Perhaps the more elaborate stochastic models recently proposed by Stasser and Taylor (1991) would be helpful here. Stasser and Taylor modeled the conversational turn taking among small groups. They showed that the probability that a particular group member will speak next during a group discussion is dependent both on the member's overall propensity to speak (included in our model) and on how recently the member last spoke. Similarly, we might develop a more complex stochastic mechanism for determining which cue a member will pool next, perhaps one in which cue pooling depends on the member's judgment policy. With such a mechanism, we would expect the model's cue pooling to more closely match the empirical data.

As we suggest earlier, the model fitting reveals some areas in which our model currently falls short. At present, our computer simulation calls into question our assumptions concerning the pooling of items of information. The data from our empirical groups suggest that pooling cannot be modeled by random sampling from the full set of cues known to a member. Such a mechanism does not model either the between-cue pooling rate differences or the within-condition relationships between cue pooling rate and cue impact. In addition, the computer simulation failed to model the absolute magnitudes of the mean cue weights in the group judgment policies. However, Hintzman (1991) argued that computer simulations should be evaluated in terms of their qualitative, rather than their quantitative performance. We could improve the quantitative fit of our computer model by tweaking parameters or by adding additional complexity. The question would remain, though, whether we had made the correct modifications or whether we were simply capitalizing on insignificant quirks of our computer algorithms. Thus, a more meaningful test of our theoretical assumptions is whether we can predict qualitative differences in group output that result from meaningful differences in input, task, or processing characteristics. Our model was relatively successful in modeling between-condition differences in cue impact, namely the common knowledge effect.

Thus, even though our information processing model, as implemented in the computer simulation, requires modification if it is to successfully mimic the empirical data, it need not be discarded. If anything, the "flawed" model makes a stronger case for our more general conclusions concerning the impact of information discussion on group judgment. Based on the SJT regression analysis of our empirical groups, we argued that biased discussion of shared information did not explain the differences in the impact of cues due to their differential distribution among group members. In the computer simulation, discussion of cues was more strongly biased by differential distribution than in our empirical groups. Yet the conclusions were the same; in the simulated "groups," as in the actual groups, the impact of cues on the group judgment was mediated by their impact on the members' opinions. Thus, even an incorrect model can teach us about the phenomena of interest.

REFERENCES

Abelson, R. P. (1968). Simulation and social behavior. In C. Lindzey & E. Aronson (Eds.), *Handbook of social psychology* (Vol. 2, pp. 274–356). Reading, MA: Addison-Wesley.

Anderson, N. H. (1981). *Foundations of information integration theory*. New York: Academic Press.

Brehmer, B., & Joyce, C. R. B. (Eds.). (1988). *Advances in psychology: Vol. 54. Human judgment: The SJT view*. North Holland: Elsevier.

Brunswik, E. (1956). *Perception and the representative design of psychological experiments*. Berkeley: University of California Press.

Einhorn, H. J., Kleinmutz, D. N., & Kleinmutz, B. (1979). Linear regression and process-tracing models of judgment. *Psychological Review, 86,* 465–485.

Gigone, D., & Hastie, R. (1993). The common knowledge effect: Information sharing and group judgment. *Journal of Personality and Social Psychology, 65,* 959–974.

Graesser, C. C. (1991). A social averaging theorem for group decision making. In N. H. Anderson (Ed.), *Contributions to information integration theory: Vol. 2. Social* (pp. 1–40). Hillsdale, NJ: Lawrence Erlbaum Associates.

Hammond, K. R. (Ed.). (1966). *The psychology of Egon Brunswik*. New York: Holt, Rinehart & Winston.

Hammond, K. R., Stewart, T. R., Brehmer, B., & Steinmann, D. (1986). Social judgment theory. In H. R. Arkes & K. R. Hammond (Eds.), *Judgment and decision making: An interdisciplinary reader* (pp. 56–76). New York: Cambridge University Press.

Hastie, R. (1988). A computer simulation model of person memory. *Journal of Experimental Social Psychology, 24,* 423–447.

Hastie, R., Penrod, S. D., & Pennington, N. (1983). *Inside the jury*. Cambridge, MA: Harvard University Press.

Hintzman, D. L. (1991). Why are formal models useful in psychology? In W. E. Hockley & S. Lewandowsky (Eds.), *Relating theory and data: Essays on human memory in honor of Bennet B. Murdock* (pp. 39–56). Hillsdale, NJ: Lawrence Erlbaum Associates.

Hovland, C. I. (1960). Computer simulation of thinking. *American Psychologist, 15,* 687–693.

Judd, C. M., & McClelland, G. H. (1989). *Data analysis: A model-comparison approach*. San Diego: Harcourt Brace.

Kalick, S. M., & Hamilton, T. E., III. (1986). The matching hypothesis reexamined. *Journal of Personality and Social Psychology, 51,* 673–682.

Lewandowsky, S. (1993). The rewards and hazards of computer simulations. *Psychological Science, 4,* 236–243.

Loftus, G. (1985). Johannes Kepler's computer simulation of the universe: Some remarks about theory in psychology. *Behavior Research Methods, Instruments, & Computers, 17,* 149–156.

Luce, R. D. (1989). Mathematical psychology and the computer revolution. In J. A. Keats, R. Taft, & S. H. Lovibond (Eds.), *Mathematical and theoretical systems* (pp. 123–137). Amsterdam: North-Holland.

Ostrom, T. M. (1988). Computer simulation: The third symbol system. *Journal of Experimental Social Psychology, 24,* 381–392.

Penrod, S. D., & Hastie, R. (1981). A computer simulation of jury decision making. *Psychological Review, 87*, 133–159.

Slovic, P., & Lichtenstein, S. (1971). Comparison of Bayesian and regression approaches to the study of information processing in judgment. *Organizational Behavior and Human Performance, 6*, 649–744.

Smith, E. R. (1988). Category accessibility effects in a simulated exemplar-based memory. *Journal of Experimental Social Psychology, 24*, 448–463.

Stasser, G. (1988). Computer simulation as a research tool: The DISCUSS model of group decision making. *Journal of Experimental Social Psychology, 24*, 393–422.

Stasser, G., & Taylor, L. A. (1991). Speaking turns in face-to-face discussion. *Journal of Personality and Social Psychology, 60*, 675–684.

Stasser, G., Taylor, L. A., & Hanna, C. (1989). Information sampling in structured and unstructured discussions of three- and six-person groups. *Journal of Personality and Social Psychology, 57*, 67–78.

Stasser, G., & Titus, W. (1985). Pooling of unshared information in group decision making: Biased information sampling during discussion. *Journal of Personality and Social Psychology, 48*, 1467–1478.

Stasser, G., & Titus, W. (1987). Effects of information load and percentage of shared information on the dissemination of unshared information during group discussion. *Journal of Personality and Social Psychology, 53*, 81–93.

Stephan, F. F., & Mishler, E. G. (1952). The distribution of participation in small groups: An exponential approximation. *American Sociological Review, 17*, 598–608.

Tesser, A. (1978). Self-generated attitude change. In L. Berkowitz (Ed.), *Advances in experimental social psychology* (Vol. 2, pp. 289–338). New York: Academic Press.

Tversky, A., & Kahneman, D. (1974). Judgment under uncertainty: Heuristics and biases. *Science, 185*, 1124–1131.

11

THE EXTENDED GROUP SITUATION THEORY (EGST): EXPLAINING THE AMOUNT OF CHANGE

Erich H. Witte
University of Hamburg, Hamburg

Finding a combination of theoretical approaches in the area of small-group research seems to be a valuable strategy toward an integration of different theoretical concepts into a more powerful middle-range approach (Witte, 1990). The similarities and dissimilarities of leading theories give us an idea of how we might integrate theoretical concepts into such an approach. The ideal, of course, is a complex theory that explains behavior in small groups—one that might address first individual behavior and then the behavior of the group as a whole. Such attempts are rare in social psychology and would lie in the tradition of what is called "theoretical" in other disciplines, or those instances in which one concept is used as a combination of different theoretical approaches typically found in natural sciences. Such an intention must not be confused with meta-theoretical approaches, which speculate as to how theories might be constructed, or with theoretical generalizations, which are intended to explain different results using a single theory. Both such approaches are both necessary and praiseworthy, but the program to be followed here differs in its goal. The idea here is that valid theoretical concepts that are able to explain empirical results and that are accepted in the literature as well-supported notions are combined into a more complex theory. One further aim is to combine concepts that have a mathematical kernel or core as a means of achieving both qualitative and quantitative theoretical predictions of individual behavior in small groups. Predicting amounts is also an unusual, but most important way for theoretical construction, for Tukey (1969) chided psychologists with the admonition: "Amount, as well as direction is vital. The physical scientists have learned much by storing up amounts, not just directions" (p. 86). Further, according to Tukey:

Measuring the right things on a communicable scale let us stockpile information about amounts. Such information can be useful, whether or not the chosen scale is an interval scale. Before the second law of thermodynamics—and there were many decades of progress in physics and chemistry before it appeared—the scale of temperature was not, in any trivial sense, an interval scale. (p. 80)

Of course, such a theoretical program is productive only if we are able to explain fundamental empirical effects in a more penetrating manner than before. For that reason three well-known empirical effects of minority influence and an interesting effect of self-categorization are explained.

This chapter is divided into the following parts: (a) the basic psychological assumptions of group situation theory (GST), (b) the development of an extended group situation theory (EGST) derived from a combination of the group situation theory with the social impact theory, (c) the integration of the theory of social decision schemes into the EGST, (d) the integration of models describing the structure of communication in small groups, (e) the explanation of three specific effects observed in minority influences, (f) the explanation of self-categorization effects of social influence, (g) a discussion of the results, and (h) some surprising predictions of the theory.

GROUP SITUATION THEORY (GST): BASIC ASSUMPTIONS

Being in a group means being under the influence of others. This is reminiscent of the difference between normative and informational social influence made by Deutsch and Gerard (1955). Deutsch and Gerard defined informational influence as "influence to accept information obtained from another as evidence about reality" (p. 629) and normative influence as "influence to conform to the positive expectations of another" (p. 629). These two kinds of influence processes have different functions in guiding an individual's behavior or judgment: The informational influence is directly connected with judgment and behavior and serves to hint at what is correct. In a broad sense, the normative information instead tells the individual how to use the information in the group situation. The general question is whether the individual should conform to the given information of the other members of the group, or to their assumed expectations of his behavior, if he has no direct information from them. One can interpret normative influence as antecedent conditions on which the type of informational influence is dependent. The informational influence is understood as a process of information integration, broadly in accordance with Anderson's (1971, 1974, 1981, 1982) considerations. The combination of these two components—informational and normative influence—leads to a model of individual choice behavior in group situations (Campbell & Fairey, 1989; Witte, 1987).

A group situation could be defined as follows: a situation in which an individual is induced by uniformity—or conformity—pressure to relate one's own judgment (reaction, valuation) to other judgments (reactions, valuations).

The first task of GST was to identify the dimensions of the informational and normative influence processes. It began with an intuitive content analysis of those variables that were often experimentally manipulated as normative dimensions, and those variables measured as a direct influence upon the reactions as informational dimensions (Witte, 1979). The normative dimensions are differentiated into:

1. *Awareness of theory* (AT), often introduced as involving more or less experienced subjects, and discussed in depth by Habermas (1966) as learning to behave after awareness of the theory that explains the behavior, is the personal transformation of GST after its knowledge in this special case here, which allows subjects to develop new behavioral strategies.

2. *Group atmosphere* (GA) includes liking and cohesion (Shaw, 1971).

3. *Distribution of individual choices* (DIC) assumes the divergence of reactions in the group, for example, a homogeneous majority against a minority of one.

4. *Verifiability of choices* (VC) describes the characteristics of the stimulus material. In the most extreme variants, it is the difference between the autokinetic effect and the lines used by Asch.

5. *Commitment to a constituency* (CC) is measured by the degree of obligation felt by negotiators to a given position.

6. *Uniformity pressure* (UP) is that degree of compulsion experienced that inclines one to consider superindividual values.

The last dimension has been differentiated with the help of the original social impact theory (Witte, 1990), but what is still needed is a theoretical integration of both concepts into an extended group situation theory (EGST; see next section).

However, the question is: How might we characterize the interplay between these normative components? We assume a hierarchical order as a heuristic device to describe complex perceptual operations. Thereby, the subsequent normative component is only introduced when the subject does not know how to interpret the group situation. This unclear situation is present when the particular component is perceived to be of medium degree. Usually, it is assumed that subjects differentiate into three degrees: positive, medium, negative or small, medium, large. Only the first component—ATI: awareness of theory—is differentiated into two degrees because it is only possible be either aware of a theory or not. (See Fig. 11.1.)

The information integration process is best described by weighting informational elements concerning their relevance in a given group situation. The informational elements are:

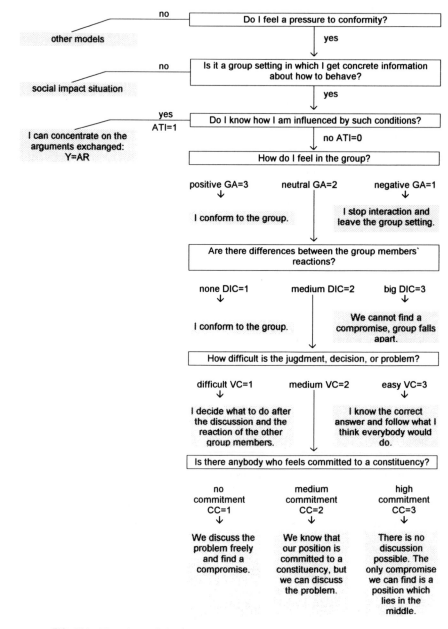

FIG. 11.1. Flowchart of the behavior in an information exchange situation: differentiation between the conditions of the normative components.

1. The *social value* as a general orientation in a group situation. This depends on the reference group and provides orientation for the social desirable or prescribed behavior: SV.

2. The *group standard*, which is the orientation given by the small group to which one must react; usually, it is the mean of the individual judgments: GS.

3. The *argumentation*, which is usually the mean of the exchanged arguments during group discussion as measured on the reaction scale. Sometimes, the arguments are weighted differently by their persuasiveness, which means that the argumentation will be a weighted average of all single arguments in the group discussion: AR.

4. The *individual value*, which is a residual category introduced as the difference between prediction and observation. It measures the idiosyncratic behavioral intention of the individual: IV.

As a general prediction of the individual reaction (Y) in a group situation we obtain:

$$Y = a * SV + b * (GS - aSV) + c * \{AR - [aSV + b(GS - aSV)]\}. \tag{1}$$

$Y' = Y + IV$ with Y' the empirically observed value and Y the theoretically predicted value. Thus $IV = Y - Y'$ is the deviation (positive or negative) between prediction and observation, or, with respect to the model, an error term. The idea here is that this deviation is to be explained by personal characteristics, and not by overindividual parameters. These personal characteristics have not been integrated into the model until now because the chosen explanation works on a more abstract level. They should be integrated after the prediction with these more general parameters and only if needed.

The informational components are in a hierarchical order according to their generalizability. On a more subjective side this means that the social support of the position determines the hierarchical order of the informational components. At first there is the social norm, which suggests what one should do in a specific situation with the greatest strength of social support by, for example, number and a more abstract cultural justification. Then follows the reactions of the group members inclusive of one's own as a more concrete reality of what to do. At the end the given arguments are considered. They are often justifications of individual reactions, which also means they represent the least relative social support of the three components. Thus the hierarchical order is organized by the amount of support inherent in the parameters themselves (see Fig. 11.2).

Their weights (a, b, c), however, can be modified by the normative components of the group situation. The standard group situation is characterized by $a = 1$, $b = \frac{1}{2}$, $c = \frac{1}{3}$ with the result that the behavior is predicted as the arithmetic mean of the three components:

$$Y = \frac{1}{3} * (SV + GS + AR). \tag{2}$$

A central question is: Why use a more complicated formula instead of a simple, arithmetic mean? The answer is fourfold. At first, information integration per se is a process, which can be modeled by the more complicated formula. The arithmetic mean is only the end result. Second, Occam's razor seems to be a

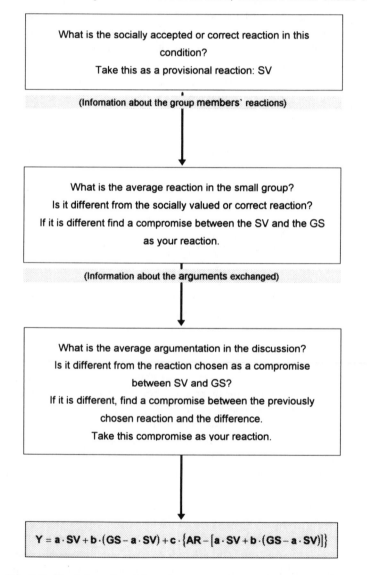

FIG. 11.2. The information integration process in an information exchange situation under standard conditions.

well-accepted norm in science, which means that if there is no modification by the more specific parameters, they are to be eliminated. However, the arithmetic mean always takes into account all three parameters. Third, it is more economic to construct theories according to more general parameters. Fourth, the assumptions about the psychological processes of the information integration must be considered: The confirmation of the special values of the weights is not the averaging process. The assumption in this case is that the subjects have a preferred rank order concerning the strength of social support, and further take into consideration the position of the informational element ($\frac{1}{1}, \frac{1}{2}, \frac{1}{3}, \ldots$) if there is no other information to modify the weighting process. This results in a standard group situation that is ambiguous and in which subjects use all the information they can get. The consequence is the often observed averaging process, if one bears in mind the SV as a general orientation, for example, the social values explanation of the choice shift (Witte & Lutz, 1982).

In all other group situations there are deviances from the simple averaging process. Under specific normative conditions one finds a different weighting pattern of the three informational elements. Such a pattern describes the way in which the group member reaches his decision. What this means is that the simple hierarchical order of the informational elements is no more valid, for the normative elements of the group situation suggest another weighting process (Witte, 1987).

The guiding principles of the weighting patterns under different normative conditions are as follows:

1. The sum of the weights must be one because the informational elements and the reaction should be measured on the same scale, without unity transformation: $a + b + c = 1$. (Remember that weights are sometimes integrated with a negative sign.) If the sum of the weights is greater or less than one, the predictions might lead to values outside the reaction scale or only restricted on a specific interval of this scale. That the measurements of the independent variables and their weighted combination remain in the same range as before is a technical demand; so it is that the dependent variable bear the same range. The differentiation between the adding and the averaging integration is a technical principle that has been discussed in attitude research.

2. The weights should be easy (i.e., bounded on rational numbers: $0, 1, \frac{1}{2}, \frac{1}{3}, \frac{1}{4}, \ldots$) because the underlying psychological process of information integration is less continuous and more categorical. This represents a principle that takes into account the ability to differentiate only between a few categories reliably, a point that is based on the research on the use of the number of categories on rating scales (Dawes & Smith, 1985).

3. The weights should qualitatively differentiate between the different information integration processes, which means that their values should be bounded on 0 and 1, if possible. This is a principle of parsimony and clear-cut differen-

tiation, with the added assumption that the most simple model should be used at the beginning.

In spite of these three restricting assumptions, there are on occasion two ways of information integration under specific normative conditions in which a predicted result can be reached (Witte, 1987). For instance, it is assumed that under a positive group atmosphere the individual reaction Y will be the group standard, for the tension to harmony leads to this compromise: Y = GS. But there are two patterns that can lead to such a compromise (remember that sometimes weights are integrated with negative sign): {a = 1, b = 1, c = 0} and {a = 0, b = 1, c = 0}. The first pattern means that the social orientation SV and the group standard GS together determine the individual reaction: The group members feel as though they are a part of their reference group and take this orientation into account. The result is that the group standard and the social value are weighted equally with the maximal weight of one. However, the group standard is the representation of the social value so that the small group is well integrated into the reference group.

The second pattern describes an isolated small group that concentrates on the reactions of its members and considers only these reactions as the basis for a compromise. In both cases the result of the individual reaction is the group standard. And in both cases the argumentation has no modifying influence on the individual reactions, although the meaning of the compromise for the individual reaction in future should be different: Under the first pattern of information integration, there are arguments that use the social value as justification. Under the second pattern, however, the group is self-determined without consideration of an external standard. The consequence may be a different degree of commitment concerning the individual reaction without the group situation, which would be comparable to the differentiation between conversion and compliance (Kelman, 1961).

Thus the process of the information integration—the patterns of the weights— and the result of this integration must be separated. Sometimes there is more than one way to reach the same result, but the different ways have a different meaning both for the stability of the individual reaction and the normative dimensions of a future group situation with the same members (Witte, 1987). Thus, the dynamics of the information integration and its final result are a necessary future step of research for the development of group situation theory.

EXTENDED GROUP SITUATION THEORY (EGST)

In the center of group situation theory one finds the classical discussion group. However, there are many other group conditions without discussions in which the subjects are influenced, for example, helping, rope pulling, stage fright, crowding, and so forth. For the most part, these group conditions are explained by the theory of social impact (Latané, 1981). Thus, a combination of both theories could expand its universe of content and explanation (see also Nowak, Szamrej, & Latané, 1990).

If we now want to combine group situation theory and social impact theory, we must select the possible informational elements involved. Generally, the original social impact theory best explains the behavior in a social situation where there is no communication between the group members that can influence the individuals directly. Thus there is no group standard (GS) and no argumentation (AR). The only parameter that influences the behavior is the social value (SV), which serves as the general behavioral orientation of the individual in this situation. The question here is whether the individuals follow this general orientation, or instead react according to their individual standards, needs or conviction (IV), thus remaining uninfluenced by the group. This means, in a technical sense, that the weight of the SV varies between one and zero (bounded on rational numbers) under a situation of positive social impact:

$$Y = a * SV \quad 0 < a < 1. \tag{3}$$

From this assumption there follows a pattern of weights for the informational components: a, 0, 0 (Witte, 1987). The variation of the parameter "a" is bounded on rational numbers between 0 and 1. (Such a restriction means a better falsification of theoretical predictions and, psychologically, a restricted differentiation between the different emotional states that determine the weights—as it is known from the research of the number of categories necessary for rating scales—Dawes & Smith, 1985). Under conditions without discussion, the influence of the SV alone is differentiated into finer grades than is the case with the other informational elements (GS and AR) acting together in a group discussion setting. The normative dimension, called uniformity pressure (UP) in the original GST, is now differentiated into strength, immediacy, and number concerning the social impact theory. These variables lead to individual impressions in a group setting that lacks discussion about what is expected. The three variables determine the amount of pressure or social impact by determining the weight of the social value as a general expectation. The direction of the individual's behavior change, however, is determined by the evaluation of the whole group setting as the independent variable. The evaluation of this setting is positive, neutral, or negative in the sense that the individual feels correct in accepting the influence or rejecting it. This is the input field, called *social force field*.

The same differentiation is necessary for the output field, which is called the *behavioral force field*. It is assumed that there also exists a differentiation into a direct (positive) transformation of the felt impact into behavior, or an inverted (negative) transformation of the felt impact into behavior. Technically, the influence of both field parameters is introduced by a change of the sign under a constant amount of impact, which is determined by immediacy, strength, and number.

It was furthermore observed, under the condition of social loafing, that the Ss shift their behavior away from the direction of the social value, and toward their individual purposes (more than they would have done under the condition of no influence). In that case, the weighting pattern is: (−a, 0, 0). These different weighting processes with a positive and a negative sign are well known within the assimilation-contrast theory (Sherif & Sherif, 1969). But this theory deals mainly with direct informational influences. Another model that explains the resistance against normative influences is reactance theory (Brehm, 1966, 1972). If people feel the loss of freedom they will react against the expectations, as well if these are socially valued in a positive manner. (For an empirical reconstruction see the section on the self-categorization effect later.)

Two processes have been identified (Witte, 1990). One is the affective-cognitive influence of the group situation, or the input transformation, a process that leads to social impact (positive weight) or social loafing (negative weight). These internal conditions are intervening variables that provoke a modification of the individual reaction for or against the social value. This affective consequence, which depends on the normative condition of the group situation, has been called the f-function of social impact theory. But, of course, the emotional state does not lead automatically to a corresponding reaction, as is known from the attitude-behavior relationship. The normative dimension of the group situation also modifies the transformation of the internal state into an external individual reaction. This transformation has been called the g-function of social impact theory (Witte, 1990). This corresponds to the differentiation between social facilitation and social inhibition.

Usually, the normative influence and the individual reaction have been observed without the two internal transformations: f- and g-function. The consequence here is that there is a two-by-two table (see Table 11.1) with four different effects. One is the classical social facilitation effect, which is observed if the social

TABLE 11.1
The Relationship of Group Situation Parameters With Impact on One Side (f - Function) and of Impact With Behavior on the Other Side (g - Function)

		Group Situation Parameters With Impact	
		Positive relationship (social impact)	Negative relationship (social loafing)
Impact With Behavior	Positive relationship Social facilitation	Social facilitation effect	Social loafing effect
	Negative relationship Social inhibition	Social inhibition and crowding effect	Self-exploration effect

impact is positive in the direction of the social value, and if the emotional state leads to a corresponding reaction. The social inhibition effect is observed if there is a positive social impact, although this internal condition leads to an overactivation with negative consequences on the reactions (e.g., the Yerkes–Dodson law).

Furthermore, the normative influence can reduce the individual effort (negative f-function), and this emotional state is then positively transformed into a reaction (positive g-function). This is a social loafing effect.

Of course, there is, logically speaking, a fourth effect, which looks like social facilitation but that is grounded on a negative f-function and a negative g-function. For instance, the emotional acceptance of the group means relaxation, and this emotion leads to more socially determined answers—for example, intrinsic motivation effect or self-exploration effect. In a recent series of experiments, Williams and Karau (1991) found a social compensation effect that seems to be comparable to this double negative relationship: If a group task is seen as meaningful then a partner with low trust, low effort, or low ability increases impact (negative input relationship) and furthermore the reduction of impact by a collective work condition, compared with a coactive, leads to a higher production rate (negative output relationship). (For further discussions, see also chapter 2 in Volume 2 of this book.)

With these two transformations in mind, we are able to model the intervening processes of social influence according to the sign of the functional relationship between normative and informational components, thus resulting in an individual reaction.

As the first normative dimension, we introduce that input transformation referred to as the social force field (SFF; see Latané, 1981). It contends with the emotional relationship (I) between the individual and the social condition as it is differentiated in social impact theory between immediacy (IN), strength (S), and number (N). The idea is that the relationship is positive with a maximum value, and then inverts into a negative relationship. This inversion process itself is not the content of EGST but the end result. It is further assumed that subjects react in correspondence to their emotional state; that is to say that they are able and willing to behave in correspondence to their emotions. Thus, as is usual in group situation theory, the SFF is differentiated into three categories, with a constant positive transformation of the emotional state into behavioral expression:

SFF = 1 is a positive social force field that has a positive relation between the parameters of the group situation and social impact under a positive transformation into behavior (a classical conformity situation):

$$
\begin{aligned}
a = v * I + w &= x * \log S + y * \log IN + z * \log N \quad (a, 0, 0) \\
x, y, z &> 0 \quad \text{and} \quad S, IN, N,
\end{aligned}
\tag{4}
$$

measured as intensities with magnitude estimation methods so that the logarithmic transformation is necessary if linear relationships are used.

The general approach of social impact theory depends on Stevens' new psychophysics, which includes magnitude estimation methods. The relation between rating scales and magnitude estimation scales is only linear following a logarithmic transformation of the magnitude scales. I (impact) is measured on an interval scale, and therefore allows any linear transformation.

$$
\begin{aligned}
&\text{SFF} = 2 \quad \text{go to BFF (behavioral force field)} \\
&\text{SFF} = 3 \quad a = v * I + w = -(r * \log S + s * \log IN + t * \log N) \quad (-a, 0, 0) \quad (5) \\
&r, s, t > 0 \quad \text{and S, IN, N measured as intensities.}
\end{aligned}
$$

The second normative dimension coming from social impact theory, in its detailed version (Witte, 1990), has to do with the transformation into a behavioral reaction that is now inverted:

$$
\begin{aligned}
&\text{BFF} = 1 \text{ (behavioral force field)} \\
&\qquad a = (-v) * I + w = x * \log S + y * \log IN + z * \log N \quad (-a, 0, 0) \\
&\text{BFF} = 2 \quad Y = IV \qquad\qquad\qquad\qquad\qquad\qquad\qquad\qquad (0, 0, 0) \qquad (6)\\
&\text{BFF} = 3 \quad a = (-v) * I + w = -(r * \log S + s * \log IN + t * \log N) \quad (a, 0, 0)
\end{aligned}
$$

This inversion of the relation between internal emotional state and behavioral reaction (or judgment) means, psychologically on the one hand, that the subjects are unable to follow their intentions, because of overactivation, and on the other hand, that there is a strong feeling of pressure to react with anticonformity (see later section on self-categorization).

The medium categories of the normative components are always arranged so that the reaction is not determined. Thus, one has to look for the next dimension or his personal standards (IV) because the situation is too ambivalent, as is assumed.

These two dimensions, newly introduced into group situation theory, describe a situation in which the influencing process is indirectly applied, without discussion, through the presence of other people. Afterward, a group situation with information exchange is considered.

One more principle has been introduced into group situation theory. This takes the form of the idea that subjects are able to learn from theories in the social sciences, which means that they change their behavior after the knowledge of the theory. This principle has to be modeled theoretically (also for the newly introduced part). For this reason, the extended group situation theory needs a new dimension, that of awareness of theory (ATS), in a situation where there is no communication:

$$
\begin{aligned}
&\text{ATS} = 1 \quad Y = IV \\
&\text{(Awareness of a theory in a social impact situation)} \qquad\qquad (7)\\
&\text{ATS} = 0 \quad \text{go to SFF.}
\end{aligned}
$$

The easiest assumption to make in this case is that such an awareness leads to the elimination of social conformity or anticonformity (see Fig. 11.3).

At this point, we have a formal integration of the social impact theory into the group situation theory. The result is the extended group situation theory (EGST) (see Table 11.2).

What is still missing, however, is the theoretical explanation of the fundamental parameters of the social impact theory: r, s, t, x, y, z. The logarithmic transformation has been explained by the perception of intensity measures and their relation to a rating scale of impact (Poulton, 1989). The logarithmic transformation is only needed if strength, immediacy, and number are measured with magnitude estimation methods. If the usual rating scales are used, there is no need for a logarithmic transformation. However, the original social impact theory stands in the tradition of the new psychophysics, which means that the logarithmic transformation has been introduced as a means of relating a rating scale

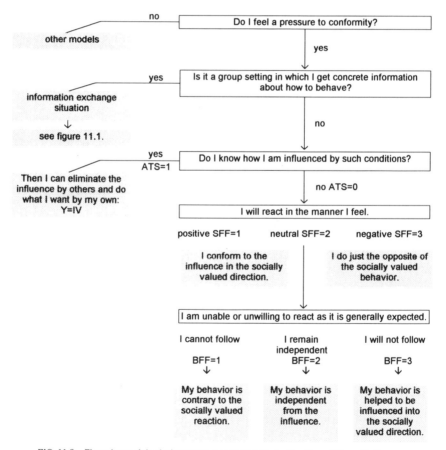

FIG. 11.3. Flowchart of the behavior in a social impact situation: differentiation between the conditions of the normative components.

TABLE 11.2
The Extended Group Situation Theory (EGST)

	if . . . ,	*then . . .*
Awareness of theory in a social impact situation	ATS = 1 ATS = 0	$Y = IV$ go to SFF
Social force field	SFF = 1 SFF = 2 SFF = 3	$Y = a * SV$ $a = v\, I + w = x * \log S + y * \log IN + 2 * \log N$ go to BFF $Y = a * SV$ $a = v * I + w = - (r * \log S + s * \log IN + t * \log N)$
Behavioral force field	BFF = 1 BFF = 2 BFF = 3	$Y = a * SV$ $a = (-v)\, I + w = x * \log S + y * \log IN + z * \log N$ $Y = IV$ $Y = a * SV$ $a = (-v)\, I + w = - (t* \log S + s * \log IN + t * \log N)$
Awareness of theory in an information exchange situation	ATI = 1 ATI = 0	$Y = AR$ go to GA
Group atmosphere	GA = 1 GA = 2 GA = 3	no social interaction go to DIC $Y = GS$
Distribution of individual choices	DIC = 1 DIC = 2 DIC = 3	$Y = GS$ go to VC group falls apart
Verifiability of choices	VC = 1 VC = 2 VC = 3	$Y = GS + 1/2 * (AR - GS)$ go to CC $Y = SV$
Commitment to a constituency	CC = 1 CC = 2 CC = 3	$Y = SV + 1/2\, (GS - SV + 1/3\, (AR - [SV + 1/2\, (GS - SV)]\}$ $Y = (SV1 + GS1 + AR1 + SV2 + GS2 + AR2)\, /6$ $Y = 1/2 * DEMAND1 + 1/2 * DEMAND2$ $= DEMAND1 + 1/2\, (DEMAND2 - DEMAND1)$

scale of social impact to a magnitude estimation of the three dimensions of social impact.

Theoretically, there are three impact variables of a social situation that determine, in combination, one internal state of individuals. This is a reduction of complexity from outside to inside. This internal state leads to a reaction of the individual—but in two different ways (directly or inverted) depending on the social and behavioral force field. These two global dimensions, which characterize a group situation, are a description of the subjects' global interpretations. Such interpretations are in the tradition of the cognitive orientation of social psychology, especially in social motivation (Weiner, 1980). Because of the relevance of these interpretations, they should be analyzed much more intensively in the future. Generally, the interpretation should take the form not of an assumption of the experimenter or theoretician, but of an empirical datum.

But how to explain the variation of the parameters? Only the sign of the integration rule has been fixed, if we take number (N) as the normative information of the group. Group size is one of the main experimentally manipulated variables in the research on social loafing, helping, and crowding. It variates from 1 to 18 with a mode around 3, 4, 5. We then get the following results as theoretical predictions:

$$Y = a * SV$$
$$a = v * I + w = z * \log N \qquad (8)$$
$$a = I = z/v * \log N - w/v.$$

Obviously, the weighting of the information is a product term that depends on both affective-cognitive (input) transformation and conative (output) expression:

$$Y = (z/v * \log N - w/v) * SV. \qquad (9)$$

If we concentrate on the relationship between logN and Y, which is in the center of impact theory, we get:

$$v * Y/SV = z * \log N - w. \qquad (10)$$

Obviously, the interpretation of z is very difficult when we recall that the whole functional relationship depends on the two weighting parameters: z as the cognitive-affective transformation, and v/SV as the behavioral expression.

Theoretically, the most interesting part of this equation is the weighting of logN: $z * SV/v$. Because there seems to be a systematic variation depending on the social situation, this parameter is the most interesting in social impact theory (Witte, 1990). The following weights were obtained in different reanalyses given by Latané (1981): $\frac{1}{4}, \frac{1}{3}, \frac{1}{2}, \frac{2}{3}$. In general, a "normal" social situation might be characterized by a weight of $\frac{1}{2}$ (Tanford & Penrod, 1984). What impact does this mean for the influence process? The direct interpretation of the parameters is only justified if we accept that the SV equals one, as in a percentage scale, and v is used as the unit transformation of the logN values into the percentage scale. At that point it is possible to interpret the coefficient of the regression line between logN and the percentage of conformity as z, or the wanted parameter that contains only the transformation from a group situation into an internal emotional state of impact. What is now preferred is to attribute this to the underlying process of impression integration. For simplification we concentrate on number as the parameter of the group situation.

There are two elements of the group situation: first, what I would do personally $N = 1$—IF(1); and second, how many people there are—IF(N). Both impressional elements are combined into an experience of impact in the following way: (f-function) under the assumption that the information integration of this impression is the same as usual:

$$I(N) = IF(1) + \frac{1}{2}[IF(N) - IF(1)]. \tag{11}$$

IF(1) is a constant that depends only on the social situation. It leads to $I(1) =$ $-w$. And IF(N) is the impressional base of the affective-cognitive transformation. The parameter is $IF(N) = logN - w$. The affective influence is modeled by the parameter z, which is the evaluation of the impression concerning the conformity pressure of the group situation. The same number of group members can be more or less influential, for example, depending on the severeness of the behavioral consequences. Both kinds of parameters together—the individual position and the accepting of the conformity pressure—give an expression of social impact. With $z = \frac{1}{2}$—the usual amount of conformity pressure felt in a group situation—we obtain the following formula:

$$I(N) = -w + \frac{1}{2}(logN - w + w) = \frac{1}{2} * logN - w. \tag{12}$$

It is very interesting to note that we get this integration rule if we combine the impressional information of normative elements. This rule describes a compromise between no impact as a result of being alone, and impact as a result of the presence of the number of group members. It is only valid if z equals $\frac{1}{2}$. However, this compromise started with the individual perspective. Only thereafter is the social influence taken into account. The integration combining the informational elements SV, GS, and AR in a group discussion to predict the reaction, begins with the social information, whereas the individual parameter is only a residual category. These different starting points of the information integration describe the specific level of comparison that is relevant under the specific conditions of impact without discussion in a group setting. In a condition without discussion, there is only the informational element of SV as a general orientation, and the other two informational elements (GS and AR) are eliminated in this setting. Under this condition the individual position is the baseline, which is modified by the social influence. Of course, in both cases the integration rule is identical with other elements. In future, perhaps, a hierarchical order of the normative impressional elements—number, immediacy, strength—will be introduced, if all three together are manipulated experimentally. Of course, there are other values of z that reflect a greater or lesser degree of influence on the part of the group members upon the individual reaction (Campbell & Fairey, 1989).

This kind of indirect information is different from the informational elements, which are direct hints of how to behave. The indirect information about impact through immediacy, strength, and number is the specific normative information about the concrete situation in which one is forced to participate. The final behavior depends on the normative field components, which are necessary to fix the sign of the integration process, and which are called the social and behavioral force field. These field components contain the relation of the subject to the group, for example, as someone in a minority position, as someone who feels reactance, as someone who is overmotivated, and so on. Under these global normative components (qualitative determination of the group setting), the situationally specific normative information is used for the quantitative determination of the emotional state of impact (input) and its quantitative transformation into behavioral conformity, with the social value as the leading orientation (output). Astonishing is that the information integration of the normative impression can be modeled in the same way as in the standard experimental condition in which the Ss get information about what to do more directly. But it is still unclear as to the conditions under which the value of z is different from $\frac{1}{2}$. Until now it has been observed as a systematic variation of this parameter (Witte, 1990), but there is no theoretical explanation of this variation.

INTEGRATION OF THE THEORY OF SOCIAL DECISION SCHEMES INTO EGST

The next step is an integration of the main theoretical approach for discussion groups, the social decision schemes, with EGST. The theory of social decision schemes allows predictions of reactions after discussion on the basis of the distribution of individual reactions before discussion. At best the theory works under the condition of two reaction alternatives (note the new development reported by Davis in chapter 3 of this volume). Under a specific distribution of individual reactions, the social decision schemes predict, with the assumption of different combination rules, the distribution of reactions following small-group discussion. The application of the model is manifold. It has been used to analyze intellectual tasks (Laughlin & Adamopoulos, 1982), mock jury decisions (Davis,

1980), attitudinal judgments (Kerr, Davis, Meek, & Rissman, 1975), and choice shifts (Laughlin & Earley, 1982).

Regarding intellectual tasks, there is one basic social combination process called *truth-supported wins*: Two correct members are necessary and sufficient for a correct group response. On the other hand, research with mock juries is best described by the social combination process called *strong majority wins*: A two-thirds majority of the group members determines the group response.

If we accept that there is only a qualitative reaction alternative, the social decision schemes are comparable with the group standard in the group situation theory. Under these conditions, the proportionality rule serves the same purpose as the group standard in group situation theory, in which the equally weighted position of the group members is usually combined into a group standard. This is the mean of a nominal scale equivalent with the proportionality rule. But because there is a deviation from this rule, the introduction of the other informational components, especially the social value as the general orientation, must model the observed reactions under the standard information integration process, specifically under those conditions in which an extremity shift or a minority influence is observed. The theory of social decision schemes concentrates on the process of information integration in such a way that there are no theoretical parameters that describe the variation of the normative dimensions of the group setting. However, it differentiates between kinds of integration rules in terms of clear-cut descriptions of the process, or the one that gives the best description of the reaction of the group after discussion. Thus, the main question is whether the different decision schemes can be modeled by the combination of the three informational parameters (SV, GS, AR) introduced by group situation theory as the underlying process of the observed group reaction.

The prediction under standard conditions runs as follows: If the argumentation of the members in the group does not introduce any new position as is often observed because of the only exchange of shared arguments (Witte & Lutz, 1982; see also chapter 5 of this volume), then we get

$$Y = SV + \frac{1}{2}(GS - SV) \tag{13}$$

with GS as the arithmetic mean of the individual reactions before group discussion.

We would like to reanalyze the data presented by Laughlin and Earley (1982), in which they applied the theory of social decision schemes on the choice shift in order to give a demonstration of the similarities and dissimilarities of both SDS and EGST. Laughlin and Earley transformed the reaction scale varying from 1 to 10 into a dichotomous reaction, with 1–5 as risky and 6–10 as cautious. After this transformation, they found two neutral items with individual reactions around 6; that indicates that there is no social value in one direction. In light of these items, they found the best prediction to be the proportionality rule. For the other items, a decision rule of "risky or cautious choice supported wins" best describes the individual reactions following discussion.

This decision rule as an average individual reaction could be modeled by the combination of SV and GS, in which GS is given by the proportionality rule. Depending on the distribution, both models give the following predictions for risky items (cautious items are predicted in the same way except that the SV supports a cautious reaction):

Distribution risky choice supported information integration wins

r	c	r	c	r	c
5	0	1.00	0.00	1.00	0.00
4	1	1.00	0.00	0.90	0.10
3	2	1.00	0.00	0.80	0.20
2	3	1.00	0.00	0.70	0.30
1	4	0.00	1.00	0.60	0.40
0	5	0.00	1.00	0.00	1.00
				(specific rule with DIC = 1)	

There are discrepancies between the two models that should be tested separately. One is the distribution (2, 3), and the other distribution (1, 4). Under the first distribution, EGST's prediction is less extreme in order that EGST might fit better than SDS. The second distribution, however, is a strong test of the influence from a social orientation, for the predictions from the two different theories are qualitatively different with the majority regarding different reactions. This is a nice test of the theories and of the influence of minorities in the direction of the zeitgeist (see later discussion).

Generally, in order to acquire a deeper impression of the psychological functioning behind the surface, the social decision schemes themselves have to be reduced to more fundamental processes and parameters. Furthermore, it is necessary to have a theory working on the interval scale level, for most of our data come from rating scales (see chapter 1 of this volume). Furthermore, the different decision schemes under various situational and stimuli conditions should be integrated into a middle-range theory. The general idea (finding a weighting process of the informational components as a means of predicting the distribution of the individual reactions after discussion) is comparable to both of the theories. Thus, the group situation theory generalizes the social decision schemes and tries to specify the underlying process as a specific informational integration of a social orientation and the consideration of the group's reactions. Therefore, the different schemes depend on both, the group standard as the distribution of the reactions on the stimulus in the small group, and the social characteristic of this stimulus. There are only a few clearly differential predictions of both concepts. One explanation of such differences could be the communication structure in the small group, for EGST determines the group standard as the arithmetic mean with equal weighting of the group members. Sometimes there are status differences in small groups that can be modeled with different weightings of the members determining the group standard. Theoretically, such ideas about status differences are introduced by models of communication structure as the observable consequence of these differences.

MODELS OF THE STRUCTURE
OF COMMUNICATION IN SMALL GROUPS

As a third way to increase the universe of content for EGST, the empirical results from small groups that concern the difference of the interaction rates must be taken seriously. These differences are theoretically modeled. These ideas can then be combined with EGST to find a more realistic approach describing behavior in small-group settings.

The extent to which group decision schemes give an impression of the weighting process depends on the characteristics of the stimulus, which is determined by the social value and the group standard. But there is another deeper weighting process spontaneously observed in natural small groups: the different speech rates of the members, which is dependent on personal characteristics as well as other features.

There are several models to describe the structural properties of the distribution of individual interaction frequencies in small groups (Goetsch & McFarland, 1980). This unequal distribution of interaction rates among the group members in a discussion is one cause of the differential influence among group members: If the one person who is dominant in a group prefers a specific reaction alternative, then the other members should be influenced more by that person than by a more submissive member. Obviously, the small-group standard (GS) should be determined by a weighting process that depends on the different rates of interaction (Bales, 1970; Stephan & Mishler, 1952; Tsai, 1977; see also chapter 8 of this volume). It was found that the following function describes the relationship between rank order (R) and interaction frequency (h):

$$\log h = -a * R + b$$
h : interaction frequency
R : rank order in the group   (14)
a, b : constants
(a is negative, because the higher the interaction frequency the smaller the rank).

These different ranks depend on personal characteristics and other individual resources (Foa & Foa, 1980).

This implicit weighting process, which depends on the members' status, must also to be integrated into the EGST, for this informational social influence, which depends on personal characteristics of the group members, has been neglected until now. It is the specific influence of a concrete distribution of the members' status that changes with the combination of new members (Borgatta & Bales, 1953). If the status distribution is known, it is sometimes possible, if the group standard (GS) is determined, to eliminate the informational component AR from the prediction of individual behavior through the different weights of the individual influence. The argumentation during group discussion is determined by the differentiation of the status. If this function between the status and the interaction frequency is valid, it is not necessary to be aware of what is said, but only how often the members have talked. The argumentation itself is a more laborious and less generalizable result of research. This is the reason why the modification of the GS through a weighting process is theoretically more promising than the influence process, which is modeled by the observed argumentation. Furthermore, such a status distribution should be more or less independent of the specific content of the discussion. Thus, if the status distribution is known, the same weightings should be used under different topics without consideration of the specific argumentation during discussion. The personal characteristics of the members—their status—partially determine their influence and therefore the average individual reaction after discussion.

This weighting process, of course, is independent of the social decision schemes, which operate under the assumption that the group members are equal but under different distributions of the individual reactions. Such an assumption seems to be true only if we observe ad-hoc groups without continuity. Natural groups, however, develop a hierarchy spontaneously, which means that such a differentiation has to be integrated into a middle-range theory of individual behavior in small groups. This is one origin of the variations observed in the prediction of the average individual reaction.

But as we can see, what is needed are weights to determine the group standard (GS) as a weighted average, which means that the weights reach a total of one. This constraint is necessary if we are to measure all informational elements on the reaction scale.

The basis is to fix the weights through the observation of the interaction frequencies, which is on a low empirical level. But if there is a linear relationship between the rank order and the logarithmic transformation of the interaction frequencies as intensity measures, then it is sufficient to know the rank order of the members concerning their interaction frequencies. The real frequencies are not necessary to determine the weights of the single members. However, there is still a more abstract fixation of the individual weights: If we know the status of the members relative to their social prestige and measure their rank order, then we should get a prediction of the interaction frequencies and thus their influence on the group standard (GS). If the rank of the status is known, the easiest quantification of the weights and the most abstract is given through the following formula, because only the rank is used as a base of the weights:

$w_i = {_i}R_{inv} * e$

w_i : the weight of the group member i.

${_i}R_{inv}$: inverted rank of group member i; that means that the highest rank gets the highest number.   (15)

  e : constant depending on the size of the group to fix the sum of the weights on 1.

For a five-member group we obtain the following weights:

$$
\begin{aligned}
&R_i \quad 1\ 2\ 3\ 4\ 5 \\
&{_i}R_{inv}\ 5\ 4\ 3\ 2\ 1 \\
&w_i \quad 0.33\ 0.27\ 0.20\ 0.13\ 0.07 \\
&e = \tfrac{1}{15} = 1/(1 + 2 + 3 + 4 + 5)
\end{aligned}
\qquad (16)
$$

These weights are used to determine the group standard (GS) in the event that there is a status difference between the group members. It is the linear transformation of the rank order differences into weight differences. Such differences are observed if either natural groups are studied, or groups that have a more continuous interaction than usual in a lab with ad-hoc groups of strangers.

Thus the relationship between the interaction frequencies (h) and the weights (w_i) is logarithmic, for such frequencies are intensity measures. This nonlinear transformation is meaningful because the frequencies are measured on a ratio scale:

$$w_i = \tfrac{e}{a} \log h - b * e. \qquad (17)$$

With the help of the last formula, it is possible to use the interaction frequencies in the tradition of Bales (1970) as indicators for the weighting process, which determines the group standard (GS) as a weighted average with a different influence of the group members depending on their status.

SPECIFIC EFFECTS OF MINORITY INFLUENCES

These theoretical integrations seem to be a first step toward a more and more general theory of behavior in small groups. However, the value of such an integration process should be demonstrated by the explanation of some empirical effects through such a theoretical concept, on the one hand, and through some surprising predictions on the other.

One of the most influential research notions in the study of small groups is the idea that innovation is fostered by minorities. During this research, three different effects have been observed: (a) the zeitgeist effect, (b) the cohesion effect, and (c) the psychologization effect. My intention is now to give an explanation that is consistent with the EGST, although these effects are also explained by the old version of the group situation theory without an extension to integrate the social impact theory (Witte, 1994).

First we have the *zeitgeist effect*, which means that a minority is very influential under positive zeitgeist conditions. The idea of group situation theory rests on the notion that a positive zeitgeist means a social value (SV) that is in favor of the position of the minority. Under these conditions—a six-person group with two members against the four-member majority, and stimulus material with medium verifiability under the standard information integration process, without modification of the arguments—we have:

$$Y = SV + \frac{1}{2}(GS - SV)$$
$$GS = \frac{2}{3}W + \frac{1}{3}R. \tag{18}$$

W means "contrary to the zeitgeist" and R means "in agreement with the zeitgeist." That means the measurement is on a nominal scale.

If the argumentation is eliminated as a further element of influence by the assumption that the arguments depend entirely on the prior positions, then we get the following result:

$$Y = R + \frac{1}{2}(\frac{2}{3}W + \frac{1}{3}R - R)$$
$$Y = 0.67R + 0.33W \tag{19}$$

This prediction, as measured on a nominal scale, means that the influence of the minority inverted the percentages of the reaction alternatives, before discussion from .67W to .67R under the standard experimental condition and an agreement of the minority with the zeitgeist. (If someone sees a contradiction to the results of the typical Asch studies, in which the increasing majority lacks an increasing influence on the minority, consult the earlier articles that have discussed these studies intensively: Witte, 1987, 1990.)

The influence of a minority against a zeitgeist is minimal and can be predicted in the following way:

$$GS = \frac{2}{3}W + \frac{1}{3}R \text{ and } SV = W$$
$$Y = W + \frac{1}{2}(\frac{2}{3}W + \frac{1}{3}R - W) \tag{20}$$
$$Y = .83W + .17R.$$

Through an experimentally controlled minority of two members, we find only 17% of naive Ss reactions that follow the minority. This has to be compared with the 67% earlier, in which the minority is in accordance with the zeitgeist. But this amount of influence is also an overestimation. Usually, it is halved (see later), and the percentage of change reaches about 8.5% of an average individual.

If it is accepted that a socially and physically determined reality are not different with respect to their influence, when their amount of verifiability is the same, then we are able to study the blue-green experiments on perception (Moscovici & Faucheux, 1972) as an empirical basis of the results derived previously. They report on a sample of people who give more than two wrong answers, and are therefore called "influenced subjects." This sample of subjects, we may assume, has changed from high verifiability (VC = 3) to medium verifiability (VC = 2). For these subjects only should the prediction of the amount of influence be correct. Their percentage of change is 18.4 and 19.3 in two experiments. For all subjects together, the easiest assumption would be that only half of them have changed their certainty, with a consequent reduction of the weight from $\frac{1}{2}$ to $\frac{1}{4}$, which means, psychologically, that the average naive subject believes more in its perception as a physical reality than in the answers of the group members. The physical determination, as it appears to the subjects, is stronger than the social determination through the other group members. Only a subsample of influenced subjects follow the predictions, because for them the verifiability of the stimulus has been reduced and the social influence is weighted equally when compared with the physical determination.

For the whole sample, the assumption is that the average naive subject lies between the state of high and medium verifiability. This also explains the results found in the Asch studies, when only a majority of two against a minority of one was introduced. Under this specific condition, it is assumed that the average naive subject also lies between high and medium verifiability, because the majority of two is not strong enough to change the certainty of the subjects, as is expected by a majority of three. Thus, under this condition, there was a reduced influence, which could be predicted in the following way:

$$Y = R + \frac{1}{4}(\frac{2}{3}W + \frac{1}{3}R - R) = .83R + .17W.$$
W means wrong line
R means right line   (21)
$GS = \frac{2}{3}W + \frac{1}{3}R$
$SV = R$

There is no further influence exercised by the arguments, because there are no arguments. The information integration is modeled by a reduced influence of the group standard (GS). The empirical result was that 12% of the answers were wrong.

At first glance, this change in certainty, or, as it is called here, change in verifiability, is a mere speculation. But in an excellent article about social influence, Stasser and Davis (1981) distinguished both aspects: opinion or choice change and certainty change. Without going into the details of this model (Witte, 1989, 1994), the assumption of a certainty change has a broader empirical base and is theoretically prolific.

The explanation of the zeitgeist effect is given by the general orientation on those social values that become relevant in a group situation.

The next point is the *cohesion effect* (Wolf, 1979, 1985). It was sometimes observed that the more cohesive the group was, the more individuals changed in the direction of the minority position. The explanation of this effect's consistency with group situation theory is as follows: Under a group atmosphere of high positive regard (GA = 3), the group tries to find a compromise among the individual standpoints:

$$Y = GS$$
$$GS = \tfrac{2}{3}W + \tfrac{1}{3}R \qquad (22)$$
$$Y = .67W + .33R$$

The influence of the minority is equivalent to its size. This is more than the influence against the zeitgeist (.17), but less than the influence under positive zeitgeist conditions with .67R.

The *psychologization effect* (Papastamou, 1986) as the third specific effect indicates a reduction of influence, because "to direct the subjects' cognitive activity towards the psychological characteristics of the minority . . . is enough to reduce its impact considerably" (p. 166). Thus, the deviation among the standpoints is not conducive to a compromise. Under this condition, group situation theory assumes that the group falls apart (DIC = 3), although the theory does not explain why. One plausible reason is that the minority will be seen as an ideologically different group, with a corresponding negative image (Papastamou, 1986). The effect is the building of subgroups. This process of falling apart sometimes begins after a short period of discussion, because the minority must first be identified. Thus the kind of argumentation produces a change in the normative dimension (DIC). This is a feedback loop from the informational to the normative components, to this point neglected in the group situation theory. This effect, and the aforementioned examples of certainty change, need a feedback loop from informational influence to normative dimensions. But this has been ignored in the theory until now.

SELF-CATEGORIZATION EFFECTS OF SOCIAL INFLUENCE

One of the most stimulating approaches of social influence research has to do with intergroup relationship and personal and social identity (Turner et al., 1987). In this tradition the classical autokinetic studies have been replicated (Abrams, Wetherell, Cochrane, Hogg, & Turner, 1990, Experiment 1). The main results of this study should be predicted by EGST. To do this the fundamental informational parameters have to be specified.

The apparatus and the setting employed in this experiment result in a norm of around 4 cm. Thus we get SV = 4. Furthermore there is a mean estimation of the confederates, which, together with the estimation of naive subjects, determines the group standard GS. Because there are three confederates and three naive subjects, the estimation of the group standard is the average of the norm, as the individual behavior and the mean estimation of the confederates. This indicates an equal weighting of all members:

$$SV = 4$$
$$GS = \tfrac{1}{2}(4 + C) \qquad \text{C: the mean estimation of the confederates.} \tag{23}$$

Under usual normative conditions the standard information integration process should predict the mean individual reaction as the dependent variable:

$$Y = SV + \tfrac{1}{2}(GS - SV)$$
$$GS = (4 + 7.8)\tfrac{1}{2} = 5.9$$
$$C = 7.8 \tag{24}$$
$$Y = 4 + \tfrac{1}{2}(5.9 - 4) = 4.95.$$

The empirical result is Y = 4.8. The difference between the prediction (4.95) and the observation (4.8) is negligible, because the range of the possible reactions in this experimental condition lies between the manipulated reactions of the confederates (7.8) on the one hand, and the social value (4.0) as the interval of possible reactions on the other. This is the range in which the prediction should be expected. The interval of possible reaction is D = 3.8, and the difference between prediction and observation is d = .15. The ratio of d/D gives something like a percentage of error, which is .03. (For a short discussion of such a strategy, see next section.)

The information integration pattern—the weights of the three informational elements—is: 1, $\tfrac{1}{2}$, 0. This is the standard condition without the influence of the arguments, because there are no arguments at all in this setting.

The next experimental manipulation introduces the salient classification into two subgroups ("grouped condition"). The idea now is that such a social situation means a social (SFF) or a behavioral force field (BFF), in which the information or the forced behavior of the subgroup is rejected. This is not totally comparable with EGST, but it will give some further suggestions when the sign of the information integration is negative, which is the technical consequence of the psychological process. For now, it is the rejection of the group standard (GS), and not the social value. This is a further extension of EGST, which is necessary as a result of the greater than usual complexity of the experimental manipulation. This, of course, requires a more complex modeling of the group setting in the light of theoretical considerations. The result is that EGST has to be modified to include this setting.

There might be a negative relation between the input and a positive relation between the internal state and the behavior (SSF = 3), or a positive impact and a negative reaction on this impact should it be transformed into behavior, that means BFF = 1. It is not possible to give the right interpretation, because there are no empirical hints. This assumption implies that the group setting of a discussion group could also be manipulated in such a way that the reaction is inverted to the information given. The general information integration pattern is: $1, -\frac{1}{2}, 0$.

However, the negative reaction is not on the social value, but on the group standard, for the group standard is the source of the influence. This kind of informational element always gets a negative sign, which is connected with the influence process. Under these assumptions the prediction is the following:

$$
\begin{aligned}
Y &= SV - \tfrac{1}{2}(GS - SV) \\
SV &= 4 \quad C = 8.6 \\
GS &= (8.6 + 4)\tfrac{1}{2} = 6.3 \\
Y &= 4 - \tfrac{1}{2}(6.3 - 4) = 2.85.
\end{aligned}
\tag{25}
$$

The empirical result is 2.50. Thus, the reaction is outside the interval of the commonly expected reactions, with the endpoints of SV = 4.0, and the manipulated reaction of the confederates, with C = 8.6. This kind of "boomerang" or contrast effect was assumed by the original researchers (Abrams et al., 1990), but the amount of change has been retrodicted by EGST under the assumption of distancing from an outgroup. Technically, this process of distancing has been modeled by a change of the sign before the group standard has been integrated into the prediction of the results. To evaluate the difference between observation and retrodiction, an interval of expected reactions must be assumed, which provides the plausible range under the specific condition. If the contrast effect is expected, then the range between 4.0 as the common individual reaction, and 2.5 as the empirical observation, is the critical region. This difference is D = 1.5, and the difference between observation and prediction is d = .35. The error percentage is d/D = .23. Under very strong preliminary assumptions about the expecting results, the error index is small enough to be satisfied with the retrodiction based on the simple formulae used in different settings. (There are many reasons a significance test should not be used here. One main point is that the significance of the deviation from a random effect is not to be evaluated, for it is the correspondence between prediction and observation, as is the case in other natural sciences, which almost never use significance tests.)

The correspondence between the predictions and the empirical data is astonishing. This seems to be a kind of corroboration of the assumptions concerning the change of the sign, but at the same time a demand for further theoretical developments to integrate into EGST subgroups and their influence in a small-group setting.

DISCUSSION

The integration of the social impact theory into the group situation theory has led to a substantial modification of the latter into an extended version: EGST. Similarily, this combination has clarified some inconsistencies of the social impact theory, especially the sign of the weights and the differentiation into two processes. Particularly astonishing was the comparable information integration of normative hints into an internal state of impact, as was observed with informational elements and their integration into a measure of reaction. However, the beginnings of both integration processes are different: The first starts with the individual level, and the second with the social.

The next step was a combination of a theory of decision schemes with the group situation theory. Here it could be shown that under many conditions the predictions seem to be comparable, but group situation theory was able to give a more subtle explanation of the underlying processes. However, the confrontation of these two theoretical concepts has not been ended. In particular, the further development of the social decision schemes into social transition schemes (Kerr, 1982) and the interaction sequence model (Stasser & Davis, 1981) must be brought into the EGST.

The often observed variation of individual interaction frequencies in longer lasting groups has to be taken into account, for such an influence leads to a modification of the average individual reaction.

Lastly, empirical effects were explained by EGST. These explanations were interesting and could offer first hints toward an understanding of the processes.

Generally, such a program of theory integration seems to be very promising, although it is very seldom followed. If theories are accepted in the scientific community, and are able to explain empirical results in similar areas, they are potential candidates for theoretical integration. The aim must be the construction of middle-range theories. But how is this possible without using the theoretical investment of the accepted smaller concepts? In any case, this program of theoretical integration is one important way to bring the group back into social psychology.

Most interesting was the reconstruction of the self-categorization effect, because the basis was a more complex than usual experimental setting as well as a clear demonstration of a change of sign before the information was integrated into a reaction. This kind of influence process is in the tradition of the classical assimilation-contrast theory as developed by Sherif (e.g., see Sherif & Sherif, 1969). The sign's change, however, was not in combination with the social value, as was the case with group settings without discussion, but with the group standard, because the experimental condition allows the influence of the reactions of the group members, as is the case in discussion groups. Under this more complex manipulation, there is an extension of the group setting, so that the normative impression is combined with informational elements coming from the small group itself, represented in the group standard. The influence process is combined with a specific normative characterization of the small-group members in a discussion setting. The information integration pattern became $(1, -\frac{1}{2}, 0)$, or more general $(1, -b, 0)$. This is more complex than the one used to explain social impact influences without discussion: $-a, 0, 0$. The main idea is that these more complex conditions can also be explained by EGST. This requires a further modification of the theory, so that a social and behavioral force field also works under conditions of group discussion. The result is that not only the social value's influence (a) can be modified by strength, immediacy, and number, but also the influence of the group standard (b). Thus the social impact theory is not reduced further on group settings without discussion. This modeling will be comparable to the one used in the group settings without discussion, but on the influence of the group standard (GS) (see Table 11.1). The concrete integration of these ideas into EGST is a task for the future. It shows, however, how a theoretical core can be used to implement more and more complex conditions.

The hitherto existing combination of the different concepts has shown those empirical effects on which each approach is grounded, and that the concepts are not counterparts, but complements explaining individual behavior in small groups. Social impact theory explains the influence of normative information on the individual reaction without further discussion, a concept that might also be extended in the future to discussion-group settings. The influence depends on that social and behavioral force field, which is a direct extension of this theory, if the theory is further specified.

The social decision schemes, on the contrary, are concentrated—from the perspective of EGST—on informational influence without normative aspects. Different rules mean a different integration of informational elements so that the basis of decision schemes are found in the transformation of individual reactions before discussion into reactions after discussion.

The research on communication structures has to do with the weighting of the individual reactions as a means of determining the group standard. This research is thus more specific than the decision schemes because the concept contains the individual characteristics of the group members.

Finally, the explanations of some interesting empirical effects, if they are accepted as such, has been a test of the EGST as a connection between theory and empirical data. In the future, many more such reconstructions and, of course, more direct predictions are necessary. EGST is only a theoretical framework within which to build a middle-range theory of individual behavior in small-group situations. Its prediction has been tested on the level of an average individual so that the individual variation has been eliminated. This corresponds with the usual test of means, which ignores the standard deviation. In the future, the individual reactions themselves have to be reconstructed or predicted. Such a strategy will lead to the introduction of personality variables and other individual characteristics as necessary predictors of individual reactions, and as a means of reducing the error variance.

In the whole theory, the principle is not to fit theoretical parameters on data before prediction, but to determine them on theoretical deductions. All weights depend on normative conditions, to ensure that they are fixed under specific situations. The research on these normative conditions as an interpretation of a social situation has to be forced in the future, because such a specific interpretation implies one or two patterns of information integration (a, b, c).

The research on these patterns of information integration is a necessary complement to the research on the end result as the mean reaction. Thus, EGST demands research on the interpretation of small-group situations and on the process of information integration, which constitutes a stimulation of empirical research from theoretical considerations.

SOME SURPRISING PREDICTIONS OF EGST

There are at least four criteria employed to evaluate a theory: (a) the potential to reconstruct data from those classical studies which constitute the accepted empirical base of a discipline, (b) the prediction of new data which corroborate the theory, (c) the integration of other accepted theoretical concepts into the theory, (d) the power for a new understanding of social phenomena.

Some predictions of the theory have been tested elsewhere (Witte, 1979), especially in combination with choice shift (Witte & Lutz, 1982). Reconstructions and theoretical integrations have been given now and before (Witte, 1987, 1990). What is still missing are some hints concerning its potential to discover new phenomena or new results as theoretical predictions resulting from the theory.

Initially some qualitative predictions can be discussed. One classical problem in small group research is the reduction of conformity, which sometimes produces a loss of problem-solving capacity within small groups. Conformity is the orientation of the individual reaction on the social value, or the group standard as super-individual points that are given before any discussion. But the idea is that the discussion is able to help the group in finding new solutions, innovations etc. Therefore, the question is: Under which conditions is the weight for the arguments maximal, and under which are the social value and the group standard eliminated? The information integration pattern should be (a = 0, b = 0, c = 1). (Remember that a, b, c are the weights for SV, GS, AR and some weights are integrated with a negative sign, so that the sum of all weights is one.) There is only one such condition: If the group members know the theory ATI = 1, then they are able to control conformity processes. This control means enlightenment in the classical sense. This strategy should be tested experimentally.

The next best condition for the weighting of arguments $(a = 0, b = 1, c = \frac{1}{2})$ leads to two normative influences: VC = 1 means that there is no social value of the material to be discussed and the individual reaction has to be formed by social exchange in a group; CC = 2 means that there are members of two reference groups with different social values finding a compromise in the small group but whose commitment to a constituency is only medium; under this condition the argumentation plays a role. This kind of social situation is a release from more conventional results. It is not necessary that the members of one reference group are in the minority position in the small discussion group. In addition, if both are equal in number, the conventionality of the average individual reaction is potentially reduced, for the argumentation as an informational element plays some role. Now it depends on the originality of the arguments—their deviance from the group standard—to reach a creative solution (Mucchi-Faina, Maass, & Volpato, 1991). This has to do with the conversion effects of minority influences (Maass, West, & Cialdini, 1987). The confrontation of two different views without a high commitment to the reference group leads potentially to higher creativity. This confrontation eliminates the importance of the two social values, but does not determine the originality of the arguments. If they are only justifications of the individual reactions, their potential influence is finally negligible. But if the subjects feel a high commitment (CC = 3) because of social pressure, there is no individual change other than a compromise demanded from outside, for example, wage negotiations. The question of whether there are one or two processes explaining majority and minority influences will be answered from EGST in following way: Under the standard experimental condition, the information integration pattern is the following ($a = 1$, $b = \frac{1}{2}$, $c = \frac{1}{3}$) and therefore different from the pattern with two subgroups. Thus the information integration processes are different. However, it is not the number that makes them different, rather the feeling of the commitment to the reference group that produces the difference. Yet both processes can be explained by one theory. Thus, we must know more about the interpretation of the normative dimensions when number is manipulated experimentally. This is a direct demand from EGST looking at the research on minority influences. This interpretation might be qualitatively different if there is a minority or a majority. But this is, of course, not the only way to get more creative solutions, or to convert the reactions of the individual members. From research in choice shift, it is known that two high-status leaders are able to find a compromise that is different from the mean of the two positions. But low-status representatives of groups are committed totally to a compromise at the middle between both positions.

Thus, the group standard determines the individual reaction after the negotiation. This is a situation with high conflict. A situation with low conflict or a positive group atmosphere (GA = 3) also leads to the same result: The individual reaction is determined by the group standard ($a = 0$, $b = 1$, $c = 0$). Now the tension to harmony prevents creative solutions. These results are discussed under the phenomenon of "group-think."

A third situation in which the individual reaction after discussion in a group is determined by the group standard is that in which all members give the same reaction individually before the group situation is created, and are then brought together in a discussion group. The result of the whole group then is the individually accepted position before discussion. Thus, the same results are expected under high emotional and cognitive conflict (CC = 3), under low emotional conflict (GA = 3) and under low cognitive conflict (DIC = 1). In all of these cases, the group is self-sufficient and the result can be predicted from the knowledge of the individual members. There are many group decisions in the political, economic, and legal fields in which the result is manipulated in such a way that the group composition has been controlled to get the expected results. The group members themselves do not feel manipulated and are well-known experts with a high moral. One such example of this kind of manipulation is technology assessment (Witte, 1991).

Under indirect influence through number, immediacy, and strength, it is necessary that the influenced subjects have the impression that they are free to determine what to do (SFF = 1). Under this condition, the behavioral consequence is in the same direction as the impact. Yet these mechanisms of influence always deal with the loss of freedom, should the subjects identify the whole situation as an influencing strategy. In that event, they will react with anticonformity, because they devalue the source of influence (SFF = 3), or they feel pushed to behave in a certain way (BFF = 1). The general consequence is that the total amount of impact is limited, because the loss of freedom begins with a higher amount of impact. Furthermore, the amount of impact of which one source is capable seems also to be limited. Thus the highest amount of impact is reached through the combination of all three sources. For example, if we want to have students with a scientific orientation, then it is necessary that many professors (N) with high prestige (strength) make them partners in research (immediacy). If science plays only a role in the examination, and/or nobody is actually doing science with the students then there will be no influence in this direction. (The general assumption is that university socialization happens in group situations.)

But the necessary condition is that scientific orientation is the behavioral norm, in terms of EGST as the social value (SV). Against the social value, there is no influence at all in this direction, except that students have to follow the impact in an examination. Then the individual reaction is controlled from outside.

The clear differentiation into the two states of the social force field (SSF = 1 and SFF = 3) is a slight deviation from the impact theory, because in the original theory there is a continuous differentiation into sources and targets, with the result that such an information integration process could lead continuously to more or less impact or release from impact. The preceding assumption is that subjects at first know which kind of situation this seems to be, and then determine the amount of impact. In impact theory, the amount of impact is the dependent variable, and the signs and weights of the three dimensions combined with sources and targets are the independent variables. In EGST, however, the signs and, in a certain way the weights as well, are the dependent variables as determined by the social situation. The basis of a specific interpretation has to be found and theoretically explicated.

If there is the feeling that subjects suffer a loss of behavioral freedom, then the reaction is contrary to the influence direction (BFF = 1). This is a well-known phenomenon of reactance. Interesting is the prediction of the amount of deviation. The amount depends on the impact and the SV as a product, which means the higher the impact, the greater the anticonformity reaction. Moreover, the greater the difference between the uninfluenced reaction to the social value, the greater the anticonformity reaction. In a situation in which subjects expected to react more freely, they will show a greater amount of anticonformity under social influence, for the usual behavior in a control condition without influence is further away from the socially valued behavior. The greater this difference, the greater the change in the direction away from the socially valued behavior. On the other hand, additional impact under conditions in which behavior lies near the social value will change the reactions minimally. Thus, the amount of change does not only depend on the social impact, but also on the interval of the feasible behavior change.

One of the most interesting conditions is the double negative relation between impact and behavioral reaction; for example, the greater the number, the smaller the impact, and the smaller the impact, the greater the conformity with the SV; or, in the symmetrical formulation, the smaller the number the greater the impact, and the greater the impact, the greater the anticonformity.

The first relationship has to do with social support of the individual position, and the second with greater adjustment to the social value with lesser impact. On the surface, this condition (BFF = 3) looks like a double positive relationship (SFF = 1). This could be a kind of therapeutical condition, in which the therapist helps the client to feel free personally, thus reducing the impact and leading the client to a more adjusted behavioral reaction. Generally, this kind of social influence has to do with the internally accepted social value as the norm to behave, under conditions without social impact to control the behavior. Then the social norm as the expected behavior and the personal norm as the individual reaction without external control become identical. This is sometimes called intrinsic motivation. Usually, intrinsic motivation can be reached by the reduction of influence. But under the conditions given in BFF = 3, there is also a negative relationship between number, strength, and immediacy with impact. Thus, the higher the influence factors, the lesser the impact. Under these assumptions, it is possible to explain the negative results of the brainstorming conditions (Diehl & Stroebe, 1987). The instruction of the brainstorming technique means a negative relation between number, strength, and immediacy as a result of the induced ignorance of the social apprehension by the other members. Furthermore, this unknown situation, in which subjects have to do two things at the same time, register what the group members have said and think about their own solutions (blocking effect), leads to a negative relation between internal state and behavior from the perspective of creativity. There are two strategies to increase creativity: First, find a positive relation between impact and behavior by reducing the complexity of the social situation, perhaps by the exchange of written propositions. Such a strategy was proposed by Moore (1987) and called "ideawriting." Second, change the negative relationship between influence factors and impact, so that the group situation increases impact through the presence of the other members. This means that there is someone to control the interaction and give feedback. The most creative results could come out by a positive relation between impact and internal state on the one hand, and internal state and behavior on the other (SFF = 1). The realization of these theoretical predictions could take the form of an individually moderated collection of ideas, combined by the moderator into a group product, and then selected individually until there is an agreement between all individuals who have taken part in this procedure. This is the inversion of the brainstorming technique.

These are some hints of qualitative predictions from EGST. But there are clear quantitative predictions, too. They are only possible if the normative elements are specified and the informational elements measured.

The first question from the research on minority influences is whether this small empirical effect is more than a random change, although it is statistically significant. Concerning EGST, the influence is often established against a majority that is certain about the right reaction, so that the minority has to change the certainty first and then the reaction. However, the certainty change, which is necessary for any behavioral change, only reaches half of the subjects, meaning that the average individual reaction's change is reduced to only $\frac{1}{4}$ —half of the usual influence. Thus the following percentage of change is predicted if it is accepted that the arguments have no further influence, and are only necessary to modify the certainty:

$$Y = SV + \tfrac{1}{4}(GS - SV)$$
$$SV : \text{a reaction against the minority R} \tag{26}$$
$$GS : \text{group standard with a minority against R}$$

Now there are several experimentally manipulated minorities: one in three, one in four, two in five, two in six. As a quantitative prediction we get:

$$GS = (2R + 1W)\tfrac{1}{3} = \tfrac{2}{3}R + \tfrac{1}{3}W$$
$$GS = (3R + 1W)\tfrac{1}{4} = \tfrac{3}{4}R + \tfrac{1}{4}W$$
$$GS = (3R + 2W)\tfrac{1}{5} = \tfrac{3}{5}R + \tfrac{2}{5}W \tag{27}$$
$$GS = (4R + 2W)\tfrac{1}{6} = \tfrac{2}{3}R + \tfrac{1}{3}W.$$

The average individual reactions under these conditions are: $Y = .92R + .08W$; $Y = .94R + .06W$; $Y = .90R + .10W$; $Y = .92R + .08W$. Obviously, the expected change—as predicted from EGST—is small under usual experimental conditions.

Why is it interesting to study such small effects? The answer is that under natural conditions such a small change can lead to a big change if time is taken into consideration and this small effect is only the first step of an innovation process (Coleman, Katz, & Menzel, 1966; Witte, 1989, 1991, 1994). But it is very difficult for a minority of one to change the certainty of the other members. Therefore, the influence of such minorities can be less than predicted. One needs a minority of two as a social force to change certainty among the assumed amount of half of the subjects. Under these circumstances, the predicted amount of change has been observed empirically.

There is, however, another strategy to increase the change—one can select high-status members as a minority. Under this condition, when the two members of a six-person group with the highest status are in the minority position (represented as W), the GS is the following:

$$GS = .47R + .53W \text{ and the reaction becomes } Y = .87R + .13W. \qquad (28)$$

There is a difference between the expected change of the majority: It increases from 8% to 13% if the highest status members are in favor of the change. On the other hand, the reduction of the influence is not negligible if the two lowest members are in favor of the minority's position:

$$Y = R + \tfrac{1}{4}(.85R + .15W - R)$$
$$Y = .96R + .04W. \qquad (29)$$

With the manipulation of the status there might be an additional effect that reduces the certainty of the lower status members, increasing the weight of GS from $\tfrac{1}{4}$ to $\tfrac{1}{2}$, which means that there is a medium certainty of all group members about the right reaction. This leads to a standard condition of influence without any influence from the arguments. Then the change increases from 13% to 27%, which is remarkable. These constitute quantitative predictions from EGST if the minority induces change against the social value.

If, on the other hand, a minority is in accordance with the social value, the amount of change is different. There are two reasons. Initially, the majority against a social value is uncertain about the reaction, and second, the socially valued or objective response is very convincing. Under the assumption that the majority is uncertain ($VC = 2$), the usual information integration is assumed:

$$Y = SV + \tfrac{1}{2}(GS - SV). \qquad (30)$$

The following group standards are assumed:

$$GS = (2W + 1R)\frac{1}{3} = \frac{2}{3}W + \frac{1}{3}R$$
$$GS = (3W + 1R)\frac{1}{4} = \frac{3}{4}W + \frac{1}{4}R$$
$$GS = (3W + 2R)\frac{1}{5} = \frac{3}{5}W + \frac{2}{5}R \qquad (31)$$
$$GS = (4W + 2R)\frac{1}{6} = \frac{2}{3}W + \frac{1}{3}R.$$

The average individual reactions are the following: $Y = .66R + .33W$; $Y = .62R + .38W$; $Y = .70R + .30W$; $Y = .66R + .33W$. Under the same relationship in the small group, the minority influence is overwhelming if the minority is in accordance with the general social orientation ($SV = R$). This dramatic alteration of the minority's influence has been observed in six-person mock-jury decisions. A preshift distribution of two (guilty) to four (not guilty) yields, empirically speaking, only a 13% change to conviction. In the other distribution of four (guilty) and two (not guilty), there is an empirical observation of 58% change in the minority's direction. The explanation is that there is an effective social orientation helping the minority to influence the majority in the direction of acquittal: "in dubeo pro reo" (Kerr & MacCoun, 1985). The predictions of EGST are 8% and 66%. The difference between observation and prediction seems to be rather small if the whole region of possible reactions is considered, which is best determined by the empirical results with $D = 58\% - 13\% = 45$. The deviation of the first prediction is $d = 5\%$ and of the second $d = 8\%$. This leads to an error rate (d/D) of 11% in the first case and of 18% in the second. The empirical results are very well predicted with simple assumptions, and without fitting theoretical parameters to data.

Until now, a boomerang effect has not been studied intensively. This effect means that the position of the arguments is rejected. This has been previously discussed under the self-categorization effect, but we would like to demonstrate now the similarity to the influence situation in which arguments are offered to change the reaction of people. If the content of these arguments has the meaning of strength (because they are well known and the subjects feel pressure), then the prediction is that the global normative orientation is $BFF = 1$. If SV is 1, as on a percentage scale, and if a normal situation is assumed, then we get: $Y = -\frac{1}{2}SV$.

There is a study by Fishbein, Ajzen, and McArdle (1980) about changing the behavior of alcoholics that is interesting because it shows a boomerang effect under the traditional influence strategy. Subjects who are willing to take part in an alcoholic treatment program are given a traditional appeal and urged to take part. After this appeal, only 50% signed up for the program. The quantitative prediction is under a normal impact condition with $a = -\frac{1}{2}$; $Y = -\frac{1}{2}SV$. This means a reduction of 50% among those willing to sign up, because the individual value is not to sign.

There is another group of subjects, unwilling to take part in the program, that are not influenced by the traditional appeal (5%). The explanation is that impact is nonexistent, because they know what is said, and then ignore the influence.

There are two other appeals with a mean change of 25%. The prediction of EGST could be that these subjects have learned to ignore such appeals but that these specific formulations are able to reach their belief system and change their behavior but only in a reduced amount. The easiest assumption, as assumed in previous studies, is that the certainty change or the change in the verifiability of choice—as it was called in EGST—has happened in only half of the subjects. Then the weight must be halved so that the prediction is: $Y = \frac{1}{4}SV$. A 25% change would thus be predicted.

In both cases, the correspondence between quantitative predictions and empirical results is surprising. Of course, we have made some necessary assumptions to reinterpret the study from the viewpoint of EGST. But no parameters are fitted to the data. The interpretation might be doubtful, but it is impossible to know what is going on in the subjects. Generally, it seems possible to predict the quantitative results of the average individual reaction. This will give us a feeling of the amount of change that could be expected under different conditions.

These qualitative and quantitative predictions offer some hints of the productiveness of EGST. Its major scope is combining old theoretical and empirical evidence to make the prediction of new results more precise, and to deepen the explanation with a more complex model. This theory, however, is not fixed in such a fashion that other more complex settings can also be modeled in the same way in the future.

REFERENCES

Abrams, D., Wetherell, M., Cochrane, S., Hogg, M. A., & Turner, J. C. (1990). Knowing what to think by knowing who you are: Self-categorization and the nature of norm formation, conformity and group polarization. *British Journal of Social Psychology, 29,* 97–119.

Anderson, N. H. (1971). Integration theory and attitude change. *Psychological Review, 78,* 171–206.

Anderson, N. H. (1974). Cognitive algebra: Integration theory applied to social attribution. In L. Berkowitz (Ed.), *Advances in experimental social psychology* (Vol. 7, pp. 1–101). New York: Academic Press.

Anderson, N. H. (1981). *Foundations of information integration theory.* New York: Academic Press.

Anderson, N. H. (1982). *Methods of information integration theory.* New York: Academic Press.

Bales, R. F. (1970). *Personality and interpersonal behaviour.* New York: Holt.

Borgatta, E. F., & Bales, R. F. (1953). Interaction of individuals in reconstituted groups. *Sociometry, 16,* 302–320.

Brehm, J. W. (1966). *A theory of psychological reactance.* New York: Academic Press.

Brehm, J. W. (1972). *Responses to loss of freedom: A theory of psychological reactance.* Morristown, NJ: General Learning Press.

Campbell, J. D., & Fairey, P. J. (1989). Informational and normative routes to conformity: The effect of faction size as a function of norm extremity and attention to the stimulus. *Journal of Personality and Social Psychology, 57,* 457–468.

Coleman, J. S., Katz, E., & Menzel, H. (1966). *Medical innovation. A diffusion study.* New York: Bobbs-Merrill.

Davis, J. H. (1980). Group decision and procedural justice. In M. Fishbein (Ed.), *Progress in social psychology*. Hillsdale, NJ: Lawrence Erlbaum Associates.

Dawes, R. M., & Smith, T. L. (1985). Attitude and opinion measurement. In G. Lindzey & E. Aronson (Eds.), *Handbook of social psychology* (pp. 509–566). New York: Random House.

Deutsch, M., & Gerard, H. B. (1955). A study of normative and informational social influences upon individual judgment. *Journal of Abnormal and Social Psychology, 51,* 629–636.

Diehl, M., & Stroebe, W. (1987). Productivity loss in brainstorming groups: Toward the solution of a riddle. *Journal of Personality and Social Psychology, 53,* 497–509.

Fishbein, M., Ajzen, I., & McArdle, J. (1980). Changing the behavior of alcoholics: Effects of persuasive communication. In I. Ajzen & M. Fishbein (Eds.), *Understanding attitudes and predicting social behavior* (pp. 217–242). Englewood Cliffs, NJ: Prentice-Hall.

Foa, E. B., & Foa, U. G. (1980). Resource theory: Interpersonal behavior as exchange. In K. J. Gergen, M. S. Greenberg, & R. H. Willis (Eds.), *Social exchange: Advances in theory and research* (pp. 70–94). New York: Plenum.

Goetsch, G. G., & McFarland, D. D. (1980). Models of the distribution of acts in small discussion groups. *Social Psychology Quarterly, 43,* 173–183.

Habermas, J. (1966). *Zur Logik der Sozialwissenschaften*. Frankfurt: Suhrkamp.

Kelman, H. C. (1961). Processes of opinion change. *Public Opinion Quarterly, 25,* 57–78.

Kerr, N. L. (1982). Social transition schemes: Model, method and applications. In H. Brandstätter, J. H. Davis, & G. Stocker-Kreichgauer (Eds.), *Group decision making* (pp. 59–79). London: Academic Press.

Kerr, N. L., Davis, J. H., Meek, D., & Rissman, A. G. (1975). Group position as a function of member attitudes: Choice shift effects from the perspective of social decision scheme theory. *Journal of Personality and Social Psychology, 34,* 282–294.

Kerr, N. L., & MacCoun, R. J. (1985). The effects of jury size and polling method on the process and product of jury deliberation. *Journal of Personality and Social Psychology, 48,* 349–363.

Latané, B. (1981). The psychology of social impact. *American Psychologist, 36,* 343–356.

Laughlin, P. R., & Adamopoulos, J. (1982). Social decision schemes on intellective tasks. In H. Brandstätter, J. H. Davis, & G. Stocker-Kreichgauer (Eds.), *Group decision making* (pp. 81–102). London: Academic Press.

Laughlin, P. R., & Earley, P. C. (1982). Social combination models, persuasive arguments theory, social comparison theory, and choice shift. *Journal of Personality and Social Psychology, 42,* 273–280.

Maass, A., West, S., & Cialdini, R. B. (1987). Minority influence and conversion. In C. Hendrick (Ed.), *Review of personality and social psychology* (Vol. 8, pp. 55–79). Beverly Hills, CA: Sage.

Moore, C. M. (1987). *Group techniques for idea building*. Beverly Hills: Sage.

Moscovici, S., & Faucheux, C. (1972). Social influence, conformity bias and the study of active minorities. In L. Berkowitz (Ed.), *Advances in experimental social psychology* (Vol. 6, pp. 149–202). New York: Academic Press.

Mucchi-Faina, A., Maass, A., & Volpato, C. (1991). Social influence: The role of originality. *European Journal of Social Psychology, 21,* 183–197.

Nowak, A., Szamrej, J., & Latané, B. (1990). From private attitude to public opinion: A dynamic theory of social impact. *Psychological Review, 97,* 362–376.

Papastamou, S. C. (1986). Psychologization and processes of minority and majority influence. *European Journal of Social Psychology, 16,* 165–180.

Poulton, E. C. (1989). *Bias in quantifying judgments*. London: Lawrence Erlbaum Associates.

Shaw, M. E. (1971). *Group dynamics*. New York: McGraw-Hill.

Sherif, M., & Sherif, C. W. (1969). *Social psychology*. New York: Harper & Row.

Stasser, G., & Davis, J. H. (1981). Group decision making and social influence: A social interaction sequence model. *Psychological Review, 88,* 523–551.

Stephan, F. F., & Mishler, E. G. (1952). The distribution of participation in small groups: An exponential approximation. *American Sociological Review, 17,* 598–608.

Tanford, S., & Penrod, S. (1984). Social influence model: A formal integration of research on majority and minority influence processes. *Psychological Bulletin, 95*, 189–225.

Tsai, Y. (1977). Hierarchical structure of participation in small groups. *Behavioral Science, 22*, 38–40.

Tukey, J. W. (1969). Analyzing data: Sanctification or detective work? *American Psychologist, 24*, 83–91.

Turner, J., et al. (1987). *Rediscovering the social group.* Oxford, England: Basil Blackwell.

Weiner, B. (1980). *Human motivation.* New York: Holt.

Williams, K. D., & Karau, S. J. (1991). Social loafing and social compensation: The effects of expectations of co-worker performance. *Journal of Personality and Social Psychology, 61*, 570–581.

Witte, E. H. (1979). *Das Verhalten in Gruppensituationen. Ein theoretisches Konzept* [Behavior in group conditions. A theoretical concept]. Göttingen, Germany: Hogrefe.

Witte, E. H. (1987). Behaviour in group situations: An integrative model. *European Journal of Social Psychology, 17*, 403–429.

Witte, E. H. (1989). Minority influences and innovation: The search for an integrated explanation from psychological and sociological models. *Arbeiten aus dem Fachbereich Psychologie, 64*, 1–65.

Witte, E. H. (1990). Social influence: A discussion and integration of recent models into a general situation theory. *European Journal of Social Psychology, 20*, 3–27.

Witte, E. H. (1991). Technologiefolgenabschätzung—Eine organisations—und sozialpsychologische Perspektive und ein methodischer Vorschlag. *Zeitschrift für Arbeits—und Organisationspsychologie, 35*, 98–104.

Witte, E. H. (1994). Minority influence and innovation: The search for an integrated explanation from psychological and sociological models. In S. Moscovici, A. Maass, & A. Mucchi-Faina (Eds.), *Minority influence* (pp. 67–93). Chicago: Nelson Hall.

Witte, E. H., & Lutz, D. H. (1982). Choice-shift as a cognitive change? In H. Brandstätter, J. H. Davis, & G. Stocker-Kreichgauer (Eds.), *Group decision making* (pp. 215–233). London: Academic Press.

Wolf, S. (1979). Behavioral style and group cohesiveness as sources of minority influence. *European Journal of Social Psychology, 9*, 381–395.

Wolf, S. (1985). Manifest and latent influence of majorities and minorities. *Journal of Personality and Social Psychology, 48*, 899–908.

12

WHEN HUMANS INTERACT LIKE ATOMS

Serge Galam
Groupe de Physique des Solides,
Université Paris

PHYSICS VERSUS SOCIAL SCIENCE

When dealing with social situations it is usually believed that one of the main difficulties comes from the rich variety of individual characteristics involved (Burnstein & Vinokur, 1973; Dion, Baron, & Miller, 1970). Along these lines the complexity of a group is expected to be an increasing function of its size. However crowds, which contain large numbers of persons, behave in some aspects like one collective individual making some behavior even simpler than in the case of one individual (Turner, 1987). This paradox suggests that within a group the individual complexity should decrease in parallel to the appearance of a new individual reality, which is the "collective dimension." In this context it is of particular importance to discriminate between, on the one hand, properties associated with purely individual characteristics, and on the other, those properties that result from the existence of a collectivity or social system (Galam & Moscovici, 1991, 1994, 1995).

Indeed, the interplay of microscopic and macroscopic levels has been most studied far from the field of social sciences. Within physics, statistical mechanics (Stanley, 1971) has been dealing with collective behavior in matter for a very long time. However, only in the last 20 years has the problem of collective phenomena been fully understood, and then only in pure systems. Inhomogeneous systems are still resisting full analysis. Modern theory of critical phenomena is based on the fundamental concepts of universality and irrelevant variables (Ma, 1976). These two concepts mean that different physical systems, like for instance a magnet and a liquid, behave the same way when passing from one macroscopic state to another macroscopic state. Well-known examples are the magnet becoming a para-magnet and the liquid, a gas. Physical characteristics of the two systems like the form of microscopic interactions and their physical nature have no effect on the so-called critical behavior that produces the physical character of the transition from one state to another state. Most of the microscopic properties of the physical compounds involved turn out to be irrelevant for describing the macroscopic change, which in turn appears to be universal. Although the number of physical systems undergoing phase transitions is infinite, all associated phase transitions can be described in terms of only a small finite number of universality classes. Only a few parameters, like space dimensionality, determine which universality class the system belongs to. The abstract and general nature of the statistical physics framework makes it tempting to extend such notions to non-physical systems, and in particular to social systems (Galam, 1982, 1986; Galam, Gefen, & Shapir, 1982), for which, in many cases, there exists an interplay between microscopic properties and macroscopic realities.

Nevertheless, the two fields of physical sciences and social sciences are rather different. In order to develop some common ground, it is useful to make some assumptions about correspondences. One possibility is to put in parallel the atom and the individual. In physics the atom defines some basic level of investigation. It is then possible to go, on the one hand, inside the atom toward elementary particles, and on the other hand, toward matter in bulk by grouping atoms. In social science, the individual human being allows us to go toward societies as well as toward the individual inside.

To implement this "atom-individual" connection, it is of interest to ask the following questions. First, is there anything common to an atom and a human being? Second, what is in common to an assembly of atoms and a group of humans? Third, are the insides of a human and an atom similar? Unfortunately or fortunately, respective answers are no, no, and no. But before giving up the "atom-individual" connection, it is worth asking a final question. What is common in the process of going in parallel from one atom and one human being to, respectively, several atoms in bulk and a group of persons? Here the answer turns affirmative. There exists much in common in the two processes of building a macrolevel from microelements. More precisely, the hypothesis behind the present approach is that these micro–macro mechanisms are universal and hold true beyond the nature of the various entities involved. The preceding series of questions aimed to clarify which problems may be addressed and which are outside the scope of the approach. It is worth stressing that we are not claiming our model will explain all aspects of human behavior. Like any modeling effort, it is appropriate only to some classes of phenomena in social science and not to others.

However, such an approach should be carefully controlled. To just map a physical theory built for a physical reality, onto a social reality, could be at best a nice metaphor, but without predictability, and at worst a misleading and wrong social theory. Physics has been successful in describing macroscopic behavior using properties of the constituent microscopic elements. The task here is to borrow from physics those techniques and concepts used to tackle the complexity of aggregations. The challenge is then to build a collective theory of social behavior along similar lines, but within the specific constraints of the psycho-social reality. The constant danger is for the theorist to stay in physics, using a social terminology and a physical formalism. The contribution from physics should thus be restricted to qualitative guidelines for the mathematical modeling of complex social realities. Such a limitation does not make the program less ambitious.

Our general approach is illustrated in the case of group decision making (Davis, 1973). We address the problem of groups for which both aspects, individual and collective, are important in the decision-making process. In particular, we study conditions that lead to either a polarization or a compromise of the group with respect to a given issue (Galam & Moscovici, 1991). Here, *polarization* means that the bulk of people move in one direction (Moscovici & Zavalloni, 1969). To keep the presentation simple, we used a model in which a group of N persons has to make a decision. Each person can choose between only two answers, for instance, "yes" and "no" or "in favor" and "against." The model is articulated around a postulate of minimum conflict individual choices. Competing interactions are introduced that generate either agreement or conflict in the group. Given a set of interactions, the postulate of minimum conflict implies the selection of a final decisional state among the 2^N configurations possible in the group.

The next section considers the simplest situation with the *bare model*. It considers horizontal interactions to account for interindividual interactions and, vertical interactions to represent the direct pressure of the social surrounding on each group member. Individual differences are included in the section Group Formation, making the model more realistic. It leads to the *dressed model,* which accounts, for a given issue, to individual representation (Moscovici, 1976) that results from cultural values, beliefs and personal experiences. The section that follows deals with the group emergence from isolated individuals to integrated group members. The *group formation process* is analyzed. In particular, we study mechanisms by which either a compromise or a polarization of the group is produced. The model is then illustrated through a few examples in the section Illustration of the Model. Cases respectively of balanced equal representation, balanced unequal representation, minorities, and leaders are analyzed. The existence of nonrational behavior is discussed in the sixth section. It is shown in particular how it enlarges qualitatively the spectrum of individual choices by creating new answers in between the two extremes yes and no. The last section contains some conclusions about the model and the approach.

THE BARE MODEL

We consider the simplest situation in which one individual has to make a choice between two answers: either yes or no, in favor or against, more or less. Such cases are indeed numerous in the social world. Moreover, cases with a larger spectrum of answers can usually be mapped at some approximative level into a two-answer case (Moscovici & Zavalloni, 1969). The individual choice can then be represented by a two-valued variable c with $c = 1$ associated to answer yes and $c = -1$ to answer no.

An assembly of N such persons is then constituted. Each individual choice is now represented by a variable c_i, where $i = 1, 2, \ldots, N$ and $c_i = \pm 1$. It is thus possible to define a collective choice of the N-person collection as the simple sum of each individual choice,

$$C = \sum_{i=1}^{N} c_i . \tag{1}$$

The outcome of considering a collection of persons is to enlarge drastically the spectrum of possible choices. It actually increases from 2 up to 2^N. However, to exist, this spectrum needs a structure to collect individual answers, to sum them up, and to display the net result. It already shows that to define a macrolevel, even reduced to a mere aggregation, requires the building of some group structure that allows an inward–outward process between the micro- and macrolevels. Moreover, to go beyond the initial two answers requires some complex internal transformation in order to associate a meaning to each one of the 2^N answers. However, the use of some rules, for instance a majority rule, can bring the collective choice back to the individual one with only two answers.

The Neutral State

The neutral state is defined as an environment in which the individual is isolated and has no reason to favor one answer over the other. Choosing yes or no does not make any difference. At this stage the notion of conflict is not yet defined. In terms of probability it means that yes and no are equiprobable. The probability distribution function is therefore,

$$p(c_i) = \tfrac{1}{2}\{\delta(c_i - 1) + \delta(c_i + 1)\}, \tag{2}$$

where δ is the Kronecker function, that is, $\delta(x = 0) = 1$ and $\delta(x \neq 0) = 0$.

Considering N such similar individuals, each person makes his choice without any interaction with others. The value of the collective choice is not even known to individuals. The probability distribution for the collection of N persons is thus,

$$p(C) = \prod_{i=1}^{N} p(c_i), \tag{3}$$

where $p(c_i)$ is given by Equation 2.

From Equations 2 and 3 the collective choice is $C = 0$. It is indeed zero only on average, with fluctuations of order $\frac{1}{\sqrt{N}}$. However this $C = 0$ result creates a new qualitative choice that did not exist at the individual level. It can be understood as the perfect compromise choice. Because the macroscopic quantity C is zero, the aggregation process turns out to have no effect at the macrolevel, which makes the associated group neutral. Perfect compromise means no group existence as such. We have only a neutral group with no link among group members.

Pair Interactions

The assumption of aggregating individuals with no exchange among them is not realistic unless they are physically isolated one from the other with no exchange of information. Interactions can indeed be introduced quite naturally.

We first notice that with a pair of persons i and j, only four different choice configurations can be produced. These are:

1. $c_i = c_j = +1$
2. $c_i = c_j = -1$
3. $c_i = -c_j = +1$
4. $c_i = -c_j = -1$

In configurations 1 and 2 they are making the same choice. The two persons i and j agree. They disagree in configurations 3 and 4, making opposite choices. It is a conflict. However, this agreement or conflict materializes only once they are both aware of the other's choice, in other words, only once they are somehow interacting.

Second, we can naturally identify a state of conflict (configurations 3 and 4) or agreement (configurations 1 and 2) using the product $c_i c_j$. It is equal to +1 for agreement and to −1 for conflict. Moreover, in both cases, it does not differentiate which choice is actually made, in accordance with being in a neutral state.

However prior to the decision itself, both individuals may, for instance, argue for a long time, or exchange written information. On the other hand, they may decide without any discussion. We thus need to introduce a quantity to measure this involvement. Let us call it exchange intensity and denote it by I. This parameter can be then incorporated into the configurational choice labeling by using the product $I c_i c_j$ instead of $c_i c_j$. An agreement state is associated with $(+I)$ whereas $(-I)$ corresponds to a conflict state. I measures the conflict intensity.

For a whole group where interactions are restricted to pairs the total degree of conflict or agreement is measured by the function,

$$G_I \equiv I \sum_{<i,j>} c_i c_j, \tag{4}$$

where we have assumed that the exchange intensity I is constant for all interacting (i, j) pairs. We call G_I the group internal conflict function and $<i, j>$ represents all interacting pairs.

The Symmetry-Breaking Concept

The internal conflict function G_I measures the degree of conflict in a group for each one of the 2^N decisional configurations. It allows one to discriminate among various possible choices, but does not indicate which one is chosen by the group. For the group decision dynamics to operate, it is necessary to invoke a criterion to select which among the possible states is favored by the group. Along these lines we introduce a postulate that gives direction to the group dynamics. Our postulate is: Each individual favors the choice that minimizes its own conflicts. It is fundamental to the operation of the whole model. Indeed, it is the only postulate at this stage of the chapter. It is a criterion that determines the direction of individual choice dynamics. Given a person, it selects which choice is favored according to a principle of minimum conflict. Justification of this postulate is beyond the scope of the present work. It is motivated a posteriori by the results obtained from the model. It is worth stressing that minimum conflict means maximum agreement.

One way to find out the final result is to start from one person. That person can decide either yes or no, at random. However, once the choice is made, all persons interacting with this particular person will make the same choice, to minimize their own conflicts. Then, for these second-generation persons, all people interacting with them will again make the same choice to favor agreement. In so doing, the whole group will end up making the same initial choice as the first person selected. The net result of these dynamics is an extreme polarization of collective choice $C = \pm N$. The sign, that is, the polarization direction, is determined by the initial individual choice, which is made randomly.

The polarization phenomenon will hold whoever is chosen to be the initial person. Only the direction will change. The main point to stress is that there exists no rule to determine who is the initial person. Indeed, in real-life situations, the aforementioned process starts simultaneously from several persons. However, somehow the group succeeds in propagating local choices at long distance, allowing everyone to minimize their own conflicts, which is realized only once everyone moved along the same choice. But the final winning choice cannot be determined a priori; it is random. Therefore, in a neutral state for which both individual choices are equiprobable (see Equation 2), we conclude that: Groups polarize themselves toward an extreme choice. The direction of that choice, however, is arbitrary. Each extreme is equiprobable.

From the definition of the group internal conflict function G_I (Equation 4) and the preceding polarization result, the postulate of individual minimum conflict turns out to be identical to a postulate of maximum G_I.

The polarization effect that results from group member interactions is identical to the *spontaneous symmetry-breaking* phenomenon well known in physics (Ma, 1976). There, it is a general concept related to the minimum energy principle. To minimize its energy, a physical system breaks spontaneously the symmetry of its ground state by selecting one particular state at random. Magnetism provides a good illustration of the phenomenon. For instance, iron is paramagnetic at high temperature. It has no magnetization although there exist local microscopic magnets. Those are indeed randomly oriented. In contrast, iron does exhibit a net and permanent magnetization at lower temperatures. This property results from a local alignment of microscopic magnets that occurs upon cooling. It is the so-called ferromagnetic state in which the microscopic moment orientation symmetry has been spontaneously broken by microscopic interactions. Repeating the cooling from high temperature down to some fixed temperature, at each cycle, the magnetization is found to be identical in intensity but may differ in direction. It shows that the alignment direction is randomly selected.

Individual interactions make the group as a whole behave as a *superperson* (Turner, 1987). It likewise chooses between two possible choices with equiprobability the isolated individual. In parallel, the individual within the group has lost his freedom of choice. He must now make a choice identical to people he interacts with. Individual freedom has turned to group freedom. It is also worth noticing that perfect compromise has disappeared as a consequence of a group-level existence. Now there exists a net effect proportional to N with $C = \pm N$ at the level of macroreality. Without interactions, the $c_i = \pm 1$ were overall self-neutralized macroscopically. Interactions have produced strong individual correlations associated with a symmetry breaking.

Our finding sheds new light on results obtained from group decision-making experiments conducted in social psychology. The polarization effect was clearly evident in data reported by Moscovici and Zavalloni (1969). However, until now, most theoretical explanations have been unconvincing in connecting choices at, respectively, the individual level (Burnstein & Vinokur, 1973), and the group level (Davis, 1973). Our proposal is that polarization effect arises quite naturally from first principles.

GROUP FORMATION

At this stage we need to formalize the internal group dynamics, which proceeds from initial individual choices toward the final collective choice. The exchange term must be modified to account for the group reality that emerges from the individual level. We first rewrite $G_I = I \sum_{i,j} c_i c_j$ as,

$$G_I = \frac{I}{2} \sum_{i=1}^{N} \left\{ \sum_{j=1}^{n} c_j \right\} c_i . \tag{5}$$

where n is the number of persons one individual interacts with. To keep the presentation simple this number is assumed equal for everyone. In cases where everyone interacts with everyone we have $n = N$. Equation 5 is just a rewriting of Equation 4. Now we modify it to account for the process of group formation. People do anticipate the emergence of a collective choice. Each individual i will thus try to project through its partner's choices, c_j (people i discusses with), its expectation of the overall final group decision. Individual i then extrapolates the j's choice, c_j, to the expected collective choice the group will eventually make without its own participation. Within this process, individual i perceives the j's choice as given by the transformation,

$$c_j \to \frac{1}{N-1}(C - c_i),\tag{6}$$

where C is the collective choice defined as before. Once this process is completed, Equation 5 becomes,

$$G_j^g = \frac{I}{2}\sum_{i=1}^{N}\left\{\sum_{j=1}^{n}\frac{1}{N-1}(C - c_i)\right\}c_i,\tag{7}$$

and,

$$G_j^g = \frac{In}{2(N-1)}\left\{C\sum_{i=1}^{N}c_i - \sum_{i=1}^{N}c_i^2\right\},\tag{8}$$

where the active anticipating process is denoted by superscript g. Using the collective choice definition, $C = \sum_{i=1}^{N} c_i$, and the property $c_i^2 = 1$, we get,

$$G_j^g = \gamma\frac{C}{N}\sum_{i=1}^{N}c_i - \gamma,\tag{9}$$

where $\gamma \equiv \frac{nIN}{2(N-1)}$ is a constant independent of the group choice. As such it is irrelevant to the collective choice. It is worth stressing that C is not yet the final decision. Rather, it is the expected final collective choice.

We can rewrite Equation 9 in the form,

$$G_j^g = S_g\sum_{i=1}^{N}c_i - \gamma.\tag{10}$$

where

$$S_g \equiv \gamma \frac{C}{N} \tag{11}$$

acts as a group field that couples with each individual choice. The field notion is a way to account for some pressure toward a given choice. Within our convention and postulate, a measure of that influence is given by the product of the field intensity and the individual choice value. Here it is $S_g c_i$. A positive field S_g favors a positive choice +1, whereas −1 is associated to a negative field. The conflict or agreement intensity is given by S_g.

We have indeed a self-consistent expression, because on the one hand, individual i wants to go along the virtual field S_g, and on the other hand, she contributes directly to this virtual field through its dependence on the collective choice C. Rewriting Equation 10 as

$$G_i^g = \gamma \frac{C^2}{N} - \gamma \tag{12}$$

shows that maximizing G_i^g results in maximizing C^2, which is obtained by $C^2 = N^2$. It is an extreme polarization with either $C = +N$ or $C = -N$. Again individual minimum conflicts appear clearly identical to the maximum of the group internal conflict function.

At this stage of the model it is worthwhile to comment on the physical basis of the approach. Underlying "group formation" is the so-called mean field theory of phase transitions. It was developed long ago to provide a theory of magnetism (Stanley, 1971). It is known to be a good approximative theory, and yields satisfactory qualitative results. However, the theory's quantitative predictions are wrong (Ma, 1976).

THE DRESSED MODEL

We are now in position to overcome two simplifying assumptions made earlier. First, most choices an individual and a group have to make are not independent of the surroundings as assumed earlier. We now account for pressure applied to the group from the outside. Second, assuming identical individuals, with no a priori individual differences in preferences about the issue, does not hold in most cases. Individual differences are now also included.

The Social State

The existence of external pressure on group members means that the equiprobability hypothesis (Equation 2) no longer holds. In that case $p(c_i = 1) \neq p(c_i = -1)$. This situation is addressed by introducing a quantity that differentiates the two possible choices, thus turning the neutral state into a social state. We call this quantity a social field and denote it S. Similarly, with the aforementioned group field S_g, each person's agreement or conflict with S is represented by the product Sc_i. Agreement is associated with $Sc_i > 0$; that is, the choice is made along the field with S and c_i having the same sign. In contrast $Sc_i < 0$ represents a conflict between the individual and the social pressure, because S and c_i have opposite signs. The surrounding group conflict measure is,

$$G_S \equiv \sum_{i=1}^{N} Sc_i. \tag{13}$$

Applying the postulate to the sum $G_i^g + G_S$ still results in an extreme polarization, but now its direction is no longer random. The group choice is $C = +N$ for $S > 0$, and $C = -N$ with $S < 0$. Under external pressure, even extremely weak, the group and the individual behave identically. They both follow the pressure induced by the external pressure. The spontaneous symmetry breaking is thus suppressed. However, symmetry breaking still occurs, but here, it is determined by the external field direction. In this case, the superperson represented by the whole group is identical to the individual person. They are both aligned along the field. This result is at contrast with the nonsocial state, where the individual loses its freedom of choice because it must make the same choice the other group members do. In parallel, the group as a whole can still choose arbitrarily.

The Representation State

To get closer to the reality it is of importance to allow individual differences in preferences concerning some issues, hereafter called *individual representations*. Moreover, a representation varies in both direction and intensity from one person to another. It depends on cultural values, past experiences, ethics, and beliefs. The representation effect can be included within our formalism by introducing an additional field. It is attached to a given individual i. We call it the internal social field S_i. Its properties are similar to those of a social field S, the difference being that the social field applies uniformly to each group member whereas an internal social field acts only on one person. As for the other fields, conflict or agreement with the internal social field is exhibited in the product $S_i c_i$. It is positive for a choice made along the representation (internal agreement with personal values), and negative otherwise (internal conflict with personal values). The group representation conflict measure is given by,

$$G_R \equiv \sum_{i=1}^{N} S_i c_i. \tag{14}$$

The distribution of individual representations is required to understand the final choice of a N-person group. The representation effect is enhanced in the isolated-person, neutral-state case where both the exchange intensity and the social external field are zero. There, from the postulate, the final decision is found to result from every individual following its own representation. It gives,

$$C = \sum_{i=1}^{N} \frac{S_i}{|S_i|},$$
(15)

where the $|\dots|$ denotes absolute value.

This equation enhances the new qualitative situation created by the existence of representations. Actual C value, which depends on the distribution of individual representations, can now be taken out of the whole spectrum of values $-N, \dots, 0, \dots, +N$. Compromise, $C = 0$, can again be an outcome. Individual representations are thus instrumental for making the whole model relevant to real situations in which collective choices are far richer than $C = \pm N$.

In other words, prior to group formation, individuals have their own representations that determine their a priori answers to the initial question. It is worth noting that all these representations result in either yes or no. Then, in the process of group formation, people start to interact through the yes and no distribution in the group. However to reach a collective choice, due to the existence of opposite representations, they must construct new answers in addition to the initial yes and no. Answers are thus enriched during group formation, due to representations. On the other hand, groups that form in the neutral state do not produce new answers. Once the final decision is reached, each group member identifies with it giving for c_i, the final value $d_i = \frac{C}{N}$, which may differ from the initial c_i, and where C is the final collective decision. In the neutral state $d_i = \pm 1$. Thus, in the process of building a new answer d_i, a new representation has been produced by the group. This new representation is integrated by the individual to yield the d_i choice. Group formation has qualitatively modified individual representations. This process shows that whereas individuals resist adopting a representation opposed to their own, via the group transformation, they will join a new common representation that accounts for the overall balance of initial representations. The preceding takes place around a new answer that did not exist prior to the group forming.

The Total State

Adding together all the effects introduced until now results in an extended group internal conflict $G = G_j^g + G_S + G_R$, which is,

$$G = I \sum_{i,j} c_i c_j + S \sum_{i=1}^{N} c_i + \sum_{i=1}^{N} S_i c_i.$$
(16)

Up to now, it has been easy to determine which state maximizes G. The extended form of Equation 16 makes this task more difficult. Competing effects may exist that make the search for the final state harder. A given individual wants to minimize own conflict with three different elements, which are:

- Interacting group members: The individual wants to come up with the same final decision as preferred by interaction partners.
- External social field: The individual wants to comply to the external pressure from immediate surroundings.
- Internal social field: The individual wants to comply to the internal pressure from personal representations.

These three elements are not necessarily satisfied simultaneously. From the postulate, the individual wants to minimize overall personal conflict. It could result in simultaneous agreement with some of the aforementioned items, and conflict with others. It is clearer to write Equation 16 as,

$$G = \sum_{i=1}^{N} S_{g,i}^{r} c_i - \gamma, \tag{17}$$

where,

$$S_{g,i}^{r} = S_g + S + S_i, \tag{18}$$

is the resulting field applied to individual i once the group formation process has been completed. From the last two equations the decision-making dynamics are seen more clearly. Applying our postulate shows that maximum G and minimum individual conflicts are achieved when each individual follows his resulting field sign. If $S_{g,i}^{r} > 0$, then $c_i = 1$ and $c_i = -1$ for $S_{g,i}^{r} < 0$. The case $S_{g,i}^{r} = 0$ results in an undetermination of the i choice as in the isolated neutral case. It is worth emphasizing that satisfying $S_{g,i}^{r}$ sign does imply satisfying simultaneously S, S_i, and S_g signs. This competing effect is the signature of the psychological complexity involved in the decision-making process.

It is worth stressing again the two steps of the group decision-making process. Each person first follows her resulting field $S_{g,i}^{r}$ to produce a collective choice C. Then this collective choice is integrated with the other individuals by $c_i \to d_i = \frac{C}{N.}$

ILLUSTRATION OF THE MODEL

To gain a deeper insight about the meaning of Equations 17 and 18, we analyze four different specific cases. Each illustrates how the model operates under certain conditions.

First Case: Two Balanced Opposite Biases

We consider an evenly divided group of N persons with no external social field; that is, $S = 0$. Half the persons have a positive representation $S_i = +S_0$, and the other half have a negative representation with the same intensity $S_j = -S_0$. The whole group thus has no net representation. Interactions are of intensity I and each person discusses with n other persons. In small, face-to-face groups, everyone usually interacts with everyone else, so $n = N$. The corresponding internal conflict function is,

$$G = -\gamma + \tfrac{\gamma}{N}C^2 + \tfrac{N}{2}(S_0 c_i^+ - S_0 c_j^-), \tag{19}$$

where c_i^+ and c_j^- are attached to persons with respectively positive and negative representation. The constant $\gamma \equiv \frac{nIN}{2(N-1)}$ was introduced earlier in the group formation section. The collective choice may be written as $C = \frac{N}{2}(c_i^+ + c_j^-)$. The actual choice is the one that maximizes G. In this case it is easily singled out, because there exist only two different kinds of persons, symbolized by c_i^+ and c_j^-. Four choice configurations are possible: (a) $c_i^+ = +1$; $c_j^- = +1$; $C = N$, (b) $c_i^+ = -1$; $c_j^- = -1$; $C = -N$, (c) $c_i^+ = +1$; $c_j^- = -1$; $C = 0$, and (d) $c_i^+ = -1$; $c_j^- = +1$; $C = 0$. The first two (a and b) are agreement and the others (c and d) are conflict. Associated internal conflict functions are: (e) $G(a) = G(b) = -\gamma + N\gamma$, (f) $G(c) = -\gamma + NS_0$, and (g) $G(d) = -\gamma - NS_0$.

Clearly $G(d) < G(c)$, reducing the choice to either a and b or c. In case $\gamma > S_0$, we have $G(a, b) > G(c)$, indicating that the interaction strength proportional to nI is stronger than S_0. The group then polarizes with $C = \pm N$. The direction of the extreme choice occurs at random. Half of the members are fully satisfied with both their representation and their partners whereas the other half is in conflict with its own representation. This result means in particular that the "losing" subgroup has to build a new representation that embodies some level of internal frustration. The "winning" part does not modify its initial representation. In this case, no new answer was built. We have $c_i \to d_i = \pm 1$.

On the other hand, strong representation—that is, $\gamma < S_0$—favors compromise, with the collective choice $C = 0$. Each member i starts from a personal representation to decide eventually through weak interactions on a medium compromise, with the creation of a new answer $d_i = 0$. Again, it is worth stressing that this compromise choice did not exist prior to the group formation. It is the result of cooperation between the group level and the individual level.

Within a balanced representation group, discussion favors a compromise. Weak exchanges result in an extreme polarization along a random direction.

Second Case: Two Unbalanced Opposite Biases

We now go back to the previous example, but consider a stronger positive representation. This is done by writing the negative representation fields as $S_j = -\alpha S_0$, with $0 < \alpha < 1$. Respective numbers of positive and negative representations are equal. Only the internal conflict function values are changed to become, respectively: (a) $G(a) = -\gamma + N\gamma + \frac{N}{2}(1-\alpha)S_0$, (b) $G(b) = -\gamma + N\gamma = -\frac{N}{2}(1-\alpha)S_0$, (c) $G(c) = -\gamma + \frac{N}{2}(1+\alpha)S_0$, and (d) $G(d) = -\gamma - \frac{N}{2}(1+\alpha)S_0$.

Because $0 < \alpha < 1$, $G(a) < G(b)$ and $G(d) < G(c)$, always. However, in the case $\gamma > S_0$, the polarization direction is determined with $C = +N$. Before, $\alpha = 1$ made the direction arbitrary, but now it is the strongest initial representation that wins. The discussion process within the forming group has made the weaker biased people align themselves with the stronger ones. Here we have $c_i \rightarrow d_i = 1$. In order for a compromise outcome to be favored, a decrease in exchanges among group members is required. For $\gamma < S_0$, the final choice is $C = 0$, which gives $c_i \rightarrow d_i = 0$.

Within an unbalanced representation group, discussion favors the initially strongest representation. Only a limitation of exchanges may produce a compromise.

Third Case: The Minority

Most cases do not have an equal number of people in two opposite subgroups. Usually there exist a majority and a minority. Let us consider a minority number M of people ($M < \frac{N}{2}$) with a positive representation $S_i = +S_0$. The majority is then $N - M$ with an unequal negative representation $S_j = -\alpha S_0$. We chose, for instance, the case of a minority more motivated than the majority. We take $0 < \alpha < 1$. Denoting c_i^+ and c_j^- the respective minority and majority choices, the collective choice is given by $C = Mc_i^+ + (N - M)c_j^-$. The internal conflict function is $G = \frac{n}{2(N-1)}IC^2 + (Mc_i^+ - (N-M)\alpha c_j^-)S_0$. Associated four choice configurations are: (a) $c_i^+ = +1$; $c_j^- = +1$; $C = N$, (b) $c_i^+ = -1$; $c_j^- = -1$; $C = -N$, (c) $c_i^+ = +1$; $c_j^- = -1$; $C = 2M - N$, and (d) $c_i^+ = -1$; $c_j^- = +1$; $C = -2M + N$. The first two (a and b) are minority–majority agreement whereas the others (c and d) are minority–majority conflict. Associated internal conflict functions are: (e) $G(a) = -\gamma + N\gamma + \{(1+\alpha)M - \alpha N\}S_0$, (f) $G(b) = -\gamma + N\gamma - \{(1+\alpha)M - \alpha N\}S_0$, (g) $G(c) = -\gamma + \frac{\gamma}{N}(2M - N)^2 + \{[(1-\alpha)M + \alpha N]S_0$, and (h) $G(d) = -\gamma + \frac{\gamma}{N}(2M - N)^2 - \{(1-\alpha)M + \alpha N\}S_0$.

Analysis of the preceding expressions is complicated because now several parameters are involved. There are N, M, nI, S_0, and α. Let us comment on some cases. Again, case d is never selected because indeed nothing is satisfied in that case, neither interactions nor representations.

First, interaction effects are winning over representation effects: The group is polarized; that is, $G(a)$ or $G(b) > G(c)$:

1. The minority wins, turning the majority to its side if $G(a) > G(b)$. It is the case if $M < (N - M)\alpha$. Condition $G(a) > G(c)$ is ensured by $nI/M > (N - 1)\alpha S_0$.
2. The majority wins, turning the minority to its side if $G(a) < G(b)$. It is the case if $M > (N - M)\alpha$. Condition $G(b) > G(c)$ is ensured by $nI/(N - M) > (N$

$- 1)S_0$. The condition does not depend on α because in both cases b and c, the majority follows its own representation $-\alpha S_0$.

Second, representation effects are winning over interaction effects: The group is balanced; that is, $G(a)$ and $G(b) < G(c)$. Condition $G(a) < G(c)$ is ensured by $nIM < (N - 1)\alpha S_0$. Condition $G(b) < G(c)$ is ensured by $nI(N - M) < (N - 1).S0$. A balanced collective choice reflecting the respective strength in numbers of each group is given by case c.

Fourth Case: The Leader

In most groups, persons are not all equal in status. The inequality can stem from either a strong character or an institutional position, like, for instance, a group president who has a double vote. To account for such situations it is enough to associate a strong individual field to the stronger person in the group. In other words, the leader case is a special case of a strong minority that reduces to one person. We can thus use the equations of the minority case discussed previously by putting $M = 1$. In the case of a charismatic leader we take $\alpha \sim 0$ with $0 < \alpha < 1$ to emphasize its subjective aspect. However, for another kind of leader, the authoritarian for instance, an external field would account for the pressure the leader applies to all group members (Galam & Moscovici, 1993).

Let us consider a leader with a positive representation $S_1 = +S_0$. The majority figure is then $N - 1$ with an unequal negative representation $S_j = -\alpha S_0$. Denoting c_0^+ and c_j^- as the respective leader and majority choices, the collective choice is given by $C = c_0^+ + (N - 1)c_j^-$. The internal conflict function is $G = \frac{n}{2(N-1)}IC^2 + (c_0^+ - (N - 1)\alpha c_j^-)S_0$. The associated four choice configurations are: (a) $c_0^+ = +1$; $c_j^- = +1$; $C = N$, (b) $c_0^+ = -1$; $c_j^- = -1$; $C = -N$, (c) $c_0^+ = +1$; $c_j^- = -1$; $C = 2 - N$, and (d) $c_0^+ = -1$; $c_j^- = +1$; $C = 2 + N$. The first two (a and b) are leader-majority agreement whereas the others (c and d) are leader-majority conflict. Associated internal conflict functions are: (e) $G(a) = -\gamma + N\gamma + \{(1 + \alpha) - \alpha N\}S_0$, (f) $G(b) = -\gamma + N\gamma - \{(1 + \alpha) - \alpha N\}S_0$, (g) $\{G(c) = -\gamma + \frac{\gamma}{N}(2 - N)^2 + \{(1 - \alpha) + \alpha N\}S_0$, and (h) $G(d) = -\gamma + \frac{\gamma}{N}(2 - N)^2 - \{(1 - \alpha) + \alpha N\}S_0$.

Analysis of preceding expressions is as complicated as in the minority case with parameters N, nI, S_0, and α. Let us comment on some cases. Again, case d is never selected because indeed nothing is satisfied in that case, neither interactions nor representations.

First, interaction effects are winning over representation effects: The group is polarized; that is, $G(a)$ or $G(b) > G(c)$:

1. The leader wins, turning the majority to its side if $G(a) > G(b)$. It is the case if $\frac{1}{\alpha} < N - 1$. Condition $G(a) > G(c)$ is ensured by $nI > (N - 1)\alpha S_0$.
2. The majority wins, turning the minority to its side if $G(a) < G(b)$. It is the case if $\frac{1}{\alpha} < N - 1$. Condition $G(b) > G(c)$ is ensured by $nI > S_0$. The condition

does not depend on α because in both cases b and c the majority follows its own representation $-\alpha S_0$.

Second, representation effects are winning over interaction effects: The group is balanced; that is, $G(a)$ and $G(b) < G(c)$. Condition $G(a) < G(c)$ is ensured by $nl < (N-1)\alpha S_0$ and condition $G(b) < G(c)$ by $nl < S_0$. A balanced collective choice reflecting the respective numerical strength of each group is given by case c.

INCLUDING NONRATIONAL BEHAVIOR

At this stage, for a given group, each particular person can make a choice by applying the postulate of minimum individual conflict. A clear-cut choice is thus determined for any issue. As such, the individual behavior obeys well-defined deterministic rules. We call it *rational* behavior. However, in real-life groups, some persons are found to act in contradiction with most people in the group. These individuals seem to be against everything the group is doing, whatever it is. In our terms, they are indeed maximizing their own individual conflict instead of reducing it, thus opposing the postulate. Such an attitude is opposite to the earlier definition of a rational behavior. On this basis, it can be defined as *nonrational* behavior. We thus conclude that up to now our model has totally ignored the possibility of nonrational behavior.

The Analogy With Physics

It is worth noticing that the exact physical equivalent of our postulate is the principle of energy minimum. However, in physics this principle is valid to determine the stable equilibrium state only when temperature, T (measured in Kelvin units), equals zero. Then, local increases of energy (fluctuations around the minimum) are not allowed. Only nonzero temperatures ($T \neq 0$) produce such fluctuations. These thermal fluctuations would be analogous to what was called previously nonrational behavior. Our analogy with statistical physics, therefore, appears to be limited to the $T = 0$ case.

At this stage of our approach, we are facing a fundamental difficulty in introducing nonrational behavior in our social model. On the one hand, nonrational behavior is a meaningful concept in social science as are thermal fluctuations and temperature in physics. However, on the other hand, the social equivalent, if any, of temperature is a real conceptual challenge. Accordingly, in the past, several attempts have been made to define a social temperature (Galam, 1982; Galam et al., 1982). But none has really gone beyond either the metaphoric level, or the ad hoc introduction of entropic effects. At this level of analysis, to keep on solid ground we can only state that a rational behavior within our social framework is the equivalent of having no fluctuations in physics. In other words, rationality is characteristic of a zero temperature situation.

On this basis it is fruitful to push the analogy further by way of a digression. First, we notice that the physical absolute zero temperature (equal to $-273\,°C$) does not exist in real-life laboratories. Only the limit of very low temperatures $T \to 0$ can be achieved, and in appropriate experimental devices. This fact can be understood by stressing that indeed the value $T = 0$ is only a limit. It is just analogous to the high temperature limit $T \to +\infty$. This analogy is quite clear within statistical mechanics where it is not the temperature that is the natural operating quantity but the parameter $\beta \equiv \frac{1}{k_B T}$ where k_B is Boltzman's constant. There, β varies from zero to infinity. $T = 0$ thus appears clearly as a limit because it is associated with $\beta \to +\infty$. Second, along these lines and within the logic of our analogy, we would be led to conclude that: Absolute rationality does not exist.

A Hint to a Social Temperature

In physics, thermal fluctuations are associated with both an increase in local energies, at the expense of the "minimum energy principle," and an increase of entropy. To account for and to balance these opposite effects, once $T \neq 0$, it is no longer the energy that is a minimum at equilibrium, but another thermodynamic function. It is called the free energy F and is defined by,

$$F = E - TS, \tag{20}$$

where E is the energy and S is the entropy (Stanley, 1971). Here the temperature T is associated to F. Therefore to be consistent within our analogy, a social temperature should be organically related to a social equivalent of the free energy (Galam & Moscovici, 1991).

Such a relationship was proposed recently in a work (Galam & Moscovici, 1994, 1995) about the genesis and development of power in societies. The new idea was to define the "social temperature" as an internal quantity that is built up from the inside of societies, at the level of its structural organization. In parallel, the social analogous of the free energy F is related to the power of the group. It is shown, in particular, that in order to increase its power (minimum of F) a society must produce and stabilize some level of individual conflicts, and this against the assumed natural trend of people toward cooperation and agreement. This level of conflicts is controlled through the "social temperature," which is the quantity of diversity generated by the society's degree of development (Galam & Moscovici, 1994, 1995). In order to produce the associated entropy (Equation 20), these individual conflicts are defined as moving "nonfixed" attitudes among people. Their density is fixed and constant, but actual persons in conflict will eventually turn back to cooperation whereas others will start to be in conflict.

In the following, this dynamics is shown to be instrumental in generating new individual choices as weighted averages over initial extreme choices. It results from oscillations between rational and nonrational behavior.

Probabilistic Nonrational Behavior

Any given group is usually embedded in a society. Using the aforementioned theory (Galam & Moscovici, 1994, 1995), we assume there exists some fixed "social temperature" T, built by the society to produce some level of conflicts. Within our group decision-making problem, a conflict (with respect to the resulting field $S_{g,i}^r$) is exactly what we defined as nonrational behavior. Because it is a dynamic effect, during the process of group formation, each person is nonrational for some of the time and rational otherwise. When individual i is nonrational, the group starts to pressure him toward rationality. Later on, the individual turns back to rationality. However, at this very moment, somebody else turns nonrational. The group then focuses on this person, repeating the same cycle as before and so on. To implement for such not individually localized, nonrational attitudes a probabilistic description is appropriate.

Given a person i, with a positive (negative) resulting field $S_{g,i}^r$ (Equation 18), we introduce a finite probability $p_i(T)$ for the choice $c_i = -1$ ($c_i = +1$). A person is thus nonrational with the finite probability $p_i(T)$), and rational with probability $[1 - p_i(T)]$. From the earlier discussion about rational behavior, we have the condition $p_i(T) = 0$ for $T = 0$. From its definition (Galam & Moscovici, 1994, 1995), $p_i(T)$ is an increasing continuous function of T. Because it is a probability, $p_i(T)$ must be smaller than or equal to one. Moreover, it turns out that cases with $p_i(T) > [1 - p_i(T)]$, that is, $p_i(T) < \frac{1}{2}$, are mathematically symmetrical with cases where $p_i(T) < [1 - p_i(T)]$, that is, $p_i(T) > \frac{1}{2}$. In other words, an excess in nonrationality is formally identical to an excess of rationality. Therefore $p_i(T)$ should have the upper limit of one half, resulting in the nonrational probability,

$$0 \leq p_i(T) \leq \tfrac{1}{2}. \tag{21}$$

Without further details, it is worth mentioning that the value T_c of the temperature at which $p_i(T_c) = \frac{1}{2}$ is singular. It is called the "critical temperature" (Stanley, 1971). At $T \geq T_c$ rationality and nonrationality are equiprobable.

Nonrationality-Driven Representation

Initially, a person has only two possible answers represented by $c_i = \pm 1$. Two opposite representations are associated with, respectively, $c_i = +1$ and $c_i = -1$. Strong interactions always spontaneously break the symmetry at the group level.

The corresponding extreme polarization is associated with one of the initial representations. However, in cases of weak interactions, it was shown in the section The Representation State that the distribution of such representations among people in a group produces, through the group formation process, an additional new answer. This answer is supported by the building of a new representation. For instance, we found in the section First Case: Two Balanced Opposite Biases that, strong and opposite convictions are a way to a balanced compromise.

A similar representation of drastic qualitative change seems also generated by nonrationality. The difference is that it is at the individual level that additional answers are created. While oscillating between rational and nonrational behavior, each person tends to reach a new stable answer, which is given by

$$\bar{c}_i = p_i(T)(-r_i) + [1 - p_i(T)]r_i, \tag{22}$$

where $r_i \equiv \dfrac{S'_{g,i}}{|S'_{g,i}|}$. This new person's choice is thus an average over its partial nonrationality. It can be written as,

$$\bar{c}_i = [1 - 2p_i(T)]r_i. \tag{23}$$

Because $p_i(T)$ varies between 0 and $\frac{1}{2}$, $\bar{c}_i$ can vary continuously from ± 1 (extreme initial choices) to 0 (perfect compromise). Within our model, nonrationality is thus shown to enlarge the individual spectrum of answers to a given issue. It allows an escape from the extreme and rough bipolarization of yes or no. To produce the answer $\bar{c}_i$, a new representation, which is a memory-induced effect of actual state of development of the surrounding society, has to be elaborated. It combines with some weights, both initial opposite representations. Equation 23 suggests that, nonrationality is an individual road in the escape from extreme choices. This nonrational individual effect makes the final collective choice $C = \Sigma_{i=1}^{N} r_i$ become,

$$C = \sum_{i=1}^{N} \bar{c}_i. \tag{24}$$

To end this section, it should be emphasized that our discussion about social temperature and nonrationality is mostly speculative. At this stage, it is only a proposal to go beyond the model for group decision making presented up to the section Illustration of the Model. More elaboration is necessary and is left for future work.

CONCLUSION

A simple model has been presented to describe group decision making using concepts from the field of statistical physics. As with any model, a large part of reality has been overlooked. However, the question is to find out if our crude description can embody some aspect of reality. The emphasis is to build a conceptual methodology rather than a final complete theory.

ACKNOWLEDGMENTS

I would like to thank S. Moscovici for stimulating discussions on the subject and J. H. Davis for fruitful comments on the manuscript.

REFERENCES

Burnstein, E., & Vinokur, A. (1973). Testing two classes of theories about group induced shifts in individual choices. *Journal of Experimental Social Psychology, 9*, 123–137.

Davis, J. (1973). Group decision and social interactions: A theory of social decision scheme. *Psychological Review, 80*, 97–125.

Dion, D. L., Baron, R. S., & Miller, N. (1970). Why do groups make riskier decisions than individuals? In L. Berkowitz (Ed.), *Advances in experimental social psychology* (Vol. 5, pp. 305–377). New York: Academic Press.

Galam, S. (1982). Entropie, désordre et liberté individuelle. *Fundamenta Scientiae, 3*, 209–213.

Galam, S. (1986). Majority rule, hierarchical structure and democratic totalitarianism. *Journal of Mathematical Psychology, 30*, 426–434.

Galam, S., Gefen, Y., & Shapir, Y. (1982). Sociophysics: A new approach of sociological collective behavior. *Journal of Mathematical Sociology, 9*, 1–13.

Galam, S., & Moscovici, S. (1991). Towards a theory of collective phenomena: I. Consensus and attitude change in groups. *European Journal of Social Psychology, 21*, 49–74.

Galam, S., & Moscovici, S. (1993). A theory of collective decision making in hierarchical and non-hierarchical groups. *Russian Psychology Journal, 13*, 62–68.

Galam, S., & Moscovici, S. (1994). Towards a theory of collective phenomena: II. Conformity and power. *European Journal of Social Psychology, 24*, 481–495.

Galam, S., & Moscovici, S. (1995). Towards a theory of collective phenomena: III. Conflicts and forms of power. *European Journal of Social Psychology, 25*, 217–229.

Ma, Sh-k. (1976). *Modern theory of critical phenomena*. Reading, MA: The Benjamin Inc.

Moscovici, S. (1976). *Social influence and social change*. London: Academic Press.

Moscovici, S., & Zavalloni, M. (1969). The group as a polarizer of attitudes. *Journal of Personality and Social Psychology, 12*, 125–135.

Stanley, H. E. (1971). *Introduction to phase transitions and critical phenomena*. New York: Oxford University Press.

Turner, J. C. (1987). *Rediscovering the social group*. Oxford, England: Basil Blackwell.

Concluding Remarks

James H. Davis
University of Illinois, Urbana-Champaign

The chapters of this volume have addressed the classic conceptual problem of consensual action in task-oriented groups (committees, panels, juries, etc.). Following discussion, debate, accommodation, compromise, and so on, a collective response represents a synthesis of the many to one solution, report, judgment, choice, or the like.

Some authors were especially concerned with response-biasing processes or mechanisms that are sometimes associated with collective action (e.g., chapters 5, 6, and 7). Others sought to identify subgroup structures unambiguously and associate these with outcome and interpersonal relations (e.g., chapters 7, 8, and 9). Some attempted to relate individual-level cognition to group-level actions (e.g., chapters 4, 5, 10, and 11). Others, for the first time, used information about distances between and among member opinions in predicting group-level responses from individual preferences or opinions (e.g., chapters 2 and 3). Finally, Galam (chapter 12) introduced concepts "from the physical theory of collective phenomena to describe collective behavior in human groups," thus continuing a long tradition in psychology of importing theoretical structures from other disciplines that have sometimes stimulated important new directions in research and theory (e.g., information theory concepts and early developments in cognition—Atteneave, 1959; Garner, 1962; Quastler, 1955).

Despite the variety of approaches, the theoretical notions presented here generally attempt to integrate group outcome with personal and interpersonal processes within a single conceptual system. Although past theoretical efforts have linked the individual level (individual member features) with the group response, by assuming something about the intervening interpersonal activities, the latter has now received more explicit treatment than heretofore; conceptual features of the interpersonal process are more precisely articulated in the theoretical treatments discussed here.

These developments are especially significant, because a routine—and sometimes tiresome—criticism of research and theory addressing task-oriented groups has been that social process is often underemphasized or ignored altogether. Of course, such criticisms have often presupposed the primacy of discovering immediate links between this or that facial expression and a group decision, between some index of body language and collective choice, or between some feature of the verbal stream and the group product. Upon reflection, it may not be surprising that the search for simple associative links between a potpourri of social acts and group performance has generally been unsuccessful. McGrath and Altman (1966) long ago warned that the failure to recognize the patterning and complexity of interaction probably is a major cause of repeated empirical failures to establish simple and direct relationships between group action and personality and demographic variables of members.

In short, new ideas and approaches are needed for studying interpersonal processes. The stimulation of just such new approaches to the study of interpersonal interaction and the associated internal mechanics of achieving consensus would be an additional happy consequence of current theoretical efforts.

Finally, the observation in chapter 1 that theoretical models, like the empirical research on groups, tend to be problem oriented and generally formal in character appears to be confirmed once more, by the work presented here. There are clearly a number of exciting new theoretical directions along which additional theory and empirical research can profitably develop. However, as mentioned in chapter 1, an upsurge in research projects addressing small, task-oriented groups (or any other kind) is unlikely until the mundane problem of an inadequate supply of research subjects is solved.

REFERENCES

Atteneave, F. (1959). *Applications of information theory to psychology: A summary of basic concepts, methods, and results*. New York: Holt.

Garner, W. (1962). *Uncertainty and structure as psychological concepts*. New York: Wiley.

McGrath, J. E., & Altman, I. (1966). *Small group research: A synthesis and critique of the field*. New York: Holt, Rinehart, & Winston.

Quastler, H. (Ed.). (1955). *Information theory in psychology: Problems and methods* (Proceedings of a conference on the estimation of information flow, Monticello, IL, July 5–9, 1954, and related papers). Glencoe, IL: The Free Press.

AUTHOR INDEX

SUBJECT INDEX